Religion in History: Conflict, Conversion and Coexistence

Edited by John Wolffe

Manchester

This publication forms part of an Open University course: AA307 *Religion in History: Conflict, Convergence and Coexistence*. Details of this and other Open University courses can be obtained from the Course Information and Advice Centre, PO Box 724, The Open University, Milton Keynes MK7 6ZS, United Kingdom: tel. +44 (0)1908 653231, e-mail general-enquiries@open.ac.uk

Alternatively, you may visit the Open University website at http://www.open.ac.uk where you can learn more about the wide range of courses and packs offered at all levels by The Open University.

To purchase a selection of Open University course materials visit the webshop at www.ouw.co.uk, or contact Open University Worldwide, Michael Young Building, Walton Hall, Milton Keynes MK7 6AA, United Kingdom, for a brochure: tel. +44 (0)1908 858785; fax +44 (0)1908 858787; e-mail ouwenq@open.ac.uk

Manchester University Press
Oxford Road
Manchester
M13 9NR
www.manchesteruniversitypress.co.uk

The Open University
Walton Hall, Milton Keynes
MK7 6AA

First published 2004 by Manchester University Press in association with The Open University

Distributed exclusively in the USA by Palgrave, 175 Fifth Avenue, New York, NY 10010, USA

Distributed exclusively in Canada by UBC Press, University of British Columbia, 2029 West Mall, Vancouver, BC, Canada V6T IZ2

Every effort has been made to trace all copyright owners, but if any have been inadvertently overlooked, the publishers will be pleased to make the necessary arrangements at the first opportunity.

Edited, designed and typeset by The Open University.

Printed in the United Kingdom by The Alden Group, Oxford.

British Library Cataloguing in Publication Data: data available

Library of Congress Cataloging in Publication Data: data available

ISBN 0 7190 7107 0

1.1

Contents

Preface

This volume is published by Manchester University Press in association with the Open University. Its central purpose is to provide core teaching material for a third level Open University undergraduate course, *Religion in History: Conflict, Conversion and Coexistence.* It replaces *Religion in Victorian Britain,* for which the course books are also co-published with Manchester University Press. There is a companion third level course, concerned with contemporary religion, *Religion Today: Tradition, Modernity and Change,* co-published with Ashgate. It is intended, however, that the material should also be of value to other readers seeking wide-ranging coverage of the historical impact of religion with particular reference to the headlined themes of the book.

Gwilym Beckerlegge, David Herbert, Susan Mumm, Gerald Parsons and John Wolffe are all members of the Department of Religious Studies at the Open University; Janet Huskinson is a member of the Classical Studies Department, and Anne Laurence of the History Department. Hannah Holtschneider is an affiliated lecturer at the Centre for Jewish-Christian Relations in Cambridge and Joanne Pearson, formerly a colleague at the Open University, is now a member of the Department of Religious and Theological Studies at Cardiff University.

The authors would like to acknowledge the essential contributions to the development of the volume and the course made by other staff at the Open University, notably Liam Baldwin (visual resources), Jonathan Hunt (book trade), Gill Marshall and Kate Clements (editors), Meridian and Yvonne Raw (course managers), Ray Munns (cartographer), Rich Hoyle (designer), and Sam Williams (course assistant). The chapters have benefited much from the perceptive and constructive comments of Hugh McLeod (external assessor) and Jim Pottinger (tutor assessor). They are also most grateful to the history editors at MUP, Jonathan Bevan and Alison Welsby for their encouragement and advice. Nevertheless any deficiencies that remain are the responsibility of the authors.

Introduction

John Wolffe

In the aftermath of the First World War, the poet W. B. Yeats (1865–1939) wrote 'The Second Coming', alluding to the Christian belief that Jesus Christ will return at the end of human history. He related his consciousness of the chaos and violence of the contemporary world to his perception of the negative impact of Christianity in the past. Yeats visualized the returning Jesus as a monster with a 'gaze blank and pitiless as the sun'. The poem concludes:

> ... now I know
> That twenty centuries of stony sleep
> Were vexed to nightmare by a rocking cradle,
> And what rough beast, its hour come round at last,
> Slouches towards Bethlehem to be born?
>
> (Ricks, 1999, p. 525)

This powerful and disturbing evocation of the disruptive potential of religion provides an apt starting point for this book. In the First World War, resulting in millions of deaths and enormous suffering and disruption, the language and rhetoric of Christianity had been prominent on both sides (Hoover, 1989). At the time that Yeats was writing, the seemingly irreconcilable religious conflicts of his native Ireland, which dated back to the sixteenth century, were a major factor in the entrenched nature of its political divisions. Bethlehem, venerated by Christians as the birth-place of Jesus, together with other nearby sites in Israel–Palestine, some of them sacred to Islam and Judaism as well as to Christianity, have from the first century to the twenty-first frequently been focal points for contention and actual violence. Shortly after Yeats' death the Nazi government of Germany, which professed to be a Christian country, was responsible for the genocide of six million Jews. In more recent years the spectre of international terrorism, with apparent links to 'fundamentalist'[1] religion, has loomed large and manifested itself most dramatically in the attacks on the United States on 11 September 2001. Such bald statements immediately give rise to the question of how far such conflicts are 'really' about religion, in the context of wider geopolitical struggles or inter-ethnic rivalries, but that very problem is a crucial one to address in seeking to understand the role of religion in history.

There is, however, another equally important side to the coin. Religious conflict has always been what catches the headlines, both in history books and in newspapers. Numerous states and societies, from the Roman Empire to the contemporary United States, have for long periods

---

[1] For discussion of the term 'fundamentalist', see below, pp. 297, 311–3.

experienced considerable religious diversity without significant overt conflict. Even in eras seemingly characterized by religious conflict, such as the crusades and the Reformation, for many at the grassroots daily life involved peaceful, if sometimes uneasy, coexistence with people of other faiths and traditions. In seeking to explain and understand the numerous occasions and contexts in which religion has been implicated in conflict, the historian must always therefore bear in mind that such conflict has not been an inevitable result of religious diversity, but was rather contingent on particular combinations of circumstances. Meanwhile the bases of both conflict and coexistence could shift as a result of conversions from one tradition to another.

All the chapters in this book are concerned either with historic interactions between major religious traditions, or with relationships between different sub-groupings and tendencies within these traditions. For our purpose the traditions under consideration include not only some of the major world religions – Christianity, Hinduism, Islam and Judaism – but also paganism and secularism (as an explicit ideological force) and secularity (as a pervading latent influence in society). The words used in the title, 'conflict', 'conversion' and 'coexistence', have been selected to highlight certain prominent forms that these interactions and relationships have taken.

Conflict denotes a situation where religious differences are perceived to be irreconcilable. Such differences may be founded in incompatible convictions and ideologies, and are likely also to relate to ways in which religion is practised and to the political, ethical and customary ordering of society. In such a situation either or both parties conclude that the general ascendancy of their own religion is imperative and that the other tradition(s) must be robustly challenged. Hence, for example, Roman emperors before Constantine intermittently persecuted Christians. Such a stance can arise from specifically religious motives, from the deep conviction that matters of essential truth touching on the eternal destiny of souls are at stake, as in the conflicts of the Reformation era. If opponents are perceived to be in fundamental error on matters of this kind, attacks on them can even be presented as a matter of kindness, designed to save them from themselves and the inevitable judgement and condemnation of God. Such an attitude has fuelled the missionary imperative in Christianity. In the Muslim world a similar conviction of the righteousness of one's own faith – in particular that Islam should be the publicly dominant tradition – has sometimes led to the oppression of religious minorities. In practice such religious motivation could often be mingled with political concerns, above all with the anxiety of rulers to impose shared values and beliefs on their people and so to reduce potential for dissent and subversion.

Confrontations can take a variety of forms. In many cases they may be characterized primarily by polemical writing and speaking, but even words on their own often entrenched divisions and provided the preconditions for conflict. An observation prompted by riots between Protestants and Roman Catholics in mid-nineteenth-century England raises interesting issues: 'the feeling that prompts the educated man to the use of injurious words, will urge the ignorant man to resort to blows' (quoted, Wolffe, 1991, p. 194). There may be no correlation between education and propensity to violence. Indeed those responsible for extreme acts of violence, from the persecutions of the Reformation era to contemporary suicide bombers, have often been well educated. The quotation reminds us, however, not only that words can have great power, but that conflict could take a range of forms, through social antagonism and exclusion to persecution, civil violence and military action. Religious conflict may divide societies and states within themselves, or set a government at odds with some of those it claims to rule. Religious dissent has been seen as tantamount to treason, in contexts ranging from Diocletian's Rome, to Louis XIV's France, and present-day Saudi Arabia. Such confrontations can also lead to international hostility and war. In extreme situations, whether, for example, in seventeenth-century Europe or in the contemporary Middle East, it is, however, important to assess the extent and the ways in which religion is a factor in conflicts that may well have much wider and more complex origins.

Conversion denotes a change of religious allegiance, including change from secularity or secularism to active religious conviction and practice. It may sometimes be a direct result of religious conflict when the 'solution' imposed by the victorious or dominant party is enforcing acceptance of its own tradition upon the losers, whose only alternatives to compliance are death or exile. This was, for example, the experience of some Christians in the pagan Roman Empire and of Jews and Muslims in early modern Spain. Even when conversion is not directly coercive it may often be associated with heavy persuasion or dominating cultural and political influence, as in the spread of Islam in its early centuries in the Middle East and around the Mediterranean, or of Christian missions in the Americas and in Africa. It can also be an entirely voluntary choice by the individuals concerned, although in societies where religious diversity is not already an accepted reality such changes of allegiance are likely to be limited by social and legislative constraints. Within Christianity, conversion is also a term used to describe a change of allegiance between sub-traditions, for example from Protestantism to Roman Catholicism, and to denote a life-changing experience of intense personal encounter with God that changes the trajectory of the individual's belief and religious practice.

Coexistence in its broadest sense could be understood as subsuming the other two categories in so far as it denotes the mere presence of two or more religious traditions within the same geographical area. It may be understood in a more specific sense as indicating an absence of significant conflict or conversion. Such coexistence can take many forms. For example, there may be genuine acceptance of religious diversity (as in modern Britain), or a trend towards assimilation and synchretism (as in pagan-Christian interactions in early medieval Europe), or, again, a social and spatial structure in which different religious communities live segregated lives but without overt hostility towards each other (as in the *millet* system under the Ottoman Empire). Coexistence may be positively welcomed, but it often arises from circumstances where traditions find themselves having to live alongside each other because none of them has the power or the will to achieve dominance. Under such circumstances coexistence may well prove unstable in the longer term and give way to a situation where conflict and/or conversion are widespread, as for example in the fluctuations of Protestant–Roman Catholic relations in Ireland during the last four and a half centuries.

In exploring different forms of coexistence, an important distinction needs to be drawn between *tolerance* and *toleration*. The former is a pragmatic attitude of mind among individuals who may be aware that their neighbours have different religious practices and beliefs from their own, and accept that difference, or at least turn a blind eye to it. *Toleration* on the other hand is a matter of state policy, in which governments accept that there is religious variety among those living in the territories they rule. Although a majority or historically dominant tradition (such as Anglicanism in England, Roman Catholicism in France, or Hinduism in India) is accorded certain privileges and prominence, minority groups are allowed to have freedom of worship if not full civil rights. Thus grassroots tolerance could sometimes make limited religious coexistence possible even if, as in nearly all states before the eighteenth century, governments and religious authorities did not adopt a policy of toleration. Conversely, in the modern world, despite widespread official toleration, popular intolerance can sometimes make the situation of religious minorities very difficult. Such problems can occur even when the state moves from a stance of toleration, in which one tradition is privileged but others acknowledged, to one of pluralism, in which all religions have equal civil status.

This book is designed to illuminate the themes of conflict, conversion and coexistence through a diverse range of historical case studies. Its approach therefore differs from other recent publications (for example Kepel, 1994; Armstrong, 2000) that have focused particularly on the background to religious conflict in the contemporary world, above all the perceived threat from 'fundamentalist' Islam. While this subject will receive due attention in the final chapter, the objective in the book as a whole is to examine the complex historical record on its own terms, seeking not so much to 'explain' the present as to equip the reader to see it in a long historical perspective and from a variety of different angles. For the historian of religion, as for students of other forms of history, it is crucially important to remind oneself that today is only the accidental and temporary vantage point from which the past is viewed. Just as, when one walks up a mountain, features of the landscape that were previously invisible gradually or suddenly come into view, and landmarks that initially dominated become obscured, so the passage of time itself changes perceptions of the past. The Reformation seemed for centuries to be a key defining phase in European history, giving rise to polarized theologies and identities that could be held with passionate intensity. In the later twentieth century, however, as the real challenges for Christianity were increasingly seen as stemming from secularity and from other faiths, the Reformation became much more liable to be dismissed as an obscure family quarrel which only concerned past generations and should not be perpetuated. Unfolding events in eastern Europe, the Balkans, and the former Soviet Union gave other historic religious and ideological divisions a greater contemporary resonance. Meanwhile, in recent decades, the upsurge in modern paganism has suggested that ancient paganisms need to be seen in a new light. Despite the lack of specific continuities, it becomes apparent that paganism in any period should be regarded as an enduring religious presence, rather than, as some would argue, a merely passing phase of human spiritual development (Thomas, 1971, pp. 47–8; Hutton, 1996, pp.422–6; Pearson, 2002).

The studies in this volume are offered within the framework of the academic discipline of religious history (Brooke and others, 1985). Religion is the central and recurrent point of reference. Accordingly a reader who also wants to understand particular developments and events from primarily secular perspectives will need to study this book alongside other historical literature. Religion, however, is understood here in a broad sense as denoting not merely the ideas and activities associated with formal religious institutions, but also the wider religious experience and attitudes of ordinary people, and interactions between religion, society and culture. The authors also endeavour to view religion objectively, in a manner detached from their personal religious (or non-religious) commitments. Such objectivity cannot and should not be absolute, and the various chapters, as in any historical writing, are inevitably shaped by personal enthusiasms and perceptions. The intention, however, is to view the topics studied in the round, rather than being limited by the outlook of a particular religious tradition. History written in a clearly confessional or denominational framework is often the product of extensive scholarship, and has considerable value in illuminating a tradition's sense of its own identity. Nevertheless it is exposed to considerable pitfalls. Much earlier writing on the history of Christianity, in particular, has been vigorously criticized for its tendency to drift into propaganda and ideology (Kent, 1987).

It is especially important to strive for objectivity and balance in explaining and assessing sometimes acute and violent religious conflicts. It is not the role of the historian to judge whether people in the past were 'right' or 'wrong' to behave as they did, but rather to understand the reasons for their actions – or inactions – and the consequences that followed from them. When confronted with, for example, the crusades or the mid-twentieth-century Holocaust of European Jews, the temptation to engage in easy armchair moralizing can sometimes be a significant one. It needs, however, to be resisted. Not only is it very difficult for the later reader to enter into the particular pressures and circumstances that led people in the past to decide and act as they did, but it is also important to seek to understand the beliefs and value systems that lay behind them. Nor, to the extent that this book highlights ways in which religion can lead to conflict, should it be read as implying a negative overall view of the historical record of religion. As religious teachings themselves widely maintain, although extreme and disproportionate violence is not justified, conflict in itself is not automatically a 'bad' thing. Moreover, alongside the role of religion in stirring conflict has been its major contributions to individual fulfilment and social and civil cohesion.

Historical myths form an important part of religious belief systems. The word 'myth' can appear loaded and even offensive to some, if it is taken to mean that the ideas and narratives so recounted are being dismissed as wholly untrue and fanciful. That, though, is not the way in which the word is used here. A myth may conceivably be an account of an historical reality, but one that is impossible to verify objectively from other evidence, especially if it involves supernatural intervention. An example is the biblical and other traditions associated with the birth and parentage of Jesus Christ. Across the centuries these beliefs have had a powerful role on Christian consciousness and artistic creativity, with the peaceable image of a baby in a manger serving as a check on more militant tendencies in the Christian tradition. A myth may also be an elaboration, development and distortion of some historical reality. For example the actual burnings of Protestants in the mid-sixteenth century led to an enduring belief that, if given the opportunity, Roman Catholics would always resort to such extreme measures to root out religious opposition. In identifying myths of this kind, the intention is not to dismiss them as 'untrue', nor uncritically to accept them as 'true', but to show how they have had great influence in shaping people's religious outlooks, and therefore need to be taken very seriously by historians. There is also a need to be conscious of the journalistic myths of their own time, such as the use of religious labels as convenient shorthand for referring to complex conflicts, in, for example, Northern Ireland or the Middle East.

In order to achieve focus and coherence within a volume of manageable size, the coverage of this book has inevitably had to be restricted. There is a particular emphasis on Christianity, and five out of the ten chapters are concerned primarily with the period since 1900. The first five chapters, however, establish a broader framework for this discussion of the relatively recent past. Christianity is examined first in its encounter with paganism in its early centuries, and second in the crusades era of the eleventh to thirteenth centuries, in which confrontation with Islam was particularly intense and prolonged. Chapters 3 and 4 are concerned primarily with conflict, conversion and coexistence in relation to internal Christian diversity since the Reformation. Chapter 5 provides an important case study of the implications of internal diversity during the nineteenth century within another major world religion, Hinduism. Implicitly it raises the question of how appropriate it would be to apply to a very different tradition concepts, such as conversion, derived primarily from the analysis of Christianity.

Chapter 6, as well as moving coverage firmly into the twentieth century, introduces a further important dimension to understanding of conflict, conversion and coexistence. It explores particularly the encounter between religion and secularity in a Britain where the cultural and social ascendancy of Christianity was no longer taken for granted. Chapter 7 pursues the idea that religious diversity and tension is a matter of gender difference as well as of theological and organizational separation. The next two chapters present an analysis of two of the most seemingly violent conflicts of the twentieth century in which religion has been implicated. As Chapter 8 shows, tentative endeavours to turn coexistence between Christians and Jews into more positive cooperation had no prospect of providing a basis for effective resistance to the overwhelming tidal wave of Nazi persecution. Subsequently, as analysed in Chapter 9, religion has been an enduring and potent strand in the entrenched confrontation of Israelis and Palestinians. The final chapter contextualizes and analyses the resurgence of Islam in the later twentieth century and explores some ways in which the preceding case studies of conflict, conversion and coexistence can help us to understand the situation and impact of religion in the contemporary world.

References

Armstrong, K. (2000) *The Battle for God: Fundamentalism in Judaism, Christianity and Islam*, London, HarperCollins.

Brooke, C. and others (1985) 'What is Religious History?', *History Today*, August, pp. 43–52.

Hoover, A. J. (1989) *God, Germany and Britain in the Great War: A Study in Clerical Nationalism*, New York, Praeger.

Hutton, R. (1996) *The Stations of the Sun: A History of the Ritual Year in Britain*, Oxford, Oxford University Press.

Kent, J. (1987) *The Unacceptable Face: The Modern Church in the Eyes of the Historian*, London, SCM Press.

Kepel, G. (1994) *The Revenge of God: The Resurgence of Islam, Christianity and Judaism in the Modern World*, Cambridge, Polity Press.

Pearson, J. A. (ed.) (2002) *Belief Beyond Boundaries*, Aldershot, Ashgate.

Ricks, C. (ed.) (1999) *The Oxford Book of English Verse*, Oxford, Oxford University Press.

Thomas, K. (1971) *Religion and the Decline of Magic: Studies in Popular Beliefs in Sixteenth and Seventeenth Century England*, London, Weidenfeld and Nicolson.

Wolffe, J. (1991) *The Protestant Crusade in Great Britain, 1829–1860*, Oxford, Clarendon Press.

1   Pagan and Christian in the third to fifth centuries

Janet Huskinson

> We multiply whenever we are mown down by you: the blood of Christians is seed.
>
> (Tertullian, *Apology*, 50, 14)

> In this sign conquer!
>
> (Constantine's 'Christian' vision before his victory over Maxentius. Eusebius, *Life of Constantine*, 1.28)

> One cannot reach so great a secret by one way alone.
>
> (Symmachus (a pagan, prefect of the city of Rome), *Relatio*, 3, 10)

> Their converts have not really been changed – they only say they have.
>
> (Libanius, *Oration*, 30, 28)

'Sound bites' like these are not hard to find in ancient sources concerned with pagan–Christian relations in the third to fifth centuries when examples of conflict, conversion and coexistence abound. This is not surprising given the important historical changes which took place in this formative period in western culture. These three centuries saw what was in effect the transformation of classical Graeco-Roman society into the world of late antiquity: the whole shape of the Roman Empire was altered, not only in its physical boundaries, but in its social, economic and political structures and in how people thought about their world. They also precede, and in many respects paved the way, for the great changes that occurred in the eastern Mediterranean from the seventh century with the rise of Islam.

Against this background Christianity developed in communities across the empire. In the first three centuries of its existence its followers were intermittently persecuted, but after the Emperor Constantine took up the Christian cause in the early fourth century (whether he fully converted and was baptized is a long-standing question), their influence increased. His successors were Christian apart from Julian (the 'Apostate') who personally converted back to paganism and sought – unsuccessfully – to reinstate it in the empire. But in the fifth century this Christian empire was fragmented by invasions of barbarians who were either pagan or 'heretical' Arian Christians, and in 476 the last emperor in the west was deposed.[1]

The Roman Empire had been more than just the setting for the rise of Christianity: it was a major enabling factor. It had brought stability to a vast territory in which local cultures and religions were allowed to continue largely without intervention. The eastern part of the empire was Greek in tradition, and the west Latin. Within them were regions and cities with their own distinctive cultural identities. Religious allegiances could vary over quite a small locality, sometimes for non-religious reasons such as long-standing inter-city rivalries. Even families could be divided. In this context diversity was bound to flourish.

Also diverse are the ways in which historians have presented pagan–Christian relations. In antiquity Christians had struggled to reconcile their classical pagan past with the biblical past of their scriptures. Modern historians have tended to take an entirely Christian perspective or have studied pagans and Christians together in the period of 'late antiquity'. The publication in 1971 of Peter Brown's *The World of Late Antiquity. Marcus Aurelius to Muhammad* was influential, particularly in showing how an interdisciplinary approach to the society which pagans and Christians shared can help to chart issues such as conflict, conversion and coexistence. Classicists, archaeologists and ancient historians now work on an era once dominated by studies of the writings of the Church Fathers (Patristics).

Following this approach, this chapter is based upon four case studies which look at some 'grass roots' situations of conflict, conversion and coexistence across time and place and also draw on evidence from a variety of sources. It starts with a brief discussion of terms, as both 'pagan' and 'Christian', though useful shorthand, contain massive simplifications. How people defined themselves and others is a crucial factor in the case studies that follow, even when they draw on crude stereotypes as a way of justifying conflict or rejection.

Although 'pagans' and 'Christians' are the subject of this chapter, this dichotomy is misleading. Apart from secularism and the wider cultural concerns of later Roman society (which will be important factors in this discussion), there were other religious groups that formed part of the overall picture.[2] Judaism has a particularly interesting role here as it was another monotheistic religion which interacted with Christianity and paganism in varying ways during this period. Although it shared so much with early Christianity in terms of background, Judaism differed from it in having gained some official sanction from the Roman state, while under

---

[1] Arianism was a form of Christianity founded by Arius, an early fourth-century priest from Alexandria, which claimed that God the Son was of lower status to God the Father (see Chidester, 2001, pp. 107–13).

[2] For the value of terms such as 'culture' and 'religion', 'sacred' and 'secular' in discussions such as this see Markus, 1990, 'Introduction'.

the Christian empire Jews were often treated with hostility as if Christians found it almost harder to coexist with a competing monotheism than with surviving paganism.[3]

Pagans

The term 'pagan' was introduced by fourth-century Christians to denote non-believers in Christianity.[4] But such a monolithic term obscures a plurality of religious experience. 'Pagans' in the Roman Empire had many different ways of relating to the divine world: there was no single belief system, sacred text or ethical code, and therefore no concept of orthodoxy, heresy or unbelief in the Christian sense. Instead, 'paganism' operated on various levels, from organized cult to personal devotion and philosophical systems, and an individual might be involved in all of these without apparent personal conflict or the need to convert from one set of beliefs or practices to another. Gods might be seen as a source of personal help in times of trouble, often in quite practical ways. Even emperors cultivated particular deities as their patrons. Constantine, for instance, linked himself with the Sun-God, Sol, and continued to do so even after he had claimed victory at Milvian Bridge in 312 in the name of Christ (as the coin of 316 shows in Figure 1). By and large the afterlife was not a major concern, although certain cults (notably 'mystery religions') offered some hope of it to their followers.

Figure 1   Solidus, coin minted at Ticinum in 316. It shows twin busts of Constantine (r.) and the Sun-God (l.). © Copyright The Trustees of The British Museum

[3] For early attempts to define differences between Christianity and Judaism see Chidester, 2001, pp. 32–6; for relative numbers of Christians and Jews in the second century see Chidester, 2001, p. 47.

[4] The usual meanings of the Latin *paganus* were a countryman or a civilian.

This variety is typical of Roman religious experience from early days. But there were some common features that are significant for our understanding of pagan–Christian relations. The first is the importance of official public cult as a way of securing the gods' favour for the community (usually described by the Latin term *religio*).[5] Rome's official cults were established in towns and cities across the empire. Local magistrates presided over the rites and temples dedicated to deities such as the Capitoline Triad (Jupiter, Juno and Minerva) were built in central locations. The cult of the emperor also belongs to this social and political context, symbolizing as it did the right relationship between leader and community. Thus the proper observance of official cult lay at the centre of the empire's life: it was part of being Roman.

A second important feature of Roman 'paganism' is its inextricable link with Graeco-Roman cultural traditions. In both town and country observance of ancient rites was important to communal identity, reinforcing the past and securing the future. Images and stories of the gods pervaded Roman culture, not only in its ritual but also in the myths which were the subject-matter of so much of its art and literature. Although Christian writers regularly attacked the immorality and sheer silliness of some of their tales, contemporary evidence shows that 'thinking' people appreciated them as allegorical expressions of philosophical truths.

A third feature is the toleration which pagan cults generally showed towards each other. As well as the traditional Graeco-Roman pantheon of gods, many other deities were worshipped locally thanks to the generally inclusive approach Romans had taken to indigenous cults in territories they had conquered. This could lead to assimilation between the two, and even syncretism as gods were given additional powers and attributes of others.[6] Some of these, such as Isis, were major deities, but others were not. Figure 2 shows a third-century relief from the Roman fort at Birrens, Dumfriesshire, on which Amandus, an architect (or surveyor), dedicates (in Latin) an image of *Brigantia*, a goddess, who, though linked with a local British tribe (the Brigantes), has been given attributes of the classical goddess Minerva (the breast-plate and arms) and the oriental Juno Caelestis (the conical stone to her right).

But there were limits to this toleration. The importance attached to official cults for the well-being of the community required that action be taken when necessary against groups whose beliefs or practices appeared to threaten this. Their activities could be defined as *superstitio*, which denoted inappropriate or excessive religious practices (in contrast to *religio*.) Magic (of various kinds) and major foreign cults came into this category and so, according to some of the earliest Roman references

[5] For a discussion of *religio* and *superstitio* see below; see also Beard, North and Price, 1998, Vol. I, pp. 215–18.

[6] For further discussion of syncretism, see Chapter 5, pp.143–4.

Figure 2 Stone sculpture showing the local goddess Brigantia with attributes of Minerva and Juno Caelestis. From Birrens, Dumfriesshire. Photo © National Museums of Scotland/Scran

to it, did Christianity 'as the most undesirable and dangerous group of all' (Beard, North, and Price, 1998, Vol. I, p. 244). Such circumstances led to negative myths and stereotypes, demonizing whatever group was seen as posing a threat. Thus the kinds of outlandish behaviour that Tacitus attributed to the Jews (*Histories* V, 4–5; Beard, North and Price, 1998, Vol. II, no. 11.8a) were later used against Christians (see Minucius Felix, *Octavius* 8–9; Beard, North and Price, 1998, Vol. II, no. 11.11d).

Christians

In some essential ways Christianity provides an immediate contrast with features of paganism just described. It was a monotheistic, missionary religion with a sacred text, an ethical system and, above all, clear hope of an afterlife, which were shared by all its followers. It had beliefs, creeds and doctrines that to some extent separated its followers from the secular world (or at least posed some need for compromise or negotiation with it), and which all too soon led to internal divisions between Christians themselves. Just as Christians might distinguish themselves from pagans or Jews, so they might define themselves (and others) as orthodox or heretic, often creating strong divisions in their communities. What beliefs or practices were necessary to define a Christian was a question much debated throughout this period. So while Christianity had some potentially unifying factors, which contemporary paganism lacked, in practice it too was heterogeneous; but with its sectarian divisions and its expectation that 'right beliefs' were necessary for salvation, it could be uncompromising.[7]

According to the Acts of the Apostles 11:26 the term 'Christian' was first applied to disciples working as missionaries in Antioch on the Orontes in the mid first century. It would have distinguished them and their beliefs from the Jews in the city, and from the followers of the city's numerous pagan cults. Typically, the earliest Christian communities were urban and lower class and were stronger and more numerous in the eastern part of the empire. The conversion of cities and countryside was a central part of Christian history throughout these centuries, as the case studies will show. But for now it is important to pick up on two challenging features of contemporary paganism which Christians had no choice but to address. Once again, they did so in various ways. For local believers it might be a question of managing their lives in the context of Roman society, while intellectuals tussled to define Christianity against the demands of classical (and Jewish) traditions.

The first feature of paganism which Christians had to address was the central role played by the observance of public cult in the life of the empire and its cities, and the importance attached to it as a means of securing the community's survival. Pliny's correspondence with the Emperor Trajan (*Letters* X, 96–7) in the early second century about the punishment of Christians shows how they were seen as a threat to traditional public worship – as *superstitio* – and also how they could be 'tested' by the command to offer sacrifices to the gods and emperor. Initially Christians who refused were sent to be tried in Rome if they were Roman citizens, or executed if they were not. In 249/50 Christians were faced with widespread persecution when the emperor Decius

---

[7] In relation to uncompromising attitudes, Bowersock, 1995, p. 5, notes that the use of the Greek word *marturos* to mean 'dying for a cause' was Christian in origin.

required everyone to sacrifice, and this recurred under the emperors Valerian and Diocletian. In the fourth century the continuation of public cult remained an issue, but in a reversed situation with Christian emperors setting the pace. The Edict of Milan of 313 allowed freedom of worship to all, but subsequent legislation against pagan sacrifice became tighter, culminating in Theodosius' edict of 391 against the public celebration of pagan cults. In other words (or so it could be argued) the official conversion of the empire to Christianity turned it from *superstitio* into *religio*.

The second challenge to Christians was the strength of classical traditions which faced them. At the theatre, or in choosing how to decorate their houses, they had to reconcile the popular mythological subjects with their religion. It is fascinating to trace how individuals did this in the historical record through a wide range of sources such as sermons, letters, inscriptions, objects and buildings. Most of this kind of evidence has a strong bias. Preachers, for instance, tend to state their case with vehemence even to the converted and sermons may reflect little of the audience's actual lives. Artefacts are often useful in providing tangible evidence to complement or even sometimes contradict the written record; they usually relate to a wider social stratum than literature (which was more exclusively the domain of elite, educated males). But they too can be hard to interpret, as is shown by a mid-fourth-century floor mosaic from Hinton St Mary in Dorset (Figure 3). What did the patron intend when he chose to decorate the smaller section of the room with the mythological episode of Bellerophon and the Chimaera, and the larger with the bust of a Christian – perhaps Christ himself – identified by the Chi Rho monogram (which represents the first two letters of the Greek word for Christ)? Here paganism and Christianity apparently coexist, but did the floor also intend to depict some element of conversion, from the heroes of paganism to Christianity? We can never know.

For educated Christians the intellectual heritage of Greece and Rome was a particularly powerful challenge and remained so throughout this period, though its emphasis was affected by changing circumstances. As a religion, Christianity differed from paganism in that even as early as the third century it had an agreed body of sacred texts. Yet central though this was to Christians' religious experience, it still could not defend them from the challenge of classical culture. A central theme in Christian writing before the fourth century was an 'apologetic' attempt to find ways of reconciling classical, philosophical and historical ideas with the Christian position. Some Christians felt defensive about the poor literary quality of the Christian holy texts compared with classical masterpieces and re-cast them in classical literary forms. The challenge of the classical heritage remained not only because of the stature of its greatest works, but because of its role in educating the elite, particularly for public office. How far they could go in separating classical culture from

Figure 3   Floor mosaic from Hinton St Mary, Dorset, showing the pagan hero Bellerophon killing the Chimaera in the upper (damaged) section and a bust of a Christian man at the centre of the lower section. Mid fourth century. © 2004 The British Museum/HIP/TopFoto

religious paganism remained a difficult question for educated Christians throughout this period (Cameron, 1993b, p.141).

Rooted though they were in religious paganism, these challenges to Christianity arose mainly in the context of contemporary secular society. In meeting challenges, Christians could draw on their own distinctive religious beliefs and historical experience and on their Jewish scriptural background. These also led them to various attitudes and practices which differed from the social norms. Above all, Christians' emphasis on the afterlife gave a new value to what was done in this world, affecting matters from sex within marriage to the proper commemoration of the dead. These differences sometimes caused immediate conflict with pagan society and proved to be important factors for change in the long term.

The four case studies that follow show how such factors operated in particular historical situations across the Roman Empire, contributing to conflict, conversion and coexistence (though not to each in equal measure). They have been chosen to give a widespread view, not only of the issues at stake but also of the range of evidence that survives from this complex period of ancient history.

North Africa in the early third century

Third-century North Africa (especially modern Libya and Tunisia) was a prosperous and prominent region of the Roman Empire. Christianity had gained an early hold on the population: according to Tertullian in c. 197 (*Apology* 1.7 and 37.4) people complained that Christians were everywhere, in town and country and at every social level. One general characteristic of North African Christianity seems to have been the passion with which Christianity was espoused, and this produced many important writers, apologists, clerics, martyrs and heretics. It therefore provides some good examples of conflict, conversion and coexistence in the period before Constantine, as well as a chance to look at a particular medium of communication that became important for the development of Christianity – the written word. In having a sacred text, Christianity differed from most pagan cults (yet was closely linked with Judaism); it also drew on other types of writing to aid its missionary work, support its congregations, and to create its own history and hagiographies. This case study will focus on some key aspects of Christian life in the region during the third century and on various types of writing which provide the evidence for them.

Some of the most vivid texts relate to martyrdom, to the trials and executions of Christians who chose to die rather than to sacrifice (Bowersock, 1995). These accounts took various forms: some were apparently based on court records, others on 'eyewitness' reports of the martyr's imprisonment and death, and yet others on the martyrs' own writings in imprisonment. They were circulated around Christian communities (sometimes in various versions) to commemorate their dead and to strengthen resolve (*Passio of Perpetua and Felicitas* 1; Musurillo, 1972, pp. l–lvii). Above all, the accounts emphasize the martyrs' commitment and courage, which is often heightened by graphic descriptions of their deaths and of miracles or visions associated with them. Thus they offer a theology of martyrdom through which martyrs reproduced the passion of Christ himself. But as historical documents they are difficult to assess, partly because of the lack of other corroborative evidence and partly because some of them seem to share characteristics of contemporary fiction (Bowersock, 1995, p. 24). Yet they reflect the mixture of elements that created Christian martyrs: legal procedures, pressure from the urban crowd, and the determination of many Christians which sometimes seemed almost to invite martyrdom. Often too they show that magistrates – though cast in the role of persecutor by the Christian narrative – were patient, even reluctant to send Christians to their death.

From Carthage (see Map 2) two rather different accounts of martyrdoms survive. The 'Acts of the Scillitan Martyrs' from 180 is in fact the earliest dated document from the Latin church, and despite some later editing, it is probably close to the original court records in its series of questions and answers (Musurillo, 1972, pp. xxii–iii, pp. 86–9). The proconsul Saturninus interrogates the twelve Christians and offers them various chances to gain pardon by taking an oath to the emperor, and thirty days in which to think things over. But they persist in their faith and are led to death, thanking God for their martyrdom. In the course of the trial it is revealed that they had 'books and letters of the just man, Paul' – probably for communal use.

The *Passio of Perpetua and Felicitas* tells how two young mothers were martyred with a group of others in 203 (Musurillo, 1972, pp. 107–31; Chidester, 2001, pp. 85–9). Its narrative juxtaposes the account of their death with descriptions of the visions which Perpetua and a companion Saturus had whilst in jail. In this way the rewards of martyrdom are offered to readers to offset the graphic details of the torments in the arena. The text explains that Perpetua and Saturus wrote the passages about the visions, although another author would have completed and edited the rest. By the fourth century the *Passio* was well-known and used in church worship.

Martyrdom was also celebrated in other kinds of contemporary writing, notably the tracts and treatises of Tertullian (c. 160–c. 225). A convert to Christianity, he became a vehement and sometimes uncompromising apologist for it, and is important as one of the first Christian writers in Latin. Some of his earliest pieces tackled the practical and ethical dilemmas that confronted new converts to Christianity in their daily coexistence with secular society. Presumably these were circulated or read to Christians. Tertullian's note in the preface to his treatise *Against*

Marcion shows that in this case there had been two previous editions, of which he himself withdrew the first dissatisfied with its length and quality, while the second was stolen (by another Christian) and distributed in a wrongly copied pirate version (Gamble, 1995, pp. 118–20. For Marcion, see Chidester, 2001, pp. 48–53). This warning to the reader shows some of the practical problems associated with the production and circulation of texts at this time, and it also reveals this particular author's concern with the quality of his output.

In the *Apology*, Tertullian turned to address pagan detractors of Christianity, using literary approaches and references (to Pliny and Tacitus) that spoke to them in their own terms. Clearly Tertullian was well read in classical literature. The work is set up like an extensive legal plea and combines a defence of Christianity with a refutation of pagan accusations against it on the grounds of magic and sedition. Tertullian also attacks the credibility of pagan deities. Yet though he was concerned to engage with pagan ideas at this level, he did not take on classical philosophy, as his near-contemporary Origen did in Alexandria. 'What has Athens to do with Jerusalem, or the academy with the Church?' asked Tertullian *(De praescriptione haereticorum,* 7.9). Later, Tertullian's rigorous stance on ethics and martyrdom led him to Montanism (a Christian sect from Asia Minor which had a great following in North Africa at this time) and he turned to writing attacks on mainstream Christians.

One avid reader of Tertullian – it is alleged – was Cyprian (c. 200–258). After a classical education he converted to Christianity in 246 and two years later became bishop of Carthage, until his martyrdom ten years later. Pastoral letters form a great part of his surviving writings and it is clear from references in them that Cyprian encouraged their wide circulation through copies and collections. They show the quality of his spiritual leadership, particularly during persecutions under the emperors Decius and Valerian. Amongst the problems he had to deal with was the vexed question of whether Christians who had lapsed under persecution should be re-admitted to the Church. The 'Acts of Cyprian' (Musurillo, 1972, pp. 169–75) record his dignified death, and a posthumous account of his life – the earliest Christian biography – was written by his deacon, Pontius.

Rome in the later third and early fourth centuries: evidence from visual art

This case study looks at a turning-point in the history of Christianity when it moved from persecution to imperial favour (Chidester, 2001, Chapter 7). Central themes are conflict with paganism and the increasing conversion of society to Christianity in the course of the fourth century.

In 312 Constantine defeated his rival Maxentius at the battle of the Milvian Bridge outside Rome, allegedly inspired by a vision from the Christian God (Eusebius, *Life of Constantine*, I.28; Chidester, 2001, pp. 100–1). In the following year he and his co-ruler Licinius declared toleration for all religions through the so-called Edict of Milan. Christian fortunes began to improve, for individuals and institutions. But this was not a simple or conclusive 'victory' over paganism. Instead, the fourth century saw something of a slow testing-out of what could or should be changed for religious purposes, and what belonged to the fabric of traditional Roman culture (Beard, North and Price, 1998, Vol. 1, Chapter 6).

Pagan–Christian relations in this period have often been studied from a political or religious angle, but art also provides some special insights across a broad social range. In particular, it illustrates some of the cultural implications of religious conversion, which, given the very conservative nature of classical Graeco-Roman culture, might have seemed rather threatening to traditional society.

During the third century the city of Rome had declined in influence and prosperity, partly because emperors needed to be far closer to contested frontiers. Few new public buildings or imperial monuments were erected. Yet one group of people in the city was beginning to find art and artefacts increasingly important as a means of self-definition. In this period Christians in Rome created their own distinctive art, introducing their own religious subject-matter into conventional decorative schemes. These earliest examples are all in funerary contexts, first in the paintings in underground burial chambers (catacombs) and later on the carved marble sarcophagi used by wealthier Christians in accordance with general fashion. There has been a good deal of debate as to why Christian religious art in Rome began then (and not before). Was there some ideological shift which made Christians feel more comfortable about depicting sacred subjects than they had done in the past? Or had the Christian community in Rome only then acquired sufficient economic resources to start commissioning its own art?

The repertoire of these images, all used in a funerary context, is important not just for art-historical reasons but for what it can say here about conversion, coexistence and conflict. In this respect the newly emergent Christian religious art is especially interesting, as it drew upon some imagery and ideas that were fashionable in funerary art of the time but rejected others; and its biblical images must have owed something to Jewish illustration although there is little, if any, first-hand evidence surviving to prove this. Many of its most popular subjects were of episodes of salvation from the Old Testament, including Jonah and the whale, Daniel and the lions, and Noah's Ark, and these tended to be shown in rather emblematic or 'shorthand' compositions where the essentials of their meaning seemed more important than aesthetic considerations.

Other popular early Christian images, which also expressed the idea of salvation and ensuing peace, were directly based on Graeco-Roman art: the Good Shepherd carrying a sheep across his shoulders – a seemingly omnipresent example – recreates a figure-type found in archaic Greek art. Others were adapted from images popular in contemporary funerary art and given a Christian spiritual value, as is shown by the late third-century sarcophagi featuring a philosopher with a female companion (Figures 4 and 5). In the pagan sarcophagus (Figure 4) the pair appear together in the centre (and again perhaps as the single standing figures at the sides). In the Christian sarcophagus (Figure 5) they also occupy the centre (and, as was quite common, their heads have been left roughly blocked out for the later addition of portrait features which would commemorate a particular couple). But here there are other, explicitly Christian features: the woman is portrayed with her hands raised in prayer (in a pose that becomes frequently used for women), and they are flanked by the Good Shepherd and the biblical scenes of Jonah and the baptism of Christ. These features convert the philosopher and the woman into specifically Christian figures, and turn pagan learning into Christian devotion with its reflective learning and prayer.

This process of adoption and adaptation may be explained at various levels. As Christian art began, artists often needed to use existing models for new subjects (as, for instance, the mythological Endymion was used for the resting Jonah in Figure 5). But transcending this practicality must have been the desire to show how themes generally important to third-century Romans could have a specifically Christian dimension. Thus, the sarcophagus scenes convert pagan learning into Christian, and generic rural landscapes into the peaceful world of the Christian Good Shepherd.

That this ideological factor was of paramount importance is also suggested by the prevalence of images to do with the afterlife and salvation. For Christians who were still being persecuted these must have had a particular resonance. One popular subject was the story of the three young Hebrews who survived martyrdom in the Fiery Furnace after their refusal to worship an image of the king Nebuchadnezzar (Book of Daniel, 3): one can imagine what this story might have meant to Christians living through situations in which failure to sacrifice to the emperor could lead to death.

After the Edict of Milan in 313, which allowed Christians to worship freely, many of these same images continued to be used, but had a new emphasis. They seemed now to convey confidence and an almost worldly assertiveness, as can be seen by comparing Figure 5 with the front of a large sarcophagus made in the late fourth century, reproduced as Figure 6. Here it is Christ who is the teacher at the centre, with the apostles ranked on either side in front of a rich, urban backdrop. On the lid, flanking the affluent-looking married couple, are biblical episodes which contrast earthly kingship with divine – the three Hebrews rejecting Nebuchadnezzar and the Adoration of the Magi. Compared with the

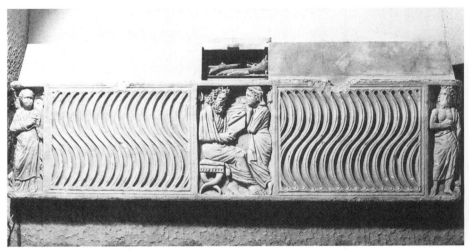

Figure 4   Pagan sarcophagus, Porto Torres, Sardinia. Photo: Koppermann, German Archaeological Institute, Rome, negative number 66.2174

Figure 5   Early Christian sarcophagus from the church of Santa Maria Antiqua, Rome, c.270. Photo: Boehringer, German Archaeological Institute, Rome, negative number 59.421

Figure 6   Front of a Christian sarcophagus, now in the church of San Ambrogio, Milan. Dated 380–400. Photo: Rossa, German Archaeological Institute, Rome, negative number 77.1088

earlier images these suggest a subtle conversion of emphasis away from the afterlife (and its possible refuge) to a new engagement with the interests of this world, reflecting some of the changes that had taken place in the earthly fortunes of the Christian community (cf. Chidester, 2001, pp. 154–6).

Christianity's new freedom, and the support it received from the emperor, gave its followers the chance to occupy positions of power in society. To display this new status they commissioned works of art for themselves and new churches for their religion. Here, too, secular culture provided both the fashions and most of the models. Biblical scenes expanded into the luxury media of silverware and ivory, yet at the same time classical traditions were so well embedded into some types of art that mythological subjects continued often like well-worn clichés. Thus, at the end of the fourth century, a Christian bride, Proiecta, had a silver toilet box decorated with the 'Toilet of Venus' and a Christian inscription enjoining her and her husband 'to live in Christ' (Shelton, 1988, pp. 72–5, no. 1).

In the last two decades of the fourth century art and artefacts become important evidence for the strength of feeling amongst leading pagans in Rome. The Senate in Rome had remained strongly pagan, which created tensions between it and the Christian emperor. A long and heated debate took place about the Altar of Victory in Rome at which senators traditionally performed official rites, and which was removed by the Christian emperor Gratian in 382 (summarized in Caseau, 1999, pp. 29–30). Even in more private contexts pagans commissioned art with a specific religious content, such as the two ivory panels probably made to commemorate a marriage between two leading pagan families, the Symmachi and Nicomachi, which each depict a pagan priestess sacrificing (Figure 7).

As these examples have shown, the visual arts were used by different religious groups and individuals in Rome to articulate their reactions to the various challenges which were involved in the development of the Christian empire. They provide some distinctive evidence for coexistence and conversion in cultural and social – as well as religious – terms.

Figure 7   Ivory panel from a diptych of the Symmachi and Nicomachi. Late fourth century, 29.9 x 12.4 cm. Photo © V & A Images, The Victoria and Albert Museum, London

Antioch in the later fourth century

This case study, set in Antioch on the Orontes in Syria (see Map 1), looks at some vital questions about the relationship between religion and civic culture, and what it might mean for a city and its citizens to become Christian. Here again coexistence and conversion are major themes.

Antioch was one of the most influential and prosperous cities of the Greek-speaking eastern Mediterranean, its importance continuing well into the sixth century. It was a Roman administrative and military centre, an important focus for its Syrian hinterland, with a large Jewish community. But its cultural traditions were strongly Greek, and fundamental to its civic life were the collective public observances of its long-established religious cults. Christianity had come to Antioch early through the missionary activities of Paul and Barnabas (Acts 11, 19:30) and flourished. By the late fourth century Christians and pagans had coexisted for several centuries, alongside other religious and ethnic groups in Antioch. But in the fourth century, with the development of the 'Christian empire', pagans and Christians were brought together on to the city council as representatives of the imperial government in the city. Thus the life of the city itself became a central issue in all kinds of debates about coexistence, between pagan and Christian, Christian and Jew, religion and secularism – all against the background of a manpower crisis in local government and economic uncertainties.[8]

Contemporary evidence for this situation, and for the tensions and compromises it involved, is particularly rich. It survives in the writings of three exceptional figures: the Emperor Julian 'the Apostate' (331–363), the pagan orator and teacher Libanius (341–c. 393), and the bishop John Chrysostom, 'the golden-mouthed' (c. 347–407). In the course of the later fourth century they all happened to live and work in the city, but it is true to say that each of them would merit a place in any general discussion of paganism and Christianity at this time. Each speaks from his own particular and passionate perspective, but between them they chart the many different levels of interaction between paganism and Christianity in contemporary Antioch. They also show quite clearly how neither of these was a monolithic religious system, but how each included disparate elements which could exist with virtual autonomy. Local Christianity, for instance, had been divided in the earlier fourth century by internal conflicts, and there were differences in religious experience between the urban church and the Christianity of the surrounding countryside.

That paganism too could mean different things to its adherents becomes clear from the experiences of the Emperor Julian, who stayed in Antioch for nine months between 362 and 363. With the zeal of a convert from Christianity he had had high hopes of his visit to Antioch's famous shrine

[8] For this see Sandwell, 2003. For a useful general survey see Harvey, 2000.

of Apollo at Daphne, but found there only an old priest who had brought his own goose from home to sacrifice (Julian, *Misopogon* 361). He thought the Antiochenes frivolous and irreligious. Libanius, writing a little later, expressed similar disappointment with his fellow citizens who did not fully share his appreciation of the value of a religious cult in underpinning the city's life and cultural traditions. For instance, he vigorously opposed the enlargement of a building in which ceremonies to do with the local games were held on the grounds that it would turn what had been a solemn and meaningful tradition into a more public and potentially disrespectful spectacle (Libanius, *Oration* 10). This shows how Libanius' concept of paganism integrated religious observance with cultural ideals – and also that many pagans in Antioch were happy to enjoy the city's traditional culture but neglected its religious aspects.

From his pulpit, John Chrysostom tackled a similar problem from a Christian angle. How to relate Christianity to life in the city was a question that existed at a collective, civic level as well as for individuals, and it had a further dimension in the need to relate the Church in the earthly city of Antioch to the Christian community in heaven. In a series of sermons written after the 'Riot of the Statues' in 387 (when the city feared retribution from Emperor Theodosius after it rose against the imposition of higher taxes), Chrysostom draws some close links between the Church and city of Antioch. He described the Church as the city's new guardian and source of its new, Christian history (see John Chrysostom, *On the Statues, Homily on Matthew* 17, 40). To individual Christians, Chrysostom gave constant reminders of the choices and challenges that continued to face them even in their largely Christianized society. How could Christians avoid the seductions of its 'pagan' life-style? How should Christian ethics affect relationships with the family and fellow citizens? Chrysostom's homilies return time and again to these central issues, warning against self-indulgent materialism and such 'pagan' pursuits as the theatre with its enactments of immoral myths.

Such examples show how these high-minded thinkers – pagan and Christian – had a common foe in the irreligiosity they perceived in contemporary life: both Libanius and Chrysostom, for instance, saw the theatre as a potential source of civic disorder (Libanius, *Oration* 19, 28; John Chrysostom, *Homily on Matthew* 37, 6–7). But by and large it seems that pagans and Christians coexisted easily in the everyday life of Antioch. Certainly Libanius numbered many Christians amongst his students, (including the young Chrysostom sent by his Christian mother) who would acquire the kind of classical education needed to fit them for public office. Even so, the city itself was becoming more Christian in its institutions. Churches were built and pagan buildings abandoned or demolished, the Christian martyr Babylas was re-interred in the suburb of Daphne, to provide a Christian parallel to its shrine of Apollo. Christian festivals were introduced alongside or to replace longstanding pagan celebrations; and as an institution in the city the church became a major benefactor, providing care for the poor and homeless as once the city's pagan elite had done. The Jewish community, which had shared a good deal of civic power in Antioch until the late fourth century, became increasingly marginalized (until the seventh century, when Jews were expelled from Antioch altogether). This may have begun as a Christian retaliation for Julian's attempt to get local Jews to side with pagans against them, but the strength of anti-Jewish invective used by Chrysostom, for instance, suggests that there may have been more to it than that. He seems to have been particularly anxious about the number of Christians with Jewish sympathies who attended synagogues, and this implies some fears for the power of Christianity in the city and perhaps too for their distinct identity (Meeks and Wilken, 1978).

In the city people could thus transfer their traditional patterns of social activity to a new religious focus, with the Church, for instance, now patronizing events that would attract the wider community. But recent historians are divided in their interpretation of changes like these. How far should they be interpreted in religious terms as a 'victory' for the Christianization of cities such as Antioch? Or is it the case that their inhabitants felt themselves so secularized that they approached these aspects of their civic life, not primarily as 'pagans' or 'Christians', but simply as members of the local community?

Outside the city Christianity had a different face. In the surrounding countryside many monks lived as ascetic 'holy men'. They were visited for their wisdom and healing by local people, though a few, such as Symeon Stylites the Elder who lived on a pillar for forty years (Chidester, 2001, p. 126), attracted visitors from far afield. They also involved themselves in the city's religious life, and John Chrysostom praised their role in working for a settlement for the city after the 'Riot of the Statues' (e.g. *On the Statues, Homily* 17). But another view of their activities is given by Libanius in a graphic communication to the Emperor Theodosius (*Oration 30. For the Temples*), made probably just a few years before the riot. He did not usually directly criticize Christianity in terms of its beliefs and doctrines, but here inveighed against the monks as lawless parasites who destroyed ancient rural shrines and threatened estates. Conflict in this instance has as much an economic and cultural basis as a religious one.

For the beliefs of the country people around Antioch, a vital source of evidence comes from inscriptions on buildings – secular as well as religious – which consecrated them to a particular divinity. A study of their particular formulae suggests that in the countryside around Antioch, pagan cults continued into the early fifth century when many temples were converted for Christian use (Trombley, 2003). Yet at the same time certain Christian phrases became popular, notably 'One God and Christ'; Antioch's Christians had shouted this overjoyed at Julian's death, and it became a popular triumphalist Christian slogan. Religious change may have been slower to happen in the countryside, but this evidence shows that it might still echo some urban concerns.

Fifth-century Gaul

Early in the fifth century a series of barbarian invasions afflicted the now
Christian western empire, bringing about some profound social and
political changes and opening up a new set of questions about pagans
and Christians. At this time there were still pagans in positions of
influence at Rome who were actively involved in cults and also
concerned with traditions of classical culture. But the longstanding
equation of paganism with classical cultural traditions was now to be
challenged by the fact that many of the invading barbarians were pagans,
but from a very different cultural background. Where did Christianity fit
into this? What were the connections between Christianity and empire in
this situation? Would it survive as the *religio* which preserved Roman
secular power, as pagan cult had done in the pre-Christian state? And if
so, how far was it also to be identified with the survival of classical
traditions? These are the kinds of tensions that underlie the instances of
conflict, conversion and coexistence in this final case study on fifth-
century Gaul.

The concept of the barbarian as the 'other' to the civilized Romans had
had a long history and was manipulated by writers and artists in various
ways, usually in polarized terms. Now it was to be used by pagan and
Christian writers as they tried to establish new identities in their changing
world. For example, paintings that celebrated a defeat of the Goths in
400 put God firmly on the side of Christian Rome by depicting 'the hand
of God driving off the barbarian' (Eunapius, *Fragment* 68). When the
Goths sacked Rome in 410 the questioning became more urgent by
pagans and Christians alike: how had the 'new' Christian empire brought
a threat to classical civilization itself? While the Roman Empire had
flourished during its many centuries of paganism, Christianity appeared
to have led it to its end after only a few generations. As a response to
this pagan criticism Augustine wrote his great work *The City of God,* in
which he set out two communities, the earthly one of those who loved
themselves, and the heavenly one of those who loved God (Chidester,
2001, pp. 143–7). He refuted pagan accusations that the barbarian
calamity had been caused by prohibitions on their cult (and in his
introduction made some pointed comments about how Christians had
given asylum to so many pagans and saved them as the Goths invaded
Rome).

Later in the fifth century, evidence from Gaul provides some valuable
insights into how the old relationships of 'barbarian' and 'Roman',
'pagan' and 'Christian' were re-configured when barbarians who had
crossed the Rhine in 407 moved southwards and settled alongside local
Romano-Gallic communities, where they converted to Christianity. Their
arrival forced the Roman authorities to leave the imperial court at Trier
(see Map 2) and to withdraw to Arles in south-eastern France. Outside
this small remaining piece of the Roman Empire in Gaul people were left

to work out new ways of coexisting and of identifying themselves and their neighbours.

In commenting on aspects of this coexistence two modern scholars provide examples of changing self-definition around the 'barbarian' and 'Roman' antithesis, illustrating how paganism and Christianity came into this new equation. Writing about how many barbarians converted to Christianity, Thompson (1963, p. 78) observed pithily how 'Their transference from the wilds of barbaria into the social relationships of Romania brought about a marked and comparatively sudden transformation in their religion.' In other words, they gave up paganism along with their old life-style and embraced Christianity as a mark of their new 'Roman' identity. Van Dam noted how even in the same region, different people defined their activities in different ways:

> the distinction in perspective between Roman and barbarian ... in many instances was equivalent to the distinction between freedom and slavery. Some men dismissed activities in marginal and troubled areas by calling them barbarian, while the men actually living there would do everything possible to remain 'free', and Roman.
>
> (1985, p. 27)

Put together these comments suggest how the inhabitants (old and new) of fifth-century Gaul had a strong urge to maintain a sense of the 'free', 'Roman' ways that had existed before the arrival of the barbarians, and that they all now looked to Christianity as a means of securing this.

The importance of Christianity within this social transformation is borne out in the lives and works of contemporary Roman writers such as Salvian and Sidonius Apollinaris. Salvian had moved south from Trier to the area of Gaul that remained Roman and had entered the monastery at Lérins. There he became famous as a teacher and writer, producing his most famous work, *The Governance of God*, around 450. This discussion of the unhappy state his country had fallen into was more moral discourse than historical analysis. As well as inveighing against the greed of the landed classes, Salvian brought the barbarians into his argument, using them as an antithesis to Christians who are only lukewarm in the practice of their faith. So, to the question of why God had allowed the defeat of the Christian empire, he gave the robust answer that Christians had deserved this punishment because of their sin (3:11; 7:1). Within this argument he turned the barbarians into exemplars of good morality despite their paganism (e.g. 4:14; 5:8; 7:9): 'What hope can there be for the Roman state when the barbarians are more chaste and more pure than the Romans?' (7:23). As a particular example he cited the 'sinful' activity of the circus (the Roman arena for chariot racing) which had eventually been ended not by pious Christians but by barbarian invaders (6:8). For Salvian, enforced coexistence with pagan invaders was, as it were, a chance for society to be re-converted to a more effective Christian morality.

The writings of Sidonius Apollinaris (c. 430–c. 484) reveal more of what it was like to live and work in the unsettled environment of mid-fifth-century Gaul.[9] They include poems for friends and panegyrics on several emperors, all written in a rather antiquarian classical style, and a large number of letters. These give some fascinating insights into religion and cultural differences from a contemporary standpoint. For instance, Sidonius portrays the Arian king of the Visigoths, Theodoric II, as a nominal Christian (*Letter* I, 2, 4), and carefully attempts to distinguish between the (positive) personal qualities of a Jewish acquaintance and the (perceived negative) aspects of his religion. The letters also show just how abandoned people in his position could feel: 'the Roman state has sunk to such an extremity of helplessness that it no longer rewards those who are devoted to it' (*Letter* III, 8, 1). This was particularly so for men such as Sidonius who came from an aristocratic class in Gaul which had traditionally defined its Roman identity through holding public office. As the opportunities for this declined they increasingly looked to the hierarchies of the Church. Bishops could become powerful local political leaders and Sidonius himself became bishop of Clermont just two years after he had been prefect of Rome in 468. Along with political ambition these aristocrats brought into the Church the classical culture that had underpinned their social status. Clerics wrote on conventional 'pagan' literary subjects as well as on Christian themes, often looking back to a 'mythical' past of Roman greatness. Gradually, though, they fostered an interest in the local Christian past and the cult of saints and relics was developed.

By the sixth century, it has been argued (by, for example, Van Dam, 1985, p. 306), the transformation had taken place in people's self-definition from 'pagan, Roman Gaul to Christian, barbarian Gaul'. Comparing this with the first case study, there is a striking contrast between the situation in the third century when Christians were seen as threats to the pagan Roman state, and these areas settled by barbarians in the fifth century where it was Christianity which became the vehicle of traditional 'Roman-ness'. Although there was undoubtedly conflict on a small scale at a local level between different groups in Gaul, coexistence was key: it seems to have led to conversions that were not only religious but also cultural and social in their impact. Christianity remained to legitimize the state, but the state and its constituents were now rather different from those of Constantine's empire.

[9] See Van Dam, 1985, pp. 156–78 for a discussion of Apollinaris' life and works.

Conflict, conversion and coexistence: some conclusions

Many ancient Christian writers give the impression that the third to fifth centuries saw the inevitable and triumphant progress of Christianity from persecution to total victory over polytheism: within such a narrative, conflict, conversion and coexistence all worked to Christian ends. Yet despite its great political power, the Christian empire did not change the religious map once and for all: it did not force through the conversion of society or replace traditional codes of behaviour with explicitly Christian ones. Instead, it was rather successful in obscuring the traces of its opponents.

Paganism and Christianity coexisted up to (and beyond) the end of this period in a 'patchwork of religious communities' (Brown, 1998, p. 641). In large cities, pagans and Christians lived side by side, but elsewhere they formed their own small separate enclaves. Christianity was often much slower to take hold in the countryside than in towns, producing the mixed religious landscape noted around Antioch, and in rural Gaul.

Various factors contributed to this high degree of unenforced coexistence. For many people, avoiding conflict could be seen as a matter of enlightened self-interest. Many individual Christians had worked out their own levels of compromise with the demands of surrounding society, and although they drew their own line at involvement with explicit polytheism, they seem to have been generally content to live and let live. There also appears to have been a good deal of general indifference to organized religion on both sides, as the comments of Libanius and Chrysostom at Antioch suggest. Festivals, feasting and spectacle are often described by religious moralists as the limits of many people's attachment to religion. Yet, it is clear from evidence at healing shrines, for instance, that many ordinary people went much further in their search for divine help. Their faith was a major factor in the development of pilgrim sites around the tombs of saints and martyrs, or visits to living holy men.

Above all, both Christians and pagans were held together by the strong bonds of a common culture, and one that had taken a traditionally inclusive approach to what constituted 'Roman-ness', particularly in terms of religion. The earlier empire had generally been open to the practice of religions that did not threaten its integrity, and it is possible to see similar ideals continuing in the fourth century, as for instance in the legislation that supported general freedom of worship. Even tangible artefacts such as the Hinton St Mary mosaic (Figure 3) and Proiecta's toilet box may be interpreted as signs of this continuing inclusiveness at work on a domestic level.

In a comparable way paganism and Christianity coexisted in the lives of many individuals. For some this was a sequential experience, moving from one set of beliefs to another; for others it was a life-long combination of elements, balanced with or without a spiritual struggle. In paganism of the earlier empire, before the rise of Christianity, it was quite possible to follow more than one cult or set of beliefs, so conversion from one to another was not an issue. But Christianity introduced some different issues. From the start it had a mission of evangelism and proved to have mass appeal. Pagan critics accused it of targetting the socially vulnerable (Origen, *Against Celsus* 3.52), but Tertullian emphasized how people of all types were converted by the witness of martyrs. Miracles could inspire spontaneous conversion, but there were also many cases of educated people arriving at Christianity after much private thought.

After the establishment of the Christian empire similar cases can be found – witness Augustine's long process of 'conversion' decribed in his *Confessions* (Chidester, 2001, pp. 136–43), and in a reverse direction Julian's 'apostasy' to paganism. But the situation is complicated by the secular power that Christianity acquired. According to Eusebius (*Life of Constantine*, 4. 54.2), even in Constantine's lifetime some people realized that it would be expedient for them to convert to the emperor's new faith. As Christian patronage became more important in secular society, instances of this kind increased, as well as debates about how to define a Christian – through behaviour, baptism or, perhaps, buildings (Markus, 1990, Chapter 3). The advantages of conversion, though, were not all one-way: rich and influential converts were no doubt welcomed by Christians, just as it was later claimed that converted barbarians were an asset to society as they lived more peacefully with their Roman neighbours (Orosius, VII, 32.13). Mass conversions are often recorded: even under Constantine some towns and cities seem to have thought it worth their while to adopt the emperor's religion (Eusebius, *Life of Constantine* 4. 37–9), while barbarians were often 'converted' to Christianity with the conversion of their leader as part of their settlement into 'a new economic and social world' (Thompson, 1963, p. 78).

The later part of the fourth century saw many intellectual conversions from paganism to Christianity. This was a time in which the educated elite may have realized that Christianity was to remain permanently at the head of their society, particularly after Julian's failure to secure a permanent restoration of pagan cult (clearly based on his own passionately held beliefs). Christianity may also increasingly have offered them more in terms of worldly advancement. For those who were already Christians in a nominal way, 'conversion' meant an intensification of their existing faith: like Paulinus of Nola, they might be moved to renounce wealth and social status and withdraw to a more ascetic life.

Conversion also affected the landscape. In the fourth and fifth centuries, towns and countryside became increasingly influenced by Christianity.

Christians demolished many pagan centres of worship and converted others for their own use. Churches were built on top of pagan shrines, and cult statues were destroyed or appropriated as art objects or even 'christened' by the inscribing of a cross. Townscapes were changed by monumental new Christian buildings, while biblical sites in Judaea were converted by Christian building into the 'Holy Land': churches were built on sites connected with the life of Christ, such as the nativity in Bethlehem and the Church of the Holy Sepulchre in Jerusalem.[10] Many of these developments were valuable as visible statements about the presence of Christianity in society rather than evidence of the inhabitants' conversion. As Libanius astutely observed in his complaint to Theodosius about the illicit destruction of ancient pagan shrines around Antioch (*Oration 30. 26–8*), any official orders to demolish them were likely to backfire and have the effect of strengthening pagans in their beliefs rather than making any genuine converts to Christianity.[11]

Despite evidence for coexistence and conversion to Christianity, town and country saw regular bouts of conflict between pagans and Christians. As in the case of persecutions of Christians in the pre-Constantinian empire, such conflict often fused religious with political motives. Law and mob violence was invoked against particular religious groups in the name of social 'law and order', and many local sectarian conflicts between pagans, Christians or Jews seem to have been occasioned by political disputes or rivalries.

There is evidence that there were many occasions when religious differences were seen as irreconcilable – conflicting positions between Roman authorities and Christian martyrs, antagonism to the Jews, and splits within Christianity itself (which were long-lasting and famously vicious: Ammianus Marcellinus, 22, 5, 4.) After all, religion was a central issue in late antiquity, even when there were also underlying tussles for secular power (Cameron, 1993b, pp. 65–6). Revenge for past wrongs was often a potent factor, both in 'tit-for-tat' conflicts at local level and also on the wider scene. After Constantine's victory in 312, Christian writers such as Lactantius celebrated the deaths of the persecutors, while the increasing cult of martyrs in the fourth century (although martyrs were rare at that time), could only but serve as a veiled reminder to contemporary pagans of just where they stood in relation to new Christian authority. As legislation against pagan cult began to tighten in the late fourth and early fifth centuries, the actions of Christian authorities provoked pagan retaliation across the empire (Fowden, 1978). In Alexandria, for instance, the great temple of the Egyptian god Serapis was burned down in 391 by Christian monks; Christians were attacked by local Jews; and in 415 Christians murdered the pagan philosopher Hypatia (Cameron, 1993b, pp. 20–1). However, by the fifth century,

[10] See also Chapter 2 and especially Chapter 9, and Chidester, 2001, pp. 113–17.

[11] See Fowden, 1978, pp. 77–8. For a general discussion of the Christian landscape see Caseau, 1999.

pagans could claim to have right on their side, for it was the Christian empire that had brought Rome to the brink of destruction by barbarians. Sectarian conflicts of this kind involved destruction of people and property and much polemical writing.

Postscript

Inevitably chapters have dividing lines and cut-off points, and this one has concentrated on pagan–Christian relations in the third to fifth centuries. Consequently, I have had to downplay the relationships which each of those groups had with Judaism, and exclude the rise during the seventh century of another great monotheism, Islam. In doing this it would be true to say that the chapter follows what until quite recently has been a common trend amongst ancient historians, who saw the coming of Islam in the seventh century as a decisive end to the classical world (or at least, a useful point at which to finish their accounts of it): 'Of all the dividing lines set up between academic disciplines in the western intellectual tradition, the frontier between classical and Islamic studies has proved the most durable and impenetrable' (Kennedy, 1999, p. 219). Now, at the beginning of the twenty-first century, there is a great interest in exploring continuities as well as changes, particularly in the culture and society of those near eastern lands which had been part of the eastern Roman Empire.[12]

As was shown in the case of fifth-century Gaul, the coming of barbarians to settle in western territories of the empire brought about some great changes for people in the area. Many of the incomers converted to Christianity, but perhaps even more profound were the changes that occurred in mentalities and social structures as people tried to relate this new world to the old world of the Roman Empire. While this was happening in the west, the east of the empire was in fact enjoying a relatively stable and prosperous time (hinted at in the case study of Antioch). Despite constant threats to its borders, especially from the Persian Empire, the east had been better able to resist invasion and the area remained fairly peaceful until at least the later sixth century. Justinian attempted to re-conquer some of the parts of the western empire which had been lost to barbarian rule, but despite his success in recovering areas of North Africa, Italy and Spain, the empire (by now usually termed 'Byzantine') was progressively weakened. Just as had happened in the west during the fifth century, so in the east in the late sixth century, large areas fell, first to Persian and then, in the mid seventh century, to Arab invaders. The ease with which the invaders

[12] These historiographical developments are usefully summarized in, for example, Cameron, 1993b, and Bowersock, Brown and Grabar, 1999, Introduction. Kennedy, 1999, provides a useful introduction to Islam and Islamic culture in this early period.

moved in may be explained by many factors, but in the context of this chapter it is interesting that one concerns the possible role of Jewish support for the Arabs against the Byzantine Empire. Judaism had continued to flourish in the Levant despite Justinian's strong anti-Jewish measures, and Jews were thought by Byzantine Christians to have sided with the Islamic Arabs against them. Whether or not this collusion happened, it seems that compared to their time under Byzantine rule, 'under Islam the lot of the Jews of Palestine probably slightly improved' (Cameron, 1993b, p. 189). In this new context they remained second-class citizens, but this time Christians also came to be regarded as such (Kennedy, 1999, pp. 226–8).

In much of this chapter the question of the relationship between religion and state has been a major issue. I began by emphasizing how the observance of public cult was deemed essential for the continued welfare of the pre-Christian Roman state. Then, under Christian emperors, I questioned what this meant for social institutions and cultural traditions as well as for religious practice. With these great developments in the seventh-century east the same questions of relationship arise, with the distinction to be made between 'Arab' and 'Islam'. Arab tribesmen inhabited the desert areas between roughly Syria in the north and Egypt in the south. They seem to have worshipped many different pagan gods, although there were conversions to Christianity in the fifth and sixth centuries and also to Judaism, which was the main monotheistic religion in some areas. Islam was the religion of which Muhammad (c. 570–632) was the prophet. He was born in Mecca in modern-day Saudi Arabia. Receiving revelations from the angel Gabriel he preached that there was only one true God, Allah. But as his followers grew in number he had to deal with the hostile reaction of local pagans, and eventually he made a move (*hijra*, 'migration') to Medina. There a new Islamic community was set up which expanded fast in the following years, largely through victories over local warring groups. In the centuries after Muhammad's death, the territories of this 'Islamic empire' grew to cover vast areas, drawing together the different Arab peoples and stretching eventually from Spain to Afghanistan. Until about 800 it is reckoned that only the minority of its population was Islamic by religion. Christianity and Judaism were officially tolerated, and conflict, conversion and coexistence continued in another set of contexts.

References

*Beard, M., North, J. and Price, S. (1998) *Religions of Rome*, Cambridge, Cambridge University Press. (Two volumes, of history and of sources, which set paganism and Christianity in the context of religion in the Roman Empire; useful too for showing what 'religion' involved in classical society.)

Bowersock, G. W. (1995) *Martyrdom and Rome*, Cambridge, Cambridge University Press.

*Bowersock, G. W., Brown, P. and Grabar, O. (eds) (1999) *Late Antiquity: A Guide to the Postclassical World*, Cambridge, MA and London, Bellknap Press of Harvard University Press. (A volume of essays, followed by an extensive reference section on aspects of late antique society, up to the rise of Islam. The essays are also published as a separate volume: Bowersock, G. W., Brown P. and Grabar, O. (2001) *Interpreting Late Antiquity: Essays on the Postclassical World*, Cambridge, MA and London, Bellknap Press of Harvard University Press.)

*Brown, P. (1971) *The World of Late Antiquity: Marcus Aurelius to Muhammed*, London, Thames & Hudson. (A highly readable general history of the period which has been very influential in defining 'late antiquity' as a period in its own right.)

Brown, P. (1998) 'Christianization and religious conflict' in A. Cameron and P. Garnsey (eds) *Cambridge Ancient History XIII, The Late Empire, A.D. 337–425*, Cambridge, Cambridge University Press, pp. 632–64.

*Cameron, A. (1993a) *The Later Roman Empire (AD 284 –430)*, Fontana History of the Ancient World, London, Fontana Press, and *Cameron, A. (1993b) *The Mediterranean World in Late Antiquity AD395–600*, London and New York, Routledge History of the Ancient World, London, Routledge. (Two excellent surveys of different time-spans within this period.)

Caseau, B. (1999) 'Sacred landscapes' in Bowersock, Brown and Grabar (eds) pp. 21–59.

Chidester, D. (2001) *Christianity: A Global History*, Harmondsworth, Penguin.

*Curran, J. (2000) *Pagan City and Christian Capital. Rome in the Fourth Century*, Oxford, Clarendon Press.

*Elsner, J. (1998) *Imperial Rome and Christian Triumph: The Art of the Roman Empire 100–450*, Oxford History of Art, Oxford, Oxford University Press. (Discusses visual art of the period from the second to fifth centuries and the development of Christian art in the context of Roman culture.)

Fowden, G. (1978) 'Bishops and temples in the eastern Roman Empire: AD 320 –435', *Journal of Theological Studies*, vol. 29, pp. 53–78.

Gamble, H. Y. (1995) *Books and Readers in the Early Church: A History of Early Christian Texts*, New Haven and London, Yale University Press.

Harvey, S. A. (2000) 'Antioch and Christianity' in C. Kondoleon, *Antioch: The Lost Ancient City*, Princeton, NJ, Princeton University Press, pp. 39–49.

Kennedy, H. (1999) 'Islam' in Bowersock, Brown and Grabar (eds) pp. 219–37.

*Lane Fox, R. (1986) *Pagans and Christians in the Mediterranean World from the Second Century AD to the Conversion of Constantine*, Harmondsworth, Penguin. (A rich account of pagan and Christian attitudes and relationships in the period before Constantine. Detailed and readable.)

Markus, R. (1990) *The End of Ancient Christianity*, Cambridge, Cambridge University Press.

Meeks, W. A. and Wilken, R. L. (1978) *Jews and Christians in Antioch in the First Four Centuries of the Common Era*, SBL Sources for Biblical Study 13, Missoula, Montana.

Musurillo, H. (1972) *Acts of the Christian Martyrs*, Oxford, Clarendon Press.

Sandwell, I. (2003) 'Christian self-definition in the fourth century AD: John Chrysostom on Christianity, Imperial rule and the City' in Sandwell and Huskinson (eds), pp. 35–58.

Sandwell, I. and Huskinson, J. (eds) (2003) *Culture and Society in Later Roman Antioch*, Oxford, Oxbow.

Shelton, K. (1988) *The Esquiline Treasure*, London, British Museum Publications.

Thompson, E. A. (1963) 'Christianity and the Northern Barbarians' in A. Momigliano (ed.) *The Conflict between Paganism and Christianity in the Fourth Century*, Oxford, Clarendon Press, pp. 56–78.

Trombley, F. (2003) 'Christian demography in the territorium of Antioch (4th–5th c.): observations on the epigraphy' in Sandwell and Huskinson (eds), pp. 59–85.

Van Dam, R. (1985) *Leadership and Community in Late Antique Gaul*, Berkeley, Los Angeles and London, University of California Press.

Asterisked items are particularly recommended for further reading.

2 Islam, Christianity and the crusades: rival monotheisms and monotheistic rivals

Jo Pearson

> The Crusades, that extraordinary series of holy wars, that long struggle in the Levant between East and West, Christendom and Islam, which began so theatrically in the eleventh century and petered out so ignominiously in the thirteenth, were described by Gibbon as 'the World's Debate'. The world has debated about them a good deal since and will no doubt go on debating.
>
> (Trevor-Roper, 1966, p. 101)

This chapter focuses on the complexities of what has become known, in European religious history, as the crusading era. Seen in simple terms, the crusades of the eleventh to the thirteenth centuries can be characterized as a rivalry for power between Christianity and Islam. As such, the struggle has many perceived parallels, not least in the post-11 September 2001 stand-off between the United States of America and Osama bin Laden, and the subsequent American invasions of Afghanistan and Iraq, seen by many as representing confrontations between Christianity and Islam. Of course, such situations, then as now, are vastly more complex. The power struggle (if such it was) was neither inevitable nor inherent in Christianity or Islam, and it was not contained within the framework of Christian–Islam encounters in the eastern Mediterranean. Rival monotheisms existed within Christianity and the crusades were undertaken against this 'enemy within', against heretical sects, and against the remaining bastions of European paganism/heathenism.

Yet it was the monotheistic rivals of Christianity and Islam that played the major part in the early and most expansive crusades, and in the development of the idea of 'the crusade' in the course of the twelfth century. For the

> 'crusade idea' was fed by rivulets which sprang from diverse and sometimes unlikely starting-points, which trickled slowly and uncertainly in their early courses: it did not flow in a single, strong current ... until the better part of a century had passed since Urban's pontificate.
>
> (Fletcher, 1998, p. 486)

This chapter therefore concentrates on the encounter between Christianity and Islam, rather than on those crusades undertaken against heresies, such as the Albigensian Crusade against the Cathars in southern France, or the Baltic Crusades against the last remaining pagans.

The crusades were so named because of the spontaneous adoption of a cross made from strips of material torn from clothing by those who heard the first preaching of the crusade at Clermont by Pope Urban II on 27 November 1095. Urban had become Pope in 1088, during a time in which church authority in relation to the secular rulers of Europe was controversial. Conflicts with the kings of Germany (also known as Holy Roman Emperors) were particularly long running, Pope Gregory VII having deposed King Henry IV in 1076 and 1080, who in return drove him from Rome to die in exile. As a result of the feud, few German bishops recognized Urban's pontificate, and much of Germany and north and central Italy, including Rome, was controlled by Henry's anti-pope, Clement III. However, Urban was able to build up support in the west and in Byzantium; by 1094 Henry was losing ground in Italy and his son, Conrad, rebelled against him and became Urban's vassal in 1095. Urban's preaching of the First Crusade was thus politically significant:

> when he called on the army of Christ to recover Christian land, Urban was, consciously or unconsciously, assuming for himself the imperial function of directing the defence of the Christian Republic at a time when he did not recognise Henry as emperor. Gregory VII had deposed a king; Urban II took over the prime duty of a temporal ruler.
>
> (Riley-Smith, 2002, p. 33)

Those who answered his call became the *cruciata* or *cruce signati*, meaning those marked by the cross, wearing what became the insignia of the scarlet cross, and willing to fight in the name of Christianity. As such, they came under papal authority, gaining for the duration of the crusade pilgrim status which made them temporary ecclesiastics; and this made the crusades 'papal instruments, the most spectacular expressions of the Papal Monarchy' (ibid., p. 50). The military expeditions in which the crusaders were involved were led against Muslim territories in an attempt to recapture the Holy Land, as well as against other non-Christians, against Christian heretics, and against Christian lords who stood against the papacy. When the crusades were initiated in 1095, they were, as Fletcher suggests, far from being a creation out of nothing. Instead, the forces that led to Urban's preaching of the First Crusade came from diverse points in history and did not come together until well into the twelfth century. This gradual growth of an idea reflected the increasing interaction between Christendom and the newer, Islamic monotheism – a novel[1] and, to Christians, unnecessary religion, which was even characterized as a Christian heresy by John of Damascus (675–749) (see Chidester, 2001, p. 190).

---

[1] In non-Islamic terms. For Muslims, Islam is the original religion.

Islam as an organized religious tradition originated in the revelations received by the Prophet Muhammad (c. 570–632), who lived in Mecca and Medina in what is now Saudi Arabia. These revelations from the one God, Allah, were collected in the Qur'ān and claimed an inheritance from Abraham, Islam being the final revelation of God, succeeding Judaism and Christianity, with Muhammad being the 'seal of the prophets', superseding Moses, Abraham and Jesus. As Chidester (2000, p. 188) reminds us:

> As disclosed to Muhammad, the Qur'an transcended the sacred texts, the Torah of the Jews and the Gospel of the Christians, that had been revealed to previous messengers of God, Moses and Jesus. Since those sacred texts had allegedly been corrupted and distorted over the centuries, the revelation of the Qur'an was necessary, not only for the conversion of unbelievers, but also to call believing Jews and Christians back to the pure faith of Islam that had been revealed to Abraham, Moses, and Jesus.

Within a century of Muhammad's death, Islam had spread from Mecca to the Atlantic in one direction and to China in the other, under the first four caliphs[2] and their successors, the Ummayad dynasty. In 638 Jerusalem (hitherto controlled by the Christian Byzantine Empire) fell to the Muslims led by Caliph Omar. In the eighth century, Muslim armies conquered the Visigothic kingdom of Spain, where they were to maintain a presence until the end of the fifteenth century. This rapid spread was a direct result of Islam's mission to reveal the word and will of Allah for the world, building a single *'umma* (community), united in submission to God. A mere one hundred years after Muhammad's death, in 732, the Muslims fought the Frankish[3] army of Charles Martel at the Battle of Tours in central France. Victory went to the Franks, but the force of Islam could not be ignored by a Christendom already divided between east and west, and by internal political fighting in western Europe. With much of Spain remaining under Islamic rule throughout the Middle Ages, it is hardly surprising that the massive early expanse of Islam posed such a psychological threat to medieval Europe, particularly when coupled with the occupation of the Christian Holy Land by Muslim forces and the divisions within Christendom itself.

By the time of the First Crusade, Christianity had had eleven hundred years in which to develop, grow and establish bitter, internal rivalries. The schism between the Christian east and west, which eventually became the division between Orthodox and Catholic was, however, a gradual process, taking place over a long history, before communion

---

[2] This word comes from the Arabic *khalifah,* meaning successor (of the Prophet Muhammad). Like Muhammad, the caliphs claimed both civil and religious authority.

[3] The 'Franks' was what medieval Muslims called the crusaders – *Ifranj* or *Firanj.* It was a term originally used to signify the inhabitants of Charlemagne's empire but was later widened to embrace all western Europeans.

2 ISLAM, CHRISTIANITY AND THE CRUSADES: RIVAL MONOTHEISMS AND MONOTHEISTIC RIVALS

between the two was formally broken off in 1054. The separation of the Monophysites[4] between the fifth and seventh centuries had severely weakened the ancient church of the Byzantine Empire in Syria and Egypt, whilst progressive estrangement between Rome and Constantinople led to a temporary schism under the patriarch Photius between 863 and 886 before the final split in 1054 under Michael Cerularius. Attempts at restoring communion – for instance, at the Council of Florence in 1439 – proved ineffective. After the fall of Constantinople to the Ottoman Turks in 1453, much of the eastern church came under Muslim rule.

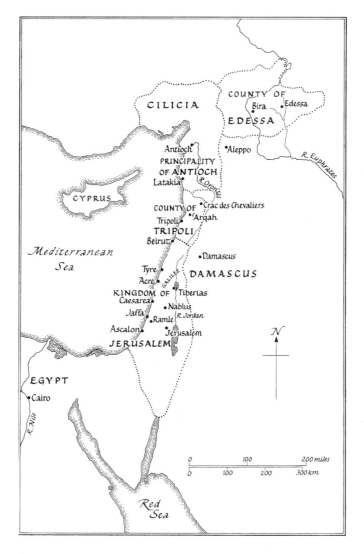

Map 1 The Latin East, 1128, from Jonathan Riley-Smith (1997) The First Crusaders, 1095–1131, Cambridge University Press (map adapted)

[4] The Monophysites were a group that believed in the single divine nature of the person of Jesus.

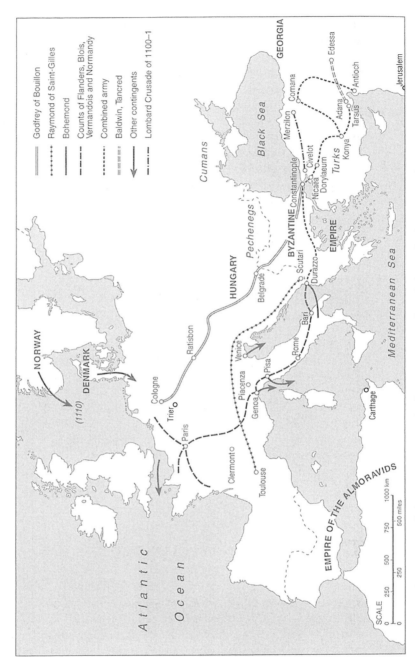

Map 2 The routes of the First Crusade from Jean Richard (1999) The Crusades, c. 1071–c. 1291,
Cambridge University Press (map adapted)

However, its geographical location at the eastern end of the
Mediterranean meant that the Greek Church had already had centuries of
contact with Islam, particularly in its patriarchates in the Holy Land. The
protection of the 'eastern brethren' and pilgrims visiting the holy sites
was one of the chief reasons given for the crusades. At the centre – and
indeed, at the centre of the world as it was imagined at the time – stood
Jerusalem, holiest of cities to both eastern and western churches, as well
as a sacred site to Jews and Muslims. For Jews it was the site of
Solomon's temple, and for Christians the place where the salvation of
humankind was secured through the death and resurrection of Jesus
Christ, and where they believed the mythical New Jerusalem would be
established at the Day of Judgement. For Muslims it was the scene of
Muhammad's 'Night Journey' recorded in the Qur'ān. During the first
centuries of Muslim rule, European pilgrims had generally been able to
visit those places sacred to Christianity in the Holy Land, including
Jerusalem. Two routes were available to them: the sea route to Egypt or
Palestine, and the land route via the Balkans, Anatolia and Syria.
However, from the early eleventh century there is some evidence of
persecution of Christians in Syria and Palestine: for example, the
destruction of the Church of the Holy Sepulchre in Jerusalem in
1009–1010, and some disruption to Christian pilgrimage to the Holy
Land. This was undoubtedly a contributing factor to Christian Europe's
desire to rescue what they saw as their holy sites. Byzantium's appeals
for European help after the Battle of Manzikert in 1071 and in the 1090s
moved the Papacy of Urban II to do something to lift the oppression of
the Near Eastern Christians and liberate the holy city of Jerusalem. Thus,
as we have seen, the first preaching of a crusade took place in Clermont
on 27 November 1095, and by 1097 a Christian army from different parts
of western Europe had reached Constantinople and begun the journey
overland towards Jerusalem. The idea of the crusade had begun.

The idea of the crusade

The whole idea of the crusade was a western phenomenon. We should
therefore be cautious in our treatment of it. There is undoubtedly a
Muslim perspective, but the idea itself was born of western Christian –
not eastern, Christian or otherwise – ideology, and the bulk of
scholarship on the crusades has been, in the words of Carole
Hillenbrand, 'unabashedly Eurocentric' (1999, p. 2). Yet

> there is great benefit to be derived from an examination of the
> way in which one medieval religious ideology shaped history by
> confronting another similarly deep-felt religious ideology ... The
> Crusades shaped western European perceptions of the Muslim
> world just as decisively as they formed Muslim views of the West.

(ibid., pp. 2–3)

However, because the idea of the crusade is a western one, with no particular resonance to Muslims,[5] Islamic scholarship has not been particularly concerned with it, and it was not treated as an isolated topic in extant Muslim work (Hillenbrand, 1999, p. 9). Indeed, it was not until the mid nineteenth century that Arabs coined the term *Hurub al-Salibiyya* to refer to the crusades. For western Europeans, on the other hand, the crusade was 'legitimized by the pope as head of Christendom and representative of Christ, rather than by a temporal ruler, and being Christ's own enterprise it was positively holy' (Riley-Smith, 2002, p. 87). This is reflected in the euphemisms used for crusades – pilgrimage (*peregrinatio*), holy war (*bellum sacrum; guerre sainte*), expedition of the Cross (*expeditio crucis*), or the business of Jesus Christ (*negotium Jhesu Christi*).

The 'business of Jesus Christ' related, of course, to the entirety of Christendom rather than to any temporal state. 'It was not the property of the Byzantine Empire or the Kingdom of Jerusalem that was to be liberated or defended, but territory belonging by right to Christendom or to Christ. It was not Spaniards or Germans, but Christians, who were imperilled by the Moors and Slavs' (ibid., p. 23). Christendom itself was regarded as 'a universal state, the Christian Republic, transcendental in that it existed at the same time in heaven and on earth' (ibid., p. 24). Fighting on behalf of the kingdom of Christ and the Church against the enemies of God was thus a religious obligation, not merely justified but holy – the cause

> related to the Church, to Christendom, seen as a political entity, and to Christ, the monarch of the universal Christian state ... those taking part saw themselves doing their duty by Christ as in other circumstances they might by their temporal lord or king.
>
> (ibid., p. 26)

Brief outline of the crusades

From a western perspective, the crusades have been portrayed as a series of at least eight Christian military campaigns undertaken to liberate, and bring under their protection, Jerusalem and other sites sacred to Christendom. They began, technically, with Urban II's call for a war of liberation in 1095 and lasted beyond the fifteenth century. Although the fall of Acre in 1291 is often declared to be the end of serious crusader activity against Islam in the Levant, some scholars argue that the crusading movement only ended with the surrender of Malta to Napoleon Bonaparte on 13 June 1798 by the Knights Hospitallers of St

---

[5] But see below, pp. 54–5 and 289–90, for discussion of the distinctive Islamic concept of *jihād*.

John, the last military order ruling a state still engaged in naval warfare against Islam. As we shall see later in this chapter, crusading imagery and rhetoric are, in fact, still employed today, but for now we shall concentrate on the central centuries of crusading warfare.

The First Crusade was by far the most successful. Even before the army reached the Holy Land, it gained important victories, capturing the Seljuq[6] capital of Iznik in June 1097 and defeating Seljuq forces at the Battle of Dorylaeum in July of the same year. The crusading army laid siege to Antioch in October 1097, and conquered the Christian Armenian city of Edessa in March 1098, establishing the first crusader state in the Near East. In June 1098 Antioch fell, and Jerusalem itself was taken on 15 July 1099. Tripoli fell to the Franks ten years later, becoming the final of the four crusader principalities: Jerusalem, Edessa, Antioch and Tripoli.

This initial success lasted until the middle of the twelfth century, at which point Edessa fell to a Muslim force under Zengi (d. 1146). In 1147–48 a Second Crusade, commanded by the German Emperor Conrad III and the French King Louis VII made an unsuccessful attempt to take Damascus. Zengi's son, Nur al-Din (d. 1174) conquered the city in 1154 and made himself 'supreme Muslim ruler in Syria' (Hillenbrand, 1999, p. 23). The death of Nur al-Din in 1174 allowed for the continuing rise of the most well-known Muslim of the crusading era, the Kurdish leader Salah al-Din (Saladin). Saladin subjugated his Muslim rivals between 1174 and 1187, thus ensuring a united Muslim front before, in July 1187, successfully fighting King Guy of Lusignan's crusading army at the Battle of Hattin. This was followed with the reconquest of Acre, and finally of Jerusalem on 2 October 1187. Saladin's family dynasty, the Ayyubids, ruled the major cities and territories, but the fall of Jerusalem and the defeat at Hattin triggered more crusading zeal in western Europe.

In 1191, Richard I of England (the 'Lionheart'), Philip II of France, and Frederick Barbarossa of the Holy Roman Empire – the three most powerful monarchs of western Europe – took Acre in the Third Crusade. Yet despite crusader victories, the crusade ended in 1192 with a truce – the Franks held most of the coastal strip but, crucially, Jerusalem remained in Muslim hands, albeit with rights of pilgrimage for Christians safeguarded. In 1193 Saladin died, having failed to take Tyre and drive the crusading Christians from the Levant.

From then on, the crusaders focused their attention on Egypt, believing it to be the key to the retaking of Jerusalem. Egypt was the original intended target of the Fourth Crusade in 1202, but instead of fighting Muslims it ended with the conquest of Constantinople in April 1204, resulting in the establishment of the Latin empire of Constantinople

[6] Descendants of Tughril I, who conquered Iran and Iraq in the name of Sunni orthodoxy and ruled on behalf of the Sunni 'Abbasid caliphs, descended from Muhammad's uncle, al'Abbas, 1055–1194. The Seljuqs were the first to use the title 'Sultan', signifying executive power under the caliph.

which lasted until 1261. The Fifth Crusade arrived on the Nile delta in 1218, and took Demietta in 1219, although it was regained a mere two years later by Saladin's nephew, al-Kamil. Threatened by internal troubles, al-Kamil negotiated a treaty with Frederick II of Sicily in 1229, a year after Frederick had arrived on crusade in Palestine. By this treaty, the crusaders regained control of Jerusalem, Bethlehem and Nazareth, for which al-Kamil was fiercely criticized within the Muslim world. However, Jerusalem reverted to Muslim rule in 1244, and Frankish decline continued, despite the Seventh Crusade of Louis IX of France who recaptured Damietta in 1249. He marched on towards Cairo, but was forced to surrender in al-Mansura.

In 1250, the Islamic counter attack was revitalized as the Mamluks of Egypt, once slave-soldiers who made up Saladin's elite fighting forces, overthrew Saladin's Ayyubid dynasty. The Mamluk sultan, Baybars (d. 1277), united Syria and Palestine, and between 1265 and 1271 conquered many Frankish possessions, including Antioch in 1268 and Krak de Chevaliers in 1271. Later sultans conquered or destroyed the remaining crusader cities, culminating in the fall of Acre in 1291. But although the crusade against Muslims in the east to protect the Holy Land was all but over, the idea of the crusade had really only just solidified. The streams that Fletcher characterized as trickling 'slowly and uncertainly in their early courses' had undergone a process of codification as successive papal courts since Urban II's pontificate sought to justify and control holy war.

The crusading idea was not going to simply disappear; in fact, it continued in one form or another until the end of the fifteenth century, played out in a variety of arenas – Palestine and the eastern Mediterranean, North Africa and Spain, Poland, Hungary, the Baltic, and the Balkans – as crusaders engaged in campaigns against Muslims, pagans, heretics, Orthodox Russians and Greeks, and Catholic political opponents of the papacy. Thus, whilst the Spanish *Reconquista* (reconquest) against the Moors until their final expulsion from Granada in 1492 retained Islam as the enemy, crusades were also fought against the Cathars in France (the Albigensian Crusade of 1209–29), the Wends in what is now north-east Germany (the Wendish Crusade of 1147), and on the Baltic frontier between 1150 and c. 1500. Although this chapter focuses on the threat to Christendom from Muslim forces, these crusades reveal the threat to Christendom that was seen to be posed by heresy and the continuation of paganism. But if the Christian world was beset with division and internal conflict, so too was the Muslim world, and this allowed Christendom to pose an unexpected threat.

'A strange and unexpected enemy':[7] the Muslims and the crusades

At the end of the eleventh century, the Muslim world was in political turmoil; whether he knew it or not, Urban II could not have chosen a better time to launch a crusade into Muslim territory. Deaths and divisions meant that any chance of a unified Muslim response was an impossibility, and the First Crusade thus came as an extremely unwelcome surprise. On the eve of the First Crusade, Muslim disunity and weakness proved invaluable to the crusaders. Ten years earlier, and unified resistance from the last of the three great Seljuq sultans, Malikshah, would almost certainly have limited, if not prevented their early success. As it was, by 1095 'the Islamic world was bereft of unity and catastrophically weakened both by a complete lack of powerful leadership and by religious schism' (Hillenbrand, 1999, p. 33). In the three years immediately prior to Urban's preaching of the crusade, all the major political figures of the Islamic world, Seljuq and Fatimid, Sunni and Shi'a, were swept from the board and it is hardly surprising that the Mamluk historian Ibn Taghribirdi calls 1094 'the year of the death of caliphs and commanders' (*Nurjum*, V, 139, cited in Hillenbrand, 1999, p. 33). The Seljuq and Fatimid empires – the two key power centres of the Muslim world – had both disintegrated in the space of two years, giving way to disorientation and anarchy.

However, it was not just politics that had caused two power centres to arise in the Islamic world during the eleventh century: there was also the important matter of religion. Two main divisions of Islam had emerged over the question of succession to the Prophet Muhammad – Sunni and Shi'a/Shi'i. Sunni Islam, which accounts for the majority of Muslims, took its name from the *Sunna*, the orally transmitted words and deeds of Muhammad which shaped Islamic law and guided individual conduct. It recognized religious authority as lying in the consensus of the community. Shi'a is a general name for a group of Muslim sects, who see the ultimate political and religious authority rather as embodied in Ali, the Prophet's son-in-law, and his descendants and spiritual successors, the Imams. Further divisions occurred within Shi'a Islam in relation to this line of Imams, with Twelvers awaiting the return of the Hidden (twelfth) Imam, believing that ultimate spiritual authority went into abeyance after the death of the eleventh Imam in 874, whilst the Isma'ili Seveners hold that the succession came to an end with the disappearance of the seventh Imam, Isma'il, in 760. Shi'a Islam also included the famous extremist Nizari Isma'ilis, or Assassins, who broke away from the Isma'ili

---

[7] Hitti, 1951, pp. 135–6. Owing to the lack of scholarship on the crusades from the Muslim perspective, this section and that concerned with Islamic uses of crusade imagery and rhetoric are heavily indebted to the work of Hillenbrand.

Fatimid caliphate in Cairo and operated during the crusading era using religious assassination as a weapon.

For the most part Sunnis and Shi'as coexisted peacefully in Muslim cities in Syria, Lebanon and Palestine during the time of the crusades, with Sunnis making up the majority although the Shi'a minority was relatively large. Indeed, as Irwin points out, 'the distinctions between Sunni and Shi'ite doctrines and rituals were not always very clear and many Sunnis had Shi'ite leanings, while there were many Shi'as who had no compunctions about taking service with the Abbasid caliphs and the Seljuk sultans' (1995, p. 219). On individual and local community levels, then, coexistence was the norm, but on a political level in terms of rival dynasties, Sunni and Shi'a were opposed militarily in the fight for power and territory.

The Fatimid Isma'ili Shi'ite caliphate of Cairo had set itself up in the tenth century in direct opposition to the 'Abbasid Sunni caliphate in Baghdad and held city states in Aleppo, Damascus and Mosul which were in an almost constant state of war with each other. Rivalry between the Fatimids and 'Abbasids continued throughout the eleventh century, and even though the Seljuqs, under Alp Arslan, found time to rout the Byzantines under Emperor Romanus Diogenes IV at the Battle of Manzikert in 1071, their chief military efforts were reserved for their Fatimid enemy. This focus on threats within the Islamic community led inevitably to the neglect of external threats. Here, religious differences acted as salt in the wound of dynastic rivalries, resulting in protracted fighting in Syria and Palestine. When the crusaders arrived there, it was unthinkable for Seljuq Sunni and Fatimid Shi'ite to form a unified front against a common enemy from outside. This is apart from the fact that, despite the turbulence of the wars, schisms, nomadic invasions and plague in Egypt in 1097 and again in 1099–1100, an invasion from western Europe was the last thing anyone in the Muslim world expected. As Irwin explains, the late eleventh century was a time of acute insecurity in the Near East for Muslims, Christians and Jews, with fears about the end of the world prevailing amongst Muslims as well as hope for a renewal of Islam, and a desire for a decisive victory between the Fatimids and Seljuqs fighting in Syria; '[w]hatever people were expecting it certainly was not a religiously inspired invasion of peoples from western Europe' (1995, p. 218).

The deaths of powerful leaders led to internal conflicts which used up precious military resources and left neither time nor motivation for involvement in Jerusalem and the Levant. Power struggles to gain territory were far more important endeavours than marching over the mountains to fight the crusaders in Syria and Palestine. Any alliances between Muslim rulers were ephemeral, and the schism between Sunni and Shi'ite had a habit of preventing any alliance between neighbouring states of different persuasion. Nevertheless, some action was taken unilaterally. In 1097–98, the Fatimid vizier and de facto ruler, al-Afdal, led his army in a pre-emptive strike of Palestine and seized Jerusalem from Turcoman Seljuq vassals. We do not know whether al-Afdal had some prior knowledge of crusader plans – perhaps through an agreement with the Christian Byzantine emperor with whom the Muslims were long familiar – or whether he was acting in alliance with them, but only a year later the crusaders routed his army at Ascalon and took Jerusalem.

It may well be the case that, given the choice between the new crusader enemy and the old Seljuq rivals, al-Afdal chose to favour the former, hoping that the Franks would act as a buffer zone between Egypt and the Turks. However, as it became obvious that Jerusalem was the prize aimed for by the crusaders, any collaboration would have fallen by the wayside. Certainly, the Fatimids were more concerned with defending their own territories against their traditional enemy than fighting the new threat from western Europe. Even before the fall of Jerusalem, Muslim states were prepared to collaborate with the new enemy against their traditional fellow-Muslim rivals. This trend was a persistent feature of crusader–Muslim relations throughout the crusading era.

As we have seen, Muslim religious identity was not uniform. In addition, there were also long-established Jewish and Christian communities, the latter also of varying affiliations – Armenians, Jacobites, Maronites, Melkites and Nestorians, as well as the Coptic minority in Egypt. Jerusalem was a pilgrimage centre not only for Christians and Jews, but also for Muslims who could not make the journey to Mecca, and it was an important meeting place for scholars of all three faiths. It seems that, in the eleventh century, local Christians and Jews were not generally persecuted by their Muslim rulers, and pilgrimage for Christians from Byzantium and western Europe was not, as a rule, prevented. However, there was certainly harassment at times and, as mentioned above, the Church of the Holy Sepulchre had been destroyed in 1009/1010. A letter written in 1100 by a Jewish pilgrim reveals that he had been stranded in Egypt, having tried for five years to reach Jerusalem.

Yet to the Muslims, the arrival of the crusaders was not understood in religious terms, nor were the invaders' motives understood to be religious. In fact, it seems that the invasion at first was not taken very seriously at all. Thus, when Baldwin of Boulogne took Edessa, the first of the crusader states, in 1098, it seems to have aroused little comment – perhaps it was already a Christian city state – and it certainly did not stir any Muslim faction to military activity. The siege of Antioch in 1097–98, on the other hand, was treated more seriously and activated a relieving army led by the ruler of Mosul, Kirbogha. The relief effort failed, and was defeated by the crusaders in battle, but the strategic position and size of Antioch had at least provoked some Muslim response. Disunity and the inevitable infighting had prevented what should have been a relatively easy success for the Muslim forces, but 'in the decentralised political climate of the day they were unable even to stay together long enough to achieve a victory. After Antioch, the way to Jerusalem lay open to the Crusaders' (Hillenbrand, 1999, p. 59).

Despite establishing the four crusader states, by 1110, the Franks were a minority. The major cities of Aleppo and Damascus remained in Muslim hands, as did Egypt, but the Muslims were unable and unwilling to unite and expel the remaining Franks, thus enabling the crusaders to fortify themselves and continue to receive reinforcements from western Europe. As Frankish expansion in the area continued, Muslim leaders remained cut off from each other by religious differences, and although some ephemeral alliances were made, more often than not agreements were made with the crusaders. Local Muslim rulers 'had no intention whatsoever of sacrificing their own political interests for the sake of some nebulous ideal of Islamic solidarity' (Hillenbrand, 1999, p. 82).

After the loss of Jerusalem, some Muslim commentators, aware of the role played by Muslim division in crusader success, called for reunification. The arrival of the crusaders had caused confusion and Muslim responses inevitably varied. However, by 1105 a treatise on Holy War, the *Kitab al-jihād*, had been produced by 'Ali ibn Tahir al-Sulami (1039–1106), a Sunni Muslim religious scholar in Damascus. In this work, he not only blamed the moral and political problems of Islam for the success of the Christians, but regarded their arrival as a Christian '*jihād*' from the west, occurring within a context of religious struggle between Islam and Christianity stretching across the Mediterranean – from Spain, Sicily and North Africa to Palestine and Syria. Al-Sulami was blunt in his appeal:

> Even now they are continuing their effort to enlarge their territory; their greed is constantly growing as they see the cowardice of their enemies who are happy to live away from danger. Moreover, they hope now for sure to make themselves masters of the whole country and to take its inhabitants captive. Would to God that, in His goodness, He would frustrate them in their aspirations by re-establishing the unity of the community.
>
> (cited in Hillenbrand, 1999, p. 73)

The Islamic concept of *jihād* denotes struggle on the part of Muslims – both inner struggle against one's own moral failings (the greater *jihād*) and religious war – and is authorized in a number of suras in the Qur'an:

> Fight those who believe not in God and the Last Day and do not forbid what God and his Messenger have forbidden – such men as practise not the religion of truth, being of those who have been given the Book – until they pay tribute out of hand and have been humbled.
>
> ...
>
> And fight the unbelievers totally even as they fight you totally; and know that God is with the god-fearing.
>
> (Qur'ān, ix, pp. 29, 36)

Emile Tyan states that *jihād* stems from the principle that Islam 'ought to embrace the whole universe, if necessary by force ... [it is] a religious duty' (in Mottahedeh and al-Sayyid, 2001, p. 23). It was this deeply embedded concept of being sanctioned to establish rule by God's law on earth that had motivated the massive early Islamic conquests. At the same time, this expansion had helped to codify theories of *jihād* which were generally accepted throughout the period of the crusades. Whereas the expansionist sense of *jihād* seems, initially, to have been seen merely as a 'permissable act', 'in no sense a duty of a Muslim', it later came to be understood by some as 'obligatory aggressive war' (ibid., p. 26), justified by the destruction of unbelief within and outside Islam. By the time of the crusades, '*jihād* had become an unpredictable variable in the internal politics of Islamic lands just as it had become in their relations with non-Islamic lands' (ibid., p. 29).

Notwithstanding the personal, interior *jihād*, the exterior *jihād* could be both offensive and defensive, each having different claims on the individual Muslim. As Irwin explains, the offensive *jihād*

> is a collective duty imposed on the Muslim community to extend the Muslim territories (*Dar al-Islam*) ... all Muslims are obliged to support [those who fight] with money and approbation ... the defensive jihad [is] to drive out aggressors who have occupied territory held by the Muslims. This sort of defensive war is an obligation that falls on every able-bodied adult Muslim.

(1995, p. 227)

In Shi'a Islam, only the imam may call for offensive *jihād*; since there will be no imam until the Last Days, the duty of external *jihād* is in abeyance[8]. This did not mean that Shi'a Muslims did not fight against the crusaders, merely that their battles were not understood as *jihād*. In addition, most Shi'as and Sufis emphasized the primacy of internal, rather than external *jihād*. As a result of Sufi preaching, particularly under Zangi and his successors in Syria, 'rulers and the religious élite devoted themselves to stamping out corruption and heterodoxy in the Muslim community, as part of a grand *jihād* which had much wider aims than merely the removal of the Franks from the coastline of Palestine' (Irwin, 1995, pp. 229–30).

As a result, the conflict between the Franks and local Muslim rulers, such as it was, gave way to coexistence. Over time, Muslims became accustomed to the crusader presence, and they had always lived side by side with eastern Christians in Syria, Palestine and Egypt. The politics of survival, particularly of maintaining independent status vis-à-vis traditional rivalries, led to opportunistic alliances with the Franks despite religious and ideological differences. The existence of the Franks helped

---

[8] Shi'ites believe that there have been either seven or twelve imams in history and that another will come as we approach the 'Last Days' or day of judgement.

Muslim cities such as Aleppo to preserve their independent status, as Muslim rivalries that existed before the First Crusade continued. Thus, from 1099 to 1109, 'the Muslims of the Levant had to learn to adjust to these unexpected and powerful invaders who did not go away but stayed to put down roots in what was traditionally Islamic territory' (Hillenbrand, 1999, p. 84).

As stated above, Muslims and eastern Christians had coexisted for some three hundred years before the arrival of the western Christian crusaders. Some Muslim rulers were concerned as to how the local Christian population would respond to the new arrivals – would they side with them or remain loyal to the local Muslims with whom they lived? It is, of course, difficult to generalize. Just as some Muslim lords negotiated with the Franks, so some local Christians betrayed Muslim forces to the crusaders, and Byzantium, which had called for western aid in the first place, tried at times to make alliances with the Muslims to drive out the Franks in order, like the Muslims, to retain their independence. Others, of course, were glad the Franks had arrived to protect pilgrimage and liberate the Holy Land. Because the Franks stayed, however, they came to constitute yet another 'local' population who had to coexist with the other groupings already there – Muslims, Christians and Jews. Islam had a policy of toleration towards peoples of the book and so, theoretically speaking, it was possible for Christians and Jews to live and worship peacefully in Muslim-ruled lands. To Muslims, the beliefs of Jews and Christians were, to put it simply, merely an incomplete version of what Muslims believed, Islam being the final and perfect revelation of Allah through Muhammad, the Seal of the Prophets. In practice, however, there was much in Christianity that Islam despised, both in doctrine and in worship, and much of the Islamic negative perception was religious, although there were also non-religious stereotypes of western Europeans to be added to this. When the two were combined in the form of the crusaders, greater familiarity could only breed contempt – frequent contact with the Franks did little to prove earlier perceptions inaccurate.

Crusader/Muslim coexistence

Western Europe held little attraction for medieval Muslims, secure in the superiority of their own culture and the perfection of Christianity by Islam. If other religions were at best incomplete, and at worst simply wrong, then what would be the point in studying them? Muslims paid little attention to the Christians under their rule or in neighbouring Byzantium, and they certainly had no interest in Christianity in western Europe. The reason for this attitude towards western Europe lay partly in Ptolemaic geography, introduced to the Islamic world by the Muslim scholar al-Khwarazmi in the tenth century. This divided the world into seven latitudinal zones or climes which predisposed certain

characteristics to those living in each one. The third and fourth zones –
in which lay the central lands of the Arab world, North Africa, Iran and
parts of China – were most harmonious and balanced. The sixth clime,
on the other hand – which contained the Franks, Slavs and Turks –
dictated a melancholy and savage temperament in filthy and treacherous
war-mongering peoples, though they were also courageous, disciplined
and organized. Al-Mas'udi (d. 956), an 'Abbasid writer, described the land
of the Franks in detail and is worth quoting at some length:

> As regards the people of the northern quadrant, they are the
> ones for whom the sun is distant from the zenith, those who
> penetrate to the North, such as the Slavs, the Franks, and those
> nations that are their neighbours. The power of the sun is weak
> among them because of their distance from it; cold and damp
> prevail in their regions, and snow and ice follow one another in
> endless succession. The warm humour is lacking among them;
> their bodies are large, their natures gross, their manners harsh,
> their understanding dull, and their tongues heavy. Their colour is
> so excessively white that it passes from white to blue; their skin
> is thin and their flesh thick. Their eyes are also blue, matching
> the character of their colouring; their hair is lank and reddish
> because of the prevalence of damp mists. Their religious beliefs
> lack solidity, and this is because of the nature of cold and the
> lack of warmth.
>
> (Hillenbrand, 1999, p. 270)

Other Muslim writers confirmed these characteristics, stressing the
courage of the Franks in fighting but also their unhygienic habits,
ignorance and barbarity, some even asserting that they shed their hair
annually like animals. By the time the crusaders arrived, the Muslim
perception of the Franks was characterized by three themes: moral
baseness and laxity; lack of personal hygiene; and courage in war. They
perceived them to be barbarians. And as Hillenbrand observes, '[c]loser
acquaintance with the Franks was to enhance such feelings of Muslim
exclusivity rather than modify this rigid edifice of preconceived and
vague opinions and prejudices' (1999, p. 274).

To this, however, needs to be added the religious dimension. Personal
hygiene, for Muslims, is tied up intricately with Islam: ablutions are part
of daily religious worship and purity is an integral part of the religion.
Public bathhouses were important to this society, but although eastern
Christians and, in time, the Franks made use of them, they remained, in
essence, unclean to Muslims: 'the Orientalised Franks are "better" than
the Franks who dwell in northern Europe, since the former have lived
for some time in Muslim lands which are situated in a more favourable
clime ... [but] They are irrevocably unclean' (Hillenbrand, 1999, p. 282).

Given the centrality of purity – outer cleanliness being a reflection of inner purity – it is hardly surprising that Muslims considered the Franks to be primarily polluters.

> In the Muslim portrayal of the Franks ... symbols of pollution and impurity abound. These reflect wellsprings of Muslim religious revulsion at a deep psychological level, and relate to the breaking of taboos and the primeval fear that they would be cut off from God.
>
> (Hillenbrand, 1999, p. 285)

Frankish occupation defiled sacred space, particularly religious buildings in Jerusalem such as the Dome of the Rock and the Aqsa Mosque. This was not just military occupation, but 'an invasion and desecration of religious sanctity' (ibid., p. 286). The positioning of the Christian cross on the Dome of the Rock and the Knights Templar's use of the Aqsa Mosque, for example, constituted defilement of the utmost order.

In addition, the crusaders were considered, in Muslim thought, to be polytheists – the Trinity could not be accepted as a doctrine reflecting one God by strictly monotheistic Islam. The Trinity was ridiculed and the oneness of God emphasized by the stress on select Qur'ānic verses – 'Praise be to Allah, who hath not taken unto Himself a son, and who hath no partner in the sovereignty' (Sura 17), and,

> Say, He is Allah, the One!
> Allah, the eternally Besought of all!
> He begetted not nor was begotten.
> And there is none comparable unto Him.
>
> (Sura 112)

Christian depictions of 'God' as a child in their iconography of Jesus went against deeply entrenched attitudes towards both anthropomorphism and any portrayal of God. Thus, as well as being polytheists (*mushrikun*), the Franks were called 'the enemies of God', 'worshippers of crosses', 'people of the Trinity' and 'servants of the messiah', as well as devils, dogs and pigs. The crusading armies also posed a threat to the traditional pilgrimage routes between Damascus (one of the main gathering points for the *hajj* – the annual Muslim pilgrimage to Mecca, one of the five pillars of Islam) and Mecca. Once the crusaders were ousted from their territories, it was necessary to reclaim Islamic sacred sites on a spiritual as well as a physical level, removing all Christian trappings and purifying with rose water and incense. At the reconquest of Jerusalem, for example, Ibn Zaki's sermon included purification: 'I praise Him ... for His cleansing of His Holy House from the filth of polytheism and its pollutions'. He called on the faithful to 'purify the rest of the land from this filth which hath angered

God and His Apostle' (cited in Hillenbrand, 1999, p. 301). Breaking crosses reclaimed Muslim holy sites, but also symbolized the defeat of Christianity by Islam.

Extended contact with the Franks had only intensified anti-Christian dogmatic arguments. How can God protect the crusaders when he could not protect himself from crucifixion? 'Anyone who believes that his God came out of a woman's privates is quite mad; he should not be spoken to, and he has neither intelligence nor faith' (*Sea of Precious Virtues*, 231, cited in Hillenbrand, 1999, p. 313). Coexistence did not bring about an end to the conflict between Islam and Christianity.

The end of the crusades?

This chapter has mentioned the tendency of crusade historians to see the fall of Acre in 1291 as the end of the crusades. Later historians, we have suggested, have been well aware of the lack of any definitive cut-off point, and indeed, we have seen that the crusades went on beyond the end of the thirteenth century, in different arenas, in different eras, and against different foes. As Hillenbrand explains, 'there was no sudden or decisive end to the crusades, whose reverberations continued to echo long after the withdrawal of the European military presence from the Levant' (1999, p. 589). Christian and Muslim offensives continued to be launched, with Holy Leagues being formed to fight the Ottoman Turks from the fifteenth to the seventeenth centuries, and the Spanish *Reconquista* seeing battles against the Moors until the final explusion of Islam from Granada in 1492.

The year 1291 did not, therefore, see the final expulsion of European military presence from the Levant, and nor did it see an end to crusading. Spain had already been an arena of conflict between Islam and Christianity for two centuries before Urban II preached the First Crusade, and although Urban's main focus was the Muslims in the Near East, he also treated the war against Muslims in Spain as a crusade. The following centuries saw many crusades proclaimed in Spain – for example, those in 1096, 1122, 1197 and 1229 – offering the same remission of sins to those fighting on this western frontier of Christendom as those defending the eastern church. Crusading ideas and methods strengthened the Holy War in Spain, and the *Reconquista* came to be equated with crusading. After some 400 years of mixed fortunes, by the end of the thirteenth century only Granada remained in Muslim control. The unification of Aragon and Castile under Ferdinand and Isabella into the kingdom of Spain in 1479, after fifty years of civil war, led to the end of Muslim rule in Granada. Inspired by crusading ideas and techniques, using the latest artillery, and playing rival sultans off against each other, Granada was slowly conquered; the city of Granada lay under siege from April 1490 until it surrendered to the Spanish on 2

January 1492. The Moors were expelled from Spain, as were the Jews, and in the same year, with the blessing of Ferdinand and Isabella, Christopher Columbus set out from Palos in Spain on his voyages of discovery, aiming not only to convert with crusading zeal, but to gain wealth to finance a new crusade to reclaim Jerusalem. This crusading mentality continued to inspire Spanish and Portuguese overseas expansion throughout the sixteenth and seventeenth centuries.

At the same time as the Muslim world in Palestine was suffering from the effects of the crusading centuries and Spain was still fighting against Muslim occupation, the Sunni Ottoman Turkish Empire went from strength to strength. It began its rise to power in the fourteenth century, took Constantinople in 1453, and continued to expand until the end of the seventeenth century. An Italian observer at the time of the fall of Constantinople to the Ottoman Sultan Mehmed recorded the sultan's declared intent to 'advance from East to West as in former times the westerners advanced into the Orient. There must ... be only one empire, one faith, and one sovereignty in the world' (in Irwin, 1995, p. 254). Clearly, the crusades had not completely checked Muslim military power, and the Ottomans certainly used modern technological developments, such as cannon, perhaps as early as the 1380s, whilst the conquest of Constantinople gave them control of the Black Sea and hence the opportunity to develop further their skills in naval warfare.

By the mid sixteenth century, '[t]he Ottoman Empire under Suleyman the Magnificent (1520–66) can be seen as the Muslim equivalent of the universal Christian empire of Charles V [the Holy Roman Emperor]' (Irwin, 1995, p. 255), controlling Greece, Cyprus, Rhodes and Trebizond as well as Constantinople, advancing into the Balkans and taking Hungary (1526), and even threatening Vienna. This was in addition to the Muslim lands of the eastern Mediterranean which had been united under the Ottomans, and the annexing of the whole of North Africa with the exception of Morocco. Suleyman and Charles V, the leaders of the Muslim and Christian worlds respectively, fought each other in what was in essence an imperial, rather than a holy war, although the rhetoric of *jihād* and holy war was used. The subsequent Christian victory in 1571 at the Battle of Lepanto in the Gulf of Corinth was hailed as 'a mighty triumph over the infidel' (ibid., p. 256). Nevertheless, the Ottoman resources were so vast that this defeat made little impact, and it was not until the Peace of Karlowitz in 1699 that the empire was defeated and began to decline.

The memory of the crusades was 'reinforced in the nineteenth and twentieth centuries as imperial Europeans once again arrived to subjugate and colonize territories in the Middle East' (Akbar Ahmed, *Living Islam*, London, 1995, p. 76, cited in Hillenbrand, 1999, p. 590), triggering disputes between France and Russia over the guardianship of the Christian Holy Places, and leading to the Crimean War. Crusader imagery was then used during the First and Second World Wars. As

Elizabeth Siberry (2000, p. 87) has pointed out, such imagery was not predominant and nor did its use escape criticism in the face of heavy casualties, horror and suffering in the trenches. Yet its use was pervasive, crossing national and religious boundaries, and its aim was similarly diverse, the Germans as well as various Muslim forces being the target. According to Siberry, 'the concept of the war as a holy war seems to have originated in sermons preached by Anglican clergymen, such as Bishop Winnington-Ingram of London, the so-called Bishop of the Battlefields' (ibid., p. 87), who spoke of the honour of fighting in a holy war against the Antichrist – 'to kill Germans: to kill them not for the sake of killing, but to save the world' (Advent sermon, 1915). Lloyd George claimed in 1916 that the young men of Britain had flocked 'to the standard of international right, as to a great crusade' (Snape and Parker, 2001, p. 402), whilst Bishop Percival of Hereford in 1915 characterized Britain and her allies as 'the predestined instruments to save the Christian civilisation of Europe from being overcome by a brutal and ruthless military paganism' (ibid., p. 401). Basil Bourchier, who served with the Red Cross in 1914 and was an army chaplain in 1915–16, perhaps also traded the Muslim infidel for German paganism when, in one of his 1915 pastoral addresses, he asserted that 'Odin is ranged against Christ. Berlin is seeking to prove its supremacy over Bethlehem' (ibid., p. 88). Specifically, he saw the Dardanelles campaign against Turkey – Germany's Muslim ally – as a crusade; indeed, 'the latest of the crusades ... A vision arises before the mind of Byzantium [Constantinople/Istanbul] once again a Christian city; St Sophia once again the home of Christian worship, and who knows, once again the Holy Land rescued from the defiling grip of the infidel' (ibid.).

Crusading imagery was, however, most pronounced in First World War efforts in Palestine. Captain Ralph Adams entitled his account of the campaign *The Modern Crusaders* (1920), and Edward Thompson wrote of the *Crusader's Coast* (1929) south of Haifa. Further parallels with the crusade were undoubtedly strengthened by the capture of Jerusalem in December 1917. When Edmund Allenby entered Jerusalem in triumph,[9] he is reputed to have said, 'today the wars of the crusaders are completed', and a *Punch* cartoon from December 1917, entitled 'The Last Crusade', depicted Richard the Lionheart gazing down on Jerusalem with the caption, 'At last my dream comes true'. This is despite the fact that Muslims, such as the Egyptian camel corps, served in Allenby's army and orders were issued forbidding the soldiers to call themselves crusaders. But Major Vivian Gilbert's memoir, *The Romance of the Last Crusade – With Allenby to Jerusalem* (1923) depicted the men fighting in Palestine as successors to the crusaders, for

> The spirit of the Crusaders was in all these men of mine ... was
> not their courage just as great, their idealism just as fine, as that

[9] Twenty years earlier, Kaiser Wilhelm II had ridden into Jerusalem on horseback dressed as a medieval crusader.

of knights of old who set out with such dauntless faith under the leadership of Richard the Lionhearted to free the Holy Land.

(cited in Siberry, 2000, p. 96)

War memorials depicted First World War soldiers alongside or looked over by crusading knights, and the 'khaki crusaders' were depicted as part of a continuing struggle in this 'last and holiest and greatest of all crusades' (F. H. Cooper, *The Khaki Crusaders*, 1919, cited in Siberry, 2000, p. 101).

Holy war, however, was also promoted in Germany, with exhortations to Muslims to rise against British rule in India and the Russians in the Caucasus. For example, one leaflet intercepted by the Russians read:

The time has come to free ourselves from infidel rule. The caliph has powerful allies. This war was sent by God to give Muslims their freedom, so those who do not join in are the enemies of God. If force of arms is not used against the infidels now, then we will never be free.

(cited in Siberry, 2000, p. 102)

The crusade image, as Siberry argues, 'had a widespread and international currency, not only amongst those who could romanticize in safety from afar, but also with participants in some of the bloodiest theatres of war' (ibid., p. 103). And crusading imagery and rhetoric did not end with the First World War. For his memoirs of the Second World War, the American General Eisenhower chose the title *The Crusade in Europe* (1948), and the Eighth Army had two official newspapers: the daily *Eighth Army News* and the weekly *Crusader.*

Throughout the twentieth century and into the twenty-first, the image of the crusades continues for both the western world and Islam. After the Second World War, crusading rhetoric was used against Communism in the Cold War through such bodies as the House Un-American Activities Committee which operated throughout the 1950s. It also found expression in 1950s evangelical crusades such as Campus Crusade, Christian Crusade, and Billy Graham's evangelism, which used an opposition between Christ and Communism – Graham declared that 'either communism must die or Christianity must die because it is actually a battle between Christ and Anti-Christ' (in Chidester, 2001, p. 560). There were also fundamentalist Christian crusades in the US in the 1960s, which continued throughout the 1980s as 'a Christian crusade against the moral, social, and political evils ... threatening American society' (Chidester, 2001, p. 571).

But crusade imagery is also to be found in modern Islamic political ideologies. Throughout the nineteenth century, the progress of European imperialism in the Middle East had made crusading parallels seem more and more appropriate: the Ottoman Sultan Abd al-Hamid II (ruled

1876–1909) repeatedly asserted that Europe was conducting a crusade against the Ottoman Empire. In the period immediately after the First World War, during the British Mandate, and then particularly after the creation of the State of Israel after the Second World War, 'Saladin's victory over the Crusaders at Hattin became a central theme in the Palestinians' political struggle against Zionists' (Hillenbrand, 1999, p. 594). Saladin himself was increasingly portrayed as 'the prototypical religio-political fighter against foreign oppression' (ibid.), to the extent that he is now the greatest fighter for Islam against western aggression and 'Arab political leaders vie to become the "Second Saladin"' (ibid., p. 595).

Not surprisingly, claims Hillenbrand, 'the Crusades are seen through an anti-imperialist prism and the Islamic response in the twelfth and thirteenth centuries is viewed as the blueprint for modern Arab and Islamic struggles for independence from western colonialist aggression, above all from Israel and the United States' (1999, p. 595).

Modern Islamic activists make great use of the idea of crusade, seeing Israel as the latest Middle Eastern crusader state, and interpreting all Christian attacks on Islam throughout its history as crusades – from

Figure 1   Saddam Hussein, as the heir of Saladin, propaganda picture, probably 1980s.
Photo © Rex Features Limited

opposition to Islamic conquerors in Syria and Palestine in the seventh century, to the *Reconquista* of medieval Spain, to more recent times. For the Egyptian Muslim Brothers, for example, the post-1947 United Nations' activities in Palestine were regarded as 'a new declaration of Zionist-Crusading war against the Arab and Islamic peoples' (Al-Shihab, 14 November 1947, pp. 86–8, cited in Hillenbrand, 1999, p. 601). As Hillenbrand explains, 'Zionism was fully identified with Crusading Western imperialism and the terms "European Crusading" (*al-salibiyya al-urubiyya*) and "Jewish Crusading" were interchangeable' (1999, p. 601). Sayyid Qutb, the principal spokesman for a faction of the Muslim Brothers after its dissolution in 1954 until his execution for treason in 1966, warned of 'the financial influence of the Jews of the United States ... Anglo-Saxon guile ... [and the] vital element in the question ... the Crusader spirit which runs in the blood of all Westerners' (S. Qutb, *Al-'adalat al-ijtima'iyya fi'l-Islam,* 1995, p. 235, in Hillenbrand, 1999, pp. 601–2).

Likewise, for other Islamic radicals the crusades have not ended either for the Christians – who in their view are still determined to destroy Islam – or for Muslims. Osama bin Laden's umbrella organization is called The World Islamic Front for Crusade against Jews and Christians. Hamas,[10] founded in the Israeli Occupied Territories in 1967, has as its goal the liberation of Palestine from Zionist occupation and the re-establishment of an Islamic state. It regards western attempts to take Palestine in the First World War as merely another example of crusading incursions. Meanwhile, the Islamic Liberation Party (Hizb al-tahrir al-islami) seeks to purge the Islamic '*umma* of colonial contamination, and sees Israel as

> a colonialist bridge-head through which America and Europe perpetuate their control and their economic exploitation of the Muslim world. Israel is 'a poisoned dagger plunged deep into its breast'. The creation of the State of Israel ... was inspired by the Crusades.
>
> (Hillenbrand, 1999, p. 603)

> The Crusaders' malice remained concealed in their hearts, till they disclosed it when they succeeded in doing away with the Ottoman Caliphal state and then establishing a Jewish state in Palestine. This they deemed a two-fold revenge for their defeat at the hands of the heroic Muslim leader Salah al-Din.
>
> (Taji-Farouki, 1996, p. 41, cited in Hillenbrand, 1999, pp. 603–4)

Vengeance for the failure of the crusades is seen in the shape of colonial exploitation of the Muslim world, and it is clear that the establishment of the State of Israel after the Second World War revived awareness of the

---

[10] Harakat al-muqawama al-Islamiyya (Movements of Islamic Resistance).

crusade experience in the Arab world. As early as 1948, 'Abd al-Latif Hamza wrote: 'The struggle against Zionists has reawakened in our hearts the memory of the Crusades' (*Adab al-hurub al salibiyya*, 1949, p. 304, in Hillenbrand 1999, p. 605). From 1969 onwards, Colonel Qaddafi's regime in Libya adopted a strongly anti-Christian, anti-western, anti-imperialist stance against, in particular, 'the filth of the American Christians' – the Jews have occupied Jerusalem, backed by the United States crusaders. Christians, as in the time of the crusades, are seen as dirty pollutants of the Muslim environment; the 'filthy American pigs' have launched 'the offensive of the Cross against Islam' and are 'the leaders of the modern Crusader offensive'.[11]

Such a stance is hardly surprising given the deleterious influence of two centuries of crusader interference and proto-colonialism in the Islamic world, followed by the steady increase in power and cultural imperialism of the west which mirrored the wane of the Muslim world's earlier superiority. Despite the subsequent success of the Ottoman Empire, in Palestine the crusades had brought little benefit to the Islamic world, and in fact caused great offence to Muslims throughout the period of conflict and coexistence during the twelfth and thirteenth centuries. Thus, whilst the so-called western world may use the rhetoric of the crusades – against poverty, famine, injustice, and so on – with the assumption that crusading has God on its side and can only be beneficial – others do not share the same viewpoint. For many people – Muslims and non-Muslims – the crusades carry connotations of military, political, economic, religious and cultural oppression by a Christian hegemony, which is out of place in the global village where humanity is, ideally, supposed to coexist without conflict. Yet, as we have noted, it is often this very coexistence that brings about conflict, as 'knowledgeable ignorance' and Orientalism/Islamophobia continue.

With Palestine and the State of Israel continuing to be a focus for western interference and intervention, Islam cannot forget the crusades – their impact 'has lasted and has resulted in battle lines of misunderstanding and hostility being drawn up between East and West' (Hillenbrand, 1999, p. 613). The crusades, then, still reverberate with incredible force in relations between the Christian west and Islamic Near and Middle East nine hundred years after the First Crusade set out to capture Jerusalem for Christendom.

---

[11] Nationalist Documents to Confront the Crusader Attack on the Arab Homeland, p. 35, no date, cited in Hillenbrand, 1999, pp. 609–10.

References and further reading

Bridge, A. (1980) *The Crusades*, St Albans, Granada Publishing.

Chidester, D. (2001) *Christianity: A Global History*, Harmondsworth, Penguin.

Cipollone, G. (2001) 'From tolerance to intolerance: the humanitarian way, 1187–1216' in M. Gervers and James M. Powell (eds), *Tolerance and Intolerance: Social Conflict in the Age of the Crusades*, NY, Syracuse University Press, pp. 28–40.

*Fletcher, R. (1998) *The Conversion of Europe From Paganism to Christianity 371–1386 AD*, London, HarperCollins.

France, J. (1997) 'Patronage and the appeal of the First Crusade' in J. Phillips (ed.) *The First Crusade: Origins and Impact*, Manchester, Manchester University Press, pp. 5–20.

Gervers, M. and Powell, James M. (eds) (2001) *Tolerance and Intolerance: Social Conflict in the Age of the Crusades*, New York, Syracuse University Press.

Hillenbrand, C. (1997) 'The First Crusade: the Muslim perspective' in J. Phillips (ed.) *The First Crusade: Origins and Impact*, Manchester, Manchester University Press, pp. 130–41.

*Hillenbrand, C. (1999) *The Crusades: Islamic Perspectives*, Edinburgh, Edinburgh University Press.

Housley, N. (1992) *The Later Crusades, 1274–1580*, Oxford, Oxford University Press.

*Irwin, R. (1995) 'Islam and the Crusades, 1096–1699' in J. Riley-Smith (ed.) *Illustrated History of the Crusades*, Oxford, Oxford University Press, pp. 217–59.

Jotischky, A. (2001) 'The Frankish encounter with the Greek Orthodox in the Crusader States: the case of Gerard of Nazareth and Mary Magdelene' in M. Gervers and James M. Powell (eds), *Tolerance and Intolerance: Social Conflict in the Age of the Crusades*, NY, Syracuse University Press, pp. 100–14.

Knobler, A. (2001) 'Crusading for the Messiah: Jews as instruments of Christian Anti-Islamic Holy War' in M. Gervers and James M. Powell (eds), *Tolerance and Intolerance: Social Conflict in the Age of the Crusades*, NY, Syracuse University Press, pp. 83–9.

Mottahedeh, R. P. and al-Sayyid, R. (2001) 'The Idea of the *Jihād* in Islam before the Crusades' in A. E. Laiou and R. P. Mottahedeh (eds) *The Crusades from the Perspective of Byzantium and the Muslim World*, Washington, Dumbarton Oaks, pp. 23–9.

Murray, A. V. (2001) *Crusade and Conversion on the Baltic Frontier, 1150–1500*, Aldershot, Ashgate.

O'Shea, S. (2000) *The Perfect Heresy: The Life and Death of the Cathars*, London, Profile Books.

*Phillips, J. (ed.) (1997) *The First Crusade: Origins and Impact*, Manchester, Manchester University Press.

Riley-Smith, J. (1986) *The First Crusade and the Idea of Crusading*, London, The Athlone Press.

Riley-Smith, J. (ed.) (1991) *The Atlas of the Crusades*, London, Times Books.

Riley-Smith, J. (1997) 'Introduction' in J. Phillips (ed.) *The First Crusade: Origins and Impact*, Manchester, Manchester University Press, pp. 1–4.

Riley-Smith, J. (2002) *What Were the Crusades?*, Basingstoke, Palgrave.

Ryan, J. D. (2001) 'Toleration denied: Armenia between East and West in the era of the Crusades' in M. Gervers and James M. Powell (eds), *Tolerance and Intolerance: Social Conflict in the Age of the Crusades*, NY, Syracuse University Press, pp. 55–64.

Saunders, J. J. (1962) *Aspects of the Crusades*, Canterbury, University of Canterbury Publications.

Schwinges, R. C. (2001) 'William of Tyre, the Muslim enemy, and the problem of tolerance' in M. Gervers and James M. Powell (eds), *Tolerance and Intolerance: Social Conflict in the Age of the Crusades*, NY, Syracuse University Press, pp. 124–32.

Snape, M. and Parker, S. (2001) 'Keeping faith and coping: belief, popular religiosity and the British people' in P. Liddle, J. Bourne and I. Whitehead (eds) *The Great World War 1914–45: Vol 2 The Peoples' Experience*, London, HarperCollins, pp. 397–419.

*Siberry, E. (2000) *The New Crusaders: Images of the Crusades in the 19th and Early 20th Centuries*, Aldershot, Ashgate.

Trevor-Roper, H. (1966) *The Rise of Christian Europe*, London, Thames & Hudson.

Asterisked items are particularly recommended for further reading.

3 Post-Reformation Britain and Ireland: the churches of the British Isles 1560–1691

Anne Laurence

In the British Isles in the late sixteenth century everyone was expected to define themselves as a Christian and was required to attend the services of the established church. The practice of any other religion was punishable – by fines, imprisonment, or even death. As we shall see, however, there were various interpretations of what constituted the established church and what constituted acceptable attendance, and the enforcement of penal laws varied greatly over the period. By the late seventeenth century the situation had changed so much that it was possible to contemplate the coexistence of different Christian denominations with each other, and of Christians with non-Christian faiths, though overt expressions of unbelief continued to be unacceptable. Thus conflict, conversion and coexistence are concepts central to the religious history of the period 1560–1691, a period in which no part of the British Isles was spared civil war and religious strife. This chapter considers the varieties of religious conflict that occurred, the concerns raised by conversion, and the gradual emergence of an official policy of limited coexistence.

Religion in the British Isles

1560

In 1560, England, Wales and Ireland shared a monarch in the person of Queen Elizabeth I, at whose accession in 1558 each nation's Protestant church had been re-established following the reign of the Catholic Mary Tudor. Dissenters from these Protestant churches could be punished, whether they were Roman Catholics or people who believed that Protestant reform had not been sufficiently thoroughgoing. The Church of Ireland was in communion with the Church of England but not subject to it. These churches had a Calvinist theology and bishops, and they retained more of the ceremonies of the Roman Catholic Church than did the Church of Scotland. Unlike England, Wales and Scotland, where the established church was the church of the majority of the population, the Church of Ireland was the church of only a minority, the majority remaining Roman Catholic.

Scotland was an independent state under the rule of Mary Stuart (Queen of Scots) where in 1560 the authority of the papacy was repudiated and a

Map 3   The British Isles and Ireland. © *The Open University*

Calvinist Book of Discipline and articles of religion were adopted. Unlike the churches in England, Wales and Ireland, which substantially retained the parish organization, ministry and bishops of the pre-Reformation Catholic Church, the church in Scotland established a new organization with parishes administered by kirk sessions (meetings of ministers and lay elders). While the churches of England, Wales and Ireland underwent little reorganization until the 1640s, the organization of the Church of Scotland was constantly evolving during the period, with bishops being gradually reinstated, though without the claims for apostolic succession made for them elsewhere in the British Isles.

The Elizabethan church settlement in England and Wales was essentially a political compromise between the queen's desire for limited religious reform, with full royal control over the church, and the views of an active body of laity and clergy who wanted further reform. In the course of Elizabeth I's reign, Roman Catholicism emerged as the great popular enemy, and a well-developed conspiracy theory was used to justify a strongly anti-Catholic foreign policy. Another development, of Elizabeth I's later years, was a critique of Calvinism which was to contribute to the later emergence of a distinctive Anglican theology.

The civil wars and republic 1642–60

By the later sixteenth century, there had emerged a number of people throughout the British Isles who believed that Protestant reform had not gone far enough, who objected to the retention of bishops, to ceremonies such as the churching of women after childbirth, and to practices such as the use of the sign of the cross in baptism and the wearing of surplices by the clergy. These people, whom we call Puritans, expressed their views more and more vociferously during the early years of the seventeenth century, especially after the emergence of the movement to make worship in the churches of England, Wales and Ireland more reverential, with a greater emphasis on ceremony and sacraments. While several bishops and many members of Parliament could be accounted Puritans, the ceremonialist movement (inspired by the writings of Lancelot Andrewes) had the support not only of the Archbishop of Canterbury, William Laud, but also of King Charles I.

Opposition to ceremonies (characterized as 'innovation') erupted into violence in the late 1630s and 1640s with the outbreak of war between England and Scotland (caused by Charles I's attempt to impose the Anglican Prayer Book on the Scots), followed by civil wars in England, Wales and Scotland in which the opposing sides were defined by their attitude to reform of the church and obedience to the monarch. With war in England, censorship collapsed, bishops were abolished in the Church of England, and the Prayer Book and 39 Articles (which defined the church's theology) were replaced by a Directory of Public Worship based on the service book used in the Church of Scotland. At the same time, groups of worshippers formed themselves into associations, congregations and churches, putting forward new theologies. From these groups emerged the denominations we now recognize as Presbyterians, Congregationalists, Baptists and Quakers. In Scotland, a truly Presbyterian church, run by its hierarchy of assemblies, without bishops from 1638, came into being. Until the 1650s there had been dissension but not schism within the Church of Scotland, but the church was split irreparably over the issue of whether support for the monarchy was compatible with support for the Covenant that defined church membership. In Ireland, the Catholic majority rose against the Protestant English government in 1641. The following years of war saw many different alignments and, in the 1650s, a concerted attempt to suppress Catholicism under laws passed in England but not previously applied to Ireland.

Figure 1   The Irish Catholic rising of 1641 gave rise to many accusations that the Catholics had committed atrocities against Protestants. Anti-Catholic feeling was encouraged by the popular press. Prints from [James Cranford] (1642) The Teares of Ireland, *London. Photo used with permission from The British Library, shelfmark: c.21.b.42*

The Restoration 1660

When the monarchy was restored in 1660, so were the established churches with bishops. The Act of Uniformity in England and Wales required clergy to use the Book of Common Prayer, subscribe to the 39 Articles and pledge non-resistance to royal authority. Hopes of simplified Anglican services and a less priestly ministry were dashed despite Charles II's conciliatory Declaration of Breda offering 'liberty to tender consciences'. Congregations of Baptists, Independents (Congregationalists) and Presbyterians who had worshipped freely in England and Wales in the 1650s now found themselves the subject of legislation that prevented them from meeting or holding civic office and which singled out Quakers for active persecution. Catholics in England and Wales were the subjects of spasmodic persecution as successive plots and campaigns heightened public fears about the threat of an international Catholic conspiracy, of which the heir to the throne (James, Duke of York) was believed to be a part. Yet in Ireland, no action was taken against the Catholic hierarchy of priests and bishops and attempts were made to accommodate peaceable Catholics by trying to distinguish between loyal and disloyal Catholic laypeople. The Catholic Church in Ireland was probably in a considerably better state than the Anglican Church of Ireland, whose 'claims to be the church of the country were at variance with the predominance of Presbyterians in many parts of the north and of Catholics in most of the rest of Ireland', Ulster having been settled by substantial numbers of Scots in the early years of the century (Simms, 1978, p. 434).

The Restoration destroyed any possibility of a single, comprehensive, national Protestant church in England and Wales and in 1660–2 1,760 members of the clergy who could not accept the religious settlement (defined by subscription to the 39 Articles) left the newly re-established church, and were forbidden to worship. In Scotland, 271 Covenanting clergy left the Church of Scotland, refusing to comply with a church in which bishops had been reinstated in 1661.[1] English nonconformists endured their lot after the unsuccessful rising of the radical millenarian Fifth Monarchists in 1661[2] and increased persecution following the Rye House Plot of 1682 in which nonconformists were implicated[3]. Scots Covenanters, in contrast, were more militant and more harshly treated: the Pentland Rising in 1666 (of Covenanters against the government) and the rising culminating in defeat at Bothwell Brig in 1679 were put down

---

[1] Covenanters supported a Scottish church governed by the Covenant. In particular, they believed there was no role for the secular government in running the church.

[2] The Fifth Monarchists (or Fifth Monarchy Men) believed that Christ would come to reign on earth for 1000 years before the Day of Judgement. They sought to hasten on Christ's arrival by various revolutionary means.

[3] The Rye House Plot was a plot to assassinate King Charles II.

with considerable severity, and preaching at a conventicle was made punishable by death.

Irish Catholics were not afforded the toleration they felt they were due, but in the 1670s there were some 1,600 priests at work in the country and a general synod of Irish Catholic bishops was held in 1670. Despite their numbers, their success was much impeded by internal disputes about the precedence of bishops, between regular and secular clergy, between Gaelic Irish and Old English, and by the absence of any form of Catholic education.

The Glorious Revolution of 1688 and its aftermath

The accession in 1685 of James VII (of Scotland) and II (of England), a practising Catholic anxious to promote his co-religionists to places of influence, led to public Catholic worship in England and the advancement of Roman Catholics to positions of power in the government and army for the first time since Mary Tudor's reign. Such was the reaction against this that in 1688 James was deposed and replaced by the joint Protestant monarchy of William III and Mary. English and Welsh nonconformists were permitted freedom of worship under the Toleration Act of 1689. This act ultimately led to a diminution in nonconformist numbers, as congregations, formerly sustained by the need to survive persecution, declined because it became possible for people not to attend church at all. However, the Glorious Revolution created a new form of dissent, for six Anglican bishops and around 400 clergy declined to swear the oath of allegiance to William and Mary because they believed in James II's unalterable claims as rightful king; known as non-jurors, they put themselves outside the established church.

The Scots took longer to accept the new monarchs. After bishops were abolished in the Church of Scotland in 1690, Covenanting ministers and laity, excluded since 1662, rejoined the church. Meanwhile, supporters of episcopacy left the church to worship separately, allying themselves politically with other supporters of King James, many of whom were Roman Catholics. These episcopalians were not formally given freedom of worship until 1712, because of the suspicion that they wanted to overthrow the monarchy and reinstate the exiled house of Stuart.

In Ireland, James II was able to rally strong support against William and it was not until 1691 that the Treaty of Limerick concluded the Williamite wars. Catholics were offered some form of toleration in return for allegiance to William. However, the failure to extend the English Toleration Act to Ireland meant that Scots Presbyterians in Ulster (who were, by the 1680s, by far the most numerous of the dissenting churches in Ireland) were not permitted to worship freely. Attempts to secure legislation for their relief foundered because of Anglican suspicion of their Scots origins (Connolly, 1992, p. 170). In the course of the fifteen years following the conquest, the Anglican-dominated Irish Parliament enacted a series of laws whose intentions were to prevent Catholics from holding political power and to reduce their access to land; the practise of Catholic religion was not prohibited (only the more or less obsolete Elizabethan Act of Uniformity did that), nor was there any specific legislation proscribing the activities of the Catholic Church hierarchy until 1709.

By the end of the seventeenth century in the British Isles, the hegemony of state churches, which had characterized the early seventeenth century, had been replaced by Protestant pluralism. Public Catholic worship was not officially tolerated and Catholics (like dissenters) were excluded from civil rights by virtue of being unable to subscribe to the established church, but the persecution of Catholics was intermittent and gradually waned. In this context, the period may be seen as one during which the principal Christian denominations took on a shape that is still just about recognizable: when the division between Protestantism and Roman Catholicism was consolidated and when many of the other Christian denominations (Baptists, Quakers and Congregationalists) came into being.

However, there is a different, though not incompatible view in the thesis put forward by the distinguished historian of the English Civil War, John Morrill, who argues that the Civil War in England was not the first European revolution, but the last of the European wars of religion following the Reformation (Morrill, 1993). His views have been thoughtfully and subtly considered in an essay by the historian of the Elizabethan church, Patrick Collinson (Collinson, 1988). The conclusion of this religious war could be seen either as 1660 with the return of the monarchy and settlement of the Church of England, or as 1689 when the Toleration Act permitted Protestant dissenters from the Churches of England and Wales freedom of worship. In Scotland, though, it was not until the 1690s, with the settlement of the Church of Scotland after the Williamite conquest, that the process of reform might be said to have come to an end. And in Ireland, hopes were raised for Roman Catholics with the flight there from England of James II in 1688, but soon after dashed by King William's victories and the enactment of a penal code that excluded Catholics from the political and economic life of the country. As Nicholas Tyacke has observed, it is customary in other European countries to consider the Reformation as a much longer-term development than has been the convention in English historiography, and even the so-called revisionist accounts have not extended the idea of the English Reformation more than a few decades from the period of the main legislative provisions in the 1530s and 1540s (Tyacke, 1998, p. 1).

The vernacularization of worship

Before the Reformation, everyone used the same Latin mass (with variations for local saints and ceremonies) and the Bible was read in Latin in a version known as the Vulgate (Bossy, 1985, p. 103). Preaching (the speciality of certain religious orders such as the Dominican friars) was usually in the vernacular unless to a learned congregation in a university or monastery. With the Catholic Reformation came the imposition of uniformity on worship; with the Protestant Reformation came services, preaching and Bible-reading all in the vernacular. In the context of the British Isles, this had repercussions for the unity of Protestantism, for, at this time, this was a multi-lingual territory. Over half the population of Scotland and a much higher proportion of the population of Ireland spoke Gaelic; the use of Welsh was widespread and the populations of Cornwall and the Isle of Man spoke their own languages. The provision of vernacular Bibles, prayer books and catechisms and a clergy able to speak the same language as their congregation was vital to the successful dissemination of reformed religion.

Translations of Bible and liturgies

Despite the importance of worship in the vernacular, the production of prayer books and Bibles in the various languages was a protracted process. Christopher Hill remarked of fifteenth-century England that 'the mere fact of owning and reading the Bible in English was presumptive evidence of heresy' (1994, p. 4) and noted that the early sixteenth-century translators of the Bible into English became martyrs. Yet by the following century, 'the vernacular Bible became an institution ... the foundation of monarchical authority, of England's protestant independence, the text book of morality and social subordination' (ibid., p. 10). Even the process by which the English Bible became an institution was far from straightforward, and the non-English speaking parts of the British Isles had a protracted wait for Bibles in their own languages.

Initially, the new Protestant church saw providing the scriptures, services and preaching in the vernacular as fundamental to the programme of converting the Catholic populations of the British Isles to Protestantism. As reformed religion became more firmly established, the scriptures assumed a greater importance as the direct word of God by which Calvinist believers in the doctrine of election (part of the theology of the churches of England and Wales, Scotland and Ireland in the early seventeenth century) might understand their spiritual state.

There were more English translations of the Bible than vernacular translations into other European languages. John Wycliffe's fifteenth-

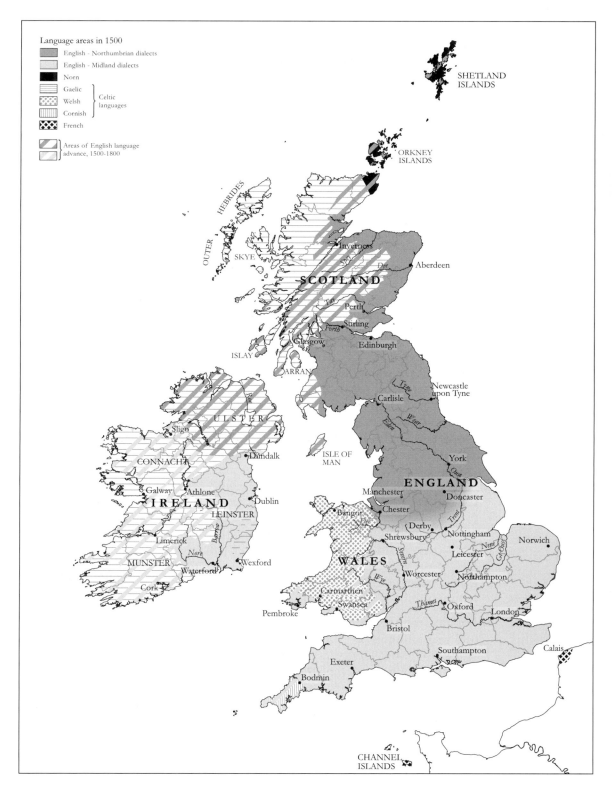

Map 4   'British languages and changes 1500–1800' from Simon Hall and John Haywood (eds) (2001) The Penguin Atlas of British and Irish History, *Harmondsworth, Penguin, p. 152. Copyright © Penguin Books, 2001. Reproduced by permission of Penguin Books Ltd*

century version was followed by the first English printed Bible of 1535 (Coverdale's); then Matthew's Bible of 1537; the 1539 Great Bible based on the work of Tyndale and Coverdale; the Geneva Bible (translated by Protestant divines exiled on the continent during Mary Tudor's reign and published in 1560); the Bishop's Bible of 1568 (a revision of the Great Bible); and the King James Authorised Version of 1611. Some translations were taken directly from the Hebrew and Greek of the originals, others from the Latin Vulgate, and some were composite works. Even after the publication of the Authorised Version, many people of Puritan leanings continued to prefer the Geneva Bible which had a strongly anti-Catholic commentary. Meanwhile, in 1582, as part of the Catholic reform effort, there appeared a Catholic translation of the New Testament, the Old Testament following in 1609. The first Book of Common Prayer (the Anglican service book in English) was produced in 1549, and a second appeared in 1552, which was revised at the beginning of Elizabeth I's reign in 1559. The version in use in England in the seventeenth century was substantially that of 1559; however, the psalms (which were not routinely printed with the Prayer Book until 1662 but formed part of the services) were from the Great Bible of 1539 and it was in this form that they were best known.

Early Protestant publications in Scotland were produced in the language known as the older Scottish tongue, a variant of English. Before the Reformation, in an attempt to avert the decline of the Catholic Church, a vernacular catechism had appeared (1552) and in 1559 a collection of vernacular prayers was published (Whyte, 1995, p. 95). John Knox's Protestant Book of Common Order, with the Psalms in metre and a translation of Calvin's catechism, was issued in 1564, and was chiefly prepared by him. Through the influence of imported Protestant publications, English linguistic forms gained much wider currency in Scotland. Reformed religion, the English language and alliance with England began to represent modernity, while the old (Catholic) religion, the older Scottish tongue and alliance with France seemed backward looking (Pittock, 2001, p. 42).

Those areas of Scotland that took least to the new religion were the western Highlands and the islands (Gaelic-speaking areas), and the north-east, which remained the centre for Latin scholarship. These areas were much more populous than they are now. A Gaelic translation of Knox's Book of Common Order was produced in 1567; a catechism and translations of the Psalms followed in the early seventeenth century, but there was no Gaelic Bible. In the 1680s, some Irish Gaelic Bibles were sent for use in Scotland, but the Scots used a different system of Gaelic orthography from the Irish, so it was not until there was a transcription into Roman type in the 1690s that Gaelic-speaking Scots had a Bible they could use (Withers, 1984, pp. 33, 43).

An Anglican Book of Common Prayer appeared in Irish in 1608. The New Testament had been translated into Irish and published in 1602 and was reprinted in 1681; the Old Testament, though actually translated in the first half of the seventeenth century, had to wait until 1685 to be published (Crowley, 2000, p. 19; Ócuív, 1978, p. 534).

William Salesbury (c.1520–1600), an enthusiast in Wales for the new religion, published in 1547 a Welsh–English dictionary intended to help Welsh speakers read the gospels in English, and in 1551 he published a Welsh translation of those sections of the epistles and gospels appointed to be read in churches throughout the year under the title 'Kynniver Llith a Ban'. The need for Welsh-language religious provision was recognized earlier than the needs of speakers of the other languages of the British Isles. In 1563, Parliament enacted that in every church in Wales there should be a Bible and a Book of Common Prayer in both Welsh and English. The first Welsh Prayer Book was published in 1567, as was a Welsh New Testament, with the Old Testament appearing in 1588.

This move to vernacularization meant that people read the words of the Bible in many different versions. In the past they had largely read them in Latin in the Vulgate, except for those few learned people who were to be found in the older centres of learning and were able to read the Hebrew Old Testament and the Greek New Testament. The Psalms, in particular, were read in numerous variants, especially with the popularity of metrical versions for singing. They also attracted the attention of poets such as Mary Sidney, Countess of Pembroke.

The Authorised Version of Psalm 137, verse 1, 'By the rivers of Babylon, there we sat down, yea we wept, when we remembered Zion' was rendered as

> At the Riuers of Babylon,
> Quhair we dwelt in Captiuitie,
> Quhen we rememberit on Sion.

in a Scottish psalter. In the 1605 Book of Common Prayer it appeared as 'By the waters of Babylon we sate downe & wept: when we remembered thee, O Sion'. In the metrical version known as Sternhold and Hopkins and used widely in English churches it appeared as

> When as we sat in Babylon,
> ye riuers rounde about:
> and in remēbraunce of Sion
> the teares for grief burst out

and in Richard Goodridge's late seventeenth-century version it appeared as

> Whilst griev'd we sate by th' Streams of Babylon,
> As the Streams glided on, our Tears ran down.[4]

The Geneva Bible of 1560 was the most widely used in England and Wales, even after the publication of the Authorised Version in 1611. However, in the 1630s Archbishop Laud, objecting to its strongly Protestant commentary, made strenuous efforts to make sure it was replaced by the Authorised Version. Nevertheless, large numbers of the earlier Bible remained in circulation and when the monopoly on printing and selling Bibles collapsed in 1640 for want of the means to enforce it, many cheap imports, some of them very inaccurate, entered the country (Hill, 1994, p. 65).

Although the ideal of the early reformers was that everyone should have direct access to the word of God, this soon appeared to senior churchmen rather a mixed blessing. Reading God's words, often expressed ambiguously and, because of the piecemeal way in which the books of the Bible had been accumulated, providing directly contradictory guidance in different passages, seemed to open up dangerous possibilities. Furthermore, people were reading the word in a wide variety of different translations and versions.

Thus Protestant reformers from the early days of the Reformation placed a great emphasis on preachers and preaching. The populace at large should have access to the word of God, but should also have direction as to how that word should be understood. Orthodoxy became not, as it had been in the Catholic Church, a matter of restricting access to the word, but of educating Christians in how the word was to be understood by means of sermons, catechisms, schooling and by enormous numbers of biblical commentaries directed at everyone from the ploughman to the bishop. The emphasis on education made it essential to speak to people in a language they could understand. At first, in much of Britain, this was taken to be the English language. London, being the most important publishing centre, naturally produced religious works in the language of south-east England.

---

[4] *Ane Cōmpendious of godlie Psalmes*, Edinburgh, 1577, p. 99; *The Booke of Common Prayer*, London, 1605, unpaginated; *The Whole Booke of Psalmes, collected into Englysh metre by T. Sternhold, I. Hopkins and others*, London, 1562, p. 350; Richard Goodridge, *The Psalter or Psalms of David Paraphras'd in Verse*, 2nd edn, Oxford 1684, p. 121. Sternhold and Hopkins's full version of the metrical psalmes first appeared in 1561 and was based on the version of the Psalms in the Geneva Bible.

Conversions and language

The impetus to religious reform in the British Isles came largely from the English-speaking populations of England and Scotland, with the result that there was a considerable association between Protestantization and Anglicization. The administrations in Westminster, Edinburgh and Dublin encouraged this; initially the new church in Ireland required its ministers to preach in English (Hayes-McCoy, 1978, p. 66). However, all the administrations had reluctantly to recognize that while ministers spoke only English, there were always going to be substantial parts of the population who could not be reached by the new religion. The authorities in Edinburgh and Dublin had mixed feelings about the use of the Gaelic language. In both Scotland and Ireland its use was associated with disloyalty to the crown, so educational schemes that forced nobles to have their children educated in English were introduced. At the same time, it was recognized that these people needed to be converted to Protestantism and that this was unlikely to happen as long as the medium of the English language was used. In the 1640s the General Assembly of the Kirk introduced a scheme for sponsoring Highland boys to be educated in Glasgow for the ministry but this, like other such schemes, was not very effective (Macinnes, 1982, p. 63).

The identification of reformed religion in Ireland with an alien language, or at least one imperfectly spoken and understood, was one of the primary sources of grievance against the English governments of Ireland and became a potent rallying cry for nationalists. In the mean time, the Gaelic- and Latin-speaking Catholic clergy in Ireland and Scotland were expelled, though they rapidly returned. In the seventeenth century, Franciscan missionaries passed freely between Ireland and the western Highlands and islands of Scotland. These were regions that had always depended on a peripatetic ministry drawn mainly from the regular orders, rather than a formal parish organization. The priests had the advantage of being able to speak to their flocks in their own languages and the experience of fitting in with the clan-based society on each side of the Irish Sea. The arrival of reformed Catholicism was associated less with traditional Gaelic Catholics, than with the Anglo-Norman families (the Old English) who professed loyalty to the monarch of England though preferred to remain Catholic (Clarke, 1987, pp. 57–72; Lennon, 1986, pp. 72–92). The first Jesuits arrived in Ireland in 1542.

In theory, the conversion of Irish Catholics to Protestantism should have been at the forefront of the Church of Ireland's policy; in practice, they had difficulty providing a ministry sufficient for people who were already Protestant. In the early seventeenth century, the church took a relaxed view about what constituted Protestantism – there were several Scots Presbyterian ministers in Church of Ireland livings. Proselytizing had never been part of the church's perceived mission, though it became a matter of greater interest after 1660. Training an Irish-speaking Protestant clergy was a concern for successive archbishops and provosts of Trinity

College, Dublin. Provost Narcissus Marsh (1638–1713), who had been instrumental in the publication of the Irish Old Testament, also arranged for instruction in Irish at the college for prospective ministers. Yet there were Protestant clergy, such as Jeremy Taylor (1613–67), Bishop of Down and Connor, who in 1664 accused the Catholic clergy of preserving the Irish language so that the population could not understand English-speaking instruction (Simms, 1978, p. 435).

The desire to convert the Irish was largely motivated by a sense that a Protestant population would be more politically submissive than a Catholic one; there would, for example, be no objection to swearing an oath of allegiance to the monarch. Conversion was also associated with an idea of progress in which economic development on the English model was to be preferred to the prevailing economic regime of Ireland. It was not until the early eighteenth century that the Irish House of Convocation (the assembly of Church of Ireland clergy) started to take any interest in providing an Irish-speaking Anglican ministry and attempting to convert the Catholic population. An ambitious scheme of 1711 to reprint the Irish New Testament, catechism and Book of Common Prayer and to equip each parish with a free school that would teach the English language and Protestant doctrine came to little (Connolly, 1992, pp. 299, 300).

Though the conversion of the population within Britain and Ireland was not a priority, there were a number of people with a wider view, and translations of the Bible into a number of other languages were made or sponsored in Britain or by Britons. The expanding world of trade is to be seen in the history of these translations: Thomas Hyde (1636–1703) published a Malay translation of the gospels and Edward Pocock (1604–1691) translated Hugo Grotius's tract *De veritate religionis Christianae* (Of the Truth of the Christian Religion) into Arabic, which was published at the expense of Robert Boyle in 1660 in the hope of converting Muslims. This scholarship was generally more concerned with converting heathens than with understanding other faiths.

Contacts with other worlds

Much of what was known about non-Christian religion came from travellers who wrote books about their experiences which were a popular form of reading matter, as for example in *A Voyage to East-India* by Edward Terry (1590–1660), written after his service as chaplain to Sir Thomas Roe, ambassador at the moghul's court in India. Terry had chapters describing both Islam and Hinduism, but said that he need not answer the 'frantick assertions' of Islam 'because that hath been done by so many hands already'(Terry, 1655, p. 261). Writing of Hindus, he dwelt chiefly on the caste system and suttee, and claimed that 'For their habits they differ very little from the Mahometans' (Terry, 1655, p. 320). Joseph

Pitts (1663–c. 1735), one of a number of men taken prisoner by Barbary pirates, was enslaved and forcibly converted to Islam in the 1680s because of the 'insatiable' cruelty of his master. He provided both a detailed description of the religion and of his reasons for converting (Vitkus, 2001, p. 312). Terry wrote of Islam containing 'much in it very pleasing to flesh and blood, and soothes up, and complies exceedingly with corrupt nature', but acknowledged that 'it cannot be denied but that there are some things in the precepts which Mahomet hath prescribed ... that are good' (Terry, 1655, p. 260). Pitts went further and commented that

> It is a shame indeed to Christians to take a view of the zeal of those poor blind Mahommetans, which in the following account will be found to be in many things very strict. If they are so strict in their false worship, it must needs be a reprimand to Christians who are so remiss in the true.

> (Vitkus, 2001, p. 223)

Members of the East India Company (founded in 1600) came across Hindus and Buddhists and learnt to speak the indigenous languages of the sub-continent, but there was little scholarly interest in those languages or religions until the second half of the eighteenth century. The *Bhagavad Gita*, for example, was not translated into English until 1785. However, amongst the noteworthy exceptions was Henry Lord, chaplain to the East India Company's factory at Surat, who in 1630 published *A Display of Two Forraigne Sects in the East Indies* and described both 'Banians' 'gathered from their Bramanes, teachers of this sect' and 'the religion of the Persees'. For safety's sake he dedicated the book to George Abbott, the Archbishop of Canterbury, to whose attention he was bringing these false beliefs 'to receive both censure and judgement', describing the Parsees' worship as 'soyled and tainted' (Lord, 1630).

The treatment of these religions was in marked contrast to that of Islam, whose holy works had reached England in the Middle Ages. Scholars in English and Scottish universities had long been interested in Arabic scholarship in science and mathematics. There were, too, extensive mercantile and diplomatic contacts with Islamic peoples, such as the meeting that took place in 1621 between a group of Carmelite monks, English merchants and Shah 'Abbās I of Iran. The Shah harangued the merchants for denying free will (Goddard, 2000, p. 118). Later in the century, the vigour of the Ottoman Empire's armies, culminating in the Turks' arrival at the gates of Vienna in 1683, aroused further interest in Islamic writings.

A Latin epitome of the Qur'ān of 1543 was widely available and the whole Qur'ān was translated from French into English by Alexander Rosse (1591–1654) in 1649 and was retranslated directly from the Arabic in a more scholarly version by George Sale (c. 1697–1736) in 1734.

Rosse's translation was a poor one, but it provoked a royalist soldier, Anthony Weldon, to denounce it to Parliament, with worse consequences for Weldon (who was arrested and exiled) than for Rosse. Abraham Whelocke (1593–1653), first professor of Arabic at Cambridge University, was said, in 1640 to be working on a refutation of the Qur'ān and in 1652 a refutation was published by Joshua Notstock. John Worthington (1618–71), Master of Jesus College Cambridge, in 1661 urged Christian missionaries to study the Qur'ān if they wanted to convert Muslims.

Growing knowledge of Islam in England led some radical reformers to suggest that Muslims, like Jews, should be included in the eschatological preparations for the second coming of Christ to earth: these required that non-Christians be converted to Christianity in advance of Christ's arrival. The suggestion seems to have been motivated by the close contacts of Britons with the Islamic world and the recognition that Islam had some admirable characteristics. Ephraim Pagitt (c.1575–1647), writing in 1645, praised Islam for not allowing Mahomet to be blasphemed and denounced the proliferation of Christian sects (Matar, 1991, pp. 60–1). Preparations for the conversion of Muslims gave a further impetus to the translation of Christian works into Arabic. In the 1660s, an Arabic catechism was produced for the benefit of Syrians and George Sale in the 1720s worked on an Arabic translation of the New Testament for the use of Syrian Christians.

Archbishop Laud

The sixteenth century was the period for the rediscovery of Greek and Hebrew language and literature and of their importance for biblical studies. Some of the foremost Greek scholars were in Scotland and Cardinal Wolsey had founded chairs of Greek and Hebrew at Oxford. The seventeenth century marked the rediscovery of Arabic. In 1631, a lectureship in Arabic was founded at Cambridge and William Bedwell (d. 1632), known as the father of Arabic studies in England, bequeathed a fount of Arabic type to Cambridge University. William Laud (1573–1645), President of St John's College, Oxford, Chancellor of Oxford University, and, from 1633, Archbishop of Canterbury, not only increased the stipend for the Oxford chair of Hebrew, but in 1635 founded a chair in Arabic, whose first incumbent was Edward Pococke (1604–91), who had been chaplain to the English merchants at Aleppo and was versed in several oriental languages.

Laud had shown an early interest in oriental languages, principally for the further pursuit of biblical studies. Although he did not know any eastern languages, he was determined to encourage scholarship in them and in 1634 obtained a royal letter to the Turkey Company requiring that every ship that returned from the east should bring one Persian or Arabic manuscript, but not a Qur'an (of which there were already sufficient copies in England). Laud was interested in patristic studies and supported the establishment in London of a Greek printing press, though he was unable to establish one in Oxford as he would have liked to do (Trevor-Roper, 1962, pp. 274–5). He was also responsible for gifts both to the university and to his own college, St John's, of oriental manuscripts and coins. In 1648, the Oxford University Press produced two works in Arabic; the first Hebrew text appeared in 1655.

One aspect of Archbishop Laud's interest in patristic studies was his concern with Greek manuscripts and he allowed Edward Pococke to travel to Greece to obtain manuscripts from the Patriarch (the head of the Greek Orthodox Church) and from Greek monasteries. In addition, Laud made contact with Cyril Lucaris, Patriarch of Alexandria, but an early interest in ecumenism was overtaken by the patriarch's interest in European Calvinism, in the wake of Protestant successes in the Thirty Years' War (Trevor-Roper, 1978, pp. 213–14, 230). Lucaris had corresponded with an earlier Archbishop of Canterbury, George Abbott, and had sent Metrophanes Kritopoulos to study at Balliol College, Oxford in 1617. The attraction of the Eastern Orthodox Church was that it seemed to offer a purer theology than the conflicting western theologies and, like the reformed churches, vested the authority of the church in councils rather than in the single person of the papacy (Patterson, 1997, p. 219).

Archbishop Laud's policies of enforcing greater conformity to a single model of worship led to an increase in the numbers of people emigrating to North America which had, from the early seventeenth century, become a destination for English Puritans who found the state of the Church of England uncongenial. A number of people, such as the minister Hanserd Knollys, went to America in the 1620s and 1630s and returned to England in the 1640s, when they learnt of the Civil War.

In 1650, there were only two places in the English-speaking part of America where toleration was explicitly permitted (Porter, 1984, pp. 197–8). In Maryland (a predominantly Catholic colony) a bill for toleration was introduced by the governor in 1649 with the arrival of a number of Puritans expelled from Anglican Virginia; Rhode Island was the only province in New England not to have an established church (Middleton, 1997, pp. 109–10). The new colonies were a haven for exiles from religious persecution in England. There was also a good deal of interest in the languages of the native population, partly for the light that study of them might throw on the underlying and supposedly universal qualities of all languages, and also for the extent that they revealed the speakers to be 'civilized'. In 1658 John Eliot (1604–90) translated and published the catechism and then a metrical version of the Psalms, and in 1663 he completed a translation of the Bible into the language of the Massachusetts Indians and concluded his work in 1660 with an Indian grammar.

Conflict

The most potent sources of religious conflict within the British Isles were Roman Catholicism, relations between church and state, the position of altars and the role of bishops. For the governments of the British Isles in this period, Roman Catholicism was synonymous with support for a foreign prince (the papacy) and with European Catholic powers who opposed the foreign policy devised in London. Differences of religious belief are difficult to disentangle from conflict about political values, since support for the papacy could be construed as treasonable or heretical. The claim that kings and the officers of the church drew their authority from God and could not be set aside by human agency had implications for secular politics as well as the government of the church.

Relations between church and state were an enduring cause of conflict, though the actual cause of war could alter. James VI (Scotland) and I (England), seared by his experiences in Scotland, where within the Church of Scotland was a party committed to separation of church and state with the church left to govern itself, firmly believed that the ultimate control of the church lay with the king.

The division amongst the Scots between Erastians (who believed that the secular authorities should play a part in the government of the church) and Covenanters (who believed that the secular government had no part to play in the regulation of the church) spread beyond Scotland, and had an impact on England, where most people were content to let Parliament regulate the church. In 1643, after the outbreak of the Civil War, Parliament concluded an alliance with the Scots, under which the Scots would provide military assistance against the king, while Parliament undertook to introduce to England the same form of church government as that in Scotland. From the outset, many supporters of Parliament felt uneasy about these terms, objecting to the implicitly theocratic nature of the Scots church. When, in 1647, the Scots allied themselves with the king, many Scots assumed that the English Parliament would continue with their plans to introduce a Presbyterian system on the Scottish model. Their failure to do so was a source of continued tension between England and Scotland in the 1650s.

Another issue was the presence of churchmen in the legislature. In England, Anglican bishops had sat in the House of Lords and were excluded in 1642, to be reinstated in 1660. As in Scotland, the presence of bishops in the Parliament was understood as a mechanism of royal control and the battleground concerned not the appointment of bishops by apostolic succession, but whether the civil power had any role at all in the government of the church. The acrimony with which the Covenanters defended their view that the government of the church should be by the General Assembly of the Kirk led to much bloodshed.

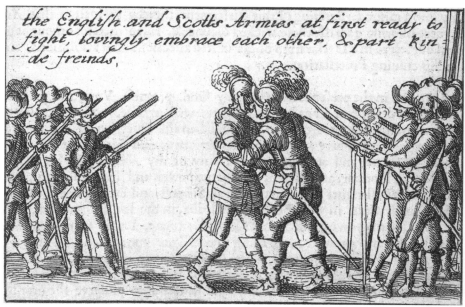

Figure 2   Initially English Puritans welcomed Scots Presbyterians in 1638 and again in 1643. Print from John Vicars, A Sight of the Transactions of these latters yeares Emblematized with engraven plates which men may read without spectacles, *London, 1646, p. 7. Photo used with permission of the British Library, shelfmark: G4092*

Another potent cause of conflict, concerning relations between church and state and the position of altars and the role of bishops, was the desire of more radical Protestants not to have to worship under the regulation of the established church. Paradoxically, some of the fiercest exchanges took place in England in the 1640s and 1650s when lack of censorship and a church organization meant that there was de facto toleration. Gathered congregations and radical Protestant congregations, for whom the only basis for a group of believers to worship together was Christ's saying 'For where two or three are gathered together in my name, there am I in the midst of them' (Matthew, 18:20), fell foul of those who wanted to reform the established church in particular ways but without opening the door to religious pluralism. The virulence of the exchanges, thanks in part to the lack of censorship, had no equivalent later in the century when the gathered congregations, now nonconformist churches, sought to secure toleration for alternative forms of worship.

Conversion

The concept of conversion had two rather different meanings in the seventeenth century. At the beginning of the period, changing people's religion to Protestantism was at the forefront of people's minds, and throughout the period, as we have seen, there was some interest in converting non-Christians to Christianity. By the 1640s and 1650s, conversion in the sense of personal experience of the divine had come to assume considerable prominence in Protestant religious life.

On the face of it, the primary form of conversion was from Catholicism to Protestantism; in reality, things were rather different. The efforts of the Catholic clergy in Ireland in the early seventeenth century to institute the reforms proposed by the Council of Trent were far more energetic than those of the Protestant clergy to secure conversions from Roman Catholicism, despite the fact that the state had adopted the view that religious uniformity was the only way of guaranteeing loyal subjects (Clarke, 1978, p. 227). More was said than done about converting Irish Catholics to Protestantism until the penal laws of 1704 and 1709, which reduced the numbers of Catholic clergy, acted as a prompt to Anglican clergy to take a greater interest in converting. However, the real pressure on Catholics to convert to Protestantism came not from an energetic proselytizing ministry but from the difficulties imposed by the legislation of 1697 and 1704 of conveying land from one Catholic to another (by descent, marriage or purchase) or from Catholics to Protestants (Connolly, 1992, pp. 269, 272).

Over the period as a whole, one might argue that more interest was shown in converting native Americans, Muslims and others to Christianity than was shown in converting Roman Catholics to Protestantism. The lack of Gaelic-speaking ministers and the absence of bibles, prayer books, catechisms and works of Protestant piety suggests that the conversion of Catholics in Ireland and the Highlands of Scotland to Protestantism was not regarded as essential to the good health of either the body politic or the souls of senior churchmen. A few religious radicals showed some interest in conversion. Two Quakers, John Love and John Perrot, travelled to Rome in 1658 to attempt to convert the Pope, while another two, Sarah Cheevers and Katherine Evans, set out for Jerusalem, but were apprehended and detained in Malta.

In England, in the millennialist fervour of the 1650s, some kind of rapprochement with the Jews was required because their conversion to Christianity was believed to be a necessary prelude to Christ's second coming.[5] England was by no means the only country to debate the subject; from 1570 onwards, many European states west of Poland considered whether to admit Jews (Israel, 1989, p. 35). Jews had been

[5] This belief finds its twenty-first century expression in the fundamentalist Christian sects who support Israeli settlements on the west bank of the Jordan.

ejected from England in 1290, but in the early 1650s there were a few living in London who petitioned Cromwell to allow them to arrange their own burials (Abbott, 1988, p. 669). In 1655 it was decided to admit Jews to England, as a result of which a number of Jewish communities were established in London and various provincial cities, a development that proved more important for coexistence than for conversion. When, in the early eighteenth century, Ashkenazi Jews began to leave eastern Europe, many settled in England and, having no language in common with the earlier Sephardic settlers, English became their common tongue.[6]

The idea of converting people from other faiths to Christianity was stronger than its execution, but it dawned on a few Christians that there was always the possibility of conversions the other way, as, for example, in the case of Joseph Pitts's conversion after being taken prisoner by Barbary pirates. Islam was considered to have affinities with Socinianism since both Muslims and Socinians denied the Trinity but recognized Christ as a prophet.

One of the most significant legacies of the religious life of the seventeenth century has been what we now call 'the Puritan conversion experience'. This was merely one aspect of a system of discipline that had profound consequences, not least for English literature. Self-examination and spiritual accounting and the recording of the individual's inner life form the origins of the autobiography as a literary form. There survive many personal accounts of conversion, of which the best known must be John Bunyan's: 'Now did my chains fall off my legs indeed, I was loosened from my affliction and irons, my temptations also fled away: so that from that time those dreadful scriptures of God left off to trouble me; now went I home rejoicing, for the grace and love of God' (Bunyan, 1987, p. 59).

Another account, by the Baptist minister Hanserd Knollys (c.1599–1691) recorded how when a student at Cambridge Knollys became

> convinced of my sinful Condition, and that I was a Child of Wrath, without Christ and Grace, &c which Work of Conviction remained strongly upon me above one year, under which I was filled with great Horrour and Temptations of the Devil.

> (Knollys, 1692, p. 3)

He withstood further doubts and temptations, renounced his Anglican ordination and, after praying in a wood, 'an answer of my Prayers was given to me ... but I heard no voice, nor did I see any Vision'. Finally,

[6] Sephardic Jews were those whose ancestors lived in Spain and who, after their expulsion in 1492, settled in North Africa and the lands of the Ottoman Empire. Ashkenazi Jews were those who in the Middle Ages lived in Germany, central and eastern Europe. Their differences were not religious but cultural, having different languages (Sephardim spoke Ladino, Ashkenazim Yiddish) and customs. Ashkenazi Jews did not start to migrate to England until the eighteenth century.

being 'fully persuaded it was an answer of my Prayers from the Lord ... I was filled with such joy, that I went on my way rejoicing, leaping and praising God' (Knollys, 1692, pp. 9, 10–11). One of the more tortured accounts is that of Oliver Cromwell.

The conversion experience itself, the moment when the individual comes to a realization of the divine presence, was given a new emphasis in the gathered congregations where individuals, as a condition of membership, gave an account of their discovery of God's presence in their lives. It is noteworthy that the basis of these congregations was not a determination to assist believers to discover God, but a shared sense of their distinctiveness from the population at large in having already undergone that experience. The pattern of the autobiography, often used as part of the process of admitting an individual to a particular religious congregation, tended to run along familiar lines: ignorance was followed by self-deception, by 'notional knowledge', by 'bitter grief for sins, by terror of the devil, by glimmerings of hope from a preacher or religious writer, by doubts and finally by a sense of homecoming in God' (Caldwell, 1983, pp. 1–2). Some of these oral accounts or testimonies were written down and published by ministers. Though somewhat formulaic and mediated by the minister's idea of the scheme they should follow, they nevertheless contain accounts of ordinary individuals' spiritual lives with a degree of detail most unusual in a society where much of the population was illiterate.

Coexistence

The concept of the coexistence of different religious groups was rarely found in the seventeenth century; and ideas of religious toleration that began to take hold in the later part of the century had a confused pre-history. In reality, there had been, since the establishment of the Elizabethan church settlement, a considerable amount of peaceful coexistence in communities such as the city of Norwich, where magistrates believed harmonious community relations to be of more importance than enforcing religious conformity (Tyacke, 1998, p. 22). We can see, in the history of the period, the emergence of the idea that it might be desirable for different religious groups to coexist, not necessarily on terms of equality, but at least without penalty. At the same time there were a number of people, including distinguished churchmen, who, while not espousing the idea of religious toleration as a principle, believed that it was wrong to persecute fellow Christians. These were ideas of moderation rather than of active support for toleration.

The claims of religious radicals in the 1650s for toleration almost always excluded Roman Catholics, and usually Anglicans as well. Cromwell urged the members of Barebone's Parliament (also known as the Nominated Parliament or the Parliament of the Saints) to take account of 'saints' of all denominations 'that we have respect unto all, though of different judgements'; as he mentions the need to tolerate Presbyterians, it seems unlikely that he was also prepared to include Catholics (Abbott, 1988, p. 62). In Ireland, after the fall of Wexford to the English forces in October 1649, he said 'I meddle not with any man's conscience. But if by liberty of conscience you mean a liberty to exercise the mass, I judge it best to use plain dealing, and to let you know, where the parliament of England have power, that will not be allowed of' (quoted in Corish, 1978, p. 342). Although nineteenth-century Whig historians, who wished to celebrate the history of political and religious freedom in England, hailed the 1640s and 1650s as the period of the foundation of ideas of religious toleration, the fact of the matter is that such toleration as existed was as much due to the inability to reach a church settlement as to a doctrinaire belief that people should be allowed freely to worship in whatever way they chose.

Doctrines that were believed to be subversive of civil order met with prompt responses from the government. The writings of the Socinian John Biddle (1615–62), who denied the divinity of Christ, provoked an ordinance in 1648 ordering the death penalty for anyone who published such beliefs; Biddle was lucky to evade execution. The Ranters, who believed, as Jacob Bauthumley (1613–c.1685) wrote, 'Men should not sin because grace abounds; but yet if they do sin, that shall turn to the prayse of God, as well as when they do wel', appeared to take delight in flouting God's ordinances (Bauthumley, 1650, p. 35).[7] The attacks on them culminated in the Blasphemy Act of 1650. The Quaker James Nayler (c.1617– 60), who in 1656 rode into Bristol on a donkey with a group of followers crying 'Holy, Holy, Holy, Lord God of Israel' (Rutt, 1828, pp. 25–6) defended himself against the charge of blasphemy by declaring that he did not believe he was Christ and he could not help it if others believed it of him (State Trials, 1810, p. 830). Nevertheless, there was in Parliament in 1656 a discussion in which Major-General Boteler said 'By the Mosiac law, blasphemers were to be stoned to death. The morality of this remains and for my part, if this sentence should pass upon him [Nayler] I should freely consent to it' (Rutt, 1828, p. 1). A similar spirit of intolerance was displayed by the first English parliament of Charles II's reign, when the hopes of moderate Presbyterians for comprehension within the established church were dashed, and a series of vindictive measures (known as the Clarendon Code) were passed to impede the free worship of anyone but Anglicans, in spite of the king's expressed desire for religious toleration. The Presbyterian minister Richard Baxter, one of 1,760 ministers in England and Wales deprived of their livings in 1660–2 for nonconformity to the Anglican settlement, wrote of 'the inundation of calamities, which in many streams

---

[7] The first phrase is taken from Romans 6:1: 'What shall we say then? Shall we continue in sin that grace may abound?'

overwhelmed thousands of godly Christians, together with their pastors' (Baxter, 1974, p. 175).

A contrast is posed by the example of Scotland whose church at this period was much less prone to schism and separation than was the Church of England (Donaldson, 1985, pp. 205–19). The ructions of the late sixteenth century over the relative importance of bishops and presbyteries did not cause anyone to break away, nor did the attempts of the 1630s to make the Church of Scotland more conformable with Anglican practice. The schisms that took place subsequently were as much to do with the politics of support for Charles I (with whom the Scots had made an alliance in 1647 which the General Assembly of the Kirk refused to accept), and for James VII and II and his successors, than with doctrine, liturgy or ecclesiology. The radical sects that appeared in Scotland with the English army of occupation in the 1650s barely survived the Restoration.

There were, nevertheless, a few people whose ideas did reach further than those of most Protestants. John Milton (1608–74) wrote *De Doctrina Christiana* (Of Christian Doctrine) with the aim of reuniting Protestants. In it, he argued that it was

> in the interests of the Christian religion that men should be free not only to sift and winnow any doctrine, but also openly to give their opinions of it, and even to write about it according to what each believes ... Without this freedom ... there is no religion and no gospel. Violence alone prevails, and it is disgraceful and disgusting that the Christian religion should be supported by violence.
>
> (Quoted in Hill, 1977, pp. 153–4)

So subversive was his work that it could not be published in his lifetime and only finally appeared in print in 1825, by which time it had rather lost its impact (Hill, 1994, p. 6). John Durie (1656–80) born in Scotland, educated in England and the Netherlands, and chaplain to English merchant companies in Germany and Sweden, was committed to the idea of a single universal Protestant church. He travelled around Europe soliciting support. This he found more readily from politicians – especially in Sweden, whose ministers hoped to secure support for a Protestant crusade to conclude the war in Germany – than from theologians. He was treated unenthusiastically by Archbishop Laud, though Laud expressed interest in the idea of dispelling the differences between Lutherans and Calvinists (Trevor-Roper, 1962, pp. 264–9). Another enthusiast for the cause was the mathematician John Pell (1611–85), and the Dutch Hugo Grotius, or de Groot (1583–1645), pursued similar aims while excluding Calvinists. The philosopher Leibnitz (1646–1716) also contributed to the debate, with his *Discourse on Metaphysics* (1686), part of his project to reunify the Catholic and

Lutheran churches.[8] While in Strasburg a publication appeared arguing for the coexistence of Catholics and Protestants (Collinson, 1991, p. 51).

Atheism was not tolerated and all the legislation of the period took it for granted that the good citizen professed a religion. Even after the Toleration Act of 1689, an act for suppressing blasphemy and profaneness of 1697 made it punishable to deny the Trinity, assert polytheism or deny the Scriptures (Berman, 1988, pp. 35–6). However, there are moments when we can see that unbelief, whether from plebeian indifference or from intellectual conviction, was recognized. Cromwell, in his speech at the opening of Barebone's Parliament in 1653, said

> Truly the judgement of truth will teach you to be as just towards an unbeliever as towards a believer; and it is our duty to do so. I confess I have often said, foolishly, I had rather miscarry to a believer than to an unbeliever.

(Abbott, 1988, p. 62)

Many people knew of the toleration of Christians and Jews in the Ottoman Empire. In some people's minds, Muslims were preferable to Catholics. After the Restoration in 1660, when conformity to the Church of England was enforced in England, nonconformists compared the regime under which they lived unfavourably to that of Islam (Matar, 1991, pp. 62–3).

Perhaps the most striking instance of coexistence relates to that of Protestants and Catholics in the British Isles, and especially in Ireland. Though officially proscribed, the proscription originating from the papacy's excommunication of Queen Elizabeth I in 1570, the persecution of Catholics by the English state was spasmodic. It could be widespread and severe, with torture of suspects and public executions. But there were also substantial periods of time when Catholics were, to a large extent, left to their own devices, provided they did not worship in public or attract notice to themselves by political opposition. Catholic Irish were permitted to sit in the Irish Parliament until 1704, though probably the last time that a Catholic MP was elected was 1660.

While Catholics and members of the Church of Ireland coexisted, in the immediate aftermath of the Restoration in 1660, Protestant ministers who would not subscribe to the Act of Uniformity (which required them to use the Book of Common Prayer) lost their livings. In Ulster, which was the province with the highest number of non-conforming Protestant ministers, over 60 were deprived.

---

[8] I owe this point to the valedictory lecture 'A philosopher looks at the past', given on 16 September 2003 by Professor Stuart Brown on the occasion of his retirement as Professor of Philosophy at the Open University.

While it is clear that this coexistence was not the product of an official ideology of toleration, one might ask the question, 'Did it come about because the state was incapable of enforcing such large-scale persecution as would have been required to enforce total adherence to the established church?' In the early years of Elizabeth I's reign it was taken for granted that it was more important for the queen to establish her rule in Ireland than that the majority of the population should abandon the Pope, provided they could be persuaded to live in peace. Serious attempts to extirpate Catholicism were made in the 1650s, under the Commonwealth, but the royal government and its agents in Dublin Castle were, after 1660, at pains to prevent the Irish House of Commons from extending English laws against Catholic religious organizations to Ireland. Even the draconian laws of the early eighteenth century against Catholic clergy in Ireland were not seriously enforced after an initial burst of activity (Connolly, 1992, p. 297)

Certainly no government considered such a wholesale elimination of adherents of one faith as was achieved either by the Spanish monarchy with the expulsion of the Moriscos or the expulsion of the Jews, or by Louis XIV's treatment of French Protestants. One might argue that proposals to remove the major part of the Irish Catholic population to the westerly province of Connacht were comparable: this was a scheme that surfaced on a number of occasions from the sixteenth century onwards. However, once it became clear that the settler population of English and Scots required domestic servants and employees to work the land and in their workshops, there was never wholehearted support for such an enforced migration.

While in the British Isles there was constant religious conflict over the period 1560–1691, there was also a considerable degree of coexistence, amounting often to de facto toleration of groups not comprehended within the established churches. Attempts to secure conversions to Protestantism supported very considerable scholarship, especially in translation studies, though it is difficult to estimate their real impact. What is unquestionable, however, is that the conversion experience became a mainstay of Christian life.

References

Abbott, W. C. (1988) *The Writings and Speeches of Oliver Cromwell*, vol. III: *The Protectorate 1653–1655*, Oxford, Clarendon Press.

Bauthumley, J. (1650) *The Light and Dark Sides of God*, London.

Baxter, R. (1974) *The Autobiography of Richard Baxter*, (ed.) N. H. Keeble, London, J. M. Dent.

Berman, D. (1988) *A History of Atheism in Britain: From Hobbes to Russell*, London, Croom Helm.

Bossy, J. (1985) *Christianity in the West*, Oxford, Oxford University Press.

Bunyan, J. (1987) *Grace Abounding to the Chief of Sinners*, (ed.) W. R. Owens, Harmondsworth, Penguin.

Caldwell, P. (1983) *The Puritan Conversion Narrative: The Beginnings of American Expression*, Cambridge, Cambridge University Press.

Clarke, A. with Edwards, R. D. (1978) 'Pacification, plantation, and the catholic question, 1603–23' in Moodie, Martin and Byrne (eds), pp. 187–232.

Clarke, A. (1987) 'Colonial identity in seventeenth century Ireland', in T. W. Moody (ed.) *Nationality and the Pursuit of National Independence*, Historical Studies XI, Belfast, Appletree Press, pp. 57–72.

*Collinson, P. (1988) 'Wars of religion' in *The Birthpangs of Protestant England: Religious and Cultural Change in the Sixteenth and Seventeenth Centuries*, Basingstoke, Macmillan, pp. 127–55, 173–6.

Collinson, P. (1991) 'The cohabitation of the faithful with the unfaithful' in O. P. Grell, J. Israel and N. Tyacke (eds) *From Persecution to Toleration: The Glorious Revolution in and Religion in England*, Oxford, Clarendon Press, pp. 51–76.

*Connolly S. (1992) *Religion, Law and Power: The Making of Protestant Ireland 1660–1760*, Oxford, Clarendon Press.

Corish, P. J. (1978) 'The Cromwellian conquest, 1649–53' in Moodie, Martin and Byrne (eds), pp. 336–52.

Crowley, T. (2000) *The Politics of Language in Ireland: A Source Book 1366–1922*, London, Routledge.

Donaldson, G. (1985) 'The emergence of schism in seventeenth century Scotland' in *Scottish Church History*, Edinburgh, Scottish Academic Press, pp. 205–19.

Goddard, H. (2000) *A History of Muslim–Christian Relations*, Edinburgh, Edinburgh University Press.

Hayes-McCoy, G. A. (1978) 'The royal supremacy and ecclesiastical revolution, 1534–47' in Moodie, Martin and Byrne (eds), pp. 39–68.

Hill, C. (1977) *Milton and the English Revolution*, London, Faber and Faber.

*Hill, C. (1994) *The English Bible and the Seventeenth-Century Revolution*, Harmondsworth, Penguin.

*Israel, J. (1989) *European Jewry in the Age of Mercantilism 1550–1750*, revised edition, Oxford, Clarendon Press.

Knollys, H. (1692) *The Life and Death of That Old Disciple of Jesus Christ, and Eminent Minister of the Gospel, Mr Hanserd Knollys*, London.

Lennon, C. (1986) 'The Counter-Reformation in Ireland 1542–1641' in C. Brady and R. Gillespie (eds) *Natives and Newcomers: The Making of Irish Colonial Society 1534–1641*, Dublin, Irish Academic Press, pp. 72–92.

Lord, H. (1630) *A Display of Two Forraigne Sects in the East Indies*, London.

Macinnes, A. (1982) 'Scottish Gaeldom, 1638–1651: the vernacular response to the Covenanting dynamic' in J. Dwyer, R. A. Mason and A. Murdoch (eds) *New Perspectives on the Politics and Culture of Early Modern Scotland*, Edinburgh, John Donald, pp. 59–94.

*Matar, N. I. (1991) 'Islam in Interregnum and Restoration England' in *The Seventeenth Century*, Vol. 6, pp. 57–71.

Middleton, R. (1997) *Colonial America: A History 1585–1776*, 2nd edn, Oxford, Blackwell.

Moodie, T. W., Martin, F. X. and Byrne, F. J. (eds) (1978) *Early Modern Ireland 1534–1691*, New History of Ireland, Vol. III, Oxford, Oxford University Press.

Morrill, J. (1993) 'The religious context of the English Civil War' in *The Nature of the English Revolution*, Harlow, Longman, pp. 45–68, reprinted from *Transactions of the Royal Historical Society*, 5th series. Vol. 34 (1984).

Ócuív, B. (1978) 'The Irish language in the early modern period' in Moodie, Martin and Byrne (eds), pp. 509–45.

Patterson, W. B. (1997) *King James VI and I and the Reunion of Christendom*, Cambridge, Cambridge University Press.

Pittock, M. G. H. (2001) *Scottish Nationality*, Basingstoke, Palgrave.

Porter, H. C. (1984) 'Americans, Puritans and American Indians: persecution or toleration?, in W. J. Sheils (ed.) *Persecution and Toleration*, Studies in Church History 21, Oxford, Blackwell, pp. 189–98.

Rutt, J. T. (ed.) (1828) *Diary of Thomas Burton Esq*, 4 vols, London.

Simms, J. G. (1978) 'The restoration, 1660–85' in Moodie, Martin and Byrne (eds), pp. 420–53.

State Trials (1810) *Cobbett's Complete Collection of State Trials*, Vol. V, London.

Terry, E. (1655) *A Voyage to East-India*, London.

Trevor-Roper, H. (1962) *Archbishop Laud*, first published in 1940, 2nd edn, London, Macmillan.

Trevor-Roper, H. (1978) 'The Church of England and the Greek church in the time of Charles I' in D. Baker (ed.) *Religious Motivation: Biographical and Sociological Problems for the Church Historian,* Studies in Church History 15, Oxford, Blackwell, pp. 213–40.

Tyacke, N. (ed.) (1998) *England's Long Reformation*, London, UCL Press.

Vitkus, D. J. (ed.) (2001) *Piracy, Slavery and Redemption: Barbary Captivity Narratives from Early Modern England*, New York, Columbia University Press.

*Whyte, I. D. (1995) *Scotland before the Industrial Revolution: An Economic and Social History c.1050–c.1750*, London, Longman.

Withers, C. W. J. (1984) *Gaelic in Scotland 1698–1981: The Geographical History of the Language*, Edinburgh, John Donald.

Asterisked items are particularly recommended for further reading.

4 Contentious Christians: Protestant–Catholic conflict since the Reformation

John Wolffe

When on 31 October 1517 Martin Luther (1483–1546) nailed his ninety-five theses on indulgences to the door of the castle church at Wittenberg, his object was to reform the Christian church rather than divide it. Only during the course of the subsequent five years did Luther emerge as the leader of a major new religious movement that was clearly on course for permanent separation from the Roman Catholic Church (McGrath, 1999, pp. 88–90). In a similar way, when in 1527 King Henry VIII of England (1491–1547) first sought a papal annulment of his marriage to Catherine of Aragon, he did so as a loyal son of the Catholic Church. There was no inevitability about the sequence of events in which Henry's marital and dynastic difficulties led in the following years to his repudiation of the authority of the papacy and the eventual creation of the Church of England. Nevertheless, within a few decades the divisions of western Christendom had become deep-rooted. When in 1545 a general council of the church was convened by Pope Paul III in the northern Italian city of Trent, there was no realistic prospect that it would provide a basis for reconciliation with the Protestant Reformers. Rather, the Council of Trent, which met intermittently until 1563, became an exercise in damage limitation and regrouping by the Roman Catholic Church, which recognized that the challenge to its universal authority was likely to be a prolonged and entrenched one.

Four and a half centuries later, despite several generations of ecumenical effort, these divisions remain. For many in the early twenty-first century, both within and outside the churches, they appear a frustrating anomaly, but in some geographical and cultural contexts, above all in Northern Ireland, they remain deeply and agonisingly meaningful. Futhermore, even where explicit Catholic–Protestant conflict is now a distant memory, it has left a profound mark on the history of the world. In the wake of the Reformation, Europe became divided between, broadly speaking, the Catholic south and the Protestant north. Religious difference was a major factor in giving rise to numerous wars, for example the Thirty Years War that ravaged western Europe between 1618 and 1648, and repeated confrontations between Britain and Roman Catholic powers such as Spain and France in the sixteenth, seventeenth and eighteenth centuries. It also contributed to civil conflicts, the French Wars of Religion in the later sixteenth century, the English Civil War in the 1640s, and the Jacobite rebellions in Britain in the eighteenth century. In Germany, which until the nineteenth century was made up of numerous small states, divisions between Protestants and Catholics were apparent not so much within the states but in the rivalries and confrontations between them. Here distrust between Protestants and Catholics was to be a significant factor hampering the eventual creation of a unitary state. Meanwhile, under British protection, a privileged Protestant minority established itself in Ireland, while the majority of the population remained Roman Catholic. Irish Protestants were therefore insecure, and the Catholics felt oppressed and degraded, a recipe for the conflicts that came to a head in the nineteenth century and culminated in the political division of the island in 1921. Between the seventeenth and nineteenth centuries too, migration to North America from all parts of Europe and by Protestant and Catholic alike brought with it the export of religious conflict to the New World. During the nineteenth century a similar tendency became apparent in other parts of the world extensively settled by Europeans, notably in Australia, New Zealand and southern Africa. In South America, the ascendancy of Roman Catholicism was unchallenged for centuries after its colonization by Spain and Portugal, but in the later twentieth century rapid growth in Protestant churches meant that there too potential for religious conflict developed.

Full-scale wars, massacres, religious riots, physical persecution and other forms of violence were the extreme expressions of a situation which otherwise varied between relatively infrequent and scattered outbursts of actual violence and long periods of mistrustful coexistence. Both Protestants and Catholics have perpetrated appalling atrocities against members of the other tradition, but more commonly they lived alongside each other in relative peace, separated though by mutual suspicion and antagonism. Nation states dominated by one tradition felt it essential for long periods to ensure the continued marginalization of the other. Neighbourhoods became segregated in Ireland and in the towns and cities of north-west England, south-west Scotland and the eastern United States. Dislike and hatred were sustained in popular culture by preaching, tracts, songs, lurid images, and annual festivals such as the celebration of St Patrick's Day (17 March) by Irish Catholics and the commemoration by Protestants of 12 July (the final defeat of Catholic forces in Ireland in 1691) and 5 November (the discovery of the Gunpowder Plot in 1605).

This chapter will provide a case study of this long-running conflict, exploring the reasons for its virulence and persistence, while also considering ways in which more overt conflict gave way to coexistence. It might readily be objected that in much of the violence, antagonism and estrangement attributed to Protestant–Catholic confessional differences, whether, for example, in late sixteenth-century France or late twentieth-century Ireland, religion was really being used as a cloak for other forces. These latter could include dynastic ambition, political ideologies, class conflict, economic competition and communal solidarity. There was even a search for boisterous entertainment by participation in street processions, or for sexual titillation through prying into the supposed secret vices of Protestant conventicles or Catholic convents.

This argument is, ironically, attractive both to secular thinkers who do not take religious motivation seriously, and to committed Christian believers who are embarrassed by actions and attitudes perpetrated in the name of God. Even if granted, however, it would still prompt the question as to why religious labels were repeatedly applied in this way. The approach to be adopted in this chapter is rather to show that Protestant–Catholic antagonisms had a genuine and sustained basis in perceived fundamental religious divergences, but that their particular manifestations owed much to other, less specifically religious, circumstances.

In order to establish a manageable agenda to cover in the space of a single chapter, it is necessary to concentrate our attention more specifically. To that end, this chapter will focus particularly on Protestant antagonism to Roman Catholicism in the English-speaking world, that is Britain, Ireland and the European settlements in what eventually became Canada and the United States. In these countries, Protestantism became not merely a religion, but also a basis for national and political identity and a prominent strand in popular culture. Accordingly, anti-Catholicism became a deeply entrenched and widely based tradition. The first section will examine the core religious basis of difference between Protestants and Catholics; the second section will show how, during the centuries after the Reformation, such theological and spiritual issues were reinforced by political and cultural factors; the third section will explore the revival and reshaping of anti-Catholicism from the later eighteenth century onwards, while the final portion of the chapter will analyse subsequent mingled decline and persistence in the late nineteenth and twentieth centuries. The main body of evidence on which this analysis is founded is in published religious, political and popular polemical literature directed against Roman Catholics, which, as we shall see, also contained striking and influential visual images. In the conclusion we shall return to consider the ways in which this study of anti-Catholicism illuminates the wider dynamics of religious conflict.

The religious basis of Protestant–Catholic antagonisms

Behind the sometimes abstruse detail of early modern theological controversies were matters of entrenched difference between Protestants and Catholics on key questions of the sources of religious authority and the means by which human beings could secure and sustain a satisfactory relationship with God. Such issues were not mere differences of opinion, but to the committed on both sides had fundamental implications for the kind of spiritual observance to be made in this life, and the destiny of one's soul for an eternity after death. Heaven and hell were vivid and eternal realities. It followed that those who held differing religious views were living a lie, and in danger of dying damned. Accordingly, they had to be convinced of their errors, or even if necessary forced to renounce them, in the interests of the salvation of their own souls.

In Catholicism, right religious belief and practice were primarily collective processes. Individuals lived and died as members of the church. Through adherence to its teachings and cradle-to-grave participation in its sacraments, its members secured a place in a spiritual community that offered them support in this world and the eventual prospect of heaven in the world to come. Immediately after death, though, God would require them to undergo a period of suffering in purgatory to cleanse them from the sins they had committed in their lives. The church, however, claimed to be able to help its adherents after death as well as in life, through the grant of indulgences which would shorten the time they had to spend in purgatory. Meanwhile the spiritual community of the saints, great Christians of the past, still laboured through their prayers to aid believers in this world in overcoming current afflictions and to lessen the pains of those in purgatory. Protestants, on the other hand, believed that men and women were fundamentally on their own before God. Their salvation was dependent on their personal faith alone and, in Calvinism, on God's preordained choice of them as individuals. Neither participation in the sacraments of the church, nor the prayers of the saints, nor even their own virtuous lives could save them from hell if that essential spiritual relationship was not in place. Purgatory was a delusion, and the only alternatives after death were heaven for those who had been accepted by God, and eternal damnation in hell for those who were not. Hence, Catholic practices that obscured this stark reality had to be remorselessly confronted. Anger at the corrupt sale of indulgences had provoked Luther's initial outburst in 1517 and, although this system was abolished by the Council of Trent, the mud still stuck. Later in the Reformation, shrines, images and relics linked to the veneration of saints were relentlessly destroyed. Protestant churches became simple, even stark, in their interior layout and decoration, while worship was purged of the ritual and sacramental elaboration that, to Catholics, symbolized and sustained the spiritual community of the church. From a Catholic perspective though, such Protestant actions were appalling and wilful destruction of sacred things and attacks on the spiritual community of the church. They subverted the basis of the Christian life in this world and meant that their perpetrators would assuredly be damned in the life to come.

Closely bound up with the approaches to religious living and the means of salvation was the question of the sources of religious authority. The medieval pre-Reformation church had developed an ambivalent attitude to the Bible. It was recognized as the foundational sacred text of Christianity and accorded great reverence. However, despite, or to a considerable extent because of, the veneration in which scripture was held, it was not seen as an appropriate object for detailed study by ordinary believers. It needed rather to be interpreted and contextualized by the traditions of the church, and by Pope, bishops and priests as its authorized teachers. In the centuries before printing and widespread literacy, moreover, such a stance was consistent with the practicalities of a situation where general circulation and reading of the Bible was not feasible. The Protestant Reformers, for their part, claimed to be restoring Christianity to its pristine 'pure' form as practised by the early church, which entailed a direct appeal to the actual text of the Bible as the essential source for the teachings and practice of the apostolic age. While the leading Reformers were uneasy about the radical potentialities of allowing every man and woman to be their own interpreter of scripture, their emphasis on individual accountability before God necessarily implied the much wider diffusion of the Bible. Hence, new translations from Latin into vernacular languages were an early priority: Luther completed a German New Testament in 1522 and William Tyndale an English one in 1525. The invention of the printing press in the later fifteenth century meant that by the time of the Reformation, for the first time in Christian history the extensive production of Bibles for use by the laity was possible. Protestants upheld the Bible as providing the essential and primary 'rule of faith', while the Roman Catholic Church maintained that the traditions and authority of the Church had to be continued alongside it. To Catholics, the Protestant attitude – given the ambiguities and difficulties of the text – was an irresponsible recipe for spiritual anarchy. Protestants, on the other hand, perceived the Catholic Church to be corrupting the essential identity of Christianity by maintaining traditions that had no basis in scripture and to be keeping its adherents in error by denying them access to the text that was the ultimate source of truth.

It was inevitable that as controversy and confrontation were maintained across many decades, positions would become polarized and caricatured. Their consistent maintenance became a matter of duty to past generations, even as understanding of the immediate sixteenth-century context of the original controversies receded. Nevertheless, the underlying issues were profound from the outset. Adherence to respective convictions was further reinforced by the atmosphere of a turbulent age in which life appeared uncertain and there was widespread belief in the imminent end of the world and of divine judgement on humankind. If God's wrath against religious heresy was liable to be manifested at any time, one needed always to be ready to demonstrate to the Almighty not only one's own rightness of belief but one's zeal against error. For that reason, intense controversy between Protestants and Catholics was liable to resurface with particular vigour at later periods of particular insecurity and apocalyptic expectation, notably in the early nineteenth century. In the meantime the words of Joseph Hall, a Church of England bishop in the troubled second quarter of the seventeenth century, can be taken as representative of the attitudes of many of his contemporaries:

> we must eternally fall out, either with God or with Rome. Since therefore neither truth can yield, nor obstinacy will yield; let us serve cheerfully under the colours of our Heavenly Leader; and both proclaim and maintain an unreconcilable war with these Romish Heresies.
>
> (Hall, 1844, p. 90)

Politics and popular culture

There were two main ways in which religion became closely associated with other ideological and cultural influences, which had already acquired a life of their own in the later sixteenth century. First, there was politics, in which religious definition and exclusion became central to the power interests of particular states or groups within them. Second, in the English-speaking world, anti-Catholicism became a pervasive feature of popular culture, evident both in print and in the annual round of celebration and commemoration, above all on 5 November. Both these factors came together in rendering anti-Catholicism a potent force in creating and sustaining national and communal identities. The particular blend of religious, political and cultural influences varied considerably from one time and one location to another.

Such specifically religious motives for antagonism rapidly became overlaid by politics. This was above all the case in England, where Henry VIII's 'break with Rome' was driven forward by his anxiety to secure a legal remarriage to Anne Boleyn in the hope of fathering a male heir. Henry and Anne's child, the future Elizabeth I (1533–1603), was illegitimate in the eyes of the Roman Catholic Church because it refused to recognize his divorce from Catherine of Aragon, who was still alive at the time of Elizabeth's birth in 1533. Hence when Elizabeth succeeded to the throne in 1558, although she was cautious in imposing Protestantism on her people, Roman Catholics still appeared committed to opposing her rule. This impression was confirmed when in 1570 Pope Pius V excommunicated her. Herein lay the justification for successive plots against Elizabeth, and most famously, the Armada of 1588 in which Philip II of Spain sent a large fleet to attack England. In 1605, Roman Catholic conspirators attempted to assassinate Elizabeth's successor, James I (James VI of Scotland), in the notorious Gunpowder Plot. At a later period, following the deposition of James II (VII of Scotland) in 1688, the Act of Settlement of 1701 prevented Catholics and anyone married to a Catholic from succeeding to the throne. Hence, when Queen Anne died in 1714, not only the exiled Jacobites descended from James II/VII, but also numerous other Roman Catholics who had a more immediate hereditary claim were passed over in favour of the Elector of Hanover, who succeeded as George I. Not until 1766, long after the two unsuccessful Jacobite rebellions in 1715 and 1745, did the Pope recognize the Hanoverians as rightful kings of Great Britain.

Even when such immediate threats of Catholic rebellion disappeared or lost their credibility, there was an enduring sense that the nation was defined and sustained by its Protestant character. Such a consciousness first developed in England in Elizabeth I's reign, and was reinforced by the events of the seventeenth and eighteenth centuries. The constitutional exclusion of the Roman Catholic minority not only from the throne, but also from holding any significant public office, came to be seen not only as a matter of prudence, but also one of the maintenance of essential national identity. Catholic acceptance of the religious authority of the Pope (who was also ruler of an independent state in central Italy) was perceived as a 'dual allegiance', which made their loyalty to the state questionable. The Union of Scotland and England in 1707 brought together in a single unitary state two countries with diverse histories and traditions, but with a common Protestant allegiance, which was highlighted in the subsequent process of forging together a united British nation (Colley, 1992). During the course of the eighteenth century, the exclusively Protestant constitutional settlements of the period between 1688 and 1714 acquired a mystique in many minds as essential supports of stability and good order, which could not be changed without risking chaos.

Meanwhile in France, which had a Roman Catholic majority and Protestant minority, events mirrored those across the Channel. The penal laws against Roman Catholics in late seventeenth- and eighteenth-century Britain had their parallel in the French King Louis XIV's decision in 1685 to revoke the Edict of Nantes under which in 1598 his grandfather Henri IV had granted a limited toleration to Protestants. While devout Catholics might see Louis's action as a means of saving souls from religious error by stimulating their conversion back to the true faith, the king himself was motivated as much by a concern to promote national unity through common religious allegiance. He equated religious dissent with treason. Out of an estimated 750,000 Protestants in France in 1685, about 200,000 emigrated to Protestant countries; the majority of the remainder professed conversion to Catholicism, while all children were compulsorily baptized and educated in the Roman Catholic Church (Carbonnier-Burkard and Cabanel, 1998, pp. 78–81). Between 1702 and 1705 there was a Protestant guerrilla uprising by the so-called Camisards in Languedoc in the south-west, which stirred an enduring climate of insecurity amongst the majority Catholic population (Doyle, 1978, p. 154). Here, as in Britain, religious difference was perceived by early modern governments as a seedbed for political subversion and social disorder.

The religious and political impulses for conflict rapidly diffused into popular culture, and established a tradition of antagonism and suspicion that acquired an enduring life of its own. A crucial factor in this process was the genuinely violent nature of religious conflict in the century after the Reformation. In England in 1553 the Roman Catholic Mary I (1516–58, daughter of Henry VIII's first marriage to Catherine of Aragon) succeeded to the throne, and began a serious attempt to reverse the advance of Protestantism that had occurred during the previous twenty years. When she encountered sustained resistance, her government revived legislation that sanctioned burning at the stake as punishment for heresy. It is estimated that between February 1555, when the burnings began, and Mary's death in November 1558, 275 people were executed in this way because of their refusal to renounce their Protestant convictions (Haller, 1963, pp. 43–4). In the context of their time the burnings were a legitimate, if extreme, reaction to the genuine religious and political challenge Protestantism presented to Mary's regime. Their legacy, however, was an abiding perception in England that Catholicism in general – rather than a specific Catholic government in particularly difficult circumstances – was inherently disposed to violent persecution. Moreover, the fact that victims, with the exception of a minority of prominent bishops and clergy, were predominantly of low social status, and included 55 women, encouraged popular identification with their stand.

This tradition was crystallized and maintained by the publication in 1563 of the *Actes and Monuments* by John Foxe (1516–87), who had lived in exile during Mary's reign. A much expanded edition was published in 1570, and was commonly known as the 'Book of Martyrs'. It recounted in graphic detail the heroism and sufferings of those who had died at the stake in the context of the portrayal of the Protestant English nation as a people chosen by God, whose spiritual freedom had been secured by the sacrifice of those who had died. As Bishop Latimer put it in the words Foxe attributed to him when he was burnt in Oxford in October 1555, 'We shall this day light such a candle by God's grace in England as I trust shall never be put out' (Haller, 1963, p. 192). Although the massive folio volumes were unlikely to be purchased and read systematically by ordinary people, copies were placed in all cathedrals and some parish churches, so many would have been able to browse through it. Their imagination would have been fuelled not only by the text, but by the illustrations, which were vivid and large in size, sometimes taking up whole pages. The frontispiece of the 1570 edition (Figure 1) vividly conveys Foxe's sense of Protestantism as the true, but persecuted church, confronted by the persecuting violence of Rome. Woodcuts emphasized the calm expressions of the victims, fortified by their Protestant faith, set against the violence of their persecutors and the cruel nature of their deaths. The 'Book of Martyrs' was republished on numerous occasions until the later nineteenth century. New editions included fresh powerful images redrawn to appeal to later generations, as in the examples

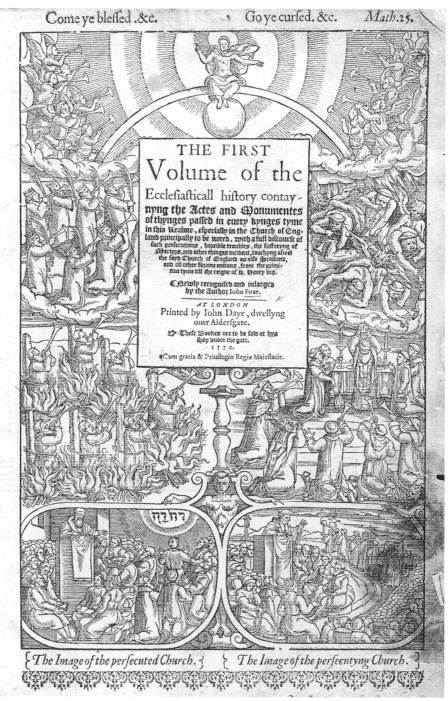

Figure 1 Foxe's sense of the theological context of his work is here highlighted: the preaching of the true Word of God is juxtaposed with the false preaching of indulgences, and the sacrifice of the martyrs with the sacrifice of the Mass. Folio frontispiece to Foxe's Actes and Monuments (Book of Martyrs), *Vol. I, 1570 edition, London. Photo used with permission from the British Library, shelfmark: J/4705.h.4*

included here from 1741 and 1814 publications (Figures 2 and 3). Its vision of Protestant courage and Catholic violence and oppression was widely diffused in popular culture, not only in Britain, but also across the Atlantic in colonial New England.

While Foxe's book ensured that the Marian persecutions had a particularly vivid place in English popular consciousness, recollection of other violent incidents served to reinforce the tradition. Particularly notable in this respect was the St Bartholomew's day massacre in Paris in August 1572, when between two and three thousand Protestants were murdered by the mob, incited by Roman Catholic clergy (Carbonnier-Burkard and Cabanel, 1998, p. 33). In Ireland in November 1641, around two thousand Protestants were massacred in a Catholic rising, and subsequent mythology greatly exaggerated the number of the dead (Brewer and Higgins, 1998, p. 27). Catholics for their part were stirred to hatred and insecurity by the execution of their co-religionists for alleged treason during Elizabeth I's reign, most notoriously Mary Queen of Scots in 1587, and by massacres of Catholics perpetrated by Oliver Cromwell's forces in Ireland in 1649. Vague awareness of such actual events,

Figure 2   Images such as this portrayal of the burning in 1556 of Thomas Cranmer, Archbishop of Canterbury under Henry VIII and Edward VI and a major driving force in the English Reformation, are important in explaining the continuing virulence of anti-Catholicism in the eighteenth century. From Foxe's Actes and Monuments *(Book of Martyrs), 1741 edition, London. Photo used with permission from the British Library, shelfmark: 1228.h.1*

Joan Horns, The Widow Hut & the pious Eliz. Thackvel, burnt in Smithfield.

Two Women & Eleven men burnt together at Stratford, in Essex.

London. Pub. by Thomas Kelly, Paternoster row. Jan.ᵗ 28ᵗʰ 1813.

Figure 3   These early nineteenth-century illustrations to Foxe emphasize the extent to which ordinary people, as well as the Protestant religious elite, suffered in the Marian persecution, and particularly highlight the martyrdoms of women, which would have appeared particularly shocking. Foxe's Actes and Monuments (Book of Martyrs)*, 1814 edition, London. Photo used with permission from the British Library, shelfmark: L.23.e.6*

transmitted by tradition across two centuries or more, with the inevitable exaggerations and distortions of legend, were seen as evidence that failure to contain one's religious opponents could have fatal consequences.

Alongside such fears of extreme religious violence, deep suspicion of the activities of religious minorities was widespread. Such attitudes were unfortunately reinforced by the understandable caution that led groups fearing persecution to keep a low profile. Such perceived secrecy was liable to be seen by the majority as confirmation that they had nefarious practices and activities to hide, rather than be recognized as a natural response to their own hostility and paranoia. In later sixteenth-century France, Roman Catholics, picking up on motifs from medieval polemic against heretics, suspected Protestant groups of holding orgies and practising infanticide. The extent of such suspicions was comically illustrated in 1562 by the case of a city councillor from Troyes, south-east of Paris, who, when accused of attending a Protestant meeting, claimed in his defence that his only motive for doing so was the hope of finding a woman for easy sex. The amused court let him go (Racaut, 2002, p. 62). Similar suspicions were excited by Roman Catholics in Britain and North America. In particular, the confessional was suspected of providing opportunities for the seduction of innocent women by lecherous priests, while convents were often believed to be, in effect, harems, where nuns provided sexual services for the nominally celibate clergy. Such allegations were most fully developed in 1836 in a book entitled *The Awful Disclosures of Maria Monk* in which the author, who claimed to be a renegade nun from the Hotel Dieu at Montreal in Canada, charged not only that there were extensive sexual relations between priests and nuns, but that the resulting infants were murdered and routinely interred in a pit under the convent (Billington, 1938, pp. 99–100). Alongside such lurid sexual speculation were fears of subversive plotting, which could be reinforced rather than lessened by the appearance of actual insignificance and obscurity. In both mid-eighteenth-century King's Lynn and mid-nineteenth-century Wick (north-east Scotland), the fact that the small number of Roman Catholics in the town received disproportionate amounts of correspondence fuelled uneasy suspicion (Haydon, 1993, pp. 151–2; Wolffe, 1991, p. 148). The harsh reality was that once paranoid attitudes of this kind were established in the popular mind they were extremely hard to shift, as Catholic professions to the contrary were liable to be interpreted rather as indications of ever deeper and double-faced plotting.

A further important factor in maintaining popular anti-Catholic attitudes, both in Britain and in colonial New England, was their association with annual festivities, above all on 5 November, the anniversary of the day in 1605 on which Guy Fawkes and his fellow conspirators planned to blow up the King and Parliament. Between the seventeenth and the nineteenth centuries, this occasion was widely marked both with church services (even when it fell on a weekday) and with street processions, including the parading and eventual burning of effigies of the Pope, as well as (or perhaps instead of) that of Guy Fawkes himself (Cressy, 1989; Storch, 1982). These could give rise to riots, which might be directed against Roman Catholics, as in Gravesend (Kent) in 1852 (Wolffe, 1991, p. 194), but were also a means for expressing social tensions and containing them by ritual expressions directed against a perceived common enemy, as in Boston, Massachusetts in the 1750s and 1760s (Cogliano, 1995, pp. 25–39).

The strength of anti-Catholicism in the English-speaking world and its persistence across the centuries stemmed from the manner in which it was stirred and sustained by such a diverse range of influences and events. Together with more specifically religious impulses there were the consequences of chronic political insecurities, the need to assert a common national ideology, the projection of fears of sexual and social subversion, and the sense of antagonism to Catholics as expressed in the rituals and celebrations of the annual round. Antagonisms could be aroused by preachers, political agitators, youths wanting an excuse for some horseplay, or even just suspicious neighbours (who might or might not actually be Roman Catholic) or unexpected gatherings in small communities. The culture of hostility extended itself across the United Kingdom, in England, Scotland and Wales, where Catholics appeared an exotic and dangerous minority, and in Ireland where they seemed a threatening if for the moment subservient majority. It crossed the Atlantic, carried by colonists imbued with a sense that in leaving Europe they were escaping from religious oppression and persecution. While the Puritan ancestors of the New England colonists had had their most immediate quarrel with the Anglican-dominated state in England, they were possessed with a sense of Roman Catholicism as the root source of religious authoritarianism. That consciousness was reinforced by the arrival of French, German and other refugees from religious persecution in continental Europe and, between 1756 and 1763 by the Seven Years War in which the British in New England confronted the forces of Roman Catholic France in the St Lawrence valley a few hundred miles to the north.

Roman Catholic anti-Protestantism has been relatively little studied, although we have noted some examples of it in France and Ireland. It is thought likely that it was less widespread than anti-Catholicism. In southern Europe, notably much of Italy, Spain and Portugal, the Roman Catholic Church had been so successful in suppressing the initial Protestant upsurge after the Reformation, that no significant Protestant presence remained to stir suspicions and antagonism. In Germany, on the other hand, the reality of a much more even balance of confessional forces appears to have induced a pragmatic readiness to accept the necessity for coexistence, once the religious wars of the sixteenth and seventeenth centuries had been fought to exhaustion. Among Roman Catholic minorities in Protestant countries, such as the estimated 80,000 in England in 1770 (Bossy, 1975, p. 298), the general approach was to seek to defuse hostility by keeping a low profile, rather than fuelling it by reciprocating it. John Henry Newman, the future convert and cardinal, recalled of his schooldays in the early nineteenth century:

> There was a Catholic family in the village, old maiden ladies we used to think; but I knew nothing of them. I have of late years heard that there were one or two Catholic boys in the school; but either we were carefully kept from knowing this, or the knowledge of it made simply no impression on our minds.
>
> (Newman, 1967, p. 16)

Nevertheless, by this period there were significant developments which were already taking Protestant–Catholic antagonisms into an important new and potentially explosive phase.

Enlightenment, revival and religious conflict

The wide-ranging cultural, social and political changes that gathered momentum in the later eighteenth century, and are conventionally seen by historians as making the dawn of the modern world, had extensive implications for anti-Catholicism. The Enlightenment, the dominant European elite intellectual and cultural movement of the age, was characterized by a rejection of religious dogmatism, and the advocacy of reason and toleration. Such attitudes, in part a reaction to the intense religious conflicts of the previous century, were associated with a perception that entrenched Protestant–Catholic hostilities reflected outdated prejudices, which now needed to be transcended in the interests of social and political harmony. The Catholic Church itself began to appear less authoritarian, notably with Pope Clement XIV's decision in 1773 to dissolve the Society of Jesus (Jesuits) who had been at the forefront of the counterattack on Protestantism during the preceding two centuries. Whereas seventeenth-century governments had resorted to violence and persecution in the vain endeavour to impose religious uniformity on their people, eighteenth-century ones increasingly recognized that minorities could not be wholly suppressed and were therefore better accommodated. In France, laws against Protestants were seldom enforced after 1760, and an edict of 1787 restored their civil status. Similarly in Britain, penal legislation against Roman Catholics fell into practical disuse, and from the 1770s steps to repeal it began to be taken.

Nevertheless powerful cross-currents remained. The trenchant critique of the Roman Catholic Church by Enlightenment philosophers such as Diderot and Voltaire initiated a tradition of a secular rather than Protestant anti-Catholicism, which was to find powerful expression in attacks on the church after the French Revolution of 1789. Those who rejected Christianity, in France and elsewhere, often adhered to a profound suspicion of the Catholic Church as authoritarian and obscurantist. More significant in the short term, however, was the reality that the advocacy of toleration by the Enlightenment intellectual elite proved to be at odds with profound and enduring suspicions amongst the populace.

This tension became very much apparent in Britain and North America in 1774, when the British government passed the Quebec Act, intended to provide for the orderly rule of the province captured from France in the Seven Years War of 1756–63. Under this legislation Roman Catholics were given a place on the colony's legislative council, and priests were allowed to hold land and to collect money from their co-religionists to support the church. From the government's point of view, this was a pragmatic and rational measure for securing consensual control of a territory with a Roman Catholic majority. From a zealous Protestant perspective, however, it constituted a major betrayal of the essential identity and interests of the British state (Haydon, 1993, p. 171). Such views were strongly held in the New England colonies to the south of Quebec, which were already increasingly at odds with Britain. The First Continental Congress of October 1774, in stating American grievances, expressed its

> astonishment that a British Parliament should ever consent to establish in that country [Canada] a Religion, that has deluged your island in blood, and dispersed impiety, bigotry, persecution, murder, and rebellion through every part of the world.
>
> (Quoted in Cogliano, 1995, p. 62)

Objection to the Quebec Act was thus a significant factor in fuelling American resentment against Britain in the build-up to the Declaration of Independence in 1776, although when the course of the subsequent war brought the new nation into alliance with Roman Catholic France, more tolerant attitudes gained ground (Cogliano, 1995, p. 154).

Americans remained very much subject to anti-papal fears. Some of the reasons for this are suggested by Map 5. Although they had the Atlantic Ocean between themselves and Rome, the strong Catholic presence in the St Lawrence valley seemed a much more immediate threat. Moreover, in the first half of the nineteenth century, Catholic influence also began to spread in the Mississippi and Ohio valleys to the west, having an entry point through the former French possession of New Orleans. Cincinnati was a particular centre of sectarian rivalry. The Protestants on the Atlantic seaboard therefore felt that they risked becoming surrounded. The significant Catholic presence in Maryland, originally founded as a Catholic colony, was a further source of anxiety.

Meanwhile in Britain, Parliament, encouraged by Catholic loyalty in the ongoing war with America, in 1778, passed an act removing some of the

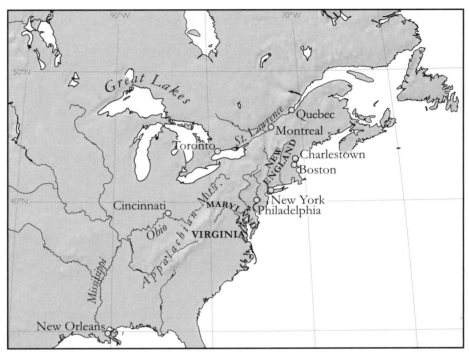

Map 5   Eastern North America showing the locations of places mentioned in the text. Note particularly the relative proximity to New England of the largely Roman Catholic St Lawrence valley

constraints placed upon them by earlier legislation. They were now allowed legally to own land, and priests and schoolmasters were no longer liable to imprisonment. These were modest concessions and Catholics were still denied the vote and full freedom of worship. Nevertheless, especially coming in the wake of the Quebec Act, the measure was sufficient to provoke a strong Protestant backlash. A sustained campaign of agitation for the repeal of the 1778 Relief Act culminated in June 1780 with the Gordon Riots, when for a week an anti-Catholic crowd took control of the streets of London, inflicting extensive damage on the property of Roman Catholics and their known sympathizers. It took 10,000 soldiers and 285 deaths to suppress the riots. There were smaller outbreaks elsewhere in the country (Haydon, 1993, pp. 204–44). Such an excess of violence, which horrified the more moderate opponents of the Relief Act, proved counterproductive in that it confirmed the perception of anti-Catholicism as itself an irrational and destabilizing force, but it also dramatically illustrated the continuing power of popular paranoia and hostility towards Rome.

As the nineteenth century dawned, there were two key factors that served not only to sustain but in many ways to revive and reshape Protestant–Catholic hostilities. First there was the situation in Ireland. The legacy of the political turmoil and wars of the seventeenth century was a position where at least three-quarters of the population was Roman Catholic, but the country was controlled by the Protestant minority (itself made up of a mixture of Anglicans and Presbyterians). Protestants enjoyed much of the wealth of the country, and a monopoly of political power, given that the penal laws excluded Catholics not only from the vote but from higher education and the professions. Such an unequal arrangement operated surprisingly peacefully for much of the eighteenth century, but once Catholic aspirations began to increase, its fundamentally problematic nature rapidly became apparent. The prospect of relaxations in the penal laws alarmed Protestants, who in Ireland, to a much greater extent than in Britain, faced an objective religious and political challenge from Roman Catholics. The insecurities of both sides gave rise in the 1790s to an upsurge of sectarian violence, centred particularly in south Ulster. Its enduring legacy was the formation of societies for mutual defence and protection of community interest, notably the Orange Order among Protestants, founded in 1795. In a significant appropriation of history to contemporary needs, Protestants began to celebrate the anniversaries of late seventeenth-century victories against Roman Catholic forces, especially the defeat of the siege of (London)Derry in 1689, and the final defeat of the Jacobites in 1691, commemorated on 12 July.[1]

In 1798, the rebellion of the United Irishmen drew support from liberal Protestants as well as Roman Catholics. After suppressing it, the British abolished the parliament in Dublin, bringing Ireland into union with Britain under the Westminster parliament. The effect of the Union of 1801 was to reinforce polarization between Protestants, who felt their security depended fundamentally on the British connection, and Roman Catholics, whose aspirations for religious equality became increasingly bound up with campaigns for the restoration of Irish political nationhood. This linkage became firmly established in the thirty years after the Union through the campaign led by Daniel O'Connell (1775–1847) for Catholic Emancipation, to admit Catholics to Parliament and other public office. This was eventually successful in 1829. Once Roman Catholics could take seats in parliament, Irish Protestants became the more conscious of their political dependence on the Protestant majority in Britain if they were to maintain their ascendancy in the face of the Catholic majority in Ireland. Sectarian tensions remained at a high pitch in the 1830s and in the 1840s when O'Connell launched a determined, albeit not immediately successful, campaign for the repeal of the Union.

The tensions in Ireland had an impact on Protestant–Catholic relations far outside Ireland itself. The centrality of Irish issues in British politics

---

[1] The decisive victory took place at the Battle of the Boyne on 1 July 1690, but after the calendar was moved on eleven days in 1752, this date corresponded to 12 July in the new style. It was also the (old style) date of a further Jacobite defeat, the Battle of Aughrim, in 1691.

throughout the nineteenth century ensured that anti-Catholic impulses in Britain itself continued to receive extensive stimulus. Meanwhile overpopulation and generally adverse social and economic conditions in Ireland led to a rising tide of emigration, which became a flood in the years after the Great Famine of 1847. By the early twentieth century, well over a million people born in Ireland had emigrated to Britain; up to seven million settled in North America; and many thousands made the long voyage to Australia (Hoppen, 1989, pp. 41, 101; Miller, 1985, p. 3; Beckett, 1981, p. 344). They settled predominantly in the burgeoning industrial cities of the Victorian age, carrying with them a strong sense of enduring identification with their native land, in which their religious allegiance was a defining feature. As at home in Belfast, in London, Liverpool and Glasgow; Boston, New York, Philadelphia and Toronto; Sydney and Melbourne, polarized Protestant and Catholic communities formed. They were separated not only by church life, but also by education, employment networks, political allegiances, popular culture and ritual. Protestants were in the minority in Ireland, but in the diaspora they found themselves supported by local co-religionists, to whom they were apt to transmit their particular ethos of hostility to Catholics, born of the mingled dominance and insecurity of their position in their homeland. Catholics found themselves doubly despised, on account of their race and their religion, a situation that fuelled their own sense of militant loyalty to their church as the one reliable source of support in a hostile world. To Protestant minds, though, the sheer number of Irish Catholic migrants, their seemingly blind devotion to their religion, and their poverty and degradation, were evidence both of threatening Catholic expansion, and of its adverse social and moral consequences.

The second key factor operative during the nineteenth century was religious revival stirring both Protestant and Roman Catholic churches. The so-called Evangelical Revival had begun to influence the Protestant churches in central Europe and the English-speaking world during the second quarter of the eighteenth century, but the 1790s and early 1800s saw a rapid expansion of its influence. Characteristic features of the movement included a sense of life-changing encounter with God in conversion, a renewed emphasis on the primacy of scripture, and zeal to spread the gospel. This missionary activism inevitably carried Evangelicals into confrontation with Roman Catholics, whom they believed to be trapped in a false religion, from which they needed to be rescued in the interests of their eternal salvation. In Ireland in the 1820s, the 'Second Reformation' movement promoted by Evangelicals seeking to convert Roman Catholics was a significant factor adding to existing religious tensions. A sense of being locked in a struggle for souls both stimulated and was reinforced by a perception that true Christianity, as it emerged at the Reformation, had been defined in opposition to Rome. Sixteenth- and seventeenth-century anti-Catholic polemic enjoyed a revival. This state of mind was further reinforced by the troubled state of the world in the two generations after the French Revolution in 1789, which led to extensive speculation about the imminence of the Second Coming of Christ. In the light of the biblical prophecies, notably in the Book of Revelation, that foretold that this event would be associated with divine judgement on all evil and false religion, perceptions of the need to confront Roman Catholicism were reinforced. In the face of impending divine wrath, it was believed that true Christians needed by their testimony to distinguish themselves clearly from error, and to seek to rescue those trapped in its delusions before it was too late.

Meanwhile, in the early nineteenth century the Roman Catholic Church also began to find new purpose and energy. A revived commitment to mission in the post-Enlightenment world was symbolized by the reinstatement of the Jesuits in 1814. This marked an important step in the growth of what is known as Ultramontanism,[2] meaning the assertion of stronger centralized authority by the papacy over the Catholic Church outside Italy. This movement was also associated with more elaborate and conspicuous worship and devotion, of a kind offensive to Protestants, notably in the veneration of the saints and the Virgin Mary, whose Immaculate Conception was proclaimed as dogma in 1854. The process was to reach its culmination with the Syllabus of Errors of 1864 in which Pope Pius IX (1792–1878) condemned liberal ideas, and the declaration of papal infallibility by the First Vatican Council in 1870.

Well before 1870, moreover, this trend was having a major impact on religious activity on the ground. In Britain and Ireland, the Roman Catholic Church gained renewed confidence from the passing of Emancipation in 1829, while Irish migration, the scale of which was imperfectly appreciated by contemporaries, led to an impression of inexorable growth in England, Scotland and the United States. A significant landmark came in 1850 when Pius IX restored a hierarchy of bishops in England and Wales (Scotland followed in 1878), with named sees and defined jurisdictions, replacing the looser missionary structure that had been operative since the Reformation. This step, however, outraged Protestant public opinion, because it was perceived as a presumptuous attempt by a foreign ruler, the Pope, to parcel out English territory. The outcry was led by the Prime Minister, Lord John Russell, and legislation passed against the new bishops, although this had only symbolic significance. Nicholas Wiseman, the flamboyant new Cardinal Archbishop of Westminster, was portrayed in the press and in caricature as a megalomaniac, as in a contemporary cartoon (Figure 4) which, despite its humour, is illustrative of underlying fears of Roman Catholic ambitions. Such apprehensions were justified to the extent that in the mid-nineteenth century, Catholics, like Protestants, were still convinced that they had a monopoly of religious truth and that their opponents must be converted. Such a point was made unequivocally by John Hughes, Archbishop of New York, who was something of an American counterpart to Wiseman. In a lecture in November 1850 he spoke

[2] The word derives from the Latin from 'beyond the mountains', i.e. the Alps.

Here you have Cardinal Foolishman sitting on the top of St Pauls, and thinking that his scarlet hat will overshadow the whole of London Westminster and Southwark.

Figure 4   This image comes from a small booklet of contemporary caricatures, and plays on the name of the new Cardinal and his pretensions, in his pastoral letter announcing his promotion to 'govern ... the counties of Middlesex, Hertford, and Essex ... Surrey, Sussex, Kent, Berkshire, and Hampshire.' From No Popery: A Protestant Roland for a Popish Oliver *by AntiGuy, 1850. Photo used with permission from The British Library, shelfmark: 3988.a.4*

provocatively of 'the decline of Protestantism' and said that it was no secret that the Roman Catholic Church's ambition was to convert the world (Hughes, 1864, p. 101).

A further destabilizing factor that added to tensions was the growth of Catholic influence within the (Anglican) Church of England. The Church of England, as it had been created in the sixteenth century, had always been something of a compromise, in that it retained some Catholic features, notably bishops. Nevertheless, during the eighteenth and early nineteenth centuries it had appeared a firmly if moderately Protestant institution. From 1833 onwards, however, the Oxford Movement (so-called because of the prominence of Oxford dons amongst its early leadership) began to reassert latent strands of Anglican identity that pointed in a much more Catholic direction. While they did not accept the authority of the Pope – and hence were not Roman Catholics – the Oxford Movement emphasized religious tradition and liturgy as channels of religious authority, and progressively their followers sought to recreate more elaborate and seemingly Catholic forms of worship and Christian practice. The conversion of some key leaders to Roman Catholicism, above all John Henry Newman in 1845, reinforced the impression amongst its critics that this was a movement subverting the Protestant identity of the Church of England and furthering the cause of Rome. The consequent controversies extended wherever Anglicanism had established a presence, in the United States as well as in Britain.

These newer factors combined with the tradition of popular antagonism inherited from past centuries to engender a period of widespread and quite intense conflict between Protestants and Roman Catholics in the English-speaking countries in the middle decades of the nineteenth century. Normally this was a conflict more of words and of simmering estrangement than of actual violence, but the latter erupted on various occasions, notably in the burning of a convent at Charlestown, Massachusetts in 1834 (see Figure 5), in the Philadelphia riots of 1844 and the Stockport riots of 1852. Prejudices were reinforced by

Figure 5   Anti-Catholic violence could stir a backlash of sympathy for Catholics, as indicated by this caricature of the attack on the Charlestown Convent in 1834, in which the Protestant rioters are portrayed as sacrilegious thugs and the nuns as innocent victims. David Claypole Johnston, 'Anti-Catholic Doings' in Scraps, *1835, no. 6, Plate 3, Boston. Courtesy of the American Antiquarian Society*

SAM ! IS OUR NEXT PRESIDENT

PERRY,

Will give his farewell Lecture on **ROMANISM**,
AT TOWN HALL, FITCHBURG,
On Thursday Evening, Jan. 11th, 1855.
☞ Doors open at 1-4 to 7, Lecture Commences at 7 1-2 ☜

Mr. P. will be happy to see his old friends once more before leaving for the West. he has recently at great expense Painted not only the thrilling scenes that come under his own observation in Papal countries but the awful tortures of Purgatory as tought by the Priests.

A Book illustrated with ten engravings of these cruel enormities can be had at the Lecture price 25 cents.

CRUELTIES OF ROMANISM!

NUNNERIES EXPOSED,

By J. A. PERRY, who has been Lecturing on Romanism, since his return from a tour in Catholic countries, where he gained access to Nunneries, and the horrid Inquisition Rooms, and witnessed scenes too cruel to be described. Has succeeded in getting the desired information from *Nunneries in New England*, having lately removed several young Ladies from these papal institutions, is prepared to give a *true* and *thrilling* expose of these *pretended* religious places.

Mr. P. has been to great expense, in illustrating his Lectures with several large Paintings, executed in a superb manner, by the best Artists; these paintings, which are so replete with startling and horrible interest, showing the *enormities* practised upon defenceless females, are correct representations of scenes that came under the observation of Mr. P. during his tour in Mexico. Each character on the canvas being painted as large as life, can be seen from any part of the room.

The manner in which Perry handles Romanism, has ever given universal satisfaction to his audiences, especially the Ladies, for he has a peculiar way of coming to the truth, without wounding the feelings of the most fastidious, which has called forth letters of commendation from many prominent Clergymen.

Tremont Temple, in Boston, was filled with ladies and gentlemen to listen to this Expose, who manifested their satisfaction by unbounded applause. Such Exposes will cause the very pillars of Popery to collapse and fall. *God speed the day !*

Sons of '76 and Lovers of Liberty Bring the Ladies !

ADMISSION 12½ Cts. to defray Expenses.

NO POSTPONEMENT.

Figure 6   Itinerant anti-Catholic lecturers were active on both sides of the Atlantic in the mid-nineteenth century. This flyer advertises a lecture in a small town in northern Massachusetts, and is suggestive evidence of how religious antagonism and sexual titillation could feed upon each other. 'Sam is our next president', flyer 11 January 1855, Broadsides collection. Courtesy of the American Antiquarian Society

perceptions of Roman Catholics as idle and degraded, and also, as in the flyer reproduced here, of abusing and corrupting women (see Figure 6). The most prominent concern however, in both Britain and the United States, was of Roman Catholicism as a political threat to national independence and free government. That fear seemed much less plausible in the nineteenth century than it had been in the sixteenth century, but it still drew credibility from the tactless grandiloquence of prelates such as Wiseman and Hughes, and from the political aspirations of Irish Catholics. Moreover, when Britons and Americans looked at Europe they perceived absolutist regimes, notably in Austria and Spain, drawing support from the Catholic Church. Americans suspected that the influx of Catholic migrants to their shores, not only from Ireland but also from continental Europe, was part of a deep-seated conspiracy, masterminded in Rome and Vienna, to subvert their hard-won Protestant and republican liberties through sheer force of numbers. Anti-Catholic paranoia in the United States reached a climax in the mid-1850s when 'Know-Nothings', who campaigned on a militantly Protestant and anti-immigrant platform, enjoyed considerable if transient electoral success.

Catholics, Protestants and liberals in the modern world

By the last quarter of the nineteenth century, the upsurge in anti-Catholicism in the British Isles and the United States had reached its peak or at least a plateau. In the United States during the 1860s the Civil War was a major distraction from such concerns; also in the 1860s the unification of Italy and the ending of the Pope's role as an Italian ruler as well as a religious leader lessened the credibility of fears regarding his political influence. While Irish migration continued, its pace slackened, and as rival urban communities became more stable and prosperous, the potential for friction diminished. Some of the more lurid allegations against Roman Catholicism were exposed as speculative or fraudulent. For example, in 1871 the committee appointed by the British House of Commons to enquire into 'conventual and monastic institutions' found no evidence at all to support the anti-Catholic charge that these were dens of oppression and sexual depravity (Arnstein, 1982).

From around 1860, the further development of liberal challenges to traditional Christian belief, notably through the influence of the theories of Charles Darwin and increasing questioning of the reliability of the Bible, began gradually to render the struggle between Protestant and Catholic a lesser priority for some. However, this process was a slow one. Moreover, there was a tendency for it to be integrated with Protestant–Catholic conflicts: Protestants claimed that reaction against alleged Catholic 'superstition' and religious authoritarianism gave rise to 'infidelity'; Catholics that Protestant insistence on the right of everyone to interpret the Bible for themselves was a root of liberalism and scepticism. The persistence well into the twentieth century of the view that Rome was more dangerous even than religious scepticism was illustrated in 1923 by an English mother who slipped into her daughter's bedroom shortly before her marriage:

> 'Darling,' said an anxious small voice, 'Father says, "Is he a Roman Catholic"?' 'No,' said Bet [her daughter] sleepily, 'he's an atheist.' 'Oh, thank goodness! I must tell Father, we couldn't sleep for worrying ...'.

(Dodds, 1977, p. 85)

The father who thus preferred having an atheist rather than a Roman Catholic for a son-in-law was an Anglican clergyman, and one of his other children was to become a bishop (ibid., p. 80).

In continental Europe, meanwhile, theological and political liberalism itself tended to fuel attacks on Roman Catholicism. In Britain, the weakening of the Protestant confessional identity of the state was associated with increasing toleration for religious minorities, including Roman Catholics. In countries such as Germany, the Netherlands and Switzerland, on the other hand, Catholics had always been sufficiently numerous for their toleration to be unavoidable. In the nineteenth century, however, the growth of liberalism at the very time that Ultramontanism seemed to be making Roman Catholicism more obscurantist and authoritarian provided fertile soil for conflict. Already in Switzerland in the 1840s the suppression of monasteries in the canton of Aargau and antagonism to the readmission of the Jesuits to the canton of Lucerne had been major factors in leading in 1847 to a brief civil war in which the liberals were triumphant (Remak, 1993, pp. 19–31). Until the 1880s Swiss Catholics remained subject to considerable suspicion and some legal repression. A similar tendency seemed to be developing in the Netherlands in the 1850s, following a hostile reaction to the restoration of the Catholic hierarchy of bishops in 1853. Here, however, Catholics and conservative Calvinists eventually made a political alliance in recognition of their common interest in resisting secular liberalism, thus highlighting the manner in which the driving force of continental anti-Catholicism at this period was quite as much liberal as Protestant. Indeed, some liberal critics of the Roman Catholic Church were themselves from Catholic backgrounds (Evans, 1999, pp. 78–92, 123–41).

The most extensive conflict, known as the *Kulturkampf* (culture struggle), occurred in Germany, where Protestant–Catholic relations had hitherto seemed less tense than in the English-speaking world. A united German state, with extensive Catholic minorities, had been formed in 1871 under the domination of Prussia, which was predominantly Protestant. The Chancellor (prime minister), Otto von Bismarck (1815–98), came to perceive the Roman Catholic Church and its political representatives, the Centre Party, as a threat to national security because of their alleged priestly and extra-territorial allegiances. His anti-papal feelings tapped into a strong vein in Protestant and liberal public opinion. He was able in 1872 to carry legislation eliminating Catholic involvement in public education and expelling the Jesuits from Germany. In 1873, stringent state controls over the Catholic Church in Prussia were established. Numerous bishops and priests were imprisoned or expelled and, in 1875, most monastic orders were banned. Within a few years it became clear that the *Kulturkampf* was proving counterproductive in that Catholics were offering united resistance rather than allowing themselves to be marginalized and assimilated, and Bismarck accordingly relaxed his repressive policies (Ross, 1998). Like French, British and American political leaders before him, Bismarck came to the pragmatic conclusion that national unity was better promoted by recognizing religious diversity rather than by making fruitless attempts to suppress it. Nevertheless the virulence of the *Kulturkampf* had both demonstrated the strength of anti-Catholic feeling in Germany and ensured a continuing legacy of estrangement and distrust, which hampered moderate attempts at nation building. The Protestant League, founded in 1887, and with a membership of half a million in 1914, espoused an exclusively Protestant vision of German identity and aligned itself with radical nationalism. The Catholic Centre Party responded by aligning itself more closely with the political right so as to secure its own nationalist credentials (Smith, 1995). Such an environment was eventually to provide an opening for those, above all Adolf Hitler (himself a nominal Roman Catholic), who directed attention to the perceived common enemy of both, the Jews.

The general trend in Protestant–Catholic relations in English-speaking countries in the late nineteenth and twentieth centuries was from conflict towards coexistence. There were, however, significant exceptions. Some were a matter of locality, in areas such as Merseyside and Clydeside that maintained a pattern of sectarian rivalry, sometimes reinforced by sporting allegiances as in the case of the 'Old Firm' Glasgow football confrontations between (Protestant) Rangers and (Catholic) Celtic. Other exceptions arose from the ongoing agitation of committed anti-Catholic organizations, some of which – such as the Protestant Reformation Society in England – were formed in the first half of the nineteenth century and were still in existence at the end of the twentieth century. There were also, as in continental Europe, particular historical contingencies that gave rise to renewed confrontation. For example, in the United States in the 1890s alarm at the perceived continuing rapid expansion of the Roman Catholic Church combined with economic insecurities and a series of specific controversies on educational matters to stir a noteworthy outburst of anti-Catholic political campaigning led by the American Protective Association (Wallace, 1990). In Scotland in the 1920s and 1930s, fringe Protestant political movements were able to enjoy shortlived successes by drawing upon an enduring tradition of anti-Catholicism in offering a populistic response to the frustration and disillusion of the Depression years (Bruce, 1985). Only after the early 1960s, when the reform of the Roman Catholic Church by the Second Vatican Council served to convince all but the most entrenched of its opponents that old ambitions to extinguish Protestantism really had been abandoned, did the potential for confrontation finally begin to disappear. This process was assisted by a fresh wave of renewal amongst the Evangelical Protestant churches of the English-speaking world, which stimulated a shift away from negative anti-Catholicism and, by widespread general secularization, meant that the historic divergences within Christianity came for many to appear an irrelevance.

The most important exception to the trend toward coexistence was Northern Ireland. As we have seen, the wider impact of sectarian tensions in Ireland was important in contributing to the general revival and reshaping of anti-Catholicism in the nineteenth century, and it is therefore not surprising that their most persistent legacy has been on Irish soil. In the decades before the outbreak of the First World War in 1914 there were repeated attempts by British governments to restore a measure of self-government to Ireland. These were frustrated, in large part due to the irreconcilable opposition of Protestants in the north of Ireland, who were terrified of becoming a minority in a Catholic-dominated state. In September 1912, nearly half a million people signed a covenant (or 'Declaration') for women affirming their reliance 'on the God whom our fathers in days of stress and trial confidently trusted' and pledging themselves to use 'all means which may be found necessary' to prevent Home Rule (Stewart, 1967, pp. 62–6). When, after the First World War, it became clear that British rule in the south of Ireland was no longer sustainable, the logic of events forced the partition of the country. In 1921, twenty-six counties achieved virtually complete independence in the Irish Free State, while six counties in the north-east formed the province of Northern Ireland, with its own Parliament under the British Crown. The boundaries of Northern Ireland (which excluded three of the nine counties making up the historic province of Ulster) were cynically drawn by the Protestants, who dominated the new state so as to ensure that they had a built-in secure majority over the Catholics, who were about a third of the population within its boundaries. The history of Northern Ireland between 1921 and the outbreak of the 'Troubles' in 1969 was characterized by blatant discrimination against the Catholic minority, which sometimes, especially in the 1920s, extended to actual state-sanctioned violence against them (Brewer and Higgins, 1998, pp. 95–6). Estrangement was reinforced by virtually complete social and cultural separation, notably through spatial segregation of housing and distinct education systems. A conflict that had its roots in religious difference was thus sustained and deepened by numerous other factors. From 1969 onwards, the seemingly inexorable cycle of terrorist and paramilitary violence further reinforced the alienation of the two communities.

There is no space here for full analysis of this very complex conflict, but three key points are worthy of emphasis in the context of this chapter. First, a balanced understanding of the role of religious difference in recent Irish history lies neither in regarding it as a mere symbolic figleaf covering other 'real' causes, nor, at the other extreme, in interpreting the whole struggle as a 'religious war'. Active religious interest and participation was certainly consistently much higher than in Britain. For example, in 1970, 75 per cent of the population of Northern Ireland, compared with 50 per cent in Great Britain described themselves as either 'very religious' or 'fairly religious'; in 1973, 92 per cent of Roman Catholics and 34 per cent of Protestants claimed to attend church at least once a week (Darby, 1976, p. 115; MacAllister, 1982). In the south of Ireland during the mid-twentieth century, social and cultural life was heavily dominated by the Roman Catholic Church, thus making the equation of Catholicism with Irish identity seem a natural one, and ensuring that among northern Protestants religious objections to a united Ireland reinforced political ones. On the other hand, the majority of religious leaders on both sides have consistently urged reconciliation rather than confrontation, and paramilitaries have tended to come from the fringes of the churches rather than from among their committed members (Wolffe, 1994, p. 114).

The extensive influence of Ian Paisley (1926–) has been a particular catalyst for the association of religion and politics (Bruce, 1986). Paisley rose to prominence in the 1960s as both a successful preacher and leader of the Free Presbyterian Church, and as a diehard opponent of any compromise with Catholicism or Irish nationalism. His theology and ideology combined his interpretation of the Reformation inheritance with his passionate commitment to the maintenance of the Protestant and British political identity of Northern Ireland. His Democratic Unionist Party (DUP) became a major force in Northern Ireland politics, bringing together many who shared his religious convictions with a wider constituency of more secular Protestants who evidently found his ideology attractive. Whilst Paisley did not explicitly condone violence, his rhetoric was a significant factor in the conditions that gave rise to it. It gave a sense of legitimacy to Protestant militants, and reinforced the perception of Roman Catholics that there could never be an equal and accepted place for them in Northern Ireland as presently constituted.

Second, the intensity of conflict in Northern Ireland in the twentieth century stemmed from the extent to which particular continuing circumstances meant that identities, now uncontroversial or even irrelevant elsewhere, remained hotly contested. Was the province to be British, royalist and Protestant or Irish, republican and Catholic? It was a polarity that mattered profoundly to many, and in which, at least until the Good Friday Agreement of 1998, there did not appear to be any credible middle ways. The wider inference to be drawn is that the decline of overt Catholic–Protestant conflict elsewhere arises from the gradual disentangling of confessional difference from wider cultural and

Figures 7 and 8   Banners carried in recent processions in Northern Ireland by a (Protestant) Loyal Orange Lodge and a (Catholic) division of the Ancient Order of Hibernians show, respectively, King William III and St Patrick in a Celtic landscape. They symbolize the importance of different readings of religious history in sustaining much later community identities and confrontations. Photos © National Museums and Galleries of Northern Ireland, Ulster Folk and Transport Museum, negative refs CX217 and DB181

political factors, especially in relation to the understanding and expression of national and communal identities. No longer did it seem that one had to be Protestant in order to be truly American, or Roman Catholic in order to be truly French.

Finally, the experience of Northern Ireland shows the importance of popular myths that combine religious conviction with a selective reading of history. Thus, on the Protestant side, there was a sense of being specially favoured by God in a covenant relationship analogous to that of Old Testament Israel (Brewer and Higgins, 1998, pp. 135–8), manifested in their seventeenth-century victories and reaffirmed in the covenant of 1912. Such a relationship was perceived as incompatible with any compromise with Roman Catholics and nationalists. Varieties of this tradition were kept vigorously alive not only by the Paisleyites, but also by the brotherhoods of the Orange Order and its associated societies, the Royal Arch Purple Chapter and the Royal Black Institution. By no means all Orangemen are regular churchgoers, but their ritual and symbolism is permeated by biblical references while their processions, banners and other images, above all on 12 July, vividly evoke their particular interpretation of Irish history (Buckley, 1989; see Figure 7). The parallel Catholic mythology is fuelled by selective dwelling on grievances, such as Cromwell's massacres in 1649, and the Famine of the 1840s, for which Protestants are held responsible, presenting a vision of Irish history and identity as inherently Catholic. The Ancient Order of Hibernians has similar functions amongst Catholics to the Orange Order among Protestants as a brotherhood that asserts and defends their perceived interests and historic traditions (Buckley and Anderson, 1988; see Figure 8). Like the Orangemen, the Hibernians do not condone sectarian violence, but the vitality of such organizations has contributed to the ongoing estrangement of the two communities.

Conclusion

How does this analysis of Protestant–Roman Catholic antagonisms contribute to the wider understanding of religious coexistence and conflict? The slow progress of generations of ecumenical endeavour is testimony to the genuine and profound nature of religious differences between Protestant and Catholic, but, as we have seen, the extent to which difference translated into conflict has varied widely across time and space. The periods of greatest conflict, whether in later sixteenth-century France and England, the mid-nineteenth-century United States, or twentieth-century Northern Ireland, can be related to particular shorter-term historical circumstances, albeit ones whose impact could last over many years or even decades. At other periods, for example, in the eighteenth century and in the twentieth century outside Ireland, peaceful, if sometimes uneasy, coexistence, was much closer to the norm. Such coexistence could be fragile, however, and might degenerate into conflict with alarming speed, as, for example, in Britain in the Gordon Riots of 1780 or in Germany in the *Kulturkampf* of the 1870s. The implication would seem to be that religious conflict, however seemingly intractable, should not be seen as inevitable and indefinite, but that, conversely, coexistence between potentially opposed traditions may well be more unstable than it appears. Comparisons might be drawn with the rapid growth of Nazi-inspired antisemitism in Germany in the 1930s, and with the rapid degeneration of relations between Catholic, Muslim and Orthodox in the former Yugoslavia in the late 1980s and 1990s.

There is also scope for identification of recurrent features in attitudes towards religious minorities. Attention has been drawn to the parallels in the early modern era between the position of Protestants in France and that of Roman Catholics in Britain. As with Jews in early twentieth-century Europe, Muslims in the late twentieth-century western world, and Christians in Islamic countries, allegations of political disloyalty and sexual deviancy were linked to religious difference as grounds for stigmatizing the minority as irredeemably hostile to the values of the majority, and hence for legitimizing persecution. The consistency of such motifs across the centuries, and in relation to a wide range of religious conflict situations, is a prompt to acknowledge the role of collective psychology and self-reinforcing prejudice in the construction of perceptions of the opposed tradition. Such a recognition is by no means to discount the reality of underlying religious differences, but it does suggest that conflicts may often have been stimulated as much by the imagination as by actual confrontations.

References

Arnstein, W. L. (1982) *Protestant versus Catholic in Mid-Victorian England: Mr Newdegate and the Nuns*, Columbia and London, University of Missouri Press.

Beckett, J. C. (1981) *The Making of Modern Ireland 1603–1923*, 2nd edition, London, Faber and Faber.

*Billington, R. A. (1938) *The Protestant Crusade, 1800–1860*, New York, Macmillan.

Bossy, J. (1975) *The English Catholic Community 1570–1850*, London, Darton, Longman and Todd.

*Brewer, J. D. and Higgins, G. I. (1998) *Anti-Catholicism in Northern Ireland, 1600–1998: The Mote and the Beam*, Basingstoke, Macmillan.

Bruce, S. (1985) *No Pope of Rome: Militant Protestantism in Modern Scotland*, Edinburgh, Mainstream.

Bruce, S. (1986) *God Save Ulster! The Religion and Politics of Paisleyism*, Oxford, Oxford University Press.

Buckley, A. (1989) '"We're Trying to Find our Identity": uses of history among Ulster Protestants' in E. Tonkin, M. McDonald and M. Chapman (eds) *History and Ethnicity*, London, Routledge.

Buckley, A. and Anderson, K. (1988) *Brotherhoods in Ireland*, Cultra, Ulster Folk and Transport Museum.

Carbonnier-Burkard, M. and Cabanel, P. (1998) *Une histoire des protestants en France*, Paris, Desclée de Brouwer.

Cogliano, F. D. (1995) *No King, No Popery: Anti-Catholicism in Revolutionary New England*, Westport, CT and London, Greenwood.

Colley, L. (1992) *Britons: Forging the Nation 1707–1837*, London, Pimlico.

*Cressy, D. (1989) *Bonfires and Bells: National Memory and the Protestant Calendar in Elizabethan and Stuart England*, London, Weidenfeld and Nicolson.

Darby, J. (1976) *Conflict in Northern Ireland: The Development of a Polarised Community*, Dublin, Gill and Macmillan.

Dodds, E. R. (1977) *Missing Persons: An Autobiography*, Oxford, Oxford University Press.

Doyle, W. (1978) *The Old European Order 1660–1800*, Oxford, Oxford University Press.

Evans, E. L. (1999) *The Cross and the Ballot: Catholic Political Parties in Germany, Switzerland, Austria, Belgium and the Netherlands, 1785–1985*, Boston, Humanities Press.

*Haller, W. (1963) *Foxe's Book of Martyrs and the Elect Nation*, London, Jonathan Cape.

*Haydon, C. (1993) *Anti-Catholicism in Eighteenth-century England, c.1714–80: A Political and Social Study*, Manchester, Manchester University Press.

Hoppen, K. T. (1989) *Ireland since 1800: Conflict and Conformity*, London and New York, Longman.

Hughes, J. (1864) *Complete Works of the Most Rev John Hughes*, vol. II, New York, American News Company.

MacAllister, I. (1982) 'The Devil, miracles and the afterlife: the political sociology of religion in Northern Ireland', *British Journal of Sociology*, vol. 33, pp. 334–50.

*McGrath, A. E. (1999) *Reformation Thought: An Introduction*, 3rd edition, Oxford, Blackwell.

Miller, K. E. (1985) *Emigrants and Exiles: Ireland and the Irish Exodus to North America*, New York and Oxford, Oxford University Press.

Newman, J. H. (1967) *Apologia Pro Vita Sua Being a History of His Religious Opinions* (originally published 1864), ed. by M. J. Svaglic, Oxford, Clarendon Press.

*Racaut, L. (2002) *Hatred in Print: Catholic Propaganda and Protestant Identity during the French Wars of Religion*, Aldershot, Ashgate.

Remak, J. (1993) *A Very Civil War: The Swiss Sonderbund War of 1847*, Boulder, Westview Press.

Ross, R. J. (1998) *The Failure of Bismarck's Kulturkampf: Catholicism and State Power in Imperial Germany, 1871–1887*, Washington, DC, The Catholic University of America Press.

Smith, H. W. (1995) *German Nationalism and Religious Conflict: Culture, Identity, Politics 1870–1914*, Princeton, Princeton University Press.

Stewart, A. T. Q. (1967) *The Ulster Crisis: Resistance to Home Rule, 1912–14*, London, Faber.

Storch, R. D. (1982) "'Please to remember the fifth of November": conflict, solidarity and public order in southern England, 1815–1900' in R. D. Storch and R. Swift (eds) *Popular Culture and Custom in Nineteenth-Century England*, London, Croom Helm, pp. 71–96.

Wallace, L. (1990) *The Rhetoric of Anti-Catholicism: The American Protective Association, 1887–1911*, New York and London, Garland.

*Wolffe, J. (1991) *The Protestant Crusade in Great Britain 1829–1860*, Oxford, Clarendon Press.

Wolffe, J. (1994) "'And there's another country ...": religion, the state and British identities, in G. A. Parsons (ed.) *The Growth of Religious Diversity: Britain from 1945*, vol. II, *Issues*, London, Routledge, pp. 85–121.

Asterisked items are particularly recommended for further reading.

5   The Hindu Renaissance and notions of universal religion

Gwilym Beckerlegge

Hinduism in a novel context

From its origins in the late seventeenth century, Calcutta grew from a British trading station on the river Hugli in Bengal to become recognized at its peak as the first city in Asia. It was a city of parks, palaces and neo-classical civic architecture, erected on top of a cluster of existing villages and embracing a temple that had long been a centre for the worship of Kali, the great Mother Goddess. Different communities typically lived in their own distinctive areas of the city. As the nineteenth century wore on, technological innovations such as trams and printing presses became part of the urban landscape. As the centre of the East India Company's administration, Calcutta reflected the wealth of its officials and indigenous trading-partners and agents. This chapter will focus on the ways in which two prominent Hindu thinkers associated with this city responded to the encounter with Christianity.

Hindus proved generally more ready to take advantage of opportunities provided through contact with the British in Bengal than Muslims, who had lost their status as former rulers and consequently many of their privileges. New wealth and social roles brought into being an expanded middle class mostly drawn from the Hindu population whose fortunes became entwined with those of the British. This minority adopted a lifestyle in the so-called 'black town' in Calcutta that rivalled that of the Europeans living in the 'white town'. For many beneath them, however, the chances of career advancement and financial improvement were limited in this new city where the British presence was felt more directly and intensely than in any other part of India. Here a western education could provide a route into the professions and government service and so attracted high-caste Hindus. Nineteenth-century Calcutta thus became 'a real metropolis for the *bhadralok* [gentlefolk], providing education, opportunities for jobs, printed books, a taste for new cultural values', but one in which the *bhadralok* 'did not yet feel at home' (Sarkar, 1997, p. 176). This narrow segment of Hindu society, and the tensions and opportunities confronting it, did much to shape the dynamic of cultural changes now referred to as the Hindu Renaissance, which will be the subject of this chapter.

Calcutta was more than a centre for trade. It felt the full impact of the complex process of acculturation, the consequences of the conjunction

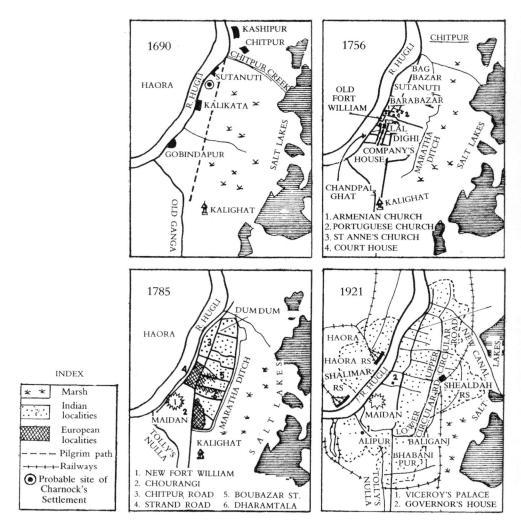

Map 6   Four stages of growth in Calcutta, from Sukanta Chaudhuri (ed.) Calcutta, The Living City, *vol. 1,* The Past. *Reproduced with the permission of the Oxford University Press India, New Delhi*

of two formerly separate cultures, which was largely the result of British settlement. In contrast to the relatively small cities found in India at the end of the Mughal era, the creation of a metropolitan centre by an alien power aided in promoting a vigorous intellectual life in which new cultural values could be created (Haldar, 1977, p. 6). Calcutta provided the setting for the generation of 'original modes of thought that have authority beyond or in conflict with old cultures or civilizations' (Redfield and Singer, 1954, p. 58). It was in this metropolitan society that a new kind of *guru* emerged, marking the 'early phase of ... transition towards an urban consumer-oriented Hinduism' (Sarkar, 1993, pp. 52, 54), and, it

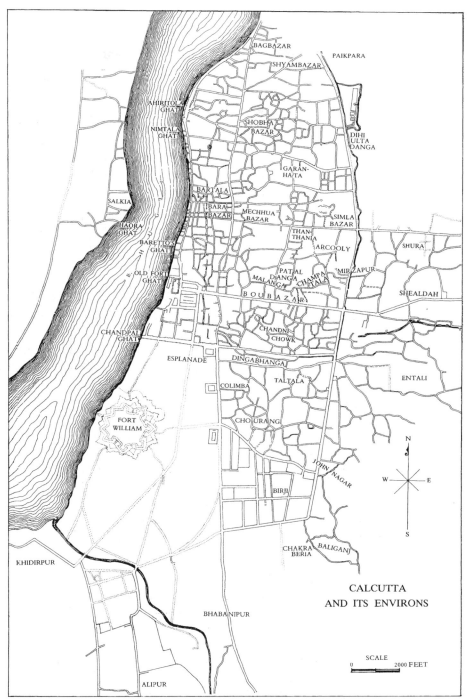

Map 7   Old Calcutta based on Upjohn's Survey 1792–3, from Sukanta Chaudhuri (ed.) Calcutta, The Living City, *vol. 1,* The Past. *Reproduced with the permission of the Oxford University Press India, New Delhi*

Figure 1   View of Clive Street, 'Native' huts facing grander buildings, by Charles D'Oyly from his book Images of Calcutta, *Dickinson and Co., London 1848. Photo with permission from The British Library, shelfmark: X905.010c*

could be argued, the beginning of a style of Hinduism that would be practised by Hindu communities outside India in the following century.

The term 'Hinduism' was created by Europeans and grew in use from the late eighteenth century. It was an attempt to label India's most common patterns of religious thought and behaviour in a way that would make sense to those familiar with the organizations and systematic statements of belief that had characterized European Christianity. In reality, Hinduism's intertwining religious traditions have embraced individuals born into specific social locations defined by caste. With this identity – familial, caste, communal and regional – has come a whole package of customs, ritual obligations and convictions, all shot through with references to the supernatural, which European observers came to agree constituted the 'religion' of 'Hinduism'.

Without a historical founder and lacking a distinct religious organization, the many variations covered by the umbrella-term 'Hinduism' have been marked by adherence to a broad world view characterized by a general conviction that a cycle of rebirth must be broken in order to achieve spiritual emancipation (*moksha*). The social ramifications of this pervasive belief have been manifested in the hierarchy of the caste system and the differentiated, social and ritual duties (*dharma*) assigned to each caste grouping, upon whose fulfilment both future spiritual progress and social standing have been seen to depend. Within the limits of these sometimes rigid and prescriptive social conventions, Hindus have adhered to a striking variety of beliefs, the majority theistic but not all. They have offered devotion to different deities but not exclusively, acknowledging many different deities and supernatural beings, and have favoured different teachers and other sources of inspiration. Simultaneously, influential schools of thought have posited a non-personal and unified reality, often referred to as Brahman, of which the deities in their personal forms are but lower and partial manifestations. The influence of early ritual and philosophical traditions, now found within the sacred text known as the Veda, has been felt more directly by the brahmin caste, which had been entrusted with the transmission of the Vedic tradition, and by those higher castes for whom the brahmins have acted as ritual specialists. For the vast majority of Hindus, many of whom to this day inhabit India's myriad villages, everyday religious life has revolved around a relationship with a deity or deities to whom devotion is offered and who may be approached for assistance with problems in the here and now, and the fulfilment of ritual and social obligations prescribed by *dharma*. It was generally not until well into the nineteenth century that religious activity came to be channelled through forms of social organization that promoted notions of discrete membership and belonging.

From its relatively recent foundation, Calcutta was very different from India's ancient cities. Many of these had developed as religious centres or as the seats of local rulers, often combining both functions. It was in this novel context that Hindu members of the 'cosmopolitan intelligentsia', rather than the traditional literati, took up the urgent task of reinterpreting *dharma* (the principles of belief and practice) in a manner meaningful to the new situation in which they found themselves. They began to reshape the tenets of Hinduism in an emergent global context, in which it could no longer be assumed that their audience would know or appreciate the particulars of Hinduism, and to create new kinds of religious organizations. They had to negotiate with a colonial power whose disapproval could impact directly on the public practice of their religion while themselves being instrumental in creating more fragmented and privatized styles of religion. A number of personalities and organizations emerged to voice the interests of sectors of the Hindu population during this time of change, challenged by the encounter with the values mediated by British administrators, traders and Christian missionaries. Their 'philosophies of encounter and acculturation, best expressed in the ideologies of comparativism and universalism' represented 'the most productive side of the Hindu intellectual response to the West' (Kopf, 1979, p. 251). The contribution of these thinkers fed into the rich variety of cultural cross-currents that have eddied subsequently between Britain and India, and which at times have been concealed by the persistence of popular images of Britain's dominance in nineteenth-century India.

In fact, the intensifying interaction between India and the west, provoking reactions ranging from abhorrence to compelling fascination, led to innovative and fascinating intellectual syntheses.[1] Some individuals at the heart of this encounter became critics of the culture and society of their birth, exploring in the process formerly alien ideas and ways of life, including religion. Two such Hindu thinkers were Rammohun Roy (c. 1772–1833) and Swami Vivekananda (1863–1902). Both were founders of important nineteenth-century Hindu movements. Their ideas, which will be examined at greater length in the second half of this chapter, provide an ideal case study for consideration under the headings of conflict, conversion and coexistence.

Conflict, conversion and coexistence

The presence of the British in India brought Hinduism and Christianity into a new phase of coexistence within the same geographical region,[2] taking the term 'coexistence' in the simplest sense defined in the Introduction (p. 7–8). Framed by a particular set of political, economic and social conditions, the relationship between Britain and colonial India was hardly one of equal partners, although Britain only ever ruled parts of the subcontinent. Britain, nevertheless, could impose its will both directly and indirectly upon much of India. It chose to do so more systematically from the early decades of the nineteenth century. Following its founding in 1600, the East India Company's merchants, protected by its soldiers, created the cities that would become associated with British rule – Madras (Chennai), Calcutta (Kolkata) and Bombay (Mumbai). Through trade and military might, the company extended its control, defeating local Indian rulers and the French who were similarly attempting to become the dominant European power in the subcontinent.[3] In the interests of trade, the East India Company adopted a policy of non-interference in local customs including, on occasion, continuing to levy tolls that traditionally went to Hindu temples. It restricted Christian ministry to British communities rather than permitting

---

[1] The term 'west' is used in the way in which it would have been understood by thinkers such as Rammohun Roy and Swami Vivekananda to refer to the United States, Britain and western Europe more generally.

[2] Small communities of Syrian Christians and Roman Catholic converts had been established in the south of India before the arrival of the British and predominantly Protestant European missionaries. See, for example, Chidester, 2001, pp. 488–95.

[3] For a fuller account of the growth of the East India Company's influence and role see, for example, Marshall, 1987, Spear, 1970 and Stein, 1998.

missionary activity among the indigenous population. The combined pressure of Evangelicals, who wished to take the gospel to millions of Hindus, and Utilitarians, who desired the reform of Indian social institutions and practices, brought about a change of policy. This led to greater freedom for Christian missionaries in company territory, legislation to abolish certain Hindu customs, and the promotion of English-language education. The denigration of Hindu religion and culture, which such initiatives implied, superimposed areas of conflict upon patterns of coexistence between Hindus and the British in India that had become established under the rule of the East India Company. One such conflict was provoked by the aim of Christian missionary organizations, actively supported by some administrators, to bring about the conversion of Hindus to Christianity. By the late 1820s, tensions also had begun to appear between different factions within Hindu society. There was increasing resistance to what was perceived as a systematic attack upon traditional beliefs and practices, even though some individuals still welcomed the window on the wider world opened by access to English learning.[4] Others were willing to make common cause with British legislative attempts to improve the lot of women and employed European norms when judging the tradition they had inherited.

Studying India's history, laws and texts was one European response to the encounter with India, as was personal reflection on the implications of a newly unveiled world view for cherished beliefs. The period between 1815 and 1825 witnessed a 'remarkable coincidence of events' in both the United States and the Indian region of Bengal where there were intellectual revolts against the prevailing religious orthodoxies (Kopf, 1979, p. 9). In Britain also, attitudes towards other religions and the whole missionary enterprise underwent considerable changes in the liberal wing of the Church of England during the latter half of the nineteenth century. Personal links were forged between prominent Hindu thinkers and religious organizations in both Britain and the United States, and in particular in New England, where the dominant form of Calvinism had been challenged by the growth of Unitarianism.

Tracing its origins back to the seventeenth century and to thinkers such as Faustus Socinus/Fausto Sozzini (1539–1604) (hence the title Socinians) and John Biddle (1612–62), Unitarianism in England took root in the dissenting chapels built after the Toleration Act of 1689, developing into a distinctive tradition in the eighteenth century. Stressing reason and religious tolerance, its characteristic belief in the unity of the Godhead constituted a rejection of Christian Trinitarian theology. Some Unitarians held to the belief that Jesus was of like, but not of the same, substance

[4] Young (1981, p. 14) emphasizes that conservative Hindu pundits did engage with the theological and philosophical dimensions of Christianity and not solely with social dimensions of the Hindu–Christian encounter.

as God the Father,[5] thus holding Jesus to be more than human. By the nineteenth century, however, this had given way to a generally held belief that Jesus was a special but purely human figure. Doctrines of eternal punishment and vicarious atonement were also abandoned. In the United States, Unitarianism similarly developed in reaction against an oppressive religious orthodoxy, although initially more driven by criticism of the Calvinistic doctrine of predestination, which had held sway in New England since the founding of the Massachusetts Bay Colony in 1630, than against Trinitarianism. Fed by many of the same intellectual currents that had shaped Unitarianism in Britain, Unitarianism in New England came to be identified with a liberal religious outlook that promoted a freer form of Christian belief and practice and refused to be bound by religious creeds. It was from within this framework of belief in a spiritual theism, transcending dogma and creeds, that Unitarians in both Britain and the United States were able to reach out to other religions in the nineteenth century, and particularly to those whom they recognized as Hindu 'reformers'.

Sensing common ground, Unitarian groups in Britain and the United States published accounts of their Hindu contacts' religious and social philosophies. Apart from establishing personal relationships through their representatives in India, they provided networks of audiences and contacts for the handful of Hindu thinkers who made the arduous journey to the west. It has been claimed that the story of the exchanges at that time between Unitarian Christians in Britain and the United States and certain Hindus reveal 'developing inter-relationships among men and women on three different continents who unexpectedly discovered they had much in common and much worth sharing' (Lavan, 1977, p. 2). This judgement could be extended to cover to varying degrees other contacts established between individual Christians and Hindus of the period.

For many Christians, it was the doctrine of salvation, rather than the exploration of differences and the celebration of common ground, that was paramount. The creation of Christian missionary organizations to take the gospel to India and so to reform Hindu society was another response to the encounter with India. In spite of the level of European and American Christian missionary activity throughout the nineteenth century, however, Hinduism did not 'crumble' (Thomas, 1997, p. 109).[6] Leaving aside questions about the effectiveness of different Christian missions, the social organization and structure of belief in Hinduism made the process of conversion, understood here as movement from one

---

[5] For this reason, this belief of early Unitarians, particularly in the United States, has been likened to Arianism, the Christian doctrine promoted by Arius (c. 250–c. 336 CE) but condemned at the Council of Nicaea in 325. See pp. 13–14 above.

[6] Discussion of the strategies and achievements of various Christian missions in India and the problems they faced may be found, for example, in Copley, 1997, Neill, 1964, and Stanley, 2002.

religious tradition (Hinduism) to another (Christianity), extremely difficult for the vast majority of Hindus to envisage, far less to undertake. Even in the nineteenth century, the specifically 'religious' aspects of Hinduism, as identified by outside observers, were largely inseparable from social identity and caste and family obligations. Consequently, to 'convert' (if such a notion had any meaning) would have implied abandoning social identity and family ties and obligations, including for eldest sons their rights of inheritance, which were tied to the performance of ritual obligations on the death of the father. Conversion 'took on the aspect of a cultural migration', and this prospect was intensified by the exclusiveness of mid-nineteenth-century mission (Copley, 1997, p. 53–4).

The extent of the 'cultural migration' required by conversion has frequently been cited as one reason why a number of Hindus who appeared to have accepted the Christian faith subsequently returned to the fold of Hinduism. In the 1880s, a limited form of organized proselytism and a formal ritual of conversion were practised within Hinduism. This came as a response from the Arya Samaj, a militant Hindu movement founded in 1875, to attempts by Christian missionaries to convert low-caste and untouchable Hindu communities. The Arya Samaj set itself the task of 'reclaiming' these converts and other Hindus it believed to have been lost previously to Islam and Sikhism, instituting a ritual of purification (*shuddhi*) to mark what in some cases was closer to 're-conversion'.[7] The lack of acceptance of this tactic by other Hindus was indicative of the novelty of such a use of ritual and other means to change socio-religious identity.

Prior to the sharper delineation of distinct religious identities and separate political goals that accompanied the movement towards independence, the boundaries between long-standing religions in India were relatively fluid in some aspects of popular belief and practice. In addition, considerable cross-fertilization had taken place in the refinement of theological and philosophical ideas. Hindu thought had a capacity for inclusivism that sought to absorb and reinterpret on its own terms (Copley, 1997, p. 57). It had 'readily absorbed aspects of other religions without feeling the need to acknowledge their existence' (Smith, 2003, p. 34). The nineteenth-century Hindu intellectuals who felt drawn into a dialogue with representatives of European religious thinking were thus embarking upon a new undertaking (Copley, 1997, p. 57; cf. Young, 1981, p. 13). Hindu 'inclusivism' also placed another

[7] The Arya Samaj, founded in 1875 by Dayananda Sarasvati, has exercised considerable influence, both directly and indirectly, over the shaping of Hindutva ('Hindu-ness' or 'Hindudom') ideology and Hindu religious nationalism, which has gained in support since the 1920s. The aim of 'reclaiming' individuals lost from Hinduism to other religions has figured in more recent debates about Indian national identity and the place of other religions in an overwhelming Hindu society. See Sharma (1977, pp. 348–50) for some discussion of senses in which earlier forms of Hinduism might be described as having a 'missionary' dimension, although not a specific ritual of 'conversion'.

obstacle in the path of the Christian missionary intent on the conversion of Hindus and, as this chapter will later show, provided Hindu thinkers with a basis upon which to construct their response to the encounter with the west.

Not only did nineteenth-century Christian missionaries fail to undermine Hinduism, but they also probably 'helped inadvertently in training men … to build the Hindu renaissance' (Thomas, 1997, p. 109). The most pervasive impact of Christianity was felt through the dissemination of English-language education provided by Christian institutions as a medium through which to introduce students to Christian teaching. In this way, Indian students developed some knowledge of Christianity, but as part of a curriculum that covered English literature and European history and philosophy. Although it has been suggested that some became 'invisible Christians' as a result (Latourette, 1971, p. 203), this education system offered the majority a different way of thinking about the world even where it failed to supplant traditional religious beliefs with Christianity. One example of this was the introduction it provided to the researches of British, American and European 'orientalists' who were then busily translating Hindu texts, reconstructing India's past, and in some cases revising their personal religious views in the process.[8] This new knowledge rekindled the pride and confidence in their own culture that many Hindus had lost after successively falling under the rule of Muslims and then British Christians. No less significant was the way in which the tools of European intellectual training were put to use in developing a critique of British rule in India, its legitimacy and benefits, and in subjecting claims made on behalf of Christianity, and its claimed superiority over Hinduism, to rational scrutiny. As Thomas notes, the convergence of these overlapping experiences and intellectual perspectives contributed to a resurgence of Hindu cultural energy commonly referred to as the 'Hindu Renaissance'.

The Hindu Renaissance

The designation 'Hindu Renaissance' is commonly applied to a period marked by a reformulation of Hindu thought, practice and organization that began approximately in the 1820s and extended until the gaining of freedom from British rule. Because of the importance of Calcutta and the surrounding region as a seat of this activity, one important stimulus to this process of change has been referred to as the 'Bengal Renaissance', in which 'Religious and social reformers, scholars, literary giants, journalists and patriotic orators, maybe a couple of scientists – all merge

---

[8] For a discussion of the work and religious attitudes of F. Max Müller and Monier Williams, see Beckerlegge, 1997, pp. 177–219 and on Müller, Beckerlegge, 2000, pp. 7–18.

to form an image of 'renaissance', *nabajagaran* (awakening) or *naba –jug* (new age) (Chaudhuri, 1990, p. 95). Most comprehensively, these changes have been said to have been tantamount to an 'Indian Renaissance'. Some commentators have linked this Renaissance more specifically to the period from the 1870s and have described this as marked by 'revivalist' activity, characterizing the concerns of the preceding era from the 1820s as 'reformist'. This chapter will refer to the Hindu Renaissance but will focus on features of the Bengal Renaissance as an important phase and component of this wider phenomenon, ranging over the period from the 1820s. It is extremely difficult in practice to maintain a consistent distinction when attempting to categorize either individuals or movements, rather than particular tendencies they may exhibit, as 'reformist' or 'revivalist', because both these inclinations may coexist in a single person or group (see Sen, 2003).

Much has been written about the 'Renaissance' in nineteenth-century India because of the impetus it is said to have given to the Hindu wing of the Indian independence movement. It affected the mindset of many who, although educated during the last quarter of the nineteenth century, came to prominence in the period leading to independence in 1947 and after. Several of its leaders, for example, Sri Aurobindo (1872–1950) and Mahatma Gandhi (1869–1948), combined roles as political and religious thinkers. Many who became bound up in the struggle for independence perpetuated the beliefs and values of its religious figureheads. They shaped a style of 'modern Hinduism' or 'neo-Hinduism' that continues to influence the English-educated, Hindu middle class. With its distinctive organizations, this style of Hinduism has been characterized by:

1 its concern with the relationship between religion and nationalism;

2 the exposure of many of its major thinkers to western ideas, education and Christianity;

3 ambivalence about the traditional use of images in religious worship or outright rejection of this practice;

4 placing greater reliance upon individual judgement, rather than the acceptance of traditional authorities, including dependence upon scriptures other than the Veda in the justification of personal belief and practice;

5 the novel reinterpretation of traditional Hindu concepts, such as *dharma* and yoga, and of philosophical systems, such as Advaita Vedanta (which will be discussed later in this chapter);

6 commitment to practical service to humanity.

Perhaps because of the flexibility of their ideas, many Renaissance and modern Hindu thinkers have found a global audience within the Hindu diaspora that has been out of proportion to their influence upon

Hinduism in India as a whole, becoming the gurus of a 'globalized' Hinduism.[9]

The social historian Sumit Sarkar has suggested that one consequence of the appeal to the middle class of the ideals and thinkers associated with the Hindu Renaissance has been the creation of a middle-class view of cultural history in which the 'renaissance' phase is seen to mark the transition from mediaeval to modern (1997, p. 160). Sarkar concedes that reference was popularly made in nineteenth-century Bengal to a 'new age' or 'awakening' (ibid., p. 161). He emphasizes, however, that Bengalis of the period both eulogized and denounced the character of the age within which they lived and the effects of British rule. Some retained the ancient Hindu theory that their own time fell within the *Kaliyuga*, the most degenerate phase in the endlessly repeating cycle of four ages (ibid., pp. 186–215). Sarkar concludes that the 'Bengal Renaissance has been very much a mid- or late-twentieth century retrospect', and in this respect is much like other 'renaissances' (ibid., p. 161). This is a useful reminder that the designation 'renaissance' is a construct, whether shaped by Indian nationalists, Christian missionaries, citizens of Calcutta or historians of religion. Sarkar also emphasizes the importance of grounding the study of this cultural phenomenon and its representations within their relevant social context (ibid.).

Accounts of the Hindu Renaissance certainly offer strikingly different judgements upon its sources, nature and significance, not least because 'The choice of a perspective is without doubt an intellectual choice, but it is also influenced by the nature of one's involvement' (Poddar, 1970, p. 1). The phrase 'Hindu Renaissance' was popularized by the publication of *Renaissance of Hinduism* by D. S. Sarma, an Indian scholar and educationist. This book first appeared in 1944 at the climax of the movement towards Indian independence. Sarma spoke of Hinduism being roused from the 'sleep' into which it had fallen as a result of enduring years of subordination to foreign rulers with alien faiths. With fresh stimulus 'The innate vitality of that religion [Hinduism] with its great and glorious past asserted itself' (1973, p. 61). This was both a 'revival' and a 'renaissance'. Applying Sarkar's principle, it is undeniable that there is a strongly apologetic slant in Sarma's presentation of this development within Hinduism. He did acknowledge the sweeping effects of English-language education upon Hindus, but resolutely maintained that this served only as a stimulus and asserted the Hindu sources of the resurgence (Sarma, 1973, p. 61). According to a seminal study of the 'idiom' of the Hindu Renaissance, it has provided the 'linguistic medium of the modern Indian apologetic', with its

---

[9] It is important not to confuse the 'modern Hinduism' stemming from the Hindu Renaissance with the far more representative kinds of recent and contemporary popular Hinduism that touch the lives of the majority of Hindus more directly on a daily basis. This distinction is explained at greater length in Beckerlegge, 2001, pp. 68–73.

uncritical glorification of India's past (Bharati, 1970, p. 268). Students of the history of India's religions are thus confronted with competing accounts of one of its most distinctive phases. The need to evaluate rival paradigms and accounts is as pressing for those writing in the postcolonial era as was the desire to describe these changes for those who experienced their impact directly.

Few recent commentators, if any, would endorse the views of an earlier writer whose work remains of historical interest because the author was resident in Calcutta at the turn of the twentieth century. J. N. Farquhar (1861–1929), a Protestant missionary-scholar, in his *Modern Religious Movements in India* (1967, first published in 1914) judged the changes he witnessed to have been largely prompted by a desire on the part of certain Hindu intellectuals to bring Indian culture into line with western ideals and Christian values. On this understanding, the stimulus for change came from Christianity as did many of the outcomes, which Farquhar regarded as wholesale assimilations of missionary Christianity, often grafted unnaturally onto existing Hindu beliefs and practices, which otherwise would have remained unchanged.[10] Farquhar's scathing treatment of aspects of this resurgence, which he believed would impede the progress of Christian mission, make plain that his work was in part a Christian polemic directed against Hinduism. It is undeniable, however, that the historical circumstances that shaped what is now known as the Hindu Renaissance were characterized by a sustained and intensive encounter between a particular segment of Hindu society and European thought, including Christianity. Consequently, the Hindu Renaissance continues to be presented in some studies as a development from Hinduism carried forward by individuals who in many cases, if not Christian in all but name, were profoundly drawn to Christian teaching.

The Indian Christian theologian, M. M. Thomas has referred to the 'acknowledged Christ' of the Indian Renaissance in what remains the standard treatment of this aspect of Hindu thought (1969, p. x). Varying degrees of affinity with Christian belief have been claimed for Raja Rammohun Roy, the founder of the Brahmo Samaj (see below), whose views, together with those of Swami Vivekananda, will be considered in more detail in the forthcoming sections. Like Rammohun Roy, a number of Hindu personalities of this period, and later, Mahatma Gandhi, were known for their close association with individual Christians and Christian organizations. Some of these Hindu leaders and thinkers visited the west

[10] Farquhar insisted that Hinduism lacked the dynamism necessary for change and that the Christian presence in India was thus a necessary and providential agent for modernization. To this extent, he implicitly endorsed an influential thesis propounded by the sociologist, Max Weber (1864–1920), who argued that the growth of Protestantism in western Europe provided a value system conducive to the rise of capitalism and active engagement in the world. Weber's argument, which took no account of the impact of European colonialism, attributed the levels of social and economic development in Asia to the absence of a comparable value system and a religious outlook characterized as 'world negating'.

to meet with religious groups or, as in the case of Gandhi, to study. The Ramakrishna Math and Mission (see below), built on the legacy of Sri Ramakrishna Paramahamsa (c. 1836–86) and Swami Vivekananda, has been described as 'Christianized Hinduism' (Lannoy, 1974, p. 244). Ramakrishna claimed to have experienced directly the presence of Jesus. His disciple, Vivekananda, received his higher education at a Christian foundation in Calcutta and later travelled extensively in the United States, England and Europe. On his return to India, he created a movement dedicated to serving humanity. What is perhaps more telling than evidence of acquaintance with Christians and Christian teaching is the way in which several of these figures drew upon Christian writings, and in some cases adapted Christian models in their forms of worship and social organizations. Consequently, it might be thought not altogether surprising that Chidester (2001, pp. 495–503), in his history of global Christianity includes discussion of the Hindu Renaissance under the overall heading of 'Hindu Christians'. This echoes a view previously expressed in different ways by others writing either from within Christianity or about Christianity and its contact with Hinduism.

Figure 2   Vivekananda in London, 1896. Courtesy of the Vedanta Society of Southern California

Figure 3   Vivekananda in San Francisco, 1900. Courtesy of the Vedanta Society of Southern California

Conflict, coexistence and religious boundaries

It is because of the very complexity of the interaction between Christianity and Hinduism that a study of the Hindu Renaissance has been included in this volume on the themes of religious conflict, conversion and coexistence. This same complexity defies unqualified 'impact of the west' explanations of its outcomes, or explanations that stress the appeal, even if unacknowledged, of Christianity both as a system of ideas and a social edifice. An approach that recognizes the role of 'strategic emulation', however, can help in understanding 'how the [Hindu] assimilation of cultural and political features of the Other [the colonial power] ... occurred under the guise of the reinterpretation of traditional institutions and values' (Jaffrelot, 1996, p. 34). Another way of understanding such a process of selective cultural assimilation and adaptation is to think in terms of 'elective affinities, rather than imitation', where convergences are sought and exploited in order to bolster existing principles or projects (Gupta, 1974, p. 34). This is a more deliberate process than the wider, largely unconscious, unplanned and often uncontrollable process of acculturation (culture change), which inevitably takes place when two cultures are brought into contact. Understanding this cultural process of 'emulation' or 'selection' entails going beyond gathering evidence of the *extent* of exposure to western and Christian influences in order to examine the *significance* of this in shaping the outlook of specific individuals, and the use to which they put motifs found in Christian thinking and other aspects associated with institutionalized Christianity.

The consequences of elements from different religions and cultural sources coming together have been regarded from certain religious and historical viewpoints as threats to the 'authenticity' or 'purity' of the religious tradition in which they coexist. The term 'syncretistic' has frequently been used to refer to systems that are judged to be 'artificial' and 'blended' to the point of losing coherence and thus integrity, rather than to denote a pervasive feature of the historical development of religions.[11] When considering whether there is a point at which expressions of a religious tradition can justifiably be held to be 'inauthentic', members of that religion often speak from their own religious convictions. An important criterion may be derived from assumptions about what constitutes the 'essence' of that religion, possibly related to judgements on originality or uniqueness that mark it out from other world-views (see Stewart and Shaw, 1994). Historians, however, are only too aware that religious traditions and communities constantly change, interacting both with each other and with non-religious

[11] For discussion of the term 'syncretism', see Stewart and Shaw, 1994, and Kraft, 2002.

influences, and that notions of the 'essence' of a religion are thus likely to prove highly problematic. Where formerly separate religions are brought into a relationship of coexistence, however, the defence of religious boundaries may well become a matter of priority for some of the parties involved. Thus, in a context where the coexistence of different elements calls out for resolution, there may be conflict between those who strive to achieve a synthesis and those who resist this. Accordingly, it has been argued that the study of syncretism should be recast as 'the politics of religious synthesis', and that this should be understood in relationship to 'anti-syncretism' (the protection of religious boundaries). Such a method would 'focus on power and agency' and ensure that 'Religious actors are not ... approached as passive victims of historical circumstances, but as intentional beings who choose, select and relate to their habitat' (Kraft, 2002, p. 149).

The encounter between Hinduism and missionary Christianity in nineteenth-century India prompted individuals to consider what constituted the 'essence' of their respective religions and the boundaries they wished to maintain. Raja Rammohun Roy and Swami Vivekananda are now both indissolubly linked to the legacy of the Hindu Renaissance and the history of the city of Calcutta. Rammohun Roy lived at the beginning of the period under discussion and is often characterized as a Hindu 'reformer', whereas Swami Vivekananda lived during what is sometimes described as the 'flowering' of the Hindu Renaissance and has been labelled a 'revivalist'. Rammohun pursued the everyday life of the householder involved in business, although born a brahmin. Vivekananda adopted the life of a *sannyasi* (an ascetic renouncer), as indicated by the title 'Swami'. Both made extensive reference to Christianity. In the remainder of this chapter, we shall examine briefly the ways in which they addressed religious organization and religious authorities and exemplars. We shall adopt a perspective that locates Rammohun and Vivekananda within the fabric of Hinduism and does not claim them as 'tacit' or 'invisible' Christians. Rather than viewing their achievements as the result of a preoccupation with the relationship between Hinduism and Christianity (for example, Chidester, 2001, p. 495), we shall focus instead on their ideas concerning 'universal religion' and factors that were conducive to the promotion of such ideas within the context of India's colonial relationship with Britain.

Religious organization

During the nineteenth century two issues forced Hindus to question the 'established structure of Hinduism': namely, missionary activity and reformism (Zavos, 2000, p. 38). Missionary activity, particularly when directed at the mass conversion of low-caste groups, raised questions about the boundaries of Hinduism and its vulnerability to external pressures. Consequently, there was a growing Hindu preoccupation during this period with *sangathan* (organization) in the spheres of both politics and religion, which we have already noted were intimately linked (ibid.). This was an important change because up until this period 'Hinduism' had typically been practised in a social framework comprising family and caste and, for some, in relationship to a particular religious teacher. Although the latter created loose clusters of devotees, these typically did not achieve the status of distinct religious organizations. The impact of British rule, it has been argued, prompted a 'discourse of organization' among Hindus who became convinced that Hindu society needed to be unified and consolidated to assert itself in political competition with India's Muslim community (ibid., pp. 15–16). In the process, at the level of religious imperatives 'organization came to be seen as an ideal to which Hindus could and should aspire, precisely because they were Hindus' (ibid., p. 15).

This brings us directly to our interest in the movements popularly associated with the Hindu Renaissance, because 'When organization is discussed as a feature of modern Hinduism, it is strongly linked to the reform movements ... and through these, to the influence of Christianity' (ibid., p. 16). Christianity, of course, manifested itself in India through the highly developed and discrete social structures of the 'Church', 'churches' and a whole range of denominational organizations. Consideration of the question of what particular features of Christian organizations, if any, Hindus of this period adapted under the pressures experienced during colonial rule thus cannot be divorced from their political aspirations. It cannot be assumed that such adaptations stemmed directly from a widespread desire by Hindus either to adopt Christian convictions or to use Christian criteria in reformulating Hinduism, although a small minority of individuals did respond to the challenge of Christianity in this way.

Raja Rammohun Roy has been referred to as the 'father' of modern India. His work and the organization he founded in Calcutta, the Brahmo Samaj (Brahman Association), are often taken as marking the beginning of the Hindu Renaissance. More specifically, he has been remembered for his commitment to areas of social reform, and in particular the abolition of *sati* (the immolation of widows), his publication of *The Precepts of Jesus* (1820) and the resultant controversy with the Serampore Baptist missionaries, and the distinctive character of the Brahmo Samaj. The Brahmo Samaj was the first expression of Hinduism 'articulated in modern organizational frameworks' (Zavos, 2000, p. 44).

The antecedent of the Brahmo Samaj was the Brahmo Sabha (Brahman Assembly), an informal organization of like-minded individuals who met on a weekly basis in a private home, which was created in 1828 by Rammohun Roy. This was soon to be followed by a more formal organization whose legal status was enshrined in a trust deed. It had its own building and its affairs were overseen by a board of trustees. Behind

Figure 4   Atul Bose, Rammohun Roy, 1960 after an old likeness, 93 x 56 ins. Photo copyright Victoria Memorial Hall, Kolkata

this phase of the Brahmo movement lay Rammohun's earlier role as a founder of the Calcutta Unitarian Committee in 1822. Another co-founder was William Adam, a former Baptist missionary whose renunciation of his former Trinitarian convictions had been triggered as a result of collaborating with Rammohun in translating the New Testament into Bengali, following the latter's criticism of flaws in two existing translations. The nature of this collaboration and its unforeseen outcome is a further example of the kind of complex interchange of religious influences then taking place in the region of Calcutta. It involved not simply the evolving religious beliefs of prominent individuals from different religious traditions brought more closely together by the discovery of shared convictions, but also the powerful interests of the Baptist Missionary Society and Unitarianism.

The evidence of Rammohun's interactions with Christians of different denominations, his preoccupation with Jesus' teaching, and the 'congregational' appearance of the movement he founded have all been taken as indicators of the extent to which he assimilated Christian influences and teaching. Just as it is difficult, however, to understand the development of Unitarianism in New England without appreciating the earlier dominance of Calvinism, so too the conditions that enabled Unitarianism to take root in Bengal were very different from those that nurtured it in Britain and the United States. It has been suggested, for example, that Unitarians and other Christian groups were attempting to define modernity but in different ways. Whereas Evangelicals put stress on Christian morality, Unitarians emphasized utility and rationality (van der Veer, 2001, p. 7). As these debates touched on India and also took place in India, Indians became participants in this process. At the centre of the East India Company's administration, intellectuals in Calcutta were exposed to the powerful voices of utilitarian and Evangelical interest groups striving to shape the future of their country and its culture. We have to consider, therefore, what a measure of identification with Unitarian principles might have signalled in early nineteenth-century Bengal. This is a point to which we shall return. First, we shall continue to examine Rammohun's creation of a modern, and indeed congregational, organizational structure, which looked so different from the ways in which Hindus had previously arranged their cultic activities.

Faced with the interventionist policies of British administrators and Christian missionaries, as the nineteenth century progressed Hindus began to organize themselves in groups to promote and where necessary to defend their religious, cultural and political interests. At much the same time as Rammohun Roy was in the throes of creating the Brahmo Samaj, a movement of radical, westernizing young intellectuals, which came to be known as Young Bengal (or the 'Derozians' after Henry Derozio, the teacher who inspired it), was sending deep shock waves through the conservative elements of Calcutta's Hindu society. By early 1830, the Dharma Sabha (Dharma Assembly) had been founded in Calcutta to defend Hindu tradition against both external and internal pressures for change. Rammohun's organizational initiative must be understood within this urban setting in which membership of similar groups, created as channels of opinion and public pressure, was fast becoming a feature of the political and professional manoeuvrings of members of the *bhadralok*, and, indeed, something of a fashionable thing to do. In addition, both the ownership of land and property and the registration of associations fell increasingly under new legislative control imposed by the British administration. This also gradually altered the social and legal parameters within which Hindu religious groups established their identity and sought recognition.

Rammohun Roy's determination to change aspects of Hinduism and Hindu society was carried forward by gathering together like-minded individuals on a basis other than caste or a shared teacher or object of devotion. The Brahmo Samaj did appear to owe something of its style to the Christian organizations that Rammohun Roy had encountered, with its congregational services, sermons and singing of specially composed hymns. Open in principle to all regardless of religion, caste and gender, the membership of the Brahmo Samaj remained Hindu and drew largely upon the higher castes.

Just before the end of the nineteenth century, Swami Vivekananda was also responsible for establishing a religious organization, the Ramakrishna Math and Mission. Founded in the name of Vivekananda's *guru*, Sri Ramakrishna Paramahamsa, the organization comprises a monastic wing (the Math) and the Mission, which is open to all. Neither is restricted to Hindus by birth. Vivekananda's decision to adopt the term 'Mission' has prompted debate about the source of the model for this movement. Like the Brahmo Samaj, the Ramakrishna Math and Mission operates as a distinct religious organization within the wider umbrella of Hinduism and has a modern organizational framework. It is still considered part of Hinduism under contemporary Indian law.[12] The Ramakrishna Mission was formed as an 'association' in 1897, and a permanent site was purchased for the Math in the following year at Belur, close to Calcutta. The Math is governed by a deed of trust and the Ramakrishna Mission has a separate legal status, although it is under the authority of the Math, which like the Mission now has many branches.

The temple later built at Belur Math consciously brings together architectural motifs from many religions, including a ground plan in the form of a cross. As we noted earlier, the novel style of this Hindu organization soon prompted claims that it owed much to Christian influence, and its stress upon philanthropy and the organization of monastic life through the ringing of bells led at least one of Vivekananda's brother-disciples to reject this new regime as western and alien to Hinduism. Vivekananda, in fact, would not have denied learning from western styles of organization, although he would have rejected any claim that he was attempting to 'Christianize' Hinduism. In the closing years of a century marked by ongoing contact between Christianity and Hinduism in Calcutta, and with the benefit of extensive, first-hand experience of travelling in the west, Vivekananda was very aware of the benefits of efficient organization. In a letter of 1898, he declared:

> We Indians suffer from a great defect, viz we cannot make a permanent organisation – and the reason is that we never like to share power with others and never think of what will come after we have gone.

> (Vivekananda, 1989, vol. VIII, pp. 456–7)

[12] For discussion of a legal challenge to the Ramakrishna Math and Mission's status as a form of Hinduism, see Beckerlegge, 2000, pp. 61–78.

Indians had to emulate the western capacity for organization because 'The secret of the success of the Westerners is the power of organization and combination' without which nothing could be achieved (Vivekananda, 1989, vol. VIII, p. 328; cf. vol. VI, pp. 301, 476–7). This insight was central to the means that Vivekananda adopted to achieve one of his goals, namely, to 'teach Hindus mutual help' through offering service to those in need (Vivekananda, 1989, vol. V, p. 67). Although some half a century earlier Rammohun Roy had not placed such explicit emphasis upon learning the secret of western-style organization, he had attributed the fall of the Mughal Empire to the self-interest of rulers who had put self-aggrandisement before the leadership of the country (Hay, 1988, p. 18).

When attempting to understand why religious leaders like Rammohun Roy and Swami Vivekananda adapted styles of religious organization reminiscent of those of western Christianity and other elements, such as forms of worship or the vestments worn by priests and ministers, we have to bear in mind the groups with whom they were attempting to communicate, what they wanted to achieve, and the lessons they had taken from their experience of colonial encounter with the British. The emulation of western religious organizations was a means to bring about changes within Hinduism. While addressing Hindus, both were also aware of the support they had received from British and American sympathizers. There was arguably an advantage to be gained from making themselves, and the style of their religious activity, *recognizable* to those familiar with a very different religious tradition, particularly to those in positions of power who had previously been exposed only to negative, stereotyped caricatures of 'popular Hinduism'. The ideas promoted respectively by Rammohun Roy and Swami Vivekananda, however, provoked hostile responses from other Hindus and Christians, both in India and the west.

Religious authority

All the judgements passed on what were undoubtedly novel elements in the ideas and organizations developed by Rammohun Roy and Swami Vivekananda, and their relationship to Hinduism raise, at least implicitly, the questions of what constitute the boundaries of Hinduism and how far these can be modified before becoming something else. Hindus schooled in their own philosophical and textual traditions had long pointed to acceptance of the Veda, an authoritative collective of ancient texts, as a feature that distinguished them from other thinkers who refused to be bound by this and its forms of argument (for example, see Young, 1981, p. 149). During the nineteenth century, when Hindus felt vulnerable to the impact of British rule and the presence of other religions, questions relating to the boundaries, organization and 'membership' of Hinduism took on a fresh significance. It was perhaps inevitable, therefore, that several of the prominent Hindus who addressed this challenge were themselves judged to have gone beyond the bounds of what others held to be 'traditional' Hinduism. One way in which to explore this tension further is to consider what authorities Rammohun Roy and Swami Vivekananda recognized and how they used them.

Rammohun Roy declared in a letter of 1824, 'I presume to think, that Christianity, if properly inculcated, has a greater tendency to improve the moral, and political state of mankind, than any other known religious system' (quoted in Richards, 1985, p. 9). This followed on the publication of *The Precepts of Jesus* (1820) in which Rammohun Roy took selected passages of the New Testament as the basis for moral guidance. Rammohun Roy, however, did not look unconditionally to Jesus as an authority and far less to the representatives of organized Christianity, although reflections on Jesus are more extensive in his writings than in those of Brahmos who made common cause with Christian groups in matters relating more exclusively to social reform. Rammohun's attempt to separate moral principles from 'the other matters contained in the New Testament', that is, its theology and supernatural claims, brought him into heated disagreement with the Baptist missionary Joshua Marshman. A key to understanding Rammohun Roy's position is to be found in 'two criteria which he applied throughout his writings ... He maintained that the canons of reason demanded universalism and freedom from contradiction of all religious statements' (Pankratz, 1998, p. 337). These were the same principles he applied to Hinduism in an earlier pamphlet written in Persian, *Tuhfat al Muwahhidin* (translated as 'A Gift to Deists'), in 1803–4. In this early work, Rammohun argued on the basis of his travels and observations that there is a general agreement about the existence of a 'supreme superintending power' and that human beings come to this recognition 'naturally'. Disagreements occur over the ways in which this Being is characterized, which Rammohun attributed to human error and falsehood. He held that there was no rational basis for exempting any religion from this judgement, and he rejected special pleading as being contrary to reason. His belief in an underlying Supreme Power behind all religions made him critical of religious leaders and convinced him that blind religious dogmatism lay behind social abuses. It also led him to prize religious tolerance and to value what could be learned from different religions (Robertson, 1995, p. 29). If one considers Rammohun's statements about Christianity in the light of his appeal to reason and notion of 'natural religion', the full implications of his dismissal of 'the other matters contained in the New Testament' become apparent. The truth that Rammohun recognized in Christian moral teaching was, according to his understanding, a powerful presentation of the universal truth contained in all religions, revealed and concealed in different ways.

While Rammohun declared the precepts taught by Jesus to be 'sublime', he also held that the truths of Christianity had been 'kept hidden under a veil of heathen doctrines and practices' introduced progressively by Jesus' followers (quoted in Richards, 1985, p. 9). Thus, although he held to the view that the propagation of Christian morality would be a powerful force for good in India, he did not identify this with what missionaries were actually offering to Hindus. As we have seen, Rammohun's appreciation of the 'essence' of Christianity demanded that its ethical teaching be stripped of Trinitarian theology and supernaturalism. His universalist convictions encouraged him to believe that all sincere religious activity was acceptable to God. When questioned whether Hindus should be converted to Christianity, his response was somewhat equivocal, but he hinted that he would have responded more positively if only Christianity could be 'properly inculcated'. He was openly critical of the methods of Christian missionaries even though he respected some as individuals.

The details of Rammohun's early life are sketchy, but it is generally assumed that his knowledge of European thought, including Christianity, deepened only after he had taken up residence in Calcutta in 1815. It is for this reason that the sources of his rationalist and universalist beliefs are attributed primarily to his own religious temperament and earlier exposure to Hinduism, Islam, Buddhism and Sikhism. His commitment to the abolition of *sati* is similarly said to have anticipated British initiatives (Crawford, 1992, p. 17). The kinds of arguments advanced by missionaries who were critical of Rammohun's version of Christian teaching and the nature of the wider missionary propaganda directed against Hinduism suggest that Rammohun would not have looked to the west as the repository of rationalism (Sarkar, 1997, p. 171). The alliance he made with Unitarians in Calcutta and his participation in a Unitarian association are most likely to have been motivated by his sense that Unitarians shared rationalist and universalist principles similar to his own and were committed to ridding Christianity of its 'heathen' supernaturalism and Trinitarian theology. If one had to categorize Rammohun's belief, there are good grounds for describing him as a 'universalist' (Lavan, 1977, p. 52).

Having subjected Hinduism to close scrutiny, Rammohun maintained that 'some changes should take place in their [Hindus'] religion, at least for the sake of their political advantage and social comfort' (quoted in Richards, 1985, p. 9). In particular, he was convinced that caste divisions, related ideas of status and elaborate ritual purifications had to be swept away, but he did not concede that Hindu 'vices' were any worse than those found in the Christian west. His arguments rested heavily on portions of the Veda categorized as *Upanishads*, speculative treatises of an often esoteric and mystical nature. It was upon these texts, together with an influential commentary upon them, the *Brahma Sutra* or *Vedanta Sutra*, that several schools of Hindu religious philosophy were later built. Rammohun identified himself with one of the most influential of these schools, Advaita Vedanta, acknowledging the authority of its

teacher, Shankara (c. eighth century).[13] He also referred to a traditional
'canon' of texts, which, in addition to the *Upanishad*s and the *Brahma
Sutra* on which he relied heavily, also included the *Bhagavadgita*, which
was of less importance to him.[14] Rammohun, nevertheless, stopped short
of acknowledging unreservedly the divine authority of the Veda (or the
sacred text of any other religion) and questioned its teachings where
these ran contrary to reason, which was his constant external criterion in
all matters relating to religion.

Rammohun undoubtedly adapted ancient Hindu sources and Advaita
Vedanta in the light of his own needs, but his style of argument 'defined
the essence of the tradition in terms of the philosophical religious texts
rather than the sectarian literature. In so doing he provided a
hermeneutical tool for a discriminating understanding of the Hindu
tradition and a rigorous response to the Christian tradition' (Pankratz,
1995, p. 339). If Rammohun's commitment to the promotion of a rational
and universalistic religious outlook and his desire to reform aspects of
Hindu society led him to forge close links with Unitarians, his creation of
the Brahmo Samaj was a declaration of the limits of that partnership and
of their common interests. Some scholars have observed that Rammohun
took a strongly utilitarian view of religion, judging it in terms of its
capacity to improve human and social conditions. It is evident that this is
precisely what he did in his examination of Christian moral teaching.

Rammohun Roy responded as a rationalist to the presence of Christianity
in the colonial setting. Swami Vivekananda's approach reflected his role
as a *sannyasi*. Even though, as we have noted, Vivekananda's
organization of the Ramakrishna Math and Mission suggests the
assimilation and adaptation of features found in institutionalized
Christianity, both solitary and communal asceticism had a long history in
Hindu India. Active during the period when opposition to British rule in
India was beginning to harden, Vivekananda's observations on
institutionalized, missionary Christianity were more bitter and cynical
than those of the earlier Rammohun Roy, and he queried both the
motives of missionaries and their right to bring anything beyond
technical and material help to India. Yet he, too, made frequent reference
to Jesus and Christian texts.

For Vivekananda (1989, vol. VII, p. 29), 'Christ and Buddha were names
of states to be attained'. This brief statement encapsulates his respect for

---

[13] Advaita Vedanta posits the identity (*advaita* – 'non-duality') of Brahman (the
unified reality that is the pervasive source and ground of everything) and *atman*
('self', the ultimate essence of the human being). Full knowledge of this, often
concealed by the phenomenal world, is held to be the goal of human existence and
the key to all perfect knowledge and action.

[14] In fact, the *Bhagavadgita*'s importance increased considerably in the latter half of
the nineteenth century and subsequently after its teaching had been given an activist
and nationalist reading. This shift was reflected, for example, in the use Vivekananda
made of this text.

the great teachers of many religions who he believed to be revealers of a universal truth, as had Rammohun Roy. Because of the comprehensive nature of the vision of this truth, they stand as exemplars on whom human beings should model themselves in order to achieve the same level of spiritual realization, but 'the names do not make much difference' (Vivekananda, 1997, p. 121). Accordingly, Vivekananda regularly referred to Jesus with respect and even in terms of adoration throughout his letters and lectures, but as one of 'The divine ones of God [who] are all my Masters. I learn of your Christ in learning of Krishna, of Buddha, in learning of Mohamet' (Burke, 1994, p. 155). Vivekananda thus cast his net wide and far beyond exclusive reference to his own master when drawing upon exemplars. Similarly, he cited a wide range of religious authorities, including the *Upanishad*s and *Bhagavadgita*. As must already be apparent, however, Vivekananda's understanding of the significance and role of Jesus was very different from that generally shared by declared Christians. Jesus had been assimilated within Vivekananda's own theory of an emergent universal religion, which owed much to Hindu assumptions, in spite of claiming to break free from the cultural forms of specific, historical traditions. Vivekananda (1989, vol. I, p. 3) hailed Hinduism as 'the mother of religions' and declared that 'Our first principle is that all that is necessary for the perfection of man and for attaining unto freedom is there in the Vedas. You cannot find anything new' (Vivekananda, 1989, vol. III, p. 250). Unlike religions that 'preach' personalities, Vivekananda claimed that the 'universal religion' can only be founded upon principles, rather than specific teachers, and traced such principles to the Veda and the Advaita Vedanta tradition of philosophy derived from this source.

It may seem at this point as though Vivekananda simply trod the same path as Rammohun Roy, appealing to the traditional philosophical school of Advaita Vedanta in support of his commitment to universal truths only partly revealed by the different religions. Rammohun Roy, however, drew upon Christian authorities and looked to Christian groups for support because he believed that Christian ethical teaching provided a powerful lever to exert pressure for social change. Vivekananda, on the other hand, portrayed Jesus primarily as an embodiment of the ideal of physical renunciation rather than as an agent for social change. Jesus 'was a Sannyasin, and his religion is essentially fit for Sannyasins only'. His teachings may be summed up as: '"Give up"; nothing more – being for the favoured few' (Vivekananda, 1989, vol. VI, p. 109). On this basis, Jesus was added to the list of paradigms that Vivekananda placed before the Indian people in order to encourage renunciation and the resultant selfless action necessary for India's spiritual and material development, which he believed could only be brought about by Indians. Emphasis upon sin and the consequent necessity of salvation was totally absent. Vivekananda followed the tradition of Advaita Vedanta in attributing human failings to the existential condition of *avidya* (lack of understanding about the true nature of reality and its ultimate identity), the source of selfish action. Accordingly, he drew upon passages from Christian texts that he believed were consistent with his version of non-dualist, Advaita philosophy. He favoured passages from the prologue to St John's Gospel, which refer to the Word being 'with God' (for example, Vivekananda, 1989, vol. VII, p. 3), and verses that record Jesus referring to his 'oneness' with God, the Father (for example, Vivekananda, 1989, vol. I, p. 322). Working from the same principles, Vivekananda was attracted to St Thomas à Kempis' *Imitation of Christ* to such an extent that he translated it into Bengali for publication. To his surprise, what he found in this Christian classic were qualities that matched the *vairagya* (renunciation) and *bhakti* (devotion) commended in the Hindu tradition (Vivekananda, 1989, vol. VI, p. 209).

It could be argued that Vivekananda's awareness of the extent of his own indebtedness led him to minimize his acknowledgement of Christian influence. His relationship to his own spiritual teacher, Ramakrishna, and his desire to assert at least the parity of Hinduism with Christianity, if not its supremacy, were probably more fundamental factors. Ramakrishna's insights flowed from altered states of consciousness experienced in his relentless quest for 'God-realization'. The record of his teaching is taken from discourses with his followers, usually prompted by their questions, and thus is spontaneous and vivid rather than systematic. In any case, Ramakrishna's charisma rested on his followers' belief that he had experienced directly the things of which he spoke. Enduring images used by Ramakrishna to explain the relationship between different religious insights refer to 'paths' up the same 'mountain' or the same 'water' known under different names and gathered in 'pots' of different styles. A rustic sage, much of Ramakrishna's experience was narrowly confined to schools of thought within Hinduism, but he was well aware of the presence of Islam and Christianity in his region and he included these traditions when exploiting this imagery. In so doing, Ramakrishna was extending insights found earlier in the Veda where it was said that the 'wise' knew that there was but one reality behind the names of the deities. It was this kind of admission, coupled with the absence of clear institutional boundaries to Hinduism and the long experience of coexistence with other religions, including those of conquerors, that gave rise to the Hindu capacity for inclusivism, which was referred to at the outset of this chapter as a further obstacle to the advance of Christian mission in India. Vivekananda's acceptance of Jesus as a *sannyasi* and of a Christian message characterized by renunciation and devotion is but another example of this at work.

As a recipient of a European-style education in Calcutta, Vivekananda found that his acquaintance with the popular application of Darwin's theory of evolution to social developments enabled him to transform the inclusivist understanding of the relationship between different religious perspectives, which had been so powerfully reinforced by Ramakrishna. Religions, still seen as paths leading individuals of different temperaments to the same goal, although at different rates, are

Figure 5   Mrs Eugene (Theodosia) Oliver, Jesus as a Yogi, 1908. Courtesy of The Vedanta Society of Southern California

themselves seen to be at various stages of development, with certain strands within them displaying higher levels of spiritual insight. Vivekananda's theory, therefore, anticipates a convergence between those elements of different religions at the highest level, revealing the previously hidden 'universal religion'. Vivekananda believed that this was to be seen most fully in the Advaita Vedanta tradition of Hinduism because of its stress upon the essential identity of the human 'self' with ultimate reality. He similarly reinterpreted this ancient affirmation of the identity of being to draw from it an ethical imperative, namely, that to serve another is in reality to serve one's 'self' because the same ultimate reality pervades and unites all beings. The Ramakrishna Mission was brought into being primarily to institutionalize this ideal.

Vivekananda relativized and subordinated cultural and historical differences, arguing that truth was to be found at the level of convergence and not in the differences that historically have lent distinctiveness to, and some would claim have defined the 'essence' of, religious traditions. This theory not only enabled him to assimilate Christianity within his brand of Hinduism but also provided the basis for a vigorous and at times aggressive defence of Hinduism in the face of Christian criticism. Once in the west, Vivekananda presented himself as a cultural and spiritual mediator who wished to facilitate an exchange between western technological and scientific knowledge and eastern spirituality between partners – not rulers and ruled.

Conclusion

The nature of Hinduism at the time of India's intensive interaction with the west during the nineteenth century make it inappropriate to categorize the changes in the beliefs of individuals such as Rammohun Roy and Swami Vivekananda as in any sense examples of 'conversion'. As this chapter has noted, the number of Hindus at that time who formally embraced membership of an institutionalized form of Christianity was very small. Nor were Rammohun and Vivekananda and others like them, who clearly were influenced by their encounter with Christianity, 'tacit Christians' or 'Hindu Christians'. Instead, this chapter has argued, their reinterpretations of their own tradition can best be understood as examples of 'strategic emulation' or the exploitation of 'elective affinities' by individuals compelled to reconsider the boundaries and core of their religion. Their reformulations of Hinduism were shaped to a significant extent by the distinctive social and political context of nineteenth-century Calcutta and the pressures of ongoing and pervasive acculturation. The selective use they made of Christianity was to a significant degree instrumental to fulfilling this need. Vivekananda's redefinition of Hinduism, in particular, could be classed as a form of 'resistance identity' (Castells, 1997, p. 8).[15]

[15] See also pp. 273, 276–81 below.

For individuals of the standing and education of Rammohun Roy and Swami Vivekananda living in a metropolitan centre like Calcutta, exposure to western and Christian influence was unavoidable. Keenly aware of social injustices within Hindu society that called out for redress, they were determined to define the place of India and Hinduism in a transformed world order. Their theories of religious universalism were different but based in common upon reworkings of the ancient Advaita Vedanta system. The development of these religious philosophies enabled them simultaneously to assert the value of the truths they found at the heart of Hinduism while not being bound by its cultural particulars or even its traditional authorities. Selectively assimilating elements from their exposure to the west and its dominant religion, these same philosophies enabled them to question claims made for the exclusivity and supremacy of Christian gospel and thus the need for Christian mission to India. This stance could easily have been adapted to fend off the challenge of another religion. The universalizing of tradition, in effect, 'pre-empted the need for any exchange' and India's 'inclusivism' could become 'the means of denying the need for any dialogue' (Copley, 1997, p. 57). When linked to interpretations that drew ethical implications from Advaita Vedanta, the sentiments of religious universalism inspired new kinds of Hindu religious organizations that were no longer confined to those born into Hinduism and in which organized philanthropic activity was given greater value than previously accorded within Hinduism.

The point was made at the outset that the religious movements associated with the Hindu Renaissance and its legacy have been untypical of recent Hinduism when taken as a whole. For many scholars, the movements associated with the Hindu Renaissance remain peripheral in relationship to the mainstream Hindu religious tradition, largely because of the limited nature of their following and the degree of their openness to western influence (for example, Smith, 2003, p. 208, n.8). Indeed, as we noted, some have questioned whether they can be treated as 'authentic' forms of Hinduism. Even while conceding that these movements are not representative, few Hindus have denied their place within the wider Hindu religious tradition. The priority these movements have given to philanthropic action has now been matched by many other popular Hindu sectarian organizations, which have also been established along the lines of the modern organization frameworks discussed in this chapter. The affirmation of the validity of all religious paths has become commonplace in more recent Hindu discourse and it exercises a lingering influence over the ideals of Indian secularism that are now under such pressure from the Hindu right. The questioning of the legitimacy of foreign missionary activity and the purpose of conversion between religions, and the affirmation of the value of the 'essence' of Hinduism, continued to be echoed during the closing days of the British Raj, for example, by Gandhi. This has been put to fresh use in recent years by Hindu nationalists in an India where Christians, and other religious communities, have to negotiate their place in the context of the politics of caste, Islamism and the Hindutva ideology of the Hindu right.

Beyond India, some of the distinctive motifs in the Renaissance reworkings of Hinduism have been channelled through the medium of organizations such as the Theosophical Society into the current of ideas that have coalesced in popular 'New Age' thinking in Europe and the United States.[16] Rammohun Roy and Swami Vivekananda contributed to the creation of modern, or neo-Vedantic thought, which has been absorbed into alternative forms of western spirituality. Swami Vivekananda's philosophy, more specifically, has influenced the popularization of yoga in Europe and the United States and writers and intellectuals, such as Romain Rolland, Aldous Huxley and Christopher Isherwood. Presented as a form of 'perennial philosophy' or universal religion by Huxley and Isherwood, modern Vedantic thought made an impact on the 'beat generation' that shaped American counter-culture in the 1950s and subsequently.[17] Today, as in the nineteenth century, the beliefs that characterized the universalist dimension of Hindu Renaissance thinking have appealed to those who have rejected what has generally passed for religious 'orthodoxy', whether in India or the west.

References

Beckerlegge, G. (1997) 'Professor Friedrich Max Müller and the missionary cause' in J. Wolffe (ed.) *Religion in Victorian Britain*, vol. V: *Culture and Empire*, Manchester and New York, Manchester University Press in association with The Open University.

Beckerlegge, G. (2000) *The Ramakrishna Mission: The Making of a Modern Hindu Movement*, New Delhi, Oxford University Press.

Beckerlegge, G. (2001) 'Hindu sacred images for the mass market' in G. Beckerlegge (ed.) *From Sacred Text to Internet*, Aldershot, Ashgate in association with The Open University.

Beckerlegge, G. (forthcoming) 'The early spread of Vedanta societies: an example of "imported localism"', in *Numen*.

Bharati, A. (1970) 'The Hindu Renaissance and its apologetic patterns', *Journal of Asian Studies*, vol. 29, no. 2, February, pp. 267–87.

[16] The term 'New Age' is popularly applied to a late twentieth-century cultural trend that drew together elements from different religions and cultural sources in exploring the relationship between mind, body and spirit. Mysticism, wholistic medicine and astrology have been important contributors. See, for example, De Michaelis (2004) and Beckerlegge (forthcoming).

[17] See Beckerlegge, 2000, for discussion of the interest shown by Rolland, Huxley and Isherwood in Vivekananda.

Burke, M. L. (1994) *Swami Vivekananda in the West: New Discoveries, His Prophetic Mission*, Part 2, 4th edn, Calcutta, Advaita Ashrama.

Castells, M. (1997) *The Power of Identity*, Oxford, Blackwell.

Chaudhuri, S. (ed.) (1990) *Calcutta*, vol. 1, Delhi, Oxford University Press.

Chidester, D. (2001) *Christianity: A Global History*, Harmondsworth, Penguin.

Copley, A. (1997) *Religions in Conflict: Ideology, Cultural Contact and Conversion in Late-colonial India*, Delhi, Oxford University Press.

Crawford, S. C. (1992) *Ram Mohun Roy: Social, Political and Religious Reform in 19th Century India*, New York, Paragon House Publishers.

De Michaelis, E. (2004) *A History of Modern Yoga: Patanjali and Western Esotericism*, London, Continuum.

Farquhar, J. N. (1967) *Modern Religious Movements in India*, Delhi, Munshiram Manoharlal.

Gupta, K. P. (1974) 'Religious evolution and social change in India: a study of the Ramakrishna Mission movement', *Contributions to Indian Sociology*, no. 8, pp. 25–50.

Haldar, M. K. (1977) 'Introduction' in B. K. Chattopadhyay, *Renaissance and Reaction in Nineteenth-Century Bengal* (trans. with an introduction by M. K. Halder), Calcutta, South Asia Books.

Hay, S. (ed.) (1988) *Sources of Indian Tradition*, vol.2, New York, Columbia University Press.

Jaffrelot, C. (1996) *The Hindu Nationalist Movement and Indian Politics, 1925 to the 1990s*, London, Hurst & Company.

*Kopf, D. (1979) *The Brahmo Samaj and the Shaping of the Modern Indian Mind*, Princeton, Princeton University Press.

Kraft, S. E. (2002) '"To mix or not to mix": syncretism and anti-syncretism in the history of theosophy', *Numen*, vol. 49, no. 2, pp. 142–77.

Lannoy, R. (1974) *The Speaking Tree*, Oxford, Oxford University Press.

Latourette, K. S. (1971) *A History of the Expansion of Christianity*, vol. 6, *The Great Century: North Africa and Asia, 1800–1914 AD*, Exeter, Paternoster Press.

Lavan, S. (1977) *Unitarians and India: A Study in Encounter and Response*, Boston, MA, Beacon Press.

Marshall, P. J. (1987) *The New Cambridge History of India*, vol. II, *Bengal: The British Bridgehead, Eastern India 1740–1828*, Cambridge, Cambridge University Press.

Neill, S. (1964) *A History of Christian Missions: The Pelican History of the Church*, vol. 6, Harmondsworth, Penguin.

*Pankratz, J. N. (1998) 'Rammohun Roy' in R. Baird (ed.) *Religion in Modern India*, 3rd rev. edn, New Delhi, Manohar, pp. 335–49.

Poddar, A. (1970) *Renaissance in Bengal: Quests and Confrontations, 1800–1860*, Simla, Indian Institute of Advanced Study.

Redfield, R. and Singer, M. (1954) 'The cultural role of cities' in *Economic Development and Cultural Change*, vol. 3, part. 1, pp. 53–73.

Richards, G. (ed.) (1985) *A Source-book of Modern Hinduism*, Richmond, Curzon.

Robertson, B. C. (1995) *Raja Rammohun Roy The Father of Modern India*, New Delhi, Oxford University Press.

Sarkar, S. (1993) *An Exploration of the Ramakrishna Vivekananda Tradition*, Shimla, Indian Institute of Advanced Study.

Sarkar, S. (1997) *Writing Social History*, New Delhi, Oxford University Press.

Sarma, D. S. (1973) *Hinduism Through the Ages*, Bombay, Bharatiya Vidya Bhavan.

Sen, A. P. (ed.) (2003) *Social and Religious Reform: The Hindus of British India*, New Delhi, Oxford University Press.

Sharma, A. (1977) 'The place of conversion in Hinduism', *Contributions to Indian Sociology*, vol. 11, no. 2, pp. 345–54.

Smith, D. (2003) *Hinduism and Modernity*, Oxford, Blackwell Publishing.

Spear, P. (1970) *A History of India*, vol. II, Harmondsworth, Penguin.

Stanley, B. (2002) *The History of the Baptist Missionary Movement, 1792–1992*, Edinburgh, T. & T. Clark.

Stein, B. (1998) *A History of India*, Oxford, Blackwell Publishers.

*Stewart, C. and Shaw, R. (1994) 'Introduction: problematizing syncretism' in C. Stewart and R. Shaw *Syncretism/Anti-syncretism: The Politics of Religious Synthesis*, London and New York, Routledge, pp. 1–26.

Thomas, M. M. (1969) *The Acknowledged Christ of the Indian Renaissance*, London, SCM Press.

Thomas, T. (1997) 'Foreign missions and missionaries in Victorian Britain' in J. Wolffe (ed.) *Religion in Victorian Britain*, vol. V: *Culture and Empire*, Manchester and New York, Manchester University Press in association with The Open University.

van der Veer, P. (2001) *Imperial Encounters: Religion and Modernity in India and Britain*, Princeton and Oxford, Princeton University Press.

(Swami) Vivekananda (1989) *The Complete Works of Swami Vivekananda*, Mayati Memorial Edition, 8 vols, Calcutta, Advaita Ashrama.

(Swami) Vivekananda (1997) *The Complete Works of Swami Vivekananda*, vol. 9, Calcutta, Advaita Ashrama.

Young, R. F. (1981) *Resistant Hinduism: Sanskrit Sources on Anti-Christian Apologetics in Early Nineteenth-century India*, Vienna, Indological Institute, University of Vienna.

*Zavos, J. (2000) *The Emergence of Hindu Nationalism in India*, New Delhi, Oxford University Press.

Asterisked items are particularly recommended for further reading.

6   How the times they were a-changing: exploring the context of religious transformation in Britain in the 1960s

Gerald Parsons

Introduction

In early 2001, a book was published with the provocative title *The Death of Christian Britain*. Written by Callum Brown, a historian then at the University of Strathclyde (and now at the University of Dundee), and building on over two decades of his work on the social history of religion in modern Britain, the book offered a bold reinterpretation of the history of the 'secularization' of British society and culture. At the same time it also presented an equally bold challenge to the predominance of theories of secularization derived from the social sciences in which the phenomenon is conceived as a long, slow process resulting – perhaps inevitably – from the impact of industrialization and modernization.

Instead of such conventional accounts of a long and slow decline of religious belief and practice in modern Britain, Brown proposed that the highly secularized society that became a characteristic and defining feature of British life and culture during the last quarter of the twentieth century was the result of a 'catastrophic and abrupt cultural revolution' during the 1960s. It was at this time that Britain's historic 'core religious and moral identity' was destroyed, profoundly rupturing the character of the nation and its people and sending organized Christianity into a spiral of decline that has taken it to the margins of social significance. More specifically, Brown argued that, quite suddenly, in the 1960s, the traditional cycle of inter-generational renewal of Christian affiliation and identity – which held British people, however loosely, to the churches and to Christian moral benchmarks – was drastically, indeed catastrophically, disrupted. Quite suddenly, and in unprecedented numbers, the British stopped going to church, marrying in church and having their children baptized, and forsook organized Christianity for 'a truly secular condition' (Brown, 2001, p. 1).[1]

---

[1] Brown therefore also emphasizes the importance of the impact of youth and pop culture in the 1960s, thus prompting the echo, in the title of this chapter, of the lyrics of one of Bob Dylan's songs that helped to define the ethos of that decade.

Brown also proposed a boldly revisionist explanation of the principal cause of the catastrophic disruption of Britain's core religious culture that occurred in the 1960s. During the nineteenth century, he argued, Britain was, in fact, a deeply Christian country characterized by high levels of churchgoing and strict religious rules of personal conduct. At the heart of this highly pervasive 'puritanism', he maintained, lay an 'evangelicalism which constructed a highly gendered conception of religiosity'. Modern Evangelicalism, Brown argued, conceived of piety as 'an overwhelmingly feminine trait', emphasizing and extolling the perceived religious role and significance of women, especially in moral matters, in contrast to the perceived moral weakness of men. Sustained by a variety of means, from tracts and sermons to obituaries, magazines and novels, this version of Christianity informed the self-understanding and personal identity of very high numbers of both men and women – though it was women who were 'the bulwark of popular support for organised Christianity' – not only in the nineteenth century, but also during the first six decades of the twentieth century. In the 1960s, however, the sexual revolution and the increasing prominence and influence of feminism prompted the collapse of this religious and moral world-view as women, especially, 'broke their relationship to Christian piety' (Brown, 2001, especially pp. 8–10, 175–80).

This chapter will examine three main aspects of the debate which has been prompted by Callum Brown's thesis in *The Death of Christian Britain*. First, it will briefly review the evidence for the sheer scale and reality of secularization and religious decline in Britain since the 1960s. Second, it will examine the historical context of the late twentieth-century collapse of the traditional Christian culture of England, Scotland and Wales,[2] exploring the extent to which the apparent strength of the 'core religious culture' that collapsed so spectacularly in, during and after the 1960s may have been more illusory than real. Third, it will ask how far the impact of feminism and the sexual revolution upon religion in Britain was in fact part of a much wider process of religious transformation in late twentieth-century Britain, in which new conflicts arose within the Christian churches, whilst an increasingly diverse variety of religious traditions and alternative and eclectic spiritualities coexisted side by side. Finally, a brief conclusion will consider how the debate about *The Death of Christian Britain* relates to the themes of conflict, conversion and coexistence upon which this volume is focused. It will explore, in particular, the extent to which, in the last four decades of the twentieth century, Britain proved a striking example of the occurrence of significant religious transformation within a context characterized

---

[2] In *The Death of Christian Britain*, Brown specifically excludes Northern Ireland from his analysis (Brown, 2001, pp. 1 and 199). In engaging with Brown's thesis, this chapter follows this precedent. For discussions of the significantly different circumstances of Northern Ireland and the much greater resilience of the 'core religious cultures' there see, for example, Davie, 1994, pp. 97–100; Bruce, 1995, pp. 60–4.

predominantly by patterns of coexistence and without sustained or overt conflict.[3]

When hell disappeared: the 1960s and the 'death of Christian Britain'

Whatever the debates about his interpretation and explanation of the process, it is unlikely that anyone will seriously disagree with Callum Brown's proposition that the 1960s witnessed the beginning of a catastrophic collapse in traditional patterns of religious commitment and participation in England, Scotland and Wales.[4] As Brown emphasizes, according to a variety of statistical indicators of religious practice and allegiance in Britain, after a peak of participation in church adherence in 1904 in England and Wales and in 1905 in Scotland, there then followed a period of relative decline during the next four decades, followed in turn by a modest but clear revival in the figures during the early 1950s. From 1956, however, the statistical indicators again began to decline, and from 1963 onwards they entered into a period of drastic decline which verged upon a state of free fall (Brown, 2001, pp. 6–7, 188). After a decade of catastrophic decrease, the rate of decline slowed again, but decline continued through the 1970s, 1980s and 1990s.

Moreover, the reality of decline was evident across a wide variety of activities and indicators. Thus, not only did the figures for church attendance – measured as a proportion of the population who attended church on a particular Sunday – decline, but so did the number of people regularly involved in active participation in the life and worship of particular Christian churches and denominations (Bruce, 2001, pp. 194–8; 2002a, pp. 63–7). Similarly, the numbers of marriages religiously solemnized in England, Wales and Scotland fell slowly in the first six decades of the twentieth century and dramatically from the 1960s onwards, a pattern that was also evident in the figures for baptisms and confirmations in the Church of England (Brown, 2001, pp. 6–7, 191; Bruce, 2001, pp. 199–200). The decline in the institution of the Sunday School – which had once occupied a key place within the Christian culture of Britain, through the dissemination to children of at least an

---

[3] Callum Brown's further reflections on the implications of his thesis concerning the 'death of Christian Britain' for issues of method and approach in the study of the social history of religion, and for the definition of 'what religion is' in both scholarship and contemporary discussion may be found in Brown, 2003.

[4] Among historians, for example, Adrian Hastings had similarly identified the 1960s as the watershed of statistical decline in indicators of participation in English Christianity (Hastings, 1991, pp. 551–2, 602–3), whilst Hugh McLeod has drawn attention to the way in which historians are increasingly focusing on the 1960s as a moment of crucial and possibly decisive change (McLeod, 2001; 2003, pp. 18–19).

elementary knowledge of Christian beliefs – was even more dramatic. In 1900, 55 per cent of British children were thus introduced to Christianity. By 1960, this had already declined to only 24 per cent, by 1980 it had fallen to 9 per cent, and by 2000 to just 4 per cent (Bruce, 2001, p. 198; 2002a, pp. 68–9; Brown, 2001, p. 188). It is true that the figures for church attendance and participation remain stronger in both Wales and – even more so – in Scotland than they do in England, where the statistics of decline are the most dramatic (Davie, 1994, pp. 47, 50). Even in Wales and Scotland, however, the trends from the 1960s onwards were, and remain, stubbornly and dramatically downwards (Morgan, 1999, pp. 251–4, 264–6, 275; Brown, 1997, pp. 159–60; Field, 2001).

The pivotal significance of the 1960s is revealed even more clearly if the example of the Roman Catholic Church in Britain is given more prominence than in Callum Brown's own analysis. Brown does not omit the Catholic case entirely from his survey, but he gives it little attention because of his emphasis upon the Evangelicalism that underpinned a particular religious narrative from 1800 onwards. Yet the impact of the cultural revolution of the 1960s upon Roman Catholicism strongly supports Brown's central contention that it was this decade that marked a crucial watershed in the decline of traditional British Christianity and the secularization of British society.

Until the 1960s, British Roman Catholicism was distinguished by its strongly exclusive fortress mentality, and its maintenance of a Catholic community and sub-culture sharply distinct from the rest of British society. With the dramatic re-orientation and opening up of the Catholic Church during the Second Vatican Council between 1962 and 1965, however, Roman Catholicism in Britain began to move into the ecumenical mainstream of British Christianity – a process that has continued until the present, despite the conservative influence of Pope John Paul II. The cardinals and bishops of the English and Scottish Catholic churches now enjoy a cultural prominence among spokespersons for the Christian community that is arguably equal to any other clerical figurehead and more prestigious than many. But the transition from exclusivity to participation in the broader Christian community of Britain was by no means the only legacy of the 1960s as far as British Roman Catholicism was concerned. The 1960s was also the decade in which the various statistics of growth and active participation in the British Catholic community first began to stall, before then beginning to decline – less sharply, certainly, than in other churches, but moving into a downward trend nonetheless (Hastings, 1991, pp. xxii–v, 580, 631–4; Hornsby-Smith, 1987, esp. pp. 208–14; 1989, esp. pp. 2–4, 38–42; 1992, pp. 123–30; Gill, 1993, pp. 209–10; Parsons, 1993a, pp. 31–55; Davie, 1994, pp. 46, 57–8). Catholics, as it was famously said, became just like everyone else – and as they did so they also began to share the experience of decline with the other major Christian churches in Britain.[5]

Moreover, at the heart of the processes of change within Roman Catholicism lay the crisis over the issue of birth control and the papal encyclical *Humanae Vitae* of 1968. It was the collision between personal sexual morality and ecclesiastical authority – located historically precisely in the context of the sexual revolution of the 1960s – that marked the moment at which, as David Lodge put it in his novel *How Far Can You Go?*, for many ordinary Catholics 'hell disappeared' and they increasingly began to choose for themselves in matters of morality and religion, rather than accepting the Catholic culture in which they had grown up (Lodge, 1980, esp. pp. 113–27; Parsons, 1992). Some of Lodge's characters in *How Far Can You Go?* remained within Catholicism, others moved away into new religious commitments or none at all – but even those who remained within their church exhibited a new propensity for the exercise of personal choice in matters of belief and morality. In this, moreover, Lodge's characters faithfully reflected trends in the actual Roman Catholic community. As Michael Hornsby-Smith has shown, many Catholics now manifest an apparently paradoxical ability to admire a strongly authoritarian Pope whilst insisting on the right to reserve substantial areas of moral judgement – particularly in matters of sexual morality – to themselves (Hornsby-Smith, 1991, esp. pp. 138–9; 1992, pp. 130–4, 140). But as Grace Davie has observed,

> the tendency to bracket out certain aspects of [a church's] teaching is, however, far more damaging than is sometimes realised, in that it becomes an ongoing process. If some formulations can be bracketed out for particular reasons, so too can others – the slippery slope is difficult to resist.

(Davie, 2000a, pp. 64–5)

David Lodge had already explored this very dilemma with his characters. What started as exploration and choice in sexual morality quickly moved on to exploration and choice in religious belief and theological opinion: 'how far can you go?' rapidly became 'where do you stop?' (Lodge, 1980; Parsons, 1992, pp. 174–8).

It remains possible, of course, to seek a silver lining within the clouds of statistical decline. Thus, those disposed to adopt a still optimistic reading of the evidence can appeal to a variety of redeeming features within the recent and contemporary situation. These may include the continuing significance of 'residual', 'folk' or 'diffusive' Christianity; the concept of

[5] Hornsby-Smith argues strongly that it is simplistic to regard the processes involved in the transformation of English Catholicism and the dissolution of the distinctive Catholic sub-culture as one of decline. That the process is not merely or simply one of decline – but also of new insights and orientation – is arguably true. But decline and crisis are also significant elements in the recent history of Roman Catholicism in Britain.

'non-churchgoing Christians' (who describe themselves as Christian in surveys and polls but do not express this self-identification through participation in Christian worship); the concept of 'believing without belonging' (the proposal that there is a substantial penumbra of 'latent' or 'residual' Christian belief that still sustains a nominal status for Christian assumptions and vocabulary, despite the decline in active Christian participation); and the concept of 'vicarious religion' (the suggestion that many people now effectively 'delegate' the maintenance of religious belief to professionals – often expecting the clergy to retain standards of orthodoxy or morality which they no longer adhere to themselves). Similarly, there may be an appeal to the numbers who still watch or listen to religious programmes on television and radio; or to the continued public response to Christian services and rituals on occasions of national mourning or commemoration after disasters or deaths of prominent figures (Wolffe, 1993, pp. 312–17; Badham, 1994, pp. 488–9, 500–1; Davie, 1994, pp. 74–116; 2000a, pp. 49, 59; 2000b, pp. 116–19; 2001, pp. 106–7). Similarly, the decline in membership and active participation in the life of the Christian churches can be set against both a broader pattern of decline in participation in public life through, for example, trades unions, political parties and voluntary organizations of various kinds, and also similar patterns of decline in attendance at football matches, whilst televised football continues to attract large audiences – 'armchair football fans' thus providing a kind of sporting equivalent to 'non-churchgoing Christians' (Badham, 1994, p. 501; Davie, 1994, p. 20; 2000a, pp. 38, 50–1, 106, 112–13; 2001, pp. 104–5; 2002, pp. 330–33).

Conversely, those persuaded by a pessimistic reading of the situation will not only continue to emphasize and reiterate both the range and variety of the statistical indicators of decline, but will also question the substance and credibility of characteristic features of the optimistic, 'silver lining' approach.[6] They will question the reality and meaning of the self-identification of 'non-churchgoing Christians': what exactly does it mean, for example, when in the national Census of 2001, 71.6 per cent of people in England and Wales identified themselves as Christian? In such a context, where respondents were merely asked to tick a box from a range of religions specified, how far does 'Christian' possess any substantial content beyond a highly residual attachment to the religion that has been historically predominant in Britain? Similarly, those persuaded by a pessimistic reading of the evidence will point to evidence of decline in even residual Christian belief in the recent surveys, acknowledging that such decline is slower than that for church

---

[6] The idea of the 'silver-lining' approach was first suggested by Bruce (1996) as a challenge to Davie's interpretation of the evidence for secularization. Whilst certainly a skilful rhetorical device, the term does not necessarily do justice to the principal aim of Davie's work which is not to provide encouragement for churchgoers but to suggest that simple versions of secularization theory probably underestimate the continuing extent of varieties of religious belief.

attendance, but suggesting that, as time passes, ceasing to 'belong' appears to lead inexorably on to ceasing to believe (Bruce, 1995, pp. 48–51; 1996, pp. 269–70; 2001, pp. 200–2; 2002a, pp. 71–3; 2002b, pp. 326–7; Gill, Hadaway and Marler, 1998; Brown, 2001, pp. 4, 190; Field, 2001, p. 164).[7] Or again, they may point to changing patterns within religious broadcasting as audiences for religious programmes have declined relative to earlier figures; appreciation of religious programmes shows signs of increasing among older people and declining among younger generations; the actual content of religious broadcasting has become less traditional and more eclectic, less devotional and more news and discussion oriented; and the once privileged times in the schedule – such as the early Sunday evening 'God Slot' – have been relinquished. Moreover, the contrast with televised football is striking here: whilst religious programming has been steadily squeezed by ratings wars, televised football has dramatically increased (Gilbert, 1994, pp. 512–13; Gunter and Viney, 1994, pp. 51–2, 63, 73; Bruce, 1996, pp. 271–2; 2002b, pp. 321–2).

The situation with regard to funerals provides a further – and possibly telling – test-case. Exponents of an optimistic view of the strength of residual Christian belief can still appeal to the fact that, even as recourse to Christian rites of baptism and marriage decline significantly, the use of Christian rites at funerals – whether in churches or at crematoria – remains extremely high (Badham, 1994, p. 501; Davie, 1994, pp. 56, 81–2). Although the option of a purely secular funeral exists, the uptake of this option still remains limited (Davie, 2000a, p. 77). Significantly, however, there are signs that, even in relation to this profound and inescapable rite of passage, there is a notable growth both in interest in and provision for secular funerals. New and specifically non-Christian rituals and ceremonies – whether embodying an alternative personal spirituality or a wholly secular celebration of the life of the deceased – are becoming more widely discussed and disseminated, both through groups such as the British Humanist Association and through more informal networks. As yet the trend remains statistically small – but the discussion of the possibility of secular funerals has become markedly more common in recent years. For example, an electronic search of references to 'secular funerals' in British newspapers over the last 20 years produced 21 such references in the last five years, but only 7 in the previous five years, and only 10 in the previous decade. Similarly, the records of the British Humanist Association show a steady rise in the

---

[7] It is important to note that Davie, in particular, does not deny that ceasing to 'belong' to a Christian church leads to a diminution of specifically Christian 'belief'. She maintains, however, that the evidence suggests that this does not lead to a simple 'loss of religious sensitivity' or 'adoption of secular alternatives', but rather to a growth in increasingly 'personal, detached and heterogeneous' forms of belief, especially among the young (Davie, 2002, p. 333).

demand for secular funerals with the assistance of a BHA officiant, from 3,000 in 1998 to 7,000 in 2002.[8] Such statistics hardly amount to a revolution, but they do suggest a changed and still changing cultural mood and context within which even the residual Christianity associated with funerals should no longer be taken for granted.

There are, moreover, other similarly suggestive signs of the way in which the traditional Christian identity of British culture has quietly been transformed. Patterns of sexual behaviour bear increasingly little resemblance to the norms of Christian sexual morality. To take one example, but a persuasive one: cohabitation before marriage – or as an alternative to it – has become increasingly common, whilst married couples are a declining percentage of the population. Thus, in the 2001 Census, whilst married couples comprised only 50.7 per cent of the total adult population in England and Wales, compared with 55 per cent in 1991, 64 per cent in 1981, and 68 per cent in 1971, the number of cohabiting couples had increased from 5.5 per cent in 1991 to 9.8 per cent. Similarly, in Scotland, the trend towards cohabitation among the young has prompted the observation that what started in the mid-1960s became, in the ensuing quarter of a century, 'the secularization of family formation' (Brown, 1997, p. 159).

Redundant and closed churches that have been converted to new uses – whether as houses or flats, as carpet warehouses or other commercial ventures, or as buildings for the use of other religious communities – constitute another highly visible sign of the decline of the historic Christian identity and culture of England, Scotland and Wales (Brown, 2001, p. 7). Moreover, just as the traditional landscape of 'Christian Britain' has been changed, so has the location of Christianity within that landscape. As part of the much longer and broader process of the privatization of religion in modern Britain, the public profile and widespread influence of Christianity in the early years of this century has declined, especially since the 1950s. Thus, it has been suggested, the position and status of Christianity can now be compared with that of a language which had long enjoyed dominance in a particular region but is now increasingly challenged by other languages. Large parts of the old language 'have dropped out of general use, but no more acceptable alternative vocabularies have been found. In some areas of life the result is simply a void. In others, the lack of any convincing alternative means that people cling to the old words' (McLeod, 1995, pp. 18–19).

At the same time, there is no longer any need to be circumspect about – and nor is there a cost to be paid for – admitting to disbelief. Whereas in the early 1960s the agnosticism of the Labour Party leader Hugh Gaitskill only became widely known after his death, by the late 1980s and early 1990s the atheism of Neil Kinnock was public knowledge but did not become a significant issue in the general elections in which he led the

---

[8] Statistics supplied to the author by the British Humanist Association.

Figure 1   A former church now being used as a carpet shop, Armley, Leeds, West Yorkshire. Photo © Roger Scruton/Collections

Labour Party (Badham, 1994, p. 501; Morgan, 1999, p. 263.). Similarly, nor did the openly acknowledged agnosticism of the Conservative leader John Major excite controversy – despite the close relationship that is traditionally perceived to exist between the Conservative Party and the Church of England. More generally, as the post-Christian feminist theologian, Daphne Hampson, observed in 1996 in the preface to her book *After Christianity*, a quiet revolution is under way in British society whereby it is increasingly common for people to say openly and publicly that they are not Christians – although they may still claim to be, in some sense, 'spiritual persons'. 'In the last decade', she noted, 'there has been a sea change. There was a time when it took much courage to say publicly in the media that one was not a Christian. Now it takes none at all' (Hampson, 1996, p. v).[9]

Finally, one may reflect on the changing nature of the British Sunday. For all the efforts of the Christian campaigns of the 1980s and early 1990s to 'Keep Sunday Special', by the late 1990s the British Sunday was well on its way to becoming – if it had not already become – a thoroughly

[9] Although not, of course, the same as proclaiming oneself not a Christian in the media, it may be significant that, in the Census of 2001, when asked about religious belief, over 9 million people in England and Wales, some 15.5 per cent of the population, chose to identify themselves explicitly,as having 'no religion' (National Statistics Online, http://www.statistics.gov.uk/census2001/default.asp, last accessed April 2004).

secularized Sabbath. Supermarkets, DIY stores and shopping centres were routinely open. Sunday Grandstand became a fixture in the television schedules and it was common not only for international cricket and rugby matches to be played on Sundays, but for the 'best' of the weekend's football and rugby fixtures to be moved to that day and given coverage on prime time television. Indeed, as a symbol of the broader transition involved one might look no further than the Sky Sports advertising campaign in the run-up to the 1997–8 football season. Cinema and television adverts and huge advertising posters portrayed a group of fans proclaiming: 'Football is our RELIGION', to which the Sky Sports advertisement responded, 'We know how you feel. We feel the same way.'

Figure 2   Sky Sports poster advertising Sky Sports' coverage of Premiership football, Mill Road, Cambridge. Photo © Diana Norman

'I'm as good a Christian as you, though I don't go to church': How 'Christian' was 'Christian Britain'?

One of the distinguishing features of Callum Brown's thesis is his emphasis on the sheer suddenness of the collapse of the core religious culture of Christian Britain in the 1960s. In so arguing, he rejects the predominant historiographical tradition that argues that the process of secularization began in the nineteenth century. Thus, in a recent discussion of secularization in western Europe, Hugh McLeod examined the evidence from France, Germany and England for the period between 1848 and 1914. In a conclusion highly relevant to the present discussion, he argued that, rather than focusing on the statistically smaller groups of the strongly religiously (or irreligiously) committed, 'the practices of the less committed provide a good indicator of the relative strength of religious and secular influences, and of varying kinds of religion and secularity' (McLeod, 2000, p. 289). On this basis, he concluded, the evidence suggests that in late nineteenth- and early twentieth-century Europe, the balance between the religious and the secular was fairly even. The mass of the people still observed Christian rites of passage, sent their children to Sunday School or catechism classes, believed in God and prayed – at least in times of crisis. But at the same time, regular church-going was becoming a minority activity, whilst the influence of the clergy was narrowing. This fine balance, McLeod argued, remained characteristic of western Europe until the 1960s – when the balance tipped in a secular direction (McLeod, 2000, p. 289).

Whilst the reference to the 1960s points forward, intriguingly, towards Callum Brown's thesis, the emphasis on the importance of the religion of 'the mass of the people' and on the nature of their less committed styles of belief relates the discussion to another theme that has been central to the discussion of secularization: namely, the extent and nature of working-class and popular belief and unbelief. For over two decades, and particularly since the publication of Jeffrey Cox's account of religious life in Lambeth between 1870 and 1930 (Cox, 1982), historians have steadily challenged the previously accepted view that the Victorian working classes were predominantly 'unchurched', 'irreligious', 'unconsciously secular' and strangers to the churches and the influence of Christianity. Instead, a succession of scholars – many of whom have exploited the techniques and evidence of oral history to particularly telling effect – have presented a different and much more nuanced account of the relationship between Christianity and the working classes.

Despite the enduring influence of their own sense – and powerful rhetoric – of failure, it is now increasingly commonly recognized that the massive investment of the Victorian churches in campaigns to evangelize, convert and make pastoral provision for the poor was remarkably successful in establishing a rich and diverse range of agencies and means by which the working classes were brought into contact with, and participated more or less closely in, Christian rituals and influences. (See, for example, Cox, 1982; McLeod, 1986; 1993, pp. 8, 27–56; 1996a, pp. 73–109; Brown, 1988; 2001, pp. 9–10, 145–61; Parsons, 1988; Williams, 1999). As a result, beyond the ranks of the minority of religiously highly committed and self-consciously 'orthodox' working-class believers, there existed also an extensive penumbra of those who espoused – in Jeffrey Cox's suggestive term – a 'diffusive Christianity'. Such diffusive Christianity was characteristically neither systematic nor precisely structured, yet it possessed its own discernible patterns of both belief and practice. In belief, diffusive Christianity set little store by doctrine and dogma. Particular doctrines – whether of the Trinity, Incarnation or Atonement – were not so much rejected as simply ignored as irrelevant or unimportant. What mattered was 'practical Christianity' conceived as ethics and morality. The Ten Commandments, the Sermon on the Mount, the parable of the Good Samaritan, doing good to one's neighbour and family, and trying to live a good life were the core beliefs of such religion. God was characteristically distant but essentially benevolent, Jesus was the supreme moral exemplar, and heaven the hoped for reward for a life lived according to this ethical creed. The living of a good life – according to such criteria – counted for more than mere church attendance; whilst church attendance without evidence of such goodness and of a practical Christianity conceived in terms of the life of Jesus and the Gospels was apt to be regarded as evidence of hypocrisy. Thus, 'a true Christian' might never go to church, but would exhibit charity and generosity to neighbours in time of need. As for its own practice, diffusive Christianity characteristically sat light to regular Sunday church-going, but nevertheless maintained the importance of a link between the churches and local communities and embraced an alternative pattern of practice centred on rites of passage, annual festivals such as Christmas, New Year Watchnight Service, Harvest Festival, or chapel and Sunday School anniversaries, perhaps supplemented by attendance at a week-night meeting in which social activities and religious devotion intermingled. Sunday School was a valued institution within such diffusive Christianity, and the Bible a source of morally and ethically uplifting teaching and example, whilst hymns provided a much loved focus of devotional expression and a reservoir of religious sentiment.[10]

The research of Sarah Williams in Southwark suggests that such diffusive Christianity may well have coexisted with the robust survival of a wide range of folk religious beliefs and practices, but this, she insists, should not obscure the extent to which diffusive Christianity indicated the importance that people attached to a particular rite or to 'the overtly Christian elements of belief associated with it'. Similarly, the determination that children should go to Sunday School, even when parents were non-churchgoers, was an indication that parents believed it important that children absorbed 'the essentials of Christianity' – although the specifics of denominational doctrines were commonly regarded as unimportant and irrelevant. Commonly, children were also taught to pray, even when parents did not do so themselves. Such expressions of commitment through one's children, together with similar expressions of attachment to a church or chapel which yet fell short of membership or regular participation, have been characterized aptly as 'religion by

[10] For particularly persuasive and evocative analyses of 'diffusive Christianity', in addition to Cox, 1982, pp. 90–105, see Williams, 1999, pp. 1, 6–7, 87–162.

deputy' (Williams, 1999, pp. 54–162). At the same time, however, it should not be overlooked that 'diffusive Christianity' and 'religion by deputy', like 'believing without belonging' in more recent decades, implies – by definition – the maintenance of a certain distance from the Christian community and therefore also from the reinforcement of specifically Christian belief which would tend to flow from regular participation in its rituals. Under these circumstances, it would not be surprising to find evidence pointing to the fragility of diffusive Christianity or to a tendency for such religious belief to become steadily more detached from the norms of church-going Christian orthodoxy.

The report on *The Army and Religion*, published in 1919 and based on an interdenominational survey, carried out by the YMCA, of attitudes to religion among British soldiers serving during the First World War, provides early evidence of just such a tendency (Cairns, 1919). The broad pattern revealed was one of rejection of official Christianity, church doctrine and regular worship, but retention of a vague theism, a practical ethics and an attachment to occasional worship. British soldiers had little time for the churches as institutions and little interest in, or knowledge of, Christian doctrine. But a belief in God was widespread, Jesus was respected as a man who suffered in a good cause (though specific ideas of atonement or incarnation were notable only by their absence), prayer was common before and after battle, but so also was a fatalistic view of providence. 'Real Christianity' consisted in a life of good will and good acts. The British soldier, according to one of the most famous lines in the report, 'has got religion, but I am not sure that he has got Christianity'. Elsewhere the report described the belief of ordinary soldiers as a 'dim and instinctive theism', existing within a state of 'spiritual anarchy', among a generation familiar with and fond of Christian hymns, yet deeply ignorant of Christian doctrine and beliefs, and for whom God was often no more than a 'relic of their days in Sunday school' (Cairns, 1919; Gill, 1993, pp. 179–82, 206; Snape and Parker, 2001, pp. 398–9).

If this survey suggested that, by the First World War, 'diffusive Christianity' was already in danger of being more diffusive than Christian, evidence from the Second World War and from the late 1940s and the 1950s suggests that, by then, such tendencies had become even more pronounced. Nationwide Mass Observation surveys during the Second World War found, above all, a state of religious confusion. Whilst the majority still expressed belief in God, the implications of such belief were rarely thought through. Beliefs and doubts were not logically related, but rather mixed up with prejudices and habits dating from childhood and pigeon-holed so that conflicts did not arise (Snape and Parker, 2001, pp. 399–400). Subsequently, in 1947, a Mass Observation survey of attitudes to religion concluded that, whilst actual hostility to religion was not widespread and an attitude of goodwill towards the idea of religion was apparent, nevertheless this coexisted with 'a hostile attitude to the Church, and a personal religious faith of an exceedingly vague and unorthodox kind'. The report concluded that for many religion had come to mean 'little more than being kind and neighbourly, doing good when opportunity arises'. Belief in the principle of treating others as you would wish them to treat you persisted, the report suggested, 'but without the sanction of faith, or any other sanction than habit and vague memories of childhood teaching' (Mass Observation, 1947, pp. 156–7).

A decade later, in his classic study of working-class life and culture, Richard Hoggart devoted several highly evocative pages to a description of working-class attitudes to religion. In terms that echo many of Sarah Williams's findings in Southwark between 1880 and 1939 – though with an arguably even greater sense of distance from the norms of official Christianity – Hoggart suggested that 'church and chapel' were still felt as 'in some sense part of the life of the neighbourhood'. People would still speak of 'our chapel' and many who did not normally attend would still go to an anniversary service or a Christmas event. Yet, he also concluded, 'even this limited sense of belonging is weakening in most of the areas I know'. Whilst they continued to use the churches for rites of passage, the ideas of working-class people, he suggested, had 'been affected by ideas which seem to have disposed of the claims of religion', whilst experience suggested that religion would not work in 'real life'. 'In so far as they think of Christianity', Hoggart maintained,

> they think of it as a system of ethics ... Christianity is morals ... Christ was a person, giving the best example of how to live; one could not expect to be able to live like that today: still, the example is there. They like to speak of 'practical Christianity'. It was widely maintained that it was not necessary to go to church or chapel to be a Christian: 'I'm as good a Christian as you, though I don't go to church' was a common saying.
>
> (Hoggart, 1957, pp. 112–19)

Hoggart wrote on the eve of the 1960s and the cultural revolution which, Callum Brown argues, finally overwhelmed the Christian culture of modern Britain. As already noted, in recent surveys there is evidence of the decline of even residual belief in specifically Christian concepts and doctrines during recent decades. In addition, particular studies of belief from the 1960s onwards have provided telling individual responses to questions and characterizations of personal religious identity which, although individually no more than isolated examples, may nevertheless convey a flavour of popular attitudes within the penumbra of residual and peripheral Christian belief in Britain in the latter decades of the twentieth century. There is, for example, a now famous response to the question, 'Do you believe in a God who can change the course of events on earth?', to which the reply was 'No, just the ordinary one' (Abercrombie *et al*, 1970, p. 160). A survey in inner-city London in the 1980s produced, among others, the following observations: of baptism '... it's a certain amount of belief in God, isn't it?, I suppose. They've got to

grow to respect other people, and things like that ... So we christened
the children, I suppose, because, I dunno ...'; or of funerals, '... it makes
it all a little bit more easier to take ... Just a ceremony that lightens the
thing for somebody'. Another person remarked: 'I do believe in
Christmas' – though the respondent saw nothing special in Jesus. Another
said: 'I just believe in a God of some sorts, I'm not too deeply into it – I
just think there's something else that kind of moves us about and guides
whatever your destiny' (Ahern, 1987, pp. 97, 99, 110).

Similarly, a survey of 'residual religiosity' on a Hull council estate in the
1980s included characteristic responses such as: baptism (or 'christening')
being frequently described as 'just what usual people do' or the 'normal
thing to do'; Christian funerals being similarly described as 'the right
thing to do', 'just to end life properly' or 'the normal thing'. The survey
also found that 'many who declared themselves atheist or agnostic were
prepared to indicate a religious preference when asked for official
purposes' – which only emphasizes that the 70 per cent who identified
themselves as 'Christian' in the 2001 Census constitutes a profoundly
ambiguous statistic – a tendency taken to the extreme by a respondent
who indicated that if asked his religion on going into hospital he would
say, 'bloody Christian, I suppose' (Forster, 1989, pp. 27–9, 38–9; 1995,
pp. 8, 14, 17). The author of the survey concluded that, whilst the survey
probably over-estimated the religiosity of the Longhill Estate – not least
because it was known that the survey was church-related and
interviewees 'no doubt exaggerated their religiosity so as to give
"answers that please"' – nevertheless hostility to Christianity was rare and
Christian practice was regarded as a useful example to set to children. At
the same time, however, the church was seen as a community facility to
be used principally in need and Christian practice was perceived to be
something one grew out of after childhood, church attendance – both
weekly and on special occasions – was as low as 5 per cent, and
Christianity was seen broadly as 'part of the English heritage' (Forster,
1989, pp. 50–3; 1995, pp. 25–6).

Extensive research conducted over more than three decades into what he
defines as 'implicit religion' has also led Edward Bailey to argue that
there remains widespread evidence of 'a doggedly persistent faith in
"Christianity", not seen as a set of dogmas but as symbolizing an intrinsic
faith or spirit'. The content of the religious faith involved, Bailey
suggests, may be summarized as: 'I believe in Christianity; I insist on the
right of everyone to make up their own mind; and I affirm the value of
values' (Bailey, 1986; 1989; 1997, pp. 261–2). Bailey accepts the value of
such belief – not least for the continuing ministry of the Christian
churches – but also accepts that the other beliefs and values of this
'creed' may be summarized as the desire for religion to be relevant to
real life, yet also kept out of politics; the opportunity to go to church,
but the non-necessity of so doing; and the moral duty of taking care of
oneself, together with a belief in 'fair play' and 'helping the underdog'
(Bailey, 1989, p. 155). It is possible to see such a creed as a late

twentieth-century lineal descendant of late nineteenth-century 'diffusive Christianity' – but it is a descendant in which the specifically Christian content of such popular religion has declined to a point that is truly residual, if indeed still meaningfully recognizable at all. Thus, as a widower remarked to a parish priest, explaining why he wanted his wife's funeral in the parish church, though he never attended its services: 'I do believe in ... Thingummy, and I've brought my children up to be Church of England' (Coombs, 1986, cited in Wolffe, 1993, p. 343).

By the 1960s, 70s and 80s, moreover, such residual contact with Christianity had clearly ceased to be a characteristic associated only, or even principally, with specifically working-class religious belief. Whilst 'diffusive Christianity' has been seen as mainly a working-class phenomenon, it is clear that an analogous form of vague and generalized Christian belief became much more widely diffused within British culture and society during the twentieth century, sustained not least by the religious broadcasting of the BBC and the religious education provided in state schools (Cox, 1982, p. 276; Parsons 1988, p. 85). Assisted by the continuation of a tendency towards a strongly practical understanding of Christianity that was already evident among middle-class late Victorian and Edwardian Christians (McLeod, 1974, pp.151–8), by the last third of the twentieth century such generalized belief had become increasingly characteristic of the Christianity of the majority of the British middle classes. If, therefore, the turmoil of the cultural revolution of the 1960s proved a decisive moment in the decline of Britain's core religious culture, the evidence of over a hundred years of 'diffusive Christianity', 'religion by deputy', and 'believing without belonging' may suggest that the core religious culture was always likely to be susceptible to the pressures of a period of intense cultural transformation.

New divisions and new diversity: the context of the death of Christian Britain

It is clear that the sexual revolution of the 1960s was a crucial factor in transforming attitudes and lifestyles, especially among the younger generations, by providing the legal framework, the social ethos, and the contraceptive technology that facilitated the increasingly widespread – and also the increasingly public – rejection of a traditional and conventional Christian sexual morality. The relaxation of the laws regarding censorship, the increase in access to contraceptive advice for unmarried – as well as married – women, the reform and liberalization of the laws regarding divorce, abortion and homosexuality, and the advent of the oral contraceptive pill, were all key parts of what has been described as a 'permissive moment' in which the primacy of restrictive public and social control of personal morality gave way to the increased role of personal choice and decision making (Weeks, 1989, pp. 249–52; Haste, 1992, pp. 205–6; Parsons, 1994a, pp. 236–40; McLeod, 2003, pp. 3–4). The sexual revolution of the 1960s was, however, by no means the only significant factor in the cultural transformation that resulted in the sudden collapse of Britain's core religious culture. At least two other factors were also of great importance: namely the controversies and conflicts within the traditional Christian churches and the growth in the sheer diversity of the religious life of Britain.

It is one of the paradoxes of the history of the Christian churches in Britain in the late twentieth century that, even as the ecumenical movement was transforming relationships between the major Christian denominations and traditions – substantially replacing remaining antagonisms by a spirit of cooperation and coexistence – yet new divisions and polarizations occurred within British Christianity. The new divisions characteristically crossed-over the old denominational differences between churches and focused instead upon the clash between theological, liturgical and moral liberals and radicals on the one hand, and theological, liturgical and moral conservatives and traditionalists on the other. The origins of these new divisions may be traced to the theological ferment that occurred within the Christian churches during the 1960s as liberals and radicals enthusiastically embraced talk of 'a new reformation', 'religionless Christianity', 'secular Christianity', 'man come of age' and 'situation ethics', whilst conservatives and traditionalists resisted such trends as dangerously secularizing influences and reasserted the claims of traditional Christian belief and practice. Increasingly, therefore, those of a liberal or radical view found more in common with liberals and radicals in other Christian denominations than with the conservatives and traditionalists in their own churches – an experience that was shared by conservatives and traditionalists who also found new allies and kindred spirits across the boundaries of the historic divisions between the churches (Parsons, 1993a, pp. 55–84).

These new divisions were anything but simple. On particular issues, such as the replacement of traditional modes of worship by more modern and contemporary forms, for example, one might easily find theologically conservative charismatic Christians enthusiastically embracing change, whilst theological liberals might champion the virtues of a traditional liturgical form of service. Two consequences of the new polarization of liberals and radicals on the one hand and conservatives and traditionalists on the other are, however, clear and relevant to the present discussion. First, it became increasingly impossible to frame, with any precision, even a broadly agreed definition of the content of contemporary Christianity. Secondly, the life of the churches increasingly became characterized by an ongoing struggle between different groups of highly 'committed' and 'activist' members – for one thing that all the various parties tended to agree upon, whether liberal, radical, conservative, traditionalist, charismatic, feminist, or whatever, was that involvement in the Christian community should be characterized by high levels of involvement, participation and religious 'self-consciousness'. But such a concept of 'committed', 'activist', 'participatory' involvement with the churches stands markedly at odds – indeed, even in conflict – with the ethos and habits of mind and practice that are characteristic of 'diffusive Christianity', 'religion by deputy' and 'believing without belonging' (Parsons, 1993a, pp. 84–7). At the popular level such tensions are habitually and characteristically expressed by the occasional attender who may remark that: 'I wish they wouldn't change all the old words in the services (or version of the Bible)', or 'I wish they'd have the good old hymns instead of all these trendy new ones.' Thus, in her research on religion in Southwark, Sarah Williams found that elderly interviewees complained about the 'newfangled modern songs' that were used in place of favourite old hymns, cited these songs as evidence that the churches had abandoned their traditional roots, and implied that this was – at least partly – why they had become alienated from the churches, whereas their own parents had not (Williams, 1999, p. 152).

Such alienation – and sheer unfamiliarity with the language of modern liturgies and versions of the Bible – must inevitably lead to the penumbra of 'believers who are not belongers' becoming at once steadily less and less at home when they do encounter the contemporary Christianity of the churches, and equally steadily more and more residual in their remaining belief. This process, moreover, has coincided with another which has also served to reduce the reservoir of Christian religious language, concepts and associations that had once sustained 'diffusive Christianity' and 'believing without belonging'. The 1960s was not only the decade in which the churches began to polarize into increasingly sharply defined liberal and conservative camps, but was also the decade in which religious education and daily acts of collective worship in schools began to change. The non-denominational religious education provided from 1870 onwards in Board Schools (and subsequently in their local authority successors) reinforced the biblical knowledge and broad awareness of Christian beliefs that were fostered by Sunday Schools, and thus also reinforced 'diffusive Christianity' (Cox, 1982, pp. 78–81, 96–7, 187–8). The 1944 Education Act continued the tradition, again making religious instruction (which was commonly assumed to mean instruction in biblical knowledge and basic non-denominational Christian belief) and a daily collective act of worship (commonly in the form of Christian hymns, bible reading and prayers) required parts of the curriculum and the school day (Parsons, 1994b, pp. 165–9).

In the 1960s, however, this began to change. The Christian element began to be supplemented by attention to other religious traditions and 'religious instruction' began to become 'religious education'. By the end of the 1960s, the movement had begun in earnest for the introduction of a much broader and less overtly Christian conception of religious education and for teaching and syllabuses that addressed all the major world religions. The characteristic 'hymns, prayers and bible reading assembly' that anyone who was at school in Britain in the 1950s and 1960s will readily remember became steadily less common (Parsons, 1994b, pp. 170–80). Moreover, although the 1988 Education Act specified that all syllabuses for religious education must 'reflect the fact that the religious traditions in Great Britain are in the main Christian', and that collective worship in schools should be 'wholly or mainly of a broadly Christian character', it also formally required that account be taken of 'the teaching and practices of the other principal religions represented in Great Britain' and left scope for the inclusion of some worship that was not Christian. If the 1988 Act thus still privileged Christianity – and also remained in important respects unclear and ambiguous – it nevertheless did so in a context that was massively different from that even a quarter of a century earlier. The particular kind of school 'RE' and 'assembly' that had been such a crucial element in sustaining diffusive Christianity for several generations was substantially consigned to history (Parsons, 1994b, pp. 183–95; Hull, 1994).[11]

The history of religious broadcasting in Britain exhibits a similar pattern. The official reports on broadcasting published in 1949 and 1962 both affirmed that the BBC was not neutral in respect of religion and that it was a duty of the BBC to promote the Christian faith, not least because Britain was a 'Christian country'. Although the latter report accepted that religious broadcasting need not be restricted to Christianity, the clear assumption was that, in practice, the overwhelming majority of such broadcasting would reflect the traditions of the 'mainstream' churches (HMSO, 1949, p. 63; 1962, pp. 88–91). By contrast, the report on broadcasting of 1977 reflected a quite different set of priorities. Written after the cultural revolution of the 1960s, the marked growth of more discursive and exploratory styles of religious broadcasting, and the emergence of a sense of the increasing religious diversity in late twentieth-century Britain, the report defined the objectives of religious broadcasting as: reflecting 'the worship, thought and action of the principal religious traditions represented in Britain, recognizing that those traditions are mainly, though not exclusively Christian'; presenting contemporary religious beliefs, ideas, issues and experiences to viewers and listeners; and meeting the religious interests and needs of those 'on the fringe of, or outside, the organised life of the Churches' (HMSO, 1977, pp. 319–21; Gunter and Viney, 1994, p. 121).

[11] It has also been noted that, from the 1960s onwards, there was a marked decline in levels of religious practice among university students, so that by the late twentieth century, 'religion was a decaying force in the universities' (Bebbington, 1992, pp. 267–8). Against this, however, it has also been argued that, as religions other than Christianity have become more prominent among students, so the 'multi-faith campus' has become a significant example of 'de-secularisation' as religiously and ethnically diverse student groups seek to assert their specifically religious identities (Gilliat-Ray, 2000).

Religious education and religious broadcasting are thus particularly effective symbols of the wider transition that has occurred in British religious life in the last four or five decades. Not only has the 'core religious culture' of 'Christian Britain' declined and become even more diluted, but at the same time the diversity of religious life in Britain has become much greater. Despite the confusion that Mass Observation surveys revealed to be characteristic of religion in Britain in the 1940s, and despite the fact that Britain had long had a well-established and flourishing Jewish community, it still remained possible then to speak of Britain as, in some sense, 'a Christian country' and to appeal, in the crises of wartime, to the 'Christian' identity and self-consciousness of the nation (Snape and Parker, 2001, pp. 401–3). By the 1980s and 1990s, however, such descriptions of Britain had simply become implausible. By then, to the existing Jewish community, there had been added increasingly prominent and substantial Hindu, Muslim, Sikh and Buddhist communities. In the half century after the Second World War, Britain had

Figure 3   Members of the local Sikh community at the Sri Guru Singh Sabha Gurdwara, Reading, Berkshire. The Gurdwara was opened in 1975 in the former Cumberland Road Methodist Church. Photo Reading Evening Post

steadily become a 'religiously plural' or 'multi-faith' society in which Christianity remained the largest single religious tradition, but in which sheer diversity had become the predominant characteristic of the nation's religious identity. Thus, in the National Census of 2001, in England and Wales, 267,000 people identified themselves as Jewish, 559,000 as Hindu, 1,591,000 as Muslim, 336,000 as Sikh, and 152,000 as Buddhist (National Statistics Online).

Nor was such religious diversity limited to the presence in Britain of communities representing a variety of major world religions. It was also expressed through a flourishing and highly diverse religious sub-culture of new religious movements, varieties of paganism, alternative spiritualities, new age beliefs and other, often highly eclectic, religious and spiritual groups. Consequently, as the traditional core religious culture of diffusive, residual Christianity diminished, the new religious pluralism of late twentieth-century Britain offered the British a rich and increasingly eclectic range of religious options. So much so, that the religious alternatives available in Britain at the dawn of the third millennium have been described as resembling both 'pick and mix religion' and 'a supermarket of faiths and ideologies' (Parsons, 1993b, p. 298; Wolffe, 1994, p. 50).

Conflict, (de)conversion and coexistence: the context of the 'death of Christian Britain' reconsidered

How does the destruction of the core religious culture of Britain that is posited by Callum Brown in *The Death of Christian Britain* relate to the themes of conflict, conversion and coexistence that are central to this book?

Conflict was most certainly a part of the turbulent transformations that took place during and after the 1960s, including the transformations in the role and status of religion in British society. But it would be thoroughly misleading to portray the religious dimension of this cultural revolution as a straightforward conflict between the traditional religious culture of Britain and the newly energized forces of secularity and permissiveness. There were, of course, those within the Christian churches who interpreted the decade in precisely that way – and whose successors continue so to interpret the legacy of the 1960s. For many conservative Christians, the liberalization of sexual morality during the 1960s was precisely a symptom of the corrosive influence of secular, permissive values. Thus, from the 1960s onwards, conservative Christians of various denominational backgrounds organized campaigns and pressure groups, such as the Nationwide Festival of Light, the Society for the Protection of the Unborn Child, and the National Viewers and Listeners Association, to combat what they perceived as the moral decline and moral pollution of British society. In subsequent decades, similar conservative Christian pressure groups emerged – such as the Christian Action Research and Education (CARE) Trust and Care Campaigns, local Community Standards Associations and a variety of other similar organizations. Such groups campaigned – and continue to campaign – over a variety of moral issues, but focus particularly on ones relating to matters such as homosexuality and gay and lesbian rights, abortion, sex education in schools, and the promotion of 'family values' (Parsons, 1994b, pp. 238–42; 1994c, pp. 149–52; Thompson, 1992; 1997).

As with other issues, however, the conflicts and controversies over sexual morality during the 1960s and subsequently were also fought out within the churches and between Christians of different theological persuasions and opinions, and were not simply between Christians and 'secular culture'. Such conflicts have continued within the churches since then, especially in relation to the issue of homosexuality, as the long-running tensions between the Gay and Lesbian Christian Movement, founded in 1974, and conservative Christian groups amply demonstrate (Parsons, 1994a, pp. 240–53). Equally, it should be noted that, during the 1960s, Christians were among those who supported the liberalizing legislative reforms in matters of personal and sexual morality (Parsons, 1994a, pp. 244–7; McLeod, 1995, pp. 15–17; 2003, p. 4). Nor should it be overlooked, in reflecting on the legacy and impact of the cultural revolution of the 1960s upon British religious life, that the roots of the growth in the influence of the charismatic movement – and of a contemporary Evangelicalism heavily influenced by it – may also be traced to the cultural ferment and counter-cultural trends of the 1960s. Although strongly conservative in theology and on issues of personal and sexual morality, these movements – which became increasingly prominent and influential within British Christianity in the last four decades of the twentieth century – were nevertheless in some respects strikingly indebted to the legacy of the 1960s. Thus, in their worship and spirituality, charismatic and Evangelical Christians increasingly celebrated the virtues of feeling, emotion and experience and rejected conventional inhibitions, thus providing, it has been suggested, a Christian version of 'doing your own thing' (Bebbington, 1989, pp. 240–8).

More recently, some commentators concerned with a variety of issues relating to questions of equality and the rights of particular groups that arise from the increased religious diversity of late twentieth-century Britain have argued that there now exists in Britain a

> three-cornered contest between a secular hegemony, a Christianity which, albeit in a dilute way, still gives to most people their understanding of divinity and moral conduct, yet is fading as an organized religion; and, thirdly, an emergent multi-faith society as the new religions establish communal and

> institutional foundations and seek accommodation from
> Christians and secularists alike.
>
> (Modood, 1994, p. 72. See also Gilliat-Ray, 2000, pp. 141–59)

At the very least, such an analysis constitutes a thought-provoking interpretation of the balance between secular and religious influences in recent and contemporary British society. It may be, however, that a more subtle and fluid model involving five broad categories – the conservative religious (of various traditional religions), the liberal religious (also of various traditional religions), the eclectically 'spiritual', the self-consciously secular, and the uncommitted – would do even greater justice to the realities of religion in contemporary Britain. Such groups now appear to exist in shifting patterns of relationship – making common cause or opposing each other in varying relationships depending on the particular issue at stake at any time. What is certainly clear is that either model amply confirms that it would be profoundly mistaken to interpret the proposed 'death of Christian Britain' as a simple conflict between a declining Christianity and an increasingly pervasive secularism.

It is also doubtful whether the proposed 'death of Christian Britain' should be seen as primarily a process of conversion – or perhaps more accurately 'deconversion'. To the extent that conversion (or deconversion) suggests a process of deliberate, decisive choice, it does not, on the whole, appear to be a particularly convincing way of describing the decline of the core religious culture of Britain. Despite the fact that the turmoil of the 1960s clearly initiated a new stage in the scale of the decline of participation and membership in the Christian churches, nevertheless this collapse does not have the character of a decisive deconversion. Rather it seems that the capacity of traditional Christian Britain to maintain itself across generations ceased. Significantly, in her analysis of religion in Southwark between 1880 and 1939, Sarah Williams concluded that 'there existed a personal, familial, and corporate familiarity with a series of religious images, teachings, and symbols which remained a vital part of popular heritage. Church based symbols were passed down from one generation to another as part of the fabric of family and communal life' (Williams, 1999, p. 147). But in the period since 1960, this process of passing on Christian symbols has been fundamentally disrupted as successive generations have had less and less contact with traditional Christian belief and practice. The decline which began in the 1960s thus resembles a collapse in the persuasive power of a received and habitual religious outlook, rather than a decisive and deliberate change – or 'conversion' – to an alternative set of beliefs and practices.

Or at least this is so except, perhaps, in one important respect. If Callum Brown is correct that a decisive factor in the 'death of Christian Britain' was the rejection by women of a particular set of definitions of female behaviour, roles and sexual morality, then there may, after all, be a sense in which one may plausibly speak of a widespread 'conversion' of women, in and since the 1960s, to the reality of greater personal choice in respect of their lifestyles, relationships and the expression of their sexuality. For whatever new ambiguities the 'permissive moment' and the pill brought for women, it also brought the possibility of new and broader choices and alternatives in matters of sexual morality and practice. Moreover, this would, as Callum Brown suggests, constitute a crucial factor in the destruction of Britain's 'core religious culture', for historians have long agreed that women did, indeed, play a much more prominent role than men both in the active life of the churches and also in diffusive Christianity (see, for example, McLeod, 1993, pp. 48–51; 1996a, pp. 156–68; 1996b, pp. 150–62; Cox, 1982, pp. 34–5; Davie, 1994, pp. 118–21; Knight, 1995, pp. 205–6; Forster, 1989, p. 50; Williams, 1999, pp. 145–6, 170–1, 175).

What, then, of coexistence? Despite the existence of particular points of conflict and contest between secular assumptions, continuing Christian influence and the claims of other religious traditions, the relationship between religious groups and traditions in Britain from the 1960s onwards can best be described as one in which an ethos of coexistence has remained predominant. As Callum Brown readily acknowledged at the end of his book, 'the death of Christian Britain' – as proposed in his thesis – did not at all imply that Christianity in Britain was dead. The Christian churches still remain significant institutions and may even be successful in fostering an increased degree of commitment and fervour among the minority of the population that continues not only to profess but also to practise Christian faith. Similarly, the decline of Christian belief and practice does not necessarily mean that religious belief as such is in decline. In Britain at the start of the third millennium, the variety of religious belief and practice available to individuals is richer and broader than ever before, as representatives and communities from all of the world's major religious traditions, and many of the more minor ones, coexist – with relatively little overt tension or conflict – alongside an immensely diverse range of alternative spiritualities and spiritually influenced lifestyle choices. But the 'culture of Christianity' – that set of assumptions about the nature of British society that once enabled people to speak of Britain as 'a Christian country' – has indeed come to an end, and with its end has come also the death of 'Christian Britain'.

References

Abercrombie, N. *et al* (1970) 'Superstition and religion: the God of the gaps', in D. Martin and M. Hill (eds), *A Sociological Yearbook of Religion in Britain*, vol. 3, London, SCM, pp. 93–129.

Ahern, G. (1987) '"I do believe in Christmas". White working-class people and Anglican clergy in inner-city London', in G. Ahern and G.

Davie, *Inner City God: The Nature of Belief in the Inner City*, London, Hodder and Stoughton, pp. 75–133.

*Badham, P. (1994) 'Religious pluralism in modern Britain', in S. Gilley and W. J. Sheils (eds) *A History of Religion in Britain*, Oxford, Blackwell, pp. 488–502. [A good short survey of the subject.]

Bailey, E. (1986) 'The religion of the people' in T. Moss (ed.) *In Search of Christianity*, London, Firethorn, pp. 177–88.

Bailey, E. (1989) 'The folk religion of the English people', in P. Badham (ed.) *Religion, State, and Society in Modern Britain*, Lampeter, Edwin Mellen, pp. 145–58.

Bailey, E. (1997) *Implicit Religion in Contemporary Society*, GA Kampen, Kok Pharos.

Bebbington, D. (1989) *Evangelicalism in Modern Britain: A History from the 1730s to the 1980s*, London, Unwin Hyman.

Bebbington, D. (1992) 'The secularization of British universities since the mid-nineteenth century', in G. Marsden and B. Longfield (eds) *The Secularisation of the Academy*, Oxford, Oxford University Press, pp. 259–77.

Brown, C. (1988) 'Did urbanisation secularize Britain', *Urban History Yearbook*, pp. 1–14.

Brown, C. (1997) *Religion and Society in Scotland since 1707*, Edinburgh, Edinburgh University Press.

*Brown, C. (2001) *The Death of Christian Britain: Understanding Secularisation 1800–2000*, London, Routledge. [The provocatively revisionist book on which this chapter has focused.]

Brown, C. (2003) 'The secularisation decade: what the 1960s have done to the study of religious history', in H. McLeod and W. Ustdorf (eds) *The Decline of Christendom in Western Europe, 1750–2000*, Cambridge, Cambridge University Press, pp. 29–46.

*Bruce, S. (1995) *Religion in Modern Britain*, Oxford, Oxford University Press. [A strong statement of the traditional argument for secularization.]

Bruce, S. (1996) 'Religion in Britain at the close of the 20th century: a challenge to the silver lining perspective', *Journal of Contemporary Religion*, vol. 11, pp. 261–75.

Bruce. S. (2001) 'Christianity in Britain, R.I.P.', *Sociology of Religion*, vol. 62, pp. 191–203.

Bruce, S. (2002a) *God is Dead: Secularization in the West*, Oxford, Blackwell.

Bruce, S. (2002b) 'Praying alone? Church-going in Britain and the Putnam thesis', *Journal of Contemporary Religion*, vol. 17, pp. 317–28.

Cairns, D. (ed.) (1919) *The Army and Religion: An Enquiry and its Bearing upon the Religious Life of the Nation*, London, Macmillan.

Coombs, M. (1986) 'Believing in thingummy', in E. Bailey (ed.) *A Workbook in Popular Religion*, Dorchester, Partners, pp. 56–7.

Cox, J. (1982) *The English Churches in a Secular Society: Lambeth, 1870–1930*, Oxford, Oxford University Press.

*Davie, G. (1994) *Religion in Britain since 1945: Believing without Belonging*, Oxford, Blackwell. [A strong statement of the view that religion in Britain remains stronger than the secularization thesis allows.]

Davie, G. (2000a) *Religion in Modern Europe: A Memory Mutates*, Oxford, Oxford University Press.

Davie, G. (2000b) 'Religion in modern Britain: changing sociological assumptions', *Sociology*, vol. 34, pp. 113–28.

Davie, G. (2001) 'The persistence of institutional religion in modern Europe', in L. Woodhead (ed.) with P. Heelas and D. Martin, *Peter Berger and the Study of Religion*, London, Routledge, pp. 101–11.

Davie, G. (2002) 'Praying alone? Church-going in Britain and social capital. A reply to Steve Bruce', *Journal of Contemporary Religion*, vol. 17, pp. 329–34.

Field, C. (2001) 'The haemorrhage of faith? Opinion polls as sources for religious practices, beliefs and attitudes in Scotland since the 1970s', *Journal of Contemporary Religion*, vol. 16, pp. 157–75.

Forster, P. (1989) *Church and People on Longhill Estate*, Occasional Paper 5, University of Hull, Department of Sociology and Social Anthropology.

Forster, P. (1995) 'Residual religiosity on a Hull council estate' in P. Forster (ed.) *Contemporary Mainstream Religion: Studies from Humberside and Lincolnshire*, Aldershot, Avebury, pp. 1–33.

Gilbert, A. (1994) 'Secularization and the future', in S. Gilley and W. J. Sheils (eds), *A History of Religion in Britain*, Oxford, Blackwell, pp. 503–21.

Gill, R. (1993) *The Myth of the Empty Church*, London, SPCK.

Gill, R., Hadaway, C. and Marler, P. (1998) 'Is religious belief declining in Britain?', *Journal for the Scientific Study of Religion*, vol. 37, pp. 507–16.

Gilliat-Ray, S. (2000) *Religion in Higher Education: The Politics of the Multi-faith Campus*, Aldershot, Ashgate.

Gunter, B. and Viney, R. (1994) *Seeing is Believing: Religion and Television in the 1990s*, London, John Libbey.

Hampson, D. (1996) *After Christianity*, London, SCM.

Haste, C. (1992) *Rules of Desire: Sex in Britain from World War II to the Present*, London, Chatto and Windus.

Hastings, A. (1991) *A History of English Christianity 1920–1990*, London, Collins.

HMSO (1949) *Report of the Broadcasting Committee*, London.

HMSO (1962) *The Committee on Broadcasting, 1960: Report*, London.

HMSO (1977) *Report of the Committee on the Future of Broadcasting*, London.

Hoggart, R. (1957) *The Uses of Literacy*, London, Chatto and Windus.

Hornsby-Smith, M. (1987) *Roman Catholics in England: Studies in Social Structure since the Second World War*, Cambridge, Cambridge University Press.

Hornsby-Smith, M. (1989) *The Changing Parish: A Study of Parishes, Priests, and Parishioners after Vatican II*, London, Routledge.

Hornsby-Smith, M. (1991) *Roman Catholic Beliefs in England: Customary Catholicism and Transformations of Religious Authority*, Cambridge, Cambridge University Press.

Hornsby-Smith, M. (1992) 'Recent transformations in English Catholicism: evidence of secularization?', in *Religion and Modernization: Sociologists and Historians Debate the Secularization Thesis*, Oxford, Oxford University Press, pp. 118–44.

Hull, J. (1994) 'Can one speak of God or to God in education', in F. Young (ed.) *Dare We Speak of God in Public*, London, Mowbray, pp. 22–34.

Knight, F. (1995) *The Nineteenth Century Church and English Society*, Cambridge, Cambridge University Press.

Lodge, D. (1980) *How Far Can You Go?*, London, Secker and Warburg.

Mass Observation (1947) *Puzzled People: A Study in Popular Attitudes to Religion, Ethics, Progress and Politics in a London Borough*, London, Victor Gollancz.

McLeod, H. (1974) *Class and Religion in the Late Victorian City*, London, Croom Helm.

McLeod, H. (1986) 'New perspectives on Victorian working-class religion: the oral evidence', *Oral History*, vol. 14, pp. 31–49.

McLeod, H. (1993) *Religion and Irreligion in Victorian England: How Secular was the Working Class?*, Bangor, Headstart History.

McLeod, H. (1995) 'The privatization of religion in modern England' in F. Young (ed.) *Dare We Speak of God in Public*, London, Mowbray, pp. 1–21.

McLeod, H. (1996a) *Religion and Society in England, 1850–1914*, London, Macmillan.

McLeod, H. (1996b) *Piety and Poverty: Working Class Religion in Berlin, London and New York 1870–1914*, New York and London, Holmes and Meier.

McLeod, H. (2000) *Secularisation in Western Europe, 1848–1914*, London, Macmillan.

McLeod, H. (2001) 'The sixties: writing the religious history of a crucial decade', *Kirchliche Zeitgeschichte*, vol. 14, pp. 36–48.

*McLeod, H. (2003) 'Introduction' in H. McLeod and W. Ustorf (eds) *The Decline of Christendom in Western Europe, 1750–2000*, Cambridge, Cambridge University Press, pp. 1–26. [A good survey and summary of current debates.]

Modood, T. (1994) 'Establishment, multicultualism and British citizenship', *Political Quarterly*, vol. 65, pp. 53–73.

Morgan, D. (1999) *The Span of the Cross: Christian Religion and Society in Wales 1914–2000*, Cardiff, University of Wales Press.

Parsons, G. (1988) 'A question of meaning: religion and working-class life' in G. Parsons (ed.) *Religion in Victorian Britain*, vol. II: *Controversies*, Manchester, Manchester University Press, pp. 63–87.

Parsons, G. (1992) 'Paradigm or period piece? David Lodge's *How Far Can You Go?* in perspective', *Literature and Theology*, vol. 6, pp. 171–90.

Parsons, G. (1993a) 'Contrasts and continuities: the traditional Christian churches in Britain since 1945', in G. Parsons (ed.) *The Growth of Religious Diversity: Britain from 1945*, vol. 1: *Traditions*, London, Routledge, pp. 23–94.

Parsons, G. (1993b) 'Expanding the religious spectrum: new religious movements in modern Britain', in G. Parsons (ed.) *The Growth of Religious Diversity: Britain from 1945*, vol. 1: *Traditions*, London, Routledge, pp. 275–303.

Parsons, G. (1994a) 'Between law and licence: Christianity, morality and "permissiveness"', in G. Parsons (ed.) *The Growth of Religious Diversity: Britain from 1945*, vol. 2: *Issues*, London, Routledge, pp. 231–66.

Parsons, G. (1994b) 'There and back again? Religion and the 1944 and 1988 Education Acts', in G. Parsons (ed.) *The Growth of Religious Diversity: Britain from 1945*, vol. 2: *Issues*, London, Routledge, pp. 161–98.

Parsons, G. (1994c) 'From consensus to confrontation: religion and politics in Britain since 1945' in G. Parsons (ed.) *The Growth of Religious Diversity: Britain from 1945, volume 2, Issues*, London, Routledge, pp. 123–59.

Snape, M. and Parker, S. (2001) 'Keeping faith and coping: belief, popular religiosity and the British people', in P. Liddle, J. Bourne and I. Whitehead (eds) *The Great World War 1914–1945*, vol. 2: *The Peoples' Experience*, London, HarperCollins, pp. 397–419.

Thompson, W. (1992) 'Britain's moral majority', in B. Wilson (ed.) *Religion: Contemporary Issues*, London, Bellew Publishing, pp. 64–91.

Thompson, W. (1997) 'Charismatic politics: the social and political impact of renewal' in S. Hunt, M. Hamilton and T. Walter (eds) *Charismatic Christianity: Sociological Perspectives*, pp. 160–83.

Weeks, J. (1989) *Sex, Politics and Society: The Regulation of Sexuality since 1800*, London, Longman.

Williams, S. (1999) *Religious Belief and Popular Culture in Southwark c.1880–1939*, Oxford, Oxford University Press.

Wolffe, J. (1993) 'The religions of the silent majority', in G. Parsons (ed.) *The Growth of Religious Diversity: Britain from 1945*, vol. 1: *Traditions*, London, Routledge, pp. 305–46.

Wolffe, J. (1994) 'How many ways to God? Christians and religious pluralism', in G. Parsons (ed.) *The Growth of Religious Diversity: Britain from 1945*, vol. 2: *Issues*, London, Routledge, pp. 23–53.

Asterisked items are particularly recommended for further reading.

7   Women, priesthood, and the ordained ministry in the Christian tradition

Susan Mumm

This chapter examines the experience of women seeking ordination in the Church of England as compared with the experiences of women in the Lutheran, Methodist and Roman Catholic churches. I have chosen to emphasize the Church of England because its public, official role as an established church gives its approach to the issue extra resonance, and because it is linked historically and theologically with the other churches under examination. In this case study, conflict does not involve physical force or threats of violence; here, conflict has been expressed verbally, symbolically and in writing. It has arisen from a mutually held conviction that those who hold the opposing view are in a state of fundamental error, which risks serious damage to the church involved. The other major theme of the chapter is coexistence, where opposing viewpoints jostle uneasily within the same faith group. In the case of some denominations, de facto segregation of the two parties has been a visible and continuing source of unease. Conversion is applicable only as a change of view within a tradition, although the decision to ordain women in the Church of England did provoke a small number of clergy and laity to join the Roman Catholic Church; an example of what John Wolffe describes elsewhere as a 'change of allegiance between sub-traditions' (see Introduction, p. 7).

A brief history

The history of women's ordination is a short one. Women's preaching and other forms of ministry go back to the early days of Christianity, in one form or another, but this is not ordination. Ordination is more than the right to preach; it implies a position which goes beyond the pulpit and conveys an authority which is normally considered to be supernatural in origin as well as life-long. It involves being in 'Holy Orders', which is a special status, and which historically was considered to set its possessor aside from lay people. The words used in the ordaining of priests underline this sense of being 'set apart' from the laity. In the service of ordination long employed in the Church of England, the bishop, placing his hands on the ordinand's head, prays:

> Receive the Holy Ghost for the office and work of a Priest in the Church of God, now committed unto thee by the imposition of our hands. Whose sins thou dost forgive, they are forgiven; and

> whose sins thou dost retain, they are retained. And be thou a
> faithful dispenser of the Word of God, and of his holy
> Sacraments;
> In the Name of the Father, and of the Son, and of the Holy
> Ghost. Amen.

While the focus of this chapter is on women as priests, it should be
remembered that women's service to Christianity is as old as the religion
itself. Women workers are mentioned throughout Acts and the Epistles. A
tradition of service continued, first as dedicated virgins and widows,
formalized into communities of women by the third century CE. In the
ninth century four groups of women – consecrated virgins, nuns,
deaconesses engaged in the service of the church, and the wives of
bishops and other men in sacred orders – were also considered to be in
a special state of life. Of these, only religious communities survived the
Middle Ages. Gradually enclosure rather than active work became the
norm, first in the Eastern Church. This was later enforced throughout the
west by Pope Boniface VII (1294–1309), a restriction reconfirmed by the
Council of Trent, and not relaxed to any great extent until the eighteenth
century. The looser discipline of Celtic Christianity appears to have
allowed at least two women, St Brigid in Ireland (c. 451–525), and Hilda
of Whitby (614–680) in England, to function as bishops. Before the
Reformation, there was a proliferation of minor orders and holy orders,
all considered 'ordained', but at the Reformation all orders below that of
deacon were abolished, and ordination was reserved for deacons and
priests. Post-Reformation, priests in holy orders ministered both with
word (preaching and prayers) and sacrament (celebrating the Eucharist).

While occasional women are recorded as preachers in England in the
period after the Reformation, they invariably belonged to religious
groups that did not set apart their clergy by specialized training leading
to ordination. Both the Quakers and early Methodists (Wesleyan
Methodists originated in the eighteenth century, with other groups
including the Primitive and Bible Christians, in the next) permitted a few
women to preach during the denomination's formation. Among the
Methodists, Wesley had been generally sympathetic to women with an
'extraordinary call', but his successors moved quickly to restrain the
preaching activities of women. Wesleyan women of the early years 'lived
out an unrepeatable situation'. They were given a greater scope of
action, especially to deal with other women, but the movement was
dominated by self-confident and omnipresent male professional clergy
(Kent, 2002, pp. 119–21). Even the women preachers had an extremely
circumscribed role.

> Women who joined the early Wesleyan societies benefited from
> the temporary tumult of a unique religious situation, but ... in the
> second generation the women found Wesleyanism more and
> more patriarchal ... John Wesley allowed a very small number of
> women to preach, but there was never any question of their

itinerating, or ... of being ordained, as some of the men were. The majority of the male itinerants disliked women preachers as powerful competitors, and stopped the practice altogether once John Wesley was dead.

(Kent, 2002, p. 121)

No woman was given the authority to join the governing bodies of the major denominations, which meant that no woman was able to make a lasting impact on religious practice at more than a very local level. While early Methodism allowed women to preach, it did not permit them to take part in the government of the church, and their early preaching role was gradually suppressed as a result of their lack of institutionally-based power. The Wesleyan ideal 'involved submission to both supernatural and pastoral authority. Charles Wesley ... combined the assertion of masculine power with an official understanding of the nature of the Anglican priesthood' (Kent, 2002, p. 111). This sense of power was passed to the Wesley's successors. As Zechariah Taft, a prominent early Methodist and author of *Biographical Sketches of the Lives and Public Ministries of Various Holy Women* (1825, 1828) expressed it:

> I believe the ordinary call of God to the ministry is to men, and the extraordinary call to females. But in this extraordinary call I do not consider *any* female strictly and fully called to the *pastoral office*, or to be the regular pastor of the Church of Christ, but I do believe that the Lord calls some females to be fellow-labourers with the *pastor* ...

(in Field-Bibb, 1991, p. 14, emphasis Taft's)

This point is central to the argument of this introduction. Taft was right in seeing the existence of women preachers as a red herring of sorts. The real issue is *admission to the fully professional ministry of the church, which includes (at least potentially) access to the highest offices and to decision-making power,* which I am describing as ordination. Preaching is not enough. The question of women as ordained to the ministry of the Methodist Church did not resurface until the 1920s, and it remained an issue creating much dissent and conflict in the Methodist Conference for several decades, as did the status of Wesleyan deaconesses. Fifty years after the subject was first seriously discussed in the twentieth century, the Methodist Conference agreed to admit women as ministers in 1973, and the first were ordained in 1974.

The Bible Christians had a longer tradition of female preachers, but this had faded before the end of the Victorian period; again, this group did not ordain, but simply permitted a few women to pursue a preaching ministry. The Salvation Army was the only British-based denomination founded before the twentieth century routinely and normatively to give women officers the same religious status as male officers prior to 1900, but they were a non-sacramental denomination and commissioned, rather than ordained, both sexes. The Quakers, as in so much else, were an exception to this pattern, with active involvement by women throughout their history. By the early twentieth century, women were being recognized as ministers in Unitarianism and Congregationalism, and the question of female clergy was under discussion in a number of the free churches. In the United States, the first woman minister to undergo a form of ordination had been Antoinette Brown Blackwell (1825–1921), who was 'ordained' as a Congregationalist by a Methodist minister in 1853; this was a situation of an individual congregation choosing their pastor. However, she served a congregation for only eight months before retiring in the face of external opposition and internal conflict (Sarna, 1996, pp. 46–7; Zikmund, 1996, p. 68).

As mentioned above, in the denominations that allowed it at all, those few women whose preaching was tolerated were those who were deemed to have a special call which exempted them temporarily from Paul's prohibitions:

> Let your women keep silence in the churches: for it is not permitted unto them to speak; but they are commanded to be under obedience as also saith the law.

(1 Corinthians 14: 34, Authorised Version)

> But I suffer not a woman to teach, nor to usurp authority over the man, but to be in silence.

(1 Timothy 2: 12, Authorised Version)

The permanent validity of the Pauline doctrine that women should keep silence in the churches remained unquestioned.

Traditional reasons for not ordaining women

Historically, the major Christian churches have not ordained women. There were three reasons commonly given for this. First, women were considered to be 'daughters of Eve', meaning that they were responsible for bringing sin into the world, and were believed to remain an ongoing source of temptation for men. The biblical accounts of the Fall were interpreted in such a way as emphasized the woman's culpability, and saw her 'punishment' for acquiring knowledge of good and evil as permanent subjection to her husband, and by implication to all men in authority. As the conduits of sin into the world, women were therefore inappropriate channels for God's grace through the sacraments.

The second reason for assuming that women were incapable of ordination was based upon a belief that they were inferior by nature and by law. This idea seems to underlie Paul's words, quoted above. Early

Figure 1 'The lustful wife tempts her virtuous husband', Medieval woodcut. The Bodleian Library, University of Oxford, shelf mark: MS Douce 195, fol. 118

Christianity was heavily influenced by Greek philosophy, which created a harsh body/spirit divide and which saw women as being intrinsically inferior to men. In addition to the intellectual influence of the Greeks, the basis for the Church's law in its formative period was Roman law, which accorded women inferior status both at home and in civic society. Some early church fathers went so far in their revision of the story of Genesis 1 and 2 as to claim that only the man was created in God's image.

Finally, in the first centuries of Christianity, women were considered tainted by beliefs that menstruation and intercourse made women ritually unclean and capable of defiling the altar. In a climate that exalted celibacy and looked upon procreation even in marriage as somehow sinful, women were considered too earthy, too close to unredeemed nature, and too tied to physical pleasure to serve as a conduit between God and the faithful. These ideas are found in the writings of the early church fathers, early church law, medieval theological treatises, and in the pronouncements of church authorities. Later, as such ideas became discredited, the churches increasingly relied on the by-then-established 'tradition of the church', which had never ordained women, as justification for not ordaining them in the modern world. (However, some Catholic authorities contest this, claiming that the early church had fully-ordained women deacons, and priests in a few provinces, such as southern Italy.)

The modern anti-ordination position

The attitude of those opposed to women's ordination to the priesthood changed radically over the first three-quarters of the twentieth century. At the beginning, it simply was not an issue. Presumably any woman who felt a calling to the Anglican, Catholic, Methodist, or Lutheran ministry either reinterpreted the calling in terms of another form of service, such as becoming a missionary or a member of a religious community, or else quietly worried about her sanity. The issue began to be formulated in terms of equality of calling about the time that the First World War ended, although it was very much a minority question at the time. Most Anglicans and others would have agreed with the *Church Times* that the very suggestion was 'grotesque'. As the historian of Anglican women, Sean Gill, reminds us, the question of ordination of women is one of very few to unite disparate elements within the theologically divided Anglican Church.

> It is because the issue of the ordination of women to the priesthood highlights so clearly the challenge of modernity, that Evangelical and Anglo-Catholic opponents of the measure have been able to make common cause with one another, even though the grounds of their opposition are not in other ways theologically compatible.
>
> (Gill, 1994, p. 233)

The arguments against the ordination of women raised a number of issues for Christians, although not all of those who objected would have agreed with the entire case. Perhaps the most widely heard objection was that it was contrary to the tradition of the church, which must be assumed to demonstrate the mind and intentions of Christ. Linked to this was the claim that the all-male discipleship of Jesus was deliberate and not simply reflective of social realities in first-century Palestine. This suggested that maleness was somehow uniquely suited to priesthood in a way that femaleness could never be. It was argued that all monotheistic religions had male priesthoods: female religious leadership was associated with pantheism, nature religions or paganism. It was asserted that the symbolism of female priests at the altar would fundamentally change the nature of the church. Some argued that God's plan for women was complementarity rather than equality, meaning that different roles for the two sexes were both appropriate and necessary. Evangelicals, in particular, placed emphasis on the claim that female 'headship' would be in conflict with their interpretation of biblical texts. An anti-feminist argument saw demands for women's ordination as another example of the unfortunate effects of secular humanism. The history of the founding of the church and its subsequent experience suggested that women could not receive Holy Orders. In addition, it would raise problems in discussions regarding reunion with some churches. Priesthood was considered to be incompatible with the duties of married women, but it would be unfair to impose celibacy on women priests alone. Finally, there would be a loss to the church if the 'specific gifts of the feminine sex' were diverted from their own ministries into the priesthood.

Early demands for an official role for women

The first demands for women's ordination within the Church of England emerged about the same time that the Methodist Conference began to consider the issue. Congregationalists had been ordaining women since the early twentieth century, but this had received little public attention until the Anglican Maude Royden (1876–1956) began her ministry in a Congregationalist church during the war years. Sean Gill summarizes the wider social pressures that brought this about as 'the movement for democracy in political life and the growth of professional paid work for women' (Gill, 1994, p. 206). The Anglican Church in particular (perhaps because of its link to the state?) was slow to acknowledge the increased role of women in public life, repeatedly refusing women to vote in parochial church council elections. When pressures to allow women the vote started to grow, the church newspaper *The Guardian* was able to reassure its anti-women-suffrage readership in 1905, that men would remain firmly in charge of the church at all levels:

> ... the most they (women) can do will be to vote for men who will vote for other men who will elect the Lay House. Moreover the other two Houses of the Representative Church Council will consist of men chosen by men.

(8 February, 1908)

In 1919, Anglican women were allowed both to vote and to serve on such councils. Historian Brian Heeney argues that this was less a victory for women's equality than an attempt to rectify the anomaly created by the 1918 Representation of the People Act, which permitted some women to vote in national elections and become members of parliament, while they were still excluded from even the most local level of government within the established church.

Best known of the early Anglican campaigners for women's ordination was Maude Royden, who came from an affluent Liverpool family and was active in advanced religious, suffragette, social hygiene and peace movements. Royden was an Oxford graduate who, during the First World War, accepted the post of Assistant Preacher at the City Temple, a congregation led by a Congregationalist, where 'her preaching filled the City Temple to the roof' (Heeney, 1988, p. 89). Remaining a life-long Anglican, she regularly preached in Anglican pulpits despite the opposition of many, including the Bishop of London (Winnington-Ingram), who objected to her preaching at the Three Hours Service held on Good Friday. Royden's view was that the church was 'so anxious to see what is safe that she loses her leadership in what is right' (cited in Gill, 1994, p. 235). Her near contemporary, Edith Picton-Turbervill (1872–1960), preached in Episcopal and Anglican services in Britain and continental Europe. She was elected as a Labour member in the 1929 General Election and was awarded an OBE. Both these women were non-militant suffragists who were active in the Church League for Women's Suffrage, which emphasized 'the deep religious significance of the women's movement' as well as the franchise. Both found that the war gave them greater opportunities to preach, but neither woman was able to progress to the fully ordained ministry to which she felt called. It is probable that we can trace the beginning of the demand for women's right to ordination within the established church to the war years, as Heeney suggests: 'women's place in the ministry of word and sacraments became associated with the question of their rights in the councils of the Church' during this time (Heeney, 1988, p. 108).

The church going public was generally hostile to the idea of women as priests. The *Church Times* claimed that the very raising of the question could be seen as a symptom of madness.

> For any sane person the thing is so grotesque that he must refuse to discuss it ... The monstrous regiment of women in politics would be bad enough but a monstrous regiment of priestesses would be a thousand fold worse. We are not inclined to treat [a proposed conference on the ordination of women] as a sane scheme; we regard it as a piece with that epidemic of hysteria which has manifested itself in the violence of feminine militants. It will pass with time.
>
> (20 July 1916)

It is clear that there was an understood connection between the demand for equal rights in the wider society and the demand for women priests. The best known of these preachers, Maude Royden, was invited to stand for election in four different constituencies, at a time when more conservative Anglican women, although they technically had the vote, deplored the fact (Heeney, 1988, p. 87). Although Royden chose not to accept any of these invitations, the fact that she sprang so readily to local committees' minds suggests that there was seen to be a relationship between women preachers and advanced, politically-active feminism. The main arm of demands for women's rights within the Church of England, the League of the Church Militant (LCM), folded in 1928, citing as its reasons that an equal franchise had been attained, and believing that their second aim, the ordination of women, had been advanced and would inevitably come to pass. In actual fact, more than half a century was to pass before the second aim of the LCM was achieved. But it is significant that this was achieved in another period when the women's cause was prominent and feminism was on the advance.

Pragmatic accommodations

The Church of England made two attempts during the interwar period to explain why women could not be priests. The first, in 1920, declares that the first generation of Christians were specially guided by the Holy Spirit, implying that their practices would be permanently normative. The second came in 1936. It was based on a peculiar argument that depicted women as passionless and men as prone to lust – and as universally heterosexual.

> We maintain that the ministration of women will tend to produce a lowering of the spiritual tone of Christian worship ... in the thoughts and desires of that sex (women) the natural is more easily made subordinate to the supernatural, the carnal to the spiritual, than is the case with men; and that the ministrations of a male priesthood do not normally arouse that side of female nature which should be quiescent during the times of adoration of almighty God. We believe, on the other hand, that it would be impossible for the male members of the average Anglican congregation to be present at a service at which a woman ministered without becoming unduly conscious of her sex.

(The Archbishops' Commission, 1936, quoted in Woolf, 1938, p. 288)

However, the 1920 discussion produced a statement that was to provide the debate for the next seventy years. This identifies the tension between the practice of the church and responsiveness to the leadership of God.

> We are profoundly conscious that the Holy Spirit teaches Christian people by those age-long precedents which we believe to be the outcome of His guidance. But sometimes it becomes our duty, faithfully retaining the lessons of the sacred past, in a very special sense to trust ourselves to His inspiration in that present which is our time of opportunity, in order that He may

> lead us into whatsoever fresh truth of thought or action is in
> accordance with the will of God.
>
> (Cited in Gill, 1994, p. 237)

It is in this period that the women seeking ordination in the Anglican
and Methodist churches launched a concerted argument for their case.
Beside the justice argument, and the voices of women convinced that
they had a vocation to the ordained ministry, there were also theological
arguments. The present situation meant that women did not have an
avenue for two-sided commitment, in that they were unable to perform
any of the roles open to clergy, even in minor orders. There was no way
in which 'called' women could become permanently and publicly
committed to the church without entering a religious community.

The first Anglican woman to be ordained priest was a deaconess. Li Tim
Oi was ordained by Bishop R. O. Hall of Hong Kong and South China on
25 January 1944, in a diocese scarred by war and invasion, and with few
men willing to serve as priests. In 1945, Bishop Hall stated 'There is no
question that Li Tim Oi has the gift of priesthood. The only thing that
remains is, is it going to be possible to ordain women with these obvious
gifts and calling to the ministry? I am convinced myself that it is right'
(cited in Gill, 1994, p. 242). The response of the Archbishop of
Canterbury was to send a letter to the bishop 'profoundly deploring' the
ordination, but the church did not break communion with the Holy
Catholic Church of China as a result. She served as a priest for four years
until the 1948 Lambeth Conference deplored her ordination and
threatened to dethrone Hall if she did not cease her priestly ministry. Li
Tim Oi voluntarily withdrew from serving publicly as a priest, but
continued to administer the sacraments when asked. She did not resign
her orders, making her the first validly ordained woman in Anglican
history. In 1971, the Anglican Consultative Councils cleared the way for
her to once again undertake the duties of a priest, by agreeing that the
national Anglican churches had the right to make their own decisions
about ordaining women. She emigrated to Toronto, Canada, in 1982 and
was active in St John's Chinese congregation until her death in 1992.

The war and interwar period were also the beginning of women's
ordination in several other traditions. Regina Jonas, the first woman
Reform rabbi, who was ordained privately in Germany in 1935, worked
increasingly publicly in synagogues throughout the early years of the
Second World War, when few male rabbis were left to serve the Jewish
community. She died in Auschwitz in 1944 (Umansky, 1996, p. 31). The
American Methodist Episcopal Church began ordaining women as early
as 1924, but only as local preachers. They did not have General
Conference membership until 1956 (Wessinger, 1996, p. 18).

The next two decades were quiet ones in the history of the ordination of
women within the Anglican communion. In 1962, the report *Gender and
Ministry* was presented to the Church of England. This raised the

Figure 2   Portrait of (Florence) Li Tim Oi. Printed with the permission of the Li Tim-Oi Foundation

question which was to become a central one in later debates in all the traditions: whether Holy Orders was still a ministry which should be set apart from all other forms of ministry. It also suggested that the priesthood was being understood less in terms of authority and 'semi-magical status', and more in terms of service. The discussion of the report identified four key questions. The first was whether the priest's ministry required biological and psychological characteristics prevalent only in men. The second question was concerned with whether sex differences were universal and unalterable. The third question discussed the symbolic importance of the priest being male and whether female priests would change the way in which the faith was perceived. The last question dealt with the persistence of 'powerful irrational motives' which might affect behaviour and attitudes. The 1968 Lambeth Conference admitted that the arguments against women's ordination were 'inconclusive' and embarked on a series of studies of the issue, as well as stating 'The New Testament does not encourage Christians to think that nothing should be done for the first time' (Field-Bibb, 1991, p. 103).

However, things were changing faster elsewhere. In 1971, the national churches within the Anglican communion were advised that bishops, with the consent of their provinces, could ordain women to the Anglican priesthood. The Bishop of Hong Kong, Gilbert Baker, promptly restored

Li Tim Oi's priestly responsibilities and ordained two teachers, Jane Hwang and Joyce Bennett. His rationale was a mixture of practical need and a distinct theological position:

> As we try to cope with the needs of a huge population ... I believe we are impelled by the Holy Spirit to make better provisions for the needs of men and women alike through a ministry more representative of humanity as a whole ... if humanity is to be fully represented before God in the priesthood it is logical to suppose that the ministry which is not limited to people of one tribe or race should not be limited to one sex.

(*Daily Telegraph*, 16 November 1971, cited in Furlong, 1991, p. 96)

In 1968, the Methodist Church in Britain produced the report *Women and the Ordained Ministry*, which recommended ordaining women on the same basis as men. Time was lost due to concerns over the effect female clergy would have on reunion until it became clear that the proposed union with the Church of England was unlikely to take place. It was then endorsed by Conference in 1973, and 17 Methodist women were ordained in 1974. The Church of Scotland began appointing women as elders in 1966, and to the ministry in 1968. The World Council of Churches reported in 1970 that 72 denominations belonging to the WCC ordained women and 143 refused to do so. The largest churches to oppose women's ordination were the major branches of Orthodoxy and Catholicism (Field-Bibb, 1991, p. 117). The Swedish Lutheran Church had in 1960 begun to ordain women after this had been to some extent forced on them by the government and the law courts. This solution led to considerable conflict and bitterness there which took several years to resolve. A number of the American Lutheran churches (most importantly ELCA, the Evangelical Lutheran Church of America) carried out its first ordinations of women in 1970. It was argued that Lutheran tradition actually made the transition easier, because of 'the insight informing the Lutheran tradition – a kind of reflexive critique – of any and all ecclesiastical pretensions that would replace the promise with human-made laws that deify particular human persons or institutions' (Malcolm, 1995, p. 294). Ultra-conservative Lutherans, however, continue to prohibit women from serving in any capacity, even in unordained roles, if it opens the possibility of them having authority over men (Brand, 1997, p. 22).

Changes worldwide

Much of the impetus for women's ordination within Anglicanism during this final stage of discussion came from the wider Anglican Communion. At this point, the focus of attention swings to the American Episcopal Church. Many women there had graduated from theological colleges, hoping that the American church would soon recognize their vocation; a number of these were veterans of the American civil rights movement, and saw it as a justice issue not dissimilar to the black rights movement.

When the American Episcopal Church's governing bodies divided on the issue (bishops in favour, laity against), three retired bishops decided to ordain women without further delay, and in July 1974, the 'Philadelphia Eleven' were ordained to the priesthood in the Church of the Advocate, Philadelphia, a church that was home to a black congregation in one of the poorest urban areas in the country. These ordinations were considered irregular, and the Episcopal Church was engulfed in a furious debate, with some bishops even threatening to sue. However, the storm was short-lived. In 1976, General Convention voted on the issue again, and this time it agreed to ordain women as well as accept the ordinations of the Philadelphia Eleven as valid. By this time the Anglican Church of Canada had been ordaining women as priests for a year, and New Zealand's Anglicans began doing the same in 1976. It has been asserted that the irregular ordinations of 1974 and 1975 were necessary in order to get women's sense of vocation taken seriously: 'the embedded message in these ordinations was that restoring equality between men and women as symbolized in priesthood was a greater good than following church discipline' (Raab, 2000, p. 223).

The US was also the location of change in another tradition. The first Jewish woman to be regularly ordained as a rabbi by the faculty of a rabbinical seminary was Sally Jane Priesand in 1972. The seminary that ordained her, the Hebrew Union College, had agreed in principle to ordain women fifty years earlier, but had refused all earlier female candidates (Zola, 1996, p. 5). It is clear from the clustering of ordinations in the Judeo-Christian tradition in the 1970s that there is a complicated relationship between demands for justice, feminist influences on the wider society, and the impact of the theology of liberation, all of which contribute to the possibility of women's priesthood.

British society, more conservative than that of North America, unsurprisingly moved more slowly. In 1975, the General Synod, in Gill's memorable phrase, 'approached its task with all the enthusiasm of men and women asked to cross a minefield wearing magnetic boots', and voted on the motion 'that this Synod considers that there are no fundamental objections to the ordination of women to the priesthood' (Gill, 1994, p. 251). This motion was carried, and its success fuelled a general sense of confidence among the supporters of women's ordination that women priests in the Church of England would soon be a reality. This was enhanced when moves to allow deaconesses to become deacons in Holy Orders were started in 1976, and by the Methodist example. However, when the 1978 General Synod debated a motion to remove the barriers to the ordination of women to the priesthood, it failed in the House of Clergy, although passing in the Houses of Bishops and Laity. It was at this point that deaconess Una Kroll, a London physician and well-known advocate of women's ordination, shouted from the gallery a protest which was to resonate with Anglican and Catholic women worldwide: 'We asked you for bread and you gave us a stone.' The Catholic wing of the church had launched a well-organized attack on the motion, fearing that it would make permanently impossible reunion with the Roman Catholic and Orthodox churches, and they were supported by some Evangelical clergy who were concerned that the ordination of women would be in conflict with their reading of the Pauline Epistles.

From the time of the failed 1978 motion, the debate on all sides was conducted with an extraordinary amount of acrimony, suspicion of opponents' motives and personal attacks. Newspapers such as the *Church Times* from this period make painful reading, as all positions engaged in vituperation. Many who had been neutral on the subject found themselves polarizing when women desiring ordination were attacked as 'witches', and 'pagan priestesses', and as plotting for the destruction of Christianity. The depths of misogyny displayed in some quarters shocked many who had never previously seen the need for women priests, into offering support. In July 1979, the Movement for the Ordination of Women (MOW) was founded. MOW contained an uneasy association of radicals and conservatives, which inevitably gave rise to conflict within the organization. As Furlong describes it, 'there was ... a basic conflict that was almost impossible to address – many supporters were very respectable people, yet the [proposed] legislation had radical implications that perhaps nobody at that time had fully perceived' (Furlong, 1991, p. 102).

> It took a lot of courage for women who had been bred to be quiet, polite and obedient, to confront their fathers in God. The most frightening aspect of it was discovering how angry we were – it felt disturbing and 'unchristian'.

(ibid.)

Tactics were also difficult to agree on: radicals advocated public demonstrations of various kinds; conservative supporters of MOW feared that such action would be counter-productive. It is a crude oversimplification to depict all advocates for women's ordination as feminist, let alone radically feminist; many were theologically and socially conservative, especially among the group seeking ordination themselves. As Gill reminds us, the Synod members who debated the issue were church activists, not social activists:

> The Houses of Synod were not, as conservatives claimed, dominated by passionate advocates of feminist theology and secular feminism, but by far more cautious and conservative members and representatives, for whom appeals to what were essentially Victorian patterns of gender identity and relationships no longer made much sense.

(Gill, 1994, p. 263)

*Figure 3   'Oh! Do not this abominable thing that I hate'
(serving other Gods – the Queen of Heaven). Anti-ordination
of women march, November 1992. Photo: David Ashdown/*
The Independent

A number of protests were organized by MOW throughout the 1980s, many of them silent. Typical was the July 1983 walkout of thirteen women deaconesses from an ordination service being held at Southwark Cathedral. They held a 'wilderness' liturgy in the street outside following their exodus, eating honey-cake and drinking milk, joined by a large number of men and women who supported MOW. At subsequent ordination ceremonies as well as meetings of General Synod, it became routine for those attending to enter the building after filing past rows of women deacons silently holding placards reading 'Waiting'. In 1981, a decade after some national churches in the Anglican Communion had begun ordaining women, and twenty years after the then-established church in Sweden had done so, the Church of England agreed to admit women to the diaconate – the lowest level of Holy Orders. (By this date, women had been admitted to Holy Orders in the Anglican Church of Canada, the Diocese of Hong Kong, the Province of New Zealand, and the Episcopal Church of the United States of America. Women priests had been approved in principle in the Anglican churches of Australia, Burma, the Province of the Indian Ocean, Ireland, the Holy Catholic Church of Japan, Kenya and the Church in Wales. A decision against ordaining women had been taken in the churches of Ceylon, Singapore, South Pacific, Tanzania, West Africa and Brazil.)

The legislation to enact this was agreed in 1987, when The Deacons (Ordination of Women) Measure closed the order of deaconess to new recruits. This made them deacons and not deaconesses, who were not then considered to be in Orders of any kind. This led to discussions of a 'permanent diaconate', a feature of Anglicanism which had not been considered necessary when only men became deacons, with the assumption that they would move on to priesthood after a year.

In 1985, opponents of the ordination of women had begun to suggest that the Anglican Church would split if women were to be ordained. In 1986, Women Against the Ordination of Women was established. It was opposed not only to the ordination of women, but also to what it felt was widespread and pervasive feminism within the Church of England.

Figure 4   Cover of The Spectator, *23 November 1985, reproduced with the permission of Nicholas Garland and* The Spectator. *'... a woman's preaching is like a dog's walking on his hinder legs. It is not done well, but you are surprised to find it done at all.' Samuel Johnson, 1763.*

Its first aim was 'to combat misplaced feminism in worship and theology'. It was also opposed to easing of the divorce laws and to homosexuality in all circumstances. Later that same year, Synod debated the measure known as 'Women Lawfully Ordained Abroad'. This permitted women from other Anglican churches to celebrate the Eucharist in England and Wales, but they were subjected to various checks which were not extended to men in the same circumstances. However, MOW welcomed this, feeling that it was better to allow women to exercise the ministry even in a limited fashion, rather than not at all, and believing that experience of women as priests would convert many waverers. This measure was rejected by the houses of Clergy and Laity (General Synod, 1988).

In 1987, the opponents of women's ordination within the Church of England founded a new group, called the Association for an Apostolic Ministry, which brought together Anglo-Catholic and Evangelicals in a common organization, despite their theological differences, which created ongoing tensions within the group. Although not all opponents of women's ordination joined it, by 1987 the Bishop of London, Graham Leonard, had compiled the names of 1,800 priests opposed to allowing women to enter the ordained ministry (Furlong, 1991, p. 113). The central problem for opponents remained the need for the priesthood to be male, symbolically as well as physically.

> An all male priesthood will be witness to those things about the nature and being of God which were signified in the particularity of Jesus' maleness: a male priesthood will continue more faithfully to represent the priesthood of Christ in the sacramental life of the Church: it will point to the role and status of men in relation to women according to the purposes of God in creation and redemption, by testifying to the headship of men over women and the proper subordination of women to men. Those of us who hold this view believe this to be an important witness to our society as men and women struggle to find new patterns of relationship and new roles for women.

(General Synod, 1988, p. 99)

The House of Bishops' report on the ordination of women was published in early 1987. It discussed theological issues, the principles for legislation, and safeguards for priests who could not accept women as full colleagues. In the Synod debate on the report, the Bishop of London described women priests as a 'virus in the bloodstream which could never be got out'. Anglo-Catholics were not the only group to fear that women priests would permanently block all possibility of reunion with Rome. The Evangelical-Catholic wing of the Evangelical Lutheran Church of America has expressed and continues to express opposition on these grounds (Grindal, 1996, p. 201). However, it was becoming clear that not all Anglo-Catholics opposed women priests. In October of 1987, eleven Anglo-Catholic bishops published a letter supporting women's ordination: 'we assert that Anglican Catholics who support the ordination of women are loyal to that tradition in which our spirituality has grown and justified in the belief that such ordinations can be a precious gift from God to enhance the catholicity of the church, and enrich her mission' (cited in Furlong, 1991, p. 125).

By the end of 1987, almost 900 women had been ordained deacon within the Church of England. About the same time a survey of priests conducted for the Association for the Apostolic Ministry indicated that approximately one in ten were opposed to the ordination of women. Threats of a split in the church were being voiced, with some claiming that an alternative church would be established, and others fearing that many would convert to Catholicism or Orthodoxy. Beginning to believe that priesthood for women was inevitable, the Cost of Conscience organization demanded financial compensation for priests who would feel compelled to leave the church when the ordination of women was legalized. Forward in Faith estimated that over a thousand priests and bishops would leave the church.[1] (In actual fact, very few parish priests left, and some of these later returned, ironically, reportedly burnt out by being employed as sacrament-dispensing machines in a Roman Church desperately short of priests.)

The Bishops' report proposed several principles to guide the formation of legislation to ordain women and to compensate those priests who wished to leave the ministry as a result, as well as providing provincial episcopal provision (commonly known as 'flying bishops') for the oversight of priests who wished to remain in post but whose diocesan bishop approved of the ordination of women. By the time of the 1988 Lambeth conference, the churches in the United States and New Zealand were close to consecrating the first women bishops. Six other provinces – Canada, Hong Kong, Brazil, Uganda, Kenya and South India, had women priests: about 1,500 in total. Australia had voted on and turned down the idea several times; it began officially ordaining women in 1992, after diocesan bishops had begun to do so on their own authority. While some argued that it was already too late, given the number of women priests in the Anglican provinces and the Free Churches in communion with Canterbury, to worry about the possible effects on reunion with Rome, others were dismayed that the Pope had sent a telegram to the 1988 conference mentioning the risk of 'new obstacles'. In February 1989, Barbara Harris was consecrated the first woman bishop in the Episcopal Church of the United States of America; the co-celebrant at her consecration was Li Tim Oi.

The final vote in November 1992 was a dramatic moment in the history of the Church of England: it passed because two former opponents of the legislation underwent a last-minute conversion. The first women to

[1] Forward in Faith is an association of Anglicans who are unable to accept the ordination of women as priests or their consecration as bishops.

be ordained to the priesthood were priested in March 1994 in Bristol Cathedral, the 'culmination of women's increasing involvement in the life of the Church over many years' (Gill, 1994, p. 267).

The uneasy consensus created by this was a two-tier Church of England, with some priests refusing the oversight of their diocesan bishops and refusing to recognize the validity of the ministry of their female colleagues. While some churches in the Anglican communion have now accepted women bishops, this still remains an area of enormous potential conflict within Anglicanism, and one where amicable resolution appears unlikely. For example, in 1997 the US General Convention passed a canon saying that all bishops must allow women to officiate in their dioceses. The Lambeth Conference passed a resolution in 1998 that said no bishop should be compelled to ordain women against his will, or license them to work in his diocese. At this date there were women in the Anglican episcopates of Canada, the United States, Polynesia, New Zealand, and the principle had been agreed in Ireland. In June 2003 the

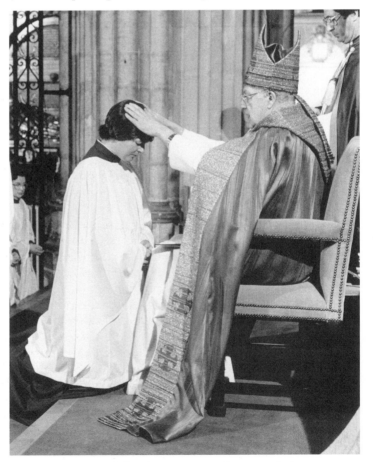

Figure 5   One of the first women deacons being ordained by the Archbishop of Canterbury, Dr Robert Runcie, April 1987, Canterbury Cathedral. Photo: Getty Images/Hulton Archive

Synod of the Scottish Episcopal Church voted 124–24 in favour of consecrating women as bishops, opening the possibility of Anglican women bishops in Great Britain within the very near future.

The Roman Catholic situation

Historically, the Roman Catholic Church, like its Anglican and Lutheran cousins, has only ordained men. Unlike the other three churches discussed in this chapter, the official Roman Catholic position on the question has not altered. The objections raised to the ordination of women are very similar to those articulated by Anglicans, although there is more emphasis on the constant tradition of the Church, and on the significance of the Marian role as symbolizing women's place in the scheme of redemption. Twentieth-century canon law, in both 1917 and 1983, repeats the same phrase: 'Only a baptised man can validly receive ordination'. Demands for women's ordination have tended to come from the more liberal national churches, particularly the Roman Catholic Churches in northern Europe and in North America. In the late 1960s and early 1970s, a number of national synods asked that the question of women's ministry be studied; in 1975, the Vatican Commission on Women in Society was established, but it was forbidden to discuss ordination. *Inter Insigniores*, a papal document of 1976, gives six reasons against women's ordination: the constant tradition of the church; the fact that Christ chose only male apostles; the practice of the apostles; the belief that the attitudes of Christ and the apostles express a permanent truth about the nature of priesthood; a belief that the priest must bear a 'natural resemblance' to Christ; and a claim that the male priesthood is part of the 'mystery' of the church and contemporary issues of gender equality do not deserve consideration in this context. Pope John Paul II's Encyclical 'on the dignity and vocation of women' explained the refusal to allow women to aspire to the priesthood in terms of the centrality of the bridegroom/bride symbolism that the church saw in the priest/laity relationship. (A number of theologians point out that this is a very recent argument, developed in the nineteenth century; see, for example, Wijngaards, 2001, pp. 113–20). There are two key documents underlying the Catholic debate, *Inter Insigniores* (1976) and *Ordinato Sacerdotalis* (1994). The first specifically excludes women from the diaconate. *Ordinato Sacerdotalis*, which was declared part of the deposit of faith in 1995 (suggesting that it is to be held as infallible), declares that 'the Church has no authority whatsoever to confer priestly ordination on women and this judgement is to be definitely held by all the Church's faithful' (*Ordinato*, 4).

The argument continued to develop. Men and women, it was argued, are ontologically equal. 'The challenge is ... to build an ecclesiology that is in harmony with its anthropology, that sees women as equally human to men, as persons made in the image of likeness of a God whose infinitude is as it implies and is not limited by sex' (Zagano, 2000, p. 22). This issue was and is always especially urgent in churches which emphasize the sacraments as a means of grace, because there are two sacraments (the Eucharist and reconciliation/confession) in which the officiant must act *in persona Christi*: must be a 'sign' of Christ and stand in his place symbolically. Advocates for the priesthood of women insisted that a single-sex clergy restricts both Christian action and theology.

> The Christian God, who encompasses male and femaleness ... is exemplar to women and to men, *precisely* because in his Incarnation he became *fully* human. That is, God did not become fully male to the exclusion of becoming fully female; God become 'man' *means* God become 'human'. To restrict the Incarnation is to restrict the act of Incarnation.
>
> (Zagano, 2000, p. 34)

There remains, however, the exclusion of women from ordained ministry (canon 1024), and therefore from the offices, functions and ministries that are restricted to clerics. To return to a point made at the beginning of the chapter, the right to preach tends to be a temporary and easily lost privilege if the preachers are outside the decision-making structures of the church. The 1983 Code of Canon Law reiterates the principle that 'only the ordained are capable of exercising the power of governance in the Church and offices that entail the exercise of that power are restricted to clerics'. It has recently been claimed that 90 per cent of Catholic theologians support women's ordination, but the centralized authority of the Vatican remains firmly opposed.

However, not all Catholics are content to accept this. Recently, scholars have claimed that there were ordained women in the early church, basing this on the prohibitions of such activity by four fourth-century Councils. In addition, increased attention has been paid to the fact that the underground churches of Communist Eastern Europe had legitimately ordained women serving as Roman Catholic priests. One of them, Ludmila Javorova, ordained in 1970, explained her position on priesthood and gender thus:

> When it is a matter of salvation or for helping souls in need, why does the hierarchy of the church object if a woman enters into the process? Who is the priest? Someone to accompany people in their joy and their suffering, who offers to go together with them, who is an experience of Christ to them, who works together with God.
>
> (www.womensordination.org)[2]

---

[2] Last accessed on 10 May 2004.

An article by a Roman Catholic advocate of women's ordination summarizes the reasons why women keep returning to the question despite repeated rebuffs.

> Some ... are energised by their own sense of call to ordination, a call they cannot ignore ... Others are driven by a sense of justice; they seek the clear and unequivocal recognition of the true equality of men and women in the church. Others emphasise the enormous problems they have with the all-male image of God which the all-male priesthood and present liturgies uphold, and hence see women's ordination as a limiting act. Others long to see the gifts of all the people of God being used in the Church's ministry. I believe we must have women at the heart of the symbolic system: going for priesthood is going for the centre of that tradition.
>
> (Uhr, 2001, p. 15)

The impact of ordained women

A study of Episcopalian women priests indicates that some perceive the difference between men and women priests as significant.

> ... when women preside at the altar, latent maternal themes in the Eucharist become apparent. Motifs of feeding and nurturing are more prominent, the sacrament is perceived as more 'embodied', women experience greater connectedness and self-affirmation, Christ and God are imaged as female ... Episcopal women clergy at the altar reveal that the impact of women priests goes deeper than attaining equality between the sexes; it extends to the *theology* of the Eucharist itself.
>
> (Raab, 2000, p. 2)

Some Anglican-oriented studies have begun to suggest that men and women accept women priests for different reasons. Men tend to articulate their acceptance as a matter of justice, women describe seeing a woman at the altar as having a perceptible impact on their view of themselves. However, it is dangerous to generalize from the small and limited studies of Anglican/Episcopal priests carried out to date, especially since the longer experience of Lutheran women priests suggests that many see no substantive difference in the experience of the Eucharist by the gender of the officiant. Women's ministry may stress the emphasis on lay ministry, as the fact that women can now be ordained reinforces the message that anybody can be called to ministry. One study of over 100 Anglican deacons suggests that the biggest difference is in leadership style, with a reduced emphasis on authority as derived from a hierarchical structure (Stevens, 1987; Francis and Robbins, 1999).

However, accounts of bullying and threats of violence, sexual and otherwise, against women priests have emerged as a disturbing theme of the first large-scale British study into the experience of women ordained within the Church of England (Thorne, 2000).

In churches with a longer history of ordaining women, the picture looks slightly different. American Lutheran women clergy generally report a low level of attention to gender as an issue in their ministry, and a general dismissal of the idea that women bring any distinctive gifts to their work as clergy. As one Lutheran pastor wrote: 'I don't struggle with my gender in ministry as much as what being a faithful pastor means for me. It includes my gender, but not at the forefront' (Lagerquist, 1999, pp. 67–8). It is true that many of these women can be described as 'minimizers', who downplay the difference between men and women in ministry and in life. It is also true that in the American context, which is generally less overtly sexist than the British, opposition to their priestly role may be somewhat muted. However, such research raises the possibility that women in churches where ordination is a more recent phenomenon may find that their awareness of gender difference in the priesthood diminishes over time, as they themselves become more accepted. Other Lutheran evidence suggests that the early ordinands' experience was very similar to that of Anglican women priests today:

> ... they encountered difficulties which can hardly be imagined today. Set into a male-defined role, they not only caused male clergy to change their self-definition, they also caused uncertainties among their sisters as everyone tried to understand and work through the radically changing role of women in the church.

(Grindal, 1995, p. 258)

However, in both the Lutheran and Anglican churches, as in Judaism, several trends are apparent. In the American Episcopal Church in 1998, there were almost 2000 women priests, constituting almost 14 per cent of all clergy; 45.8 per cent of all deacons in that year were women. Very few have reached the episcopate: 8 (2.5 per cent) bishops in 1998 were women, twenty-one years after the first ordinations. The number of full-time women clergy in both the Lutheran and Jewish traditions has also grown at a very rapid pace; so much so that some priests have articulated a fear that the profession will lose status if the influx continues and it becomes seen as a 'woman's profession'. Like Lutherans and Anglicans, what was rare in Reform Jewish seminaries twenty years ago is now the norm. All three now typically report that 50 per cent or more of those preparing themselves for ordination are women; in the Conservative Jewish tradition, one-third of the aspirants are female. While women rabbis are much less likely to describe a sense of 'calling' than their Christian counterparts, their reported experience as ordained persons is strikingly similar, both in terms of opportunities and limitations on their ministry (Raab, 2000, p. 6, Zola, 1996, p. 6; Simon,

1993, p. 67). In all of these traditions, ordained women are paid significantly less, on average, than their male equivalents; there is also evidence that they find it difficult to be promoted and tend to cluster in the least desirable posts, suggesting that discrimination in opportunities may be widespread (Raab, 2000, pp. 225–6). This problem is exacerbated in countries with a strong cultural tradition of female subordination, as experiences of women ordained as Lutheran clergy in Africa and Asia indicate; in addition, it is difficult for married women to gain acceptance as priests in these parts of the world (Mghwira, 1997; Hutabarat, 1997, pp. 142–3, 146; Kanyoro, 1997, p. 148).

Catholicism is changing too, although the Vatican continues to insist that women can never hope to be ordained. John Wijngaards sees the Second Vatican Council (1962–65) as the moment when Catholic women found their voice, although he reminds us that the St Joan's International Alliance, which was formed in 1911 to press for women's rights in the church and in society, began to discuss ordination in 1928 (Wijngaards, 2001, p. 26). One form of pressure resembles the kind of practical accommodation to necessity that the Hong Kong diocese and German Jews faced, when irregular ordinations took place as a measure of expediency as well as of conviction. The church can no longer train enough priests to serve the faithful. In American Catholicism, it has become routine for women to administer priestless parishes. The great majority of lay parish ministers are women. This has been possible since a revision of canon law in the 1980s permitted persons who are not priests to exercise pastoral care. Catholics are becoming accustomed to the sight of women at the altar. There is also the fact that women have been ordained by Catholic bishops, especially in the territories of the former Soviet Union during the Cold War.

There have been a variety of groups dedicated to furthering the cause of women's ordination within the Catholic Church. At the moment of writing, one of the most active is Women's Ordination Worldwide, an international coalition of organizations that advocates women's ordination in all denominations, but which currently focuses its activities on Roman Catholicism. In 2001, it organized the first public demonstration ever held in Rome demanding women's ordination, on the occasion of the international meeting of Roman Catholic bishops for the 10th Ordinary General Assembly of the Synods of Bishops. The banner depicted women in silhouette elevating the host,[3] with a caption reading 'Ordain Women Priests' in Italian and 'Ordain Women' in Latin, French, German, Polish, Spanish and English. Members of WOW also held a blessing liturgy and procession, wearing purple stoles, the universal symbol for women's ordination, which called on Catholic leaders to end the exclusion of women from ordination.

---

[3] The elevation of the host is part of the ritual of the sacrament, where the bread or wafer is lifted up before the eyes of the congregation.

One unintended consequence of the Vatican's position has been a reconsideration of the meaning of ministry. A growing number of Catholics are questioning the need for an ordained priest at all, focusing instead on the priesthood of all believers and the sacredness of the community gathered together. As Lavinia Byrne, a former nun and prominent advocate of women priests, argues: by refusing to ordain women there is a risk that the laity become alienated by the gulf between its teaching and its sacramental authority (Byrne, 1994). Unofficial celebrations of the Eucharist are becoming more common, involving both men and women as officiants. The best known of these is Critical Mass, which celebrates the Eucharist publicly in order to raise awareness of the issue of priesthood. For at least some Catholics, the question is shifting from 'why not women priests?' to 'why priests at all?'

Conclusion

The relationship between feminism and women's ordination is a complicated one: because women who seek to be priests are accused of wishing to further a feminist 'agenda' without having any true vocation, many women priests adopt an ambivalent stance toward feminism. 'Often the price of admission for women to institutional acceptance is the forfeiture of feminist ideas and identification' (Wessinger, 1996, p. 212). Barbara Brown Zikmund has reminded us that women's full participation in priesthood is a *process* and not a once-for-all event. The date of first ordination in any tradition is not the end of the story, and it certainly does not mark the point at which women priests become fully accepted, much less incorporated in the church's structures. Instead, these dates can be seen as marking the beginning of a second stage of struggle, to achieve full participation in a calling to religious leadership (Zikmund, 1986, cited in Wessinger, 1996, p. 31).

The story of women's ordination is a story of pain for all involved: for women who believe that their churches refuse to recognize their vocation, and for those who remain sure that women's ordination means a denial of biblical teaching and church tradition. Conflict is inevitable, and will continue, as the issues are fought out in different churches and denominations around the world in the years to come. The uneasy peace of coexistence satisfies few.

References

Brand, E. L. (1997) 'Vocation and ministry', in Kanyoro, pp. 12–27.

Byrne, L. (1994) *Woman at the Altar: The Ordination of Women in the Roman Catholic Church*, London, Mowbray.

*Field-Bibb, J. (1991) *Women Towards Priesthood: Ministerial Politics and Feminist Praxis*, Cambridge, Cambridge University Press.

Francis, L. J. and Robbins, M. (1999) *The Long Diaconate: 1987–1994. Women Deacons and the Delayed Journey to Priesthood*, Leominster, Gracewing.

*Furlong, M. (1991) *A Dangerous Delight: Women and Power in the Church*, London, SPCK.

General Synod of the Church of England (1988) *The Ordination of Women to the Priesthood: A Second Report by the House of Bishops of the General Synod of the Church of England*, London, Church House.

*Gill, S. (1994) *Women and the Church of England from the Eighteenth Century to the Present*, London, SPCK.

Grindal, G. (1995) 'Talk among yourselves: political debate among women of the ELCA', *Word & World*, vol. xv, no. 3, pp. 258–71.

Grindal, Gracia (1996) 'Women in the Evangelical Lutheran Church in America', in Wessinger, pp. 180–204.

*Heeney, B. (1988) *The Women's Movement in the Church of England 1850–1930*, Oxford, Clarendon Press.

Hutabarat, B. (1997) 'Women pastors in Indonesia', in Kanyoro, pp. 143–6.

Kanyoro, M. (ed.) (1997) *In Search of a Round Table: Gender, Theology and Church Leadership*, Geneva, World Council of Churches.

Kanyoro, M. (1997) 'The Ordination of Women in Africa', in Kanyoro, pp. 147–52.

Kent, J. (2002) *Wesley and the Wesleyans*, Cambridge, Cambridge University Press.

Lagerquist, L. D. (1999) 'Responding to the call: Lutheran women and pastoral ministry', *Dialog*, vol. 38, no. 4, pp. 264–8.

Malcolm, L. (1995) 'The gospel and feminism: a proposal for Lutheran dogmatics', *Word & World*, vol. xv, no. 3, pp. 290–8.

Mghwira, A. E. (1997) 'African Women and Lutheran tradition', in Kanyoro, pp. 133–8.

Movement for the Ordination of Women, journal 1980–1992, later issues titled *Chrysalis*, The Women's Library, Aldgate, London.

Raab, K. A. (2000) *When Women Become Priests: The Catholic Women's Ordination Debate*, New York, Columbia University Press.

*Sarna, J. D. (1996) 'From Antoinette Brown Blackwell to Sally Priesand: an historical perspective on the emergence of women in the American rabbinate', in Zola, pp. 43–53.

Simon, R. J. (1993) *Rabbis, Lawyers, Immigrants, Thieves: Exploring Women's Roles*, Westport, Praeger.

Stevens, L. (1987) 'Different voice, different voices: Anglican women in ministry', *Review of Religious Research*, vol. 30, pp. 262–75.

Thorne, H. (2000) *Journey to Priesthood: An In-Depth Study of the First Women Priests in the Church of England*, Bristol, University of Bristol.

Uhr, M. L. (2001) 'Women's ordination: barriers and boundaries', *WomenChurch*, vol. 28, pp. 1–16.

Umansky, E. M. (1996) 'Women's journey toward rabbinic ordination', in Zola, pp. 27–41.

Weber, T. (1993) 'From Maude Royden's Peace Army to the Gulf Peace Team: an assessment of unarmed interpositionary forces', *Journal of Peace Research* , vol. 30, no. 1, pp. 45–64.

*Wessinger, C. (ed.) (1996) *Religious Institutions and Women's Leadership: New Roles Inside the Mainstream*, Chapel Hill, University of South Carolina Press.

*Wijngaards, J. (2001) *The Ordination of Women in the Catholic Church*, New York, Continuum.

Woolf, V. (1938) *Three Guineas*, London, Hogarth.

www.womenpriests.org

Zagano, P. (2000) *Holy Saturday: An Argument for the Restoration of the Female Diaconate in the Catholic Church*, New York, Crossroad.

Zola, G. P. (ed.) (1996) *Women Rabbis: Exploration and Celebration*, Cincinnati, HUC-JIR Rabbinic Alumni Association Press.

Zikmund, B. B. (1996) 'Women's ministries within the United Church of Christ', in Wessinger, pp. 58–78.

Asterisked items are particularly recommended for further reading.

8 Christians, Jews and the Holocaust

K. Hannah Holtschneider

Introduction

This chapter examines the relationship between Christians and Jews during the Holocaust – the discriminatory policies of the National Socialist state towards the Jews of Europe, beginning in 1933 in National Socialist Germany, in particular, the systematic murder of Jews in mass executions, ghettos and death camps which resulted in the genocide of European Jewry (for a discussion of different terminologies see Young, 1988, pp. 85ff.; Tal, 1989, pp. 218–24). However, in order to understand Christian–Jewish relations *during* the Holocaust we need to understand their views of each other before. Only if we know about previous patterns of Christian–Jewish relations are we able to identify whether their behaviour continued or departed from that established before Nazi rule. The Holocaust affected Jews and Christians in all of Europe and, arguably, across the world. In the course of this chapter, we focus on two countries which exemplify the state of Jewish–Christian relations in Europe on the eve of the Holocaust. Germany – the country which became the Nazi state – typifies western Europe in the sense that Jews here were an acknowledged minority (Jews in Germany numbered c. 500,000, less than 1 per cent of the population) with increasing civil rights since the nineteenth century. Poland – on whose territory the murder of Jews from all over Europe was mainly carried out – exemplifies the situation in eastern Europe, where the majority of Europe's Jews lived[1] and where the First World War brought independence for many multinational states (such as Czechoslovakia and Hungary). The chapter closes with an evaluation of postwar developments in Jewish–Christian relations.

---

[1] With 3,000,000 Jews, Poland had the largest Jewish population in Europe alongside Russia where a comparable number of Jews lived. For detailed figures on the Jewish population in Europe see Benz, 1991. The majority of Jews murdered in the Holocaust were Ashkenazim ('Ashkenaz' being a Yiddish word for Germany, referring to the Jewish communities of northern and eastern Europe). However, significant Sefardi ('Sefarad' being the Hebrew word for Spain, referring to the Jewish communities originally of Spain and Northern Africa, who then migrated north and west primarily after the expulsion of Jews from Spain in 1492) communities were among the victims as well, such as the Sefardi communities of Hamburg in Germany, Amsterdam in the Netherlands, as well as communities in France, Italy, Greece and the Balkans. Cf. also Chapter 3.

In this chapter Christianity and Judaism refer to religious systems of belief and thought as well as to Christian and Jewish institutions and cultures linked with this spiritual and intellectual heritage. Christians and Jews are the people who identify themselves as such or who are identified as such by others. Thus, cultural contexts can be characterized as Christian even if the primary population do not necessarily identify themselves as such. People can be seen as Jewish by others, even when they do not regard themselves as Jewish. Conflict arising from differences between self-identification and labelling by others is an issue addressed in this chapter. While the Catholic Church in Poland could claim the committed allegiance of the majority of the non-Jewish population, the situation was different in Germany. Increasing numbers of the population had become distanced from the mainstream churches and the Jewish community, in particular since the 1890s and in the wake of the First World War. However, statistics indicate that no more than 5 per cent had left their community's religious or cultural organizations altogether (Nowak, 1995, p. 230; Barkai, 1998a, p. 31 and Honigmann, 1988, pp. 37f., on Berlin). Even the disaffected remained culturally attached to many of the values and behaviour of their previous communities (Nipperdey, 1988, pp. 124ff.). Disaffection with the mainstream churches was most prevalent in the socialist working-class community and among intellectuals and politicians. Hence, while the churches and the Jewish community were by no means able to speak for the whole of the German population, the pronouncements and actions of their leaders reflect the values and opinions of a significant part of German society throughout the period under examination. In particular, much of the pre-Weimar political climate had been dominated by Catholic–Protestant opposition (Nipperdey, 1988, pp. 156f.) and this division continued to influence post-First World War political culture in Germany. Interpreting the Holocaust as part of Christian–Jewish relations and, as such, as a conflict involving Christians and Jews, is thus justifiable even if parts of the population were disaffected from the religious communities.

Postwar developments in Christian–Jewish conversations have shaped the attitudes that religious Jews and Christians have taken to the Holocaust and to relations before and during the Third Reich. Much of the research undertaken and the subsequent theological changes made in this area were motivated by Christian remorse for centuries of religious antisemitism. Christian antisemitism[2] was recognized as the basis for

---

[2] That is, using Jews as 'negative witnesses' to the truth of Christianity; cf. Haynes, 1995, for an exploration of the influence of Augustine's concept of the 'witness people'.

racist antisemitism, which became stronger in political terms from 1870,[3] and thus for the murderous antisemitism of the Holocaust. The Christian desire to re-examine and redress the perceived Christian predisposition towards antisemitism shaped the agenda of postwar Christian–Jewish conversations. Jewish participants in these conversations, and contributors to research on Christian–Jewish relations before and during the Holocaust, largely adopted this Christian agenda and investigated the history of relations between Christians and Jews from the perspective of antisemitism. The history and conceptualization of antisemitism became the hermeneutical key to the histories of Christian–Jewish relations through the centuries, culminating in the Holocaust. Other ways of interpreting the history of Christian–Jewish interaction in Europe, such as a history of relations between a majority and a (religiously protected) minority, or a history of religious and material conflict which offered a variety of models of relations between Christians and Jews, moved to the margins of their analyses.

However, in recent years, other investigative perspectives have entered Holocaust research. While not denying the primacy of antisemitism for any interpretation of the Holocaust, scholars have begun to break down the history of the Holocaust into smaller areas, identified through geographical, temporal or conceptual limits. This has led to a greater methodological diversity in Holocaust scholarship, as well as to greater diversity in the insights being sought. Thus, complementing the existing historiography, sociology and psychology, memory studies and literary criticism have also become part of the canon of methodologies used by scholars interested in the interpretation of the Holocaust in a religious context, whether Jewish or Christian. This research has begun to create an understanding of the Holocaust that is more diverse, more complex and more detailed. The interpretative diversity also testifies to the complexity of the subject matter, and to the fact that it is difficult, if not impossible, to ascertain one key to the Holocaust which opens up the interpretation of the whole event. However, these varied perspectives on the Holocaust have yet to impact fully on the study and conceptualization of Christian–Jewish relations before and during the Holocaust.

[3] See the writings of German political activist Wilhelm Marr who coined the term antisemitism (1879), as well as specific incidences which preoccupied the public, such as the Dreyfus Affair – the trial of Dreyfus, a Jewish officer in the French army falsely accused of treason – in the 1890s and the contemporaneous dissemination of the racist pamphlet *Protocols of the Elders of Zion* alleging a Jewish conspiracy to dominate the world. For a discussion, see Cohn, 1967.

The Holocaust

> The Holocaust incorporates many different chronologies, such as
> those of its high-level perpetrators, its implementers, its victims,
> opponents and bystanders, of regions and nation states. With
> regard to the specific area of Allied responses in the war,
> knowledge and perceptions of the destruction process varied
> from country to country and between states and public.

(Kushner, 1994, p. 21)

An important dimension in the construction of a chronology of the
Holocaust is based upon the geographical context to which the timeline
is applied. In Germany, government sanctioned discrimination against
Jews and people with Jewish ancestry and heritage began in 1933,
shortly after Hitler's rise to power, pushing groups of people to the
margins of society and ultimately outside the 'universe of obligation'.[4]
Countries that came under German influence after 1933, or which were
annexed by Germany, sometimes underwent a similar process, but not
always. Governments of satellite states, such as newly 'independent'
Slovakia, implemented antisemitic policies under the influence of the
Nazis, whereas Fascist Italy protected its Jewish population from murder
until 1943, despite the implementation of 'race laws' in 1938. German-
occupied France and Vichy France followed different policies. All Jews in
the part of France occupied by Germany were subjected to policies
comparable to those Jews were subjected to in other occupied countries.
In the territory administered by the collaborationist French government
in Vichy, native French Jews enjoyed greater protection than Jewish
immigrants and refugees, despite the promulgation of antisemitic
legislation, since their French citizenship was never revoked. Denmark's
government, instituted by the Nazis, was allowed to operate
independently and saved its small Jewish population in a national effort,
evacuating them to Sweden before deportation to death camps could
begin. Holland, occupied by the Nazis from 1940, was unable to save its
Jewish population and Jewish refugees, although most of the population
did not support the Nazi regime. Bulgaria protected its native Jewish
community, while complying with Nazi orders after the Bulgarian
takeover of Macedonia in 1941, deporting the local Jewish community in
1943 to Treblinka death camp. Hungary's Jews suffered discrimination
and persecution by the Nazi-dependent government, but the Hungarian
government did resist deportation of the Hungarian Jewish community to
death camps until 1944. Hence, determining when the Holocaust began

---

[4] 'The "universe of obligation" designates the outer limits of the social territory inside
which moral questions may be asked at all with any sense. On the other side of the
boundary, moral precepts do not bind, and moral evaluations are meaningless. To
render the humanity of victims invisible, one needs merely to evict them from the
universe of obligation' (Baumann, 1989, p. 27).

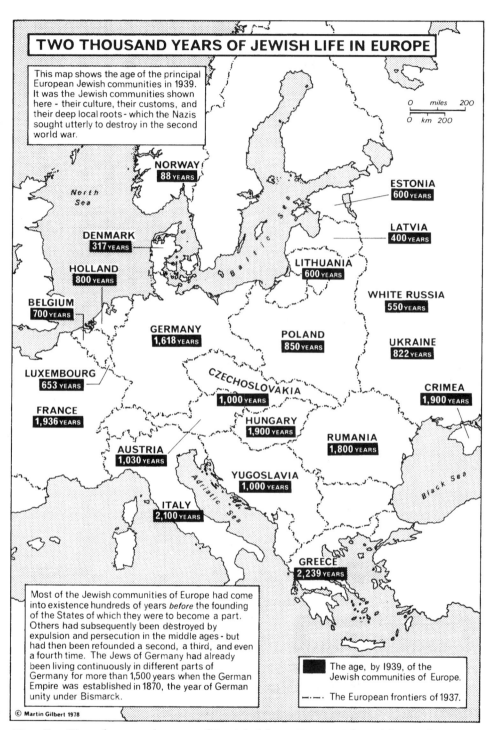

TWO THOUSAND YEARS OF JEWISH LIFE IN EUROPE

This map shows the age of the principal European Jewish communities in 1939. It was the Jewish communities shown here - their culture, their customs, and their deep local roots - which the Nazis sought utterly to destroy in the second world war.

NORWAY **88** YEARS

ESTONIA **600** YEARS

LATVIA **400** YEARS

DENMARK **317** YEARS

LITHUANIA **600** YEARS

HOLLAND **800** YEARS

BELGIUM **700** YEARS

WHITE RUSSIA **550** YEARS

GERMANY **1,618** YEARS

POLAND **850** YEARS

UKRAINE **822** YEARS

LUXEMBOURG **653** YEARS

CZECHOSLOVAKIA **1,000** YEARS

CRIMEA **1,900** YEARS

FRANCE **1,936** YEARS

HUNGARY **1,900** YEARS

RUMANIA **1,800** YEARS

AUSTRIA **1,030** YEARS

YUGOSLAVIA **1,000** YEARS

ITALY **2,100** YEARS

GREECE **2,239** YEARS

Most of the Jewish communities of Europe had come into existence hundreds of years *before* the founding of the States of which they were to become a part. Others had subsequently been destroyed by expulsion and persecution in the middle ages - but had then been refounded a second, a third, and even a fourth time. The Jews of Germany had already been living continuously in different parts of Germany for more than 1,500 years when the German Empire was established in 1870, the year of German unity under Bismarck.

The age, by 1939, of the Jewish communities of Europe.

—·—·— The European frontiers of 1937.

© Martin Gilbert 1978

Map 8 'Two thousand years of Jewish life in Europe' from The Holocaust, Maps and Photographs, *a visual narrative by Martin Gilbert, Holocaust Educational Trust, 1998. Used with permission of Martin Gilbert*

in a given geographical setting depends on the perspective adopted. Prior hermeneutical commitments of scholars determine the way in which the Holocaust is represented and talked about (for a concise discussion of the historiography of the Holocaust, cf. Engel, 2000). Similarly, the focus on Christian–Jewish relations in this chapter provides an interpretative perspective determining what evidence we are looking at, and how we do so, and thus shapes the representation of the Holocaust given below.

For the purpose of our analysis, the chronology of events leading up to the Holocaust begins at the end of the First World War and is broken into three time periods relating to the political developments in Germany and Poland. These time periods are addressed in the following three subsections of the chapter: 1918–1933/39, 1933/39–1945, 1945–. The end of the First World War marks the beginning of the interwar period with its significant changes to the political map of Europe. The beginning of the Third Reich in 1933 and of the war in 1939, when Germany occupied the western half of Poland, serve as caesuras marking a second period in the events of the Holocaust in Germany and Poland. How Christians and Jews interpreted their situations during the war is discussed in the second section. The end of the war signals another watershed, the final section addressing post-1945 developments. In this chapter 'Jews' are identified as an ethnic or cultural group, while 'Judaism' describes religious commitments subscribed to by part of the community of ethnic/cultural Jews. 'Christianity' is seen here predominantly as a nominal cultural and political identification (sometimes explicitly in opposition to Jews) of the majority of the population, while the churches are treated as the active representative organizations of Christianity.

Christians and Jews until the beginning of Nazi rule: Germany (1918–33) and Poland (1918–39)

The developments in Germany and Poland from the end of the First World War until the Nazis seized power saw a number of new efforts at Christian–Jewish relations, as well as renewed political and cultural activity in the Christian and Jewish communities of both countries. Interwar independent Poland saw an upsurge of Jewish political and religious activity which created great hopes for a Jewish future in the country. However, the interwar years in Poland proved to be the period in which hopes for a Jewish/non-Jewish coexistence in Poland were quashed, the main alternative being emigration, Palestine and the USA being favoured destinations. Weimar Germany equally saw Jewish hopes for full social and political integration, while at the same time witnessing the growth of antisemitic political parties and nationalist movements which sought to exclude Jews.

Germany 1918–33

Germany's defeat at the end of the First World War also brought the end of the monarchy. The emperor absconded to Holland and abdicated. In the resulting power vacuum, civil war ensued. When the Republic was announced, the new government had fled the troubles in Berlin to the quiet town of Weimar where it formulated a new constitution. The governments of the Weimar Republic ruled a people which was at odds with the idea of democracy. Many Germans wished for a return of the monarchy and of the imperial and national glory associated with the founding of the Reich under Prussian hegemony in the wake of the Franco-German war of 1870/71. The Reich had united the different German monarchies for the first time and thus created a political entity which reflected the idea of a German nation (though it still excluded Austria). While great hopes had rested on this new nation state, domestic political tensions between democratic and anti-democratic forces led to its downfall. Defeat in the First World War left Germany's national pride severely injured, and an extremist *revanche* plagued the Weimar Republic from its inception. Despite the difficult political and economic situation in interwar Germany, the Weimar years were a time of fervent intellectual activity. Addressing the implications of the experience of the war, but also struggling to come to terms with the changed political situation, the universities in particular were torn between progressive and conservative movements.

Along with secular political parties, the representatives of Catholics, Protestants and Jews had to take a stand towards the new political order. Catholics – just having emerged from the *Kulturkampf* under Bismarck – again faced the task of proving their allegiance to the German nation. Their primary political party, the *Zentrumspartei*, was accused of Ultramontanism, and thus of placing political loyalty to the Vatican above their loyalty to the German state.[5] Donald Dietrich's study of German Catholics under the Nazis concludes that 'anti-Semitism since 1871 had served as a vehicle bearing Catholic patriotic values' (Dietrich, 1988, p. 245). Jews were perceived to be proponents of secularism and liberalism and thereby in direct conflict with the values propagated by the Catholic Church. Many Catholics perceived themselves to be in a struggle against 'Judaism', while racialist antisemitism and violence were rejected by the official representatives of Catholicism as similarly 'secular' threats to the church. While the Centre Party, the Catholic hierarchy and a few Catholic publications played an important role in campaigning against antisemitism, the dominance of the 'Jewish question' in Weimar

---

[5] For details about the *Kulturkampf* see Chapter 4, pp. 120–1.; for a discussion of Ultramontanism, see Chapter 4, p. 115.

politics demanded that representatives of German Catholics clarify their position towards 'the Jews'. Because of the division between church and state, anti-Jewish politics and legislation could be seen as lying outside the church's realm and as being in the interest of the German people (Greive, 1987, pp. 172, 177f.). The status of Catholics in the Reich was only settled with the Concordat between the German state and the Vatican in 1933. While ensuring limited Catholic autonomy in the Reich, it thereby also ensured official Catholic silence on antisemitic policies and atrocities.

Protestants were in the majority in the new state and exhibited a strong nationalism as part of their religious identity, renowned professors of theology having signed their agreement to go to war in 1914, often even with enthusiasm. The mainstream, state-supported, Protestant churches date from the wars of religion in the wake of the Reformation and can broadly be identified as either Lutheran or Reformed in orientation. While the experience of the First World War generated new theological movements – most notably Karl Barth's dialectic theology – the conservative nationalist forces in the Protestant churches did not decline. Anti-democratic forces loomed large in the Protestant churches, since

> The majority feared that without the accustomed support of the *Obrigkeit* (authorities) they would not be able to hold their own against the antireligious and anti-ecclesiastical ideology of liberalism and socialism. They regarded democracy and universal suffrage as a danger.
>
> (Büttner, 2000, p. 433)

One of the public manifestations of this nationalist conservatism was antisemitic political agitation by pastors (Gutteridge, 1976, p. 3). This tendency reached an extreme in the publications of Wilhelm Stapel, a Lutheran publicist, who suggested the separation of the Protestant churches into Christians of 'German descent' and Christians of Jewish descent. According to Stapel, Christians of Jewish descent were unable to grasp the depths of the 'German soul', but had to be acknowledged as 'Christian brothers' (Gutteridge, 1976, p. 52). Opponents of such proposals included some significant and influential theologians, such as Eduard Lampeter, Karl Barth and Paul Tillich (Gutteridge, 1976, p. 57ff.). While some Protestants joined in dialogues with Jews, these seemed to be initiated more often by Jews than by Christians. The Protestant Churches in Weimar Germany saw the situation of Jews in German society as part of the political debate of the 'Jewish question', and only as such as a theological issue, rather than as a theological problem that is at the heart of Christian self-understanding because of the Jewishness of Jesus and the early history of the church. While showing apprehension at violence, they showed no serious opposition against the increasing antisemitic agitation inside and outside the churches, racial or otherwise (Gutteridge, 1976, p. 41).

Jewish political association in the Weimar Republic was diverse. For centuries, the Jewish community in Germany had enjoyed peaceful coexistence with the non-Jewish population. Since the founding of the Reich in 1871 and access to greater civil rights, Jews were increasingly represented in German politics, aided by a growing identification of Jews with some forms of German nationalism. Thus, more Jews acted as representatives of the socialist movement and political parties, but Jews were part of all political parties and no dominant political trend can be identified in the Jewish population at large. The Weimar years placed Jewish self-understanding under pressure, and sharpened the debate about the relationship of Jews to German nationalism. The fragmented Jewish cultural sphere did contain movements with a more national character, in the sense of German national as well as Zionist character.[6] In imitation of non-Jewish youth movements inspired by religious and national spirituality in their search for German identity, young Jews engaged in separate but similar activities, not necessarily being welcome in the non-Jewish youth groups, where German was often declared to mean Christian (Mosse, 1970, pp. 78ff.). Some politically conservative Jewish circles supported the extreme nationalist right, hoping for full integration into the *völkisch*[7] national community (Gordon, 1984, p. 47). While the Zionist movement remained small, assimilation being the dominant trend in German Jewry, the variety of Jewish political, cultural and religious organizations in Weimar Germany suggests the difficulties inherent in defining a German-Jewish identity to which a majority of the Jewish community could subscribe.

As equality in civil rights was being achieved under the Weimar constitution, liberal religious circles placed great hopes on gaining equality in the university system as well. The liberal scholarly community opposed the definition of Jewish studies as a simple ancillary to the understanding of Christianity. The achievement of statutory equality with the churches and recognition of the independence of Jewish thought and history had been much debated since the exchange between the leading liberal Christian theologian Adolf von Harnack and Rabbi Leo Baeck, who responded to Harnack's published lecture series *The Essence of Christianity* with *The Essence of Judaism*. The Institutum Iudaicum Berlin, under the leadership of Hugo Gressman, was established as an academic institution, devoted to the study of Judaism as a faith and culture in its own right.

[6] Zionism began as a nineteenth-century Jewish political movement lobbying for the creation of a Jewish nation state in Palestine. It is associated prominently with the work of Theodor Herzl (*The Jewish State*) who called the First Zionist World Congress in Vienna in 1897. Various Zionist ideologies developed, some religious, drawing on medieval writings about the yearning for Zion, transforming a spiritual concept into a political ideology.

[7] *Völkisch* nationalism, one manifestation of German nationalism, placed great emphasis on the *Volk*, conceived in racist terms as a community sharing a heritage by virtue of 'blood' ties determined through birth.

On the level of formalized Christian-Jewish dialogue, Martin Buber and Franz Rosenzweig pioneered the *Freies jüdisches Lehrhaus* (Independent House for the Study of Judaism), devoted to the education of the Jewish (and Christian) public. Buber's journal *Der Jude* devoted much space to articles by Jews on Christianity and by Christians on Judaism. Intended as an exercise in mutual recognition and reconciliation, this attempt went awry with the Christian participants refusing to recognize Judaism as a living faith alongside Christianity. Christian participants saw the series of articles as an opportunity to continue the centuries-old battleground of rivalry between the two faiths (Mendes-Flohr, 1987, pp. 109ff.). There were other endeavours in Christian-Jewish relations, such as dialogues between individual Christians and Jews sharing in a genuine voyage of religious discovery, reinterpreting the relationships between God and humanity together (Mendes-Flohr, 1987, p.132). A concrete appreciation of Jewish scholarship in Christian circles was signalled by

> the concerted effort of Christians to include Jewish scholars of Judaism among the authors of the second edition of the standard encyclopedia of theology and religious studies, *Die Religion in Geschichte und Gegenwart* (Religion in Past and Present, 1927–1933).
>
> (Mendes-Flohr, 1998, p. 168)

However, further efforts at dialogue were made impossible by the creation of the Third Reich.

These Jewish initiatives are distinct from more contemporary dialogues in which Christians have generally been the initiators of Christian–Jewish conversations (in Germany as well as in other European countries and the United States). Paul Mendes-Flohr suggests that the situation in the Weimar Republic resulted from the dominance of the 'Jewish question' in politics and society which produced an urgent need for Jews to address Jewish–Christian relations. This,

> one may assume, had the effect of dispelling decisively the bourgeois illusion of an unproblematic *modus vivendi* between Jew and Christian, and thus rendered open, uninhibited theological encounter between Jew and Christian possible.
>
> (Mendes-Flohr, 1987, p. 106)

Poland 1918–39

The peace settlements in the wake of the First World War granted Poland independence and raised Jewish hopes for greater political self-determination and national representation as part of Poland's multi-ethnic population. At the same time, legislation directed at making Poland into a mono-ethnic state curtailed such hopes right from the beginning. That Poland was forced by the victorious nations of the First World War to guarantee the rights of its minorities is a significant indicator of the political climate in the country. Parts of the Polish nationalist movement suggested that in order to be Polish one had to be Catholic, a definition that was supported by the Catholic Church in Poland which could claim the loyalty of the majority of the Polish population, in particular because of its allegiance with forms of Polish nationalism. Other Christian denominations were strongly represented in some regions only, such as the Ukrainian Orthodox and Ukrainian Catholic churches in the south-east corner of Poland and Protestant churches in the west of Poland towards the border with Germany.

Jewish history in Poland presents a long and complex story which has been interpreted in contradictory ways. Poland witnessed, on the one hand, the most ferocious antisemitism, enforced before Polish independence by Tsarist antisemitic policies which in the 1880s led to waves of Jewish emigration to Palestine and the USA. The Polish partitions, beginning in 1772 and ending with the establishment of Congress Poland at the Congress of Vienna in 1815, ended Polish independence until the end of the First World War and divided Poland between Prussia, the Austro-Hungarian Empire and Russia. This meant that Russia gained a large Jewish population which it allowed to live and settle only in a restricted territory (the Pale of Settlement, i.e. mainly Poland, the Ukraine and parts of the Baltic states)[8] and which it suppressed as 'infidels' with antisemitic legislation. On the other hand, Poland was the land which, perhaps more than others, allowed Jews to settle and prosper, intellectually as well as economically (*Polin* – 'here there is rest', as Poland is described in Jewish literature). Both descriptions are applicable to different periods in Jewish history in Poland. Poland was historically also of variable territory, often divided, notably between Prussia, Russia and Austria/Hungary, rarely independent, a country that was home to many minorities.

The relations between the different communities living on Polish territory were regulated by the various rulers and often supported the segregationist policies of the Jewish and Christian communities themselves. At other times, however, the different religious identities did not determine economic considerations. In medieval and early modern times, until the philosophies of the Enlightenment disturbed the social order by opening up unprecedented possibilities for Jews and non-Jews in politics, commerce and culture, 'Jews collectively had a special status, the nature of that collectivity usually being defined as non-Christian but also, sometimes, as non-Polish' (Hundert, 1986, p. 55). Until the rise of Polish nationalist movements in the nineteenth century, as a response to

[8] However, despite the oppressive Tsarist policies, the Jewish population in the Russian Empire rose from c. 1.5 million to c. 5.6 million (Steinlauf, 1997, p. 8).

the partition of the country between Russia and the Austro-Hungarian Empire in 1795, Poland's multi-ethnic society had generally been able to sustain different cultural and religious groups in a peaceful coexistence. While inter-group harmony was at times disturbed, such conflict as broke out had not endangered the status quo of inter-group relations. Jews joined in nationalist uprisings in the 1830s and 1860s, as did many Catholic priests, in opposition to the Catholic hierarchy, which supported acceptance of partition in obedience to the state (Modras, 1994, pp. 19ff.). However, Polish nationalists began to draw on 'Christian symbolism to idealize Poland as the Christ among nations' (Modras, 1994, p. 21) to the exclusion of Jews.

Interwar Poland saw further radicalization of Polish nationalism, driving at the exclusion of minorities. Poland was at war until 1921, needing to consolidate its borders with Lithuania in the north and the USSR in the south-east. Accommodating different cultural and religious communities, which now also expressed their identities in nationalist terms, was a priority for the Polish state. Antisemitic agitation was prominent in interwar Poland, in particular among extreme nationalist bodies like the *Endek* party, which advocated a mono-ethnic Polish state. During the interwar period, Poland was a democracy, ruled by more or less democratic forces. Dmowski and Piłsudski were the two leaders governing Poland until 1935, Dmowski proposing a 'united, monocultural and monoreligious Polish state', Piłsudski suggesting a 'multiethnic, multireligious Poland based, if not on Socialism, then at least on social justice' (Mendelsohn, 1983, p. 16). After Piłsudski, the country 'was ruled by a group of chauvinistic and antidemocratic army officers much influenced (though still to some extent rejecting) the growing native fascist movement and the growing influence of Nazism' (Mendelsohn, 1983, p. 16). Nationalist plans for dealing with the Jewish minority included enforced mass emigration. In the absence of concrete possibilities for facilitating Jewish emigration, politicians took more immediate measures, discriminating against Jewish businesses and restricting the intake of Jews in universities. Declining professional opportunities led to disillusionment, particularly among young Jews fearing for their future in Poland. Hostility to Jews in the Catholic Polish population was expressed in spontaneous and orchestrated outbreaks of violence. The Catholic Church was deeply implicated in this antisemitic agitation. At best, its representatives did nothing to contradict the political propaganda, at worst they joined forces with politicians and actively supported their campaign (Mendelsohn, 1983, pp. 71f.).

Examining the Catholic press in interwar Poland, Ronald Modras attempted a representative survey of Catholic attitudes towards Jews and

Judaism in the 1920s and 1930s.[9] The results of his study indicate a progressive sharpening of antisemitic attitudes among Catholics, including the hierarchy. While antisemitism was condemned by the Vatican, Polish Catholics appeared to find their own anti-Jewish propaganda a reasonable defence against a perceived threat from the Jewish community (Modras, 1994, pp. 154ff.). As in Germany, Jews were seen as the embodiment of secularism and hence as the personification of anti-Catholic values (ibid., p. 157). Racial ideas took hold in Catholic circles, in particular in the debate about Jewish converts to Catholicism. The argument that a Pole had to be a Catholic without Jewish ancestry implied doubting the sincerity of Jewish converts, suggesting conversion to Catholicism was simply a move towards gaining acceptance in Polish society rather than an expression of genuine religious conviction, whereas membership in the 'Jewish race' could never be relinquished (ibid., pp. 272ff., 278). However, there were dissenting Catholic voices as well, advocating conversion as a solution to the 'Jewish question'. As in Germany, the 'Jewish question' was at the top of the political and cultural agenda, dominating much of Polish politics and discussion within the Catholic Church in Poland.

Another solution advocated by many Catholics was emigration. This was supposed to be achieved by boycotting Jewish business, thereby cutting off the economic basis of Jewish life in Poland, as well as through active support of Zionism. Since many Jews were among the poorest part of the Polish population, the government explored emigration plans which would make use of colonial territory, such as the 'Madagascar Plan' suggested by the Nazi German government (Modras, 1994, p. 280).[10] However, emigration was not seen as a realistic option by the government, nor was Zionism endorsed by the Vatican. Jews also migrated into Poland in the 1930s, fleeing Germany and other Nazi-occupied territories, while many other countries were increasingly applying immigration quotas.

Interwar Poland struggled economically. One aspect of Catholic antisemitic agitation focused on promoting 'Christian business' at the

---

[9] To date this is the only historical study that examines a representative sample of data. Modras examined works published under the auspices of the Catholic Church in Poland, mainly journals, in the years 1933–39, looking for references to 'Jews, Judaism, or antisemitism' (Modras, 1994, p. xiv). He suggests that while it is 'impossible to determine the precise influence they had on their readers ... collectively they tell us not only what individual Catholic writers thought about Jews but what their readers, especially priests, were wont to think. They are indicative of the clerical mind-set at the time' (Modras, 1994, p. xiv).

[10] The 'Madagascar Plan' proposed the deportation of the Jewish population of Europe to the island of Madagascar. It was considered by some western European governments from the end of the First World War and was explored in more detail by Germany and Poland in 1937. The plan became impossible in 1940 when Germany lost the Battle of Britain.

expense of 'Jewish business', suggesting that Poland was detrimentally dominated by Jews. Catholic journals such as the *Mały Dziennik* promoted the 'nationalization' of the economy and advised its readers to drive Jews out of business by boycotting Jewish retailers. Similarly, such journals advocated curtailing the access of Jews to universities and separating Jewish from non-Jewish students in the classroom (creating 'ghetto benches'), withdrawing civil rights by introducing legislation that excluded Jews from certain professions (Aryan paragraphs) and both limiting the quota of meat slaughtered according to Jewish law and taxing it highly, aiming at the same goal of 'nationalization' (Modras, 1994, pp. 226ff.). Some of these policies were legalized and enforced by the government, and they received support from the Catholic Church in Poland, not least from Cardinal Hlond, the Polish primate. However,

> Catholic leaders insisted that such a nationalization of Polish life was to take place peacefully. Violence was unchristian and to be abhorred. Economic boycott, ghetto benches, and the exclusionary Aryan paragraphs were all seen as legitimate, non-violent forms of self-defense.
>
> (Modras, 1994, p. 300)

Polish independence had guaranteed Jews equal rights of citizenship and freedom of religious expression. During the interwar period, Polish Jewish communal politics centred on the 'Jewish question', as in Germany, and with that Jewish politics were concentrated on responses to antisemitism. Approaches to antisemitism divided Polish Jews – the small and internally divided Zionist movement advocated the preparation for a mass emigration to the *Yishuv* (the Jewish community in Palestine) and a bid for Jewish statehood, while others envisaged a Jewish future as part of the Polish nation (Mendelsohn, 1983, pp. 44ff.). The divide between religious and secular Jews ran through the Zionist and the anti-Zionist camps alike. At one extreme lay the *Hasidic* Jews of Galicia – traditional in their observance and distinct in their clothing – and at the opposite end of the spectrum the reform-minded assimilationists, each signifying to the other what they considered 'wrong' with Jewish life and tradition. Other differences can be accounted for historically, the Lithuanian Jews in the north-east of newly independent Poland – *Litvaks* – whose ideal of study and observance (*Mitnagdism*) conflicted with the more mystical approach centred on a leader – *Rebbe* – in Galician Jewry (*Hasidism*). In addition, the various socialist and communist parties each advocated their own solutions to the 'Jewish question', either favouring Jewish political independence, in Palestine or elsewhere, or consolidation with the non-Jewish Polish society (Mendelsohn, 1983, pp. 44ff.). Poland's Jews developed a rich tapestry of political and cultural activity in the interwar years, from reforms to the Jewish education system, the Yiddish press, and local political movements to the *Hehalutz* movement, training volunteers for a new life in Palestine.

In the 1930s, the pressures of the boycott, the Jewish quotas in universities and the economic restrictions placed on Polish Jewry left Jewish youth in a position of 'no hope'. While emigration had initially been favoured by many young Jews, leading to the growing strength of the Zionist parties, the restrictive immigration policy to Palestine adopted by the British in the White Paper of 1936 led to a disillusionment with Zionism. Instead, the parties that fought antisemitism and favoured a Jewish future in Poland gained more support: the secular Yiddishist working-class party, the socialist Bund, and the Communists (Mendelsohn, 1983, pp. 77ff.). The orthodox religious parties, such as *Agudas Yisroel*, advocating a Jewish future in Poland, failed to win over young Jews in the 1930s, since they also promoted a traditional Judaism opposing the movements of secularization and acculturation, values that were no longer embraced by most young Jews (ibid., p. 82).

Mendelsohn suggests that the Jewish situation in Poland was paradigmatic for Jewish/non-Jewish relations in eastern Europe between the wars:

> The combination of traditional hatred of Jews, the triumph of nationalism, internal weakness, and the role of the Jewish question in the struggle for power between the moderate right and the extreme right typified the situation not only in Poland, but in other East Central European states as well. In this respect, as with regard to internal Jewish developments – acculturation, economic decline, political divisiveness, the failure of national autonomy and Zionism to solve the Jewish question – Poland may serve as a paradigm of the Jewish experience in interwar East Central Europe.

> (Mendelsohn, 1983, pp. 82f.)

Poland was a multicultural society – coexistence being the term that seems to apply to most of Polish history, even during periods of heightened intercultural competition and religiously motivated conflict. Interwar Poland was in a state of conflict over the political and cultural future of the country, and the economic situation was consistently harsh. Christian and Jewish Poles were often engaged in this conflict in terms of their religious, cultural and economic self-definitions, arguing in the public political sphere about their different visions for the future of Poland. Religious conversations between Jews and Christians did not occupy much public space, but appear to have occurred privately between individuals such as rabbis and priests, relying on the physical closeness of Christian and Jewish communities in Poland. It thus appears legitimate to characterize the interwar period as a time of conflict between Christians and Jews, a conflict that on the political level was dominated by secular Jewish forces and secular as well as religious non-Jewish Polish nationalists. Pro-Nazi sympathies grew louder as the war approached, since, for right-wing nationalist Poles, joining forces with Hitler was perceived as a defence against communism and, hence, against Russia's desire to expand its influence once again and to occupy Poland. This situation of conflict progressively crushed Jewish hopes for a future in Poland.

The conflict in which many German Jews and Christians considered themselves involved during the Weimar years can be seen as a religious struggle in the sense that both tried to work out their relationship to each other in the German nation state, as well as their definition of and identification with the German nation. The religious dimensions of this conflict appear to lie in the extent to which some Christians, considering Jews on (racist) religious grounds as outside the German nation, aspired to drive Jews out of positions of responsibility and public office, while Jews were moving towards greater integration in German society, taking seriously their newly gained civil rights. Another, parallel dimension of the conflict occurred within the Christian and Jewish communities. Christian antisemitic agitation was countered from within the churches, though this dissenting voice failed to impact decisively on the masses. Other divisions exacerbated the political and religious marginalization of German Jews: the Catholic–Protestant division was matched by an internal Protestant division in the fight for a national church. Similarly, Jewish groups advocated wildly different notions of integration into German society and as such could not present a united front in the encounter with Nazism.

Having examined Christian and Jewish views of each other, and relations between the two communities from the end of the First World War until the beginning of Nazi rule, two of the key terms of this volume – conflict and coexistence – appear as apt descriptions of the situation. While Jews and Christians in Germany and Poland enjoyed the benefits of equal rights, Christians saw themselves engaged in a struggle against what they perceived as a powerful enemy, 'the Jews' (which often was synonymous with 'Communists' and 'Masons'). In both countries, the 'Jewish question' was prominent on the political agenda and Jews and Christians were called upon to take a political stand towards it. This led to the two communities being pitched against each other. Dissenting voices within each community advocated a Jewish future as part of the German and Polish states, though, among Christians, these were clearly in the minority. However, positive examples of Christian–Jewish relations may be seen in the efforts at creating a religious dialogue in Germany as well as in everyday life in Poland, where large parts of the population, in particular those on the political left, refused to obey the boycott of Jewish businesses.

GERMAN OFFICIAL PLANS FOR THE "FINAL SOLUTION", 20 JANUARY 1942

The number of Jews mentioned at the **Wannsee Conference**, country by country and area by area, for eventual deportation, and subsequent death. More than 14 million people were thus marked out for death.

One of the macabre features of the numerical list of the Jews submitted to the Wannsee Conference was the fact that no figure was given for the Jews of Estonia, merely a brief note that Estonia was 'Free of Jews'. This was true; the 1,000 Estonian Jews who had come under German rule in October 1941 had all been murdered during the three months before the Wannsee Conference.

ESTONIA "Free of Jews"

USSR 5 million

NORWAY 1,300

DENMARK 5,600

LATVIA 3,500

LITHUANIA 34,000

HOLLAND 160,800

BIALYSTOK DISTRICT 400,000

WHITE RUSSIA 446,484

BELGIUM 43,000

Wannsee
GERMANY 131,800 Berlin

Chelmno

GENERAL GOVERNMENT 2,284,000

420,000

FRANCE OCCUPIED ZONE 165,000

BOHEMIA AND MORAVIA 74,200

88,000

UKRAINE 2,994,684

SLOVAKIA

AUSTRIA 43,700

HUNGARY 742,800

FRANCE UNOCCUPIED ZONE 700,000

CROATIA 40,000

SERBIA 10,000

RUMANIA 342,000

ITALY 58,000

ALBANIA 200

BULGARIA

48,000

GREECE 69,600

0 miles 200
0 km 300

In December 1941, a month *before* the Wannsee Conference, the first Nazi extermination camp had already come into operation, at Chelmno, responsible for the mass-murder of Jews, Gypsies, and Soviet prisoners-of-war. After passing through corridors marked 'To the showers' and 'To the doctor', the victims were forced into a large truck which was in fact a gas-chamber, where they were killed within a few minutes. By the end of 1944 more than 360,000 Jews had been murdered in Chelmno alone.

The Wannsee Conference also specified the number of Jews in *unconquered* countries for eventual destruction, including 330,000 from Britain, 18,000 from Switzerland, 6,000 from Spain and 4,000 from Ireland.

© Martin Gilbert 1978

Map 9 'German official plans for the "Final Solution", 20 January 1942', from The Holocaust, Maps and Photographs, *a visual narrative by Martin Gilbert, Holocaust Educational Trust, 1998. Used with permission of Martin Gilbert*

Christians and Jews in Germany (1933–45) and Poland (1939–45)

Germany 1933–45

When the Nazis came to power in 1933, their antisemitic measures, laws and policies impacted on fragmented Christian and Jewish groupings, each fighting for the attention and support of their respective communities to provide what they believed to be a viable response to the political situation. While the Catholic Church protected itself through the Concordat concluded between the Nazi state and the Vatican, thereby joining its status to the 'new order', the Protestant churches became embroiled in what is known as the *Kirchenkampf* ('church conflict'). The pro-Nazi extreme formed a 'German Christian' movement, supporting Hitler's racial laws even (or perhaps particularly) where they affected church members of Jewish descent. At the other end of the spectrum lay the Confessing Church, whose members, while not necessarily anti-Nazi, objected to the state applying the 'Aryan paragraph' to the membership of the church, i.e. effectively trying to define who could be a member of the church and who could not.[11] While the Confessing Church and the Catholic Church remained concerned about Christians of Jewish descent, its concern for people defined as Jews outside the realm of the churches was minimal. As long as Christians perceived themselves to be in a situation of struggle among each other and with the regime, support for Jewish concerns not pertaining directly to the churches did not enter any official Christian agenda.

With the Nazis in government, the churches struggled first and foremost for their own survival and independence, or for consolidation of their status with the regime. Recent studies on German public opinion under Nazism reveal that Jews were at the margins of the popular consciousness and hardly entered into their decision-making processes (Kulka, 2000). While the Catholic Church remained supportive of those of its members with Jewish ancestry, the Protestant Churches were divided on this question. The German Christians wholeheartedly supported the 'Aryan clause', excluding people of Jewish descent from the church, while the Confessing Church vetoed the adoption of this clause and, at least nominally, continued to care for 'non-Aryan' Christians. At the beginning of the war, in September 1939, Jews were already considered outside the 'universe of obligation' for most Germans

---

[11] Nazi legislation, explicated in detail in the Nuremberg Laws 1935, classified people as 'Aryans' and 'non-Aryans'. 'Non-Aryans', i.e. all who had at least one Jewish grandparent, were gradually excluded from professional and social life. The application of 'Aryan paragraphs' excluded people of 'non-Aryan' descent from organizations, professions and public life.

and most Christians. While Christians mobilized opposition to the regime – Protestants notably on the question of the 'Aryan clause' for church membership, Catholics and Protestants alike on the euthanasia programme, codenamed T4 – the rights of (non-Christian) Jews were not considered an immediate Christian concern. Until the *Kristallnacht* pogrom of 1938,[12] Jewish exclusion from German society had largely been facilitated by laws, such as the 1935 Nuremberg Laws, which seemed to consolidate the regime's antisemitic propaganda into a 'reliable' legal format. Thus, many Jews opted to find an accommodation with the new political order.

The self-perception of the Catholic Church under the Nazis reveals its preoccupation with

> the defense of the remaining Catholic terrain against the totalitarian system of the Third Reich ... Catholicism and the Church wanted to remain what they had always been. They fought for the preservation of their identity. Nonconformity and perseverance, together with limited cooperation, was the motto.
>
> (Repgen, 1987, p. 206)

This striving for self-preservation meant that Catholic concern for Jews was not prominent. Konrad Repgen argues that since Catholics in the nineteenth and early twentieth centuries had been isolated by the *Kulturkampf*, and had received little support from other religious groups in the Reich, 'they did not want to damage their own interests by engaging themselves on behalf of others' (Repgen, 1987, p. 214). While some Catholic publications condemned antisemitism in the early years of Nazi rule,

> the Catholic Church remained committed to the policy which it had pursued since April 1933. That meant no positive support of the German policy toward the Jews, relief actions and occasional public disapproval, but it stopped short of open public protest with timely reference to specific acts of persecution.
>
> (Repgen, 1987, p. 219)

[12] On 9/10 November 1938, Nazi leaders organized a pogrom against the Jewish population and against property owned by the Jewish community and individuals in most German cities, in 'retaliation' for the assassination of Ernst von Rath, a member of staff at the German embassy in Paris, by a youth, Herschel Grynszpan, angered by the expulsion of his Polish-born parents from Germany. Ninety-one people were killed, many synagogues and shops destroyed (police and firefighters intervened only to protect neighbouring [non-Jewish] houses) and, in the following days, about 30,000 people were imprisoned in concentration camps. The pogrom was named *Kristallnacht*, literally 'crystal night', because of the many broken windows of synagogues, shops and houses. Because the name was invented by the Nazis to mock the destruction of Jewish property and to downplay the physical brutality against Jews, many people prefer to use the term 'November pogrom' instead. While the population mostly did not intervene to prevent the pogrom, outrage at the violence and 'barbarity' of the actions was strongly present in the media.

The 1937 papal encyclical *Mit brennender Sorge* ('With Burning Concern') can be read in the same vein, as a call for the protection of the persecuted Catholic Church and an expression of humanitarian concern for all who suffer under Nazi rule. Catholics in positions in the church hierarchy continued to support individual Jews, through agencies such as the *Caritasbund* (a social welfare charity) and similar organizations. Before the war, these organizations had helped to facilitate emigration – mainly of Christians who were defined as Jewish under the Nuremberg Laws. This aid continued during the war. Some clergy spoke out openly against antisemitic measures, notably against the *Kristallnacht* pogrom, and some even wrote letters to the government, making clear their opposition to the persecution of the Jews. Although it was by no means safe for Catholics to do so – many were brought to trial for their aid activities – the Concordat afforded clergy and church institutions a certain freedom. Without concrete guidance from Rome, clergy were left on their own to make decisions about resistance and rescue. Regarding Catholic–Jewish relations, Donald Dietrich concludes that

> The majority of people who had been outraged over the euthanasia issue, because it touched their friends and relatives, failed to react sufficiently when their Jewish neighbors were exposed to discrimination, ghettoization, deportation, and execution ... That German public opinion and the Church were a force to be reckoned with in principle and could have played a more positive role in averting the Jewish disaster as well is a lesson to be derived from the failure of Hitler's euthanasia efforts.
>
> (Dietrich, 1988, p. 243)

While individual Catholics reached out to Jews in rescue activities and protected Catholics with Jewish ancestry, on the whole the Catholic Church remained silent about the persecution of Jews. Although Christian–Jewish relations in the Weimar Republic had been perceived as a struggle engaging the truth of Christianity, this aspect of relations between Jews and Christians was absent in the face of the humanitarian crisis of the Jews in the Third Reich, particularly in the face of Catholic fear for their own interests and safety.

Amongst Protestants, the split between the German Christians and the Confessing Church took up much of the energy of clergy and involved lay people. Individual clergy voiced their opposition to the persecution of Jews in sermons, as Catholics did, notably after the *Kristallnacht* pogrom, but these were isolated efforts. Richard Gutteridge concludes that 'The Church as a whole kept silent. No bishop, Church government or synod spoke out in public at this time on behalf of the persecuted Jews' (Gutteridge, 1987, p. 230). The 1934 synod in Barmen, which founded the Confessing Church, defined 'true Christianity' in opposition to the German Christians, issuing 'The Theological Declaration of Barmen' which addressed head-on the church–state relationship. While defining the principles according to which Christians ought to make decisions about their actions and loyalties, the declaration remained abstract. 'There was no criticism of Nazi racial ideology. The Jews were not so much as mentioned. Due expression was given of political loyalty to the divinely sanctioned State' (ibid., p. 234). Subsequent synods dealt with the defence of the church and showed little concern for the plight of the Jews. Only a few, such as Dietrich Bonhoeffer, called for programmatic action of the Confessing Church on behalf of Jews.

While the Confessing Church continued to support Christians of Jewish ancestry among its members, their support was far from unconditional. The conflict with Jewry in which large parts of the Protestant churches had seen themselves during the Weimar years now found an outlet in antisemitic policies. While wishing to safeguard the church's right to set out standards of Christian behaviour, members of the Confessing Church also supported the exclusion of Christians of Jewish ancestry from 'Aryan' communities, suggesting that such 'Jewish Christians' ought to form their own parishes.

> Certain Parish Councils (*Gemeinderäte*) were in favour of an embargo upon the christening of Jews. The thorny question appears to have been whether a Jew who sought baptism was to be regarded, if and when baptized, as thereby gaining entry not only into the *Christian* Church but also into the *German* Church with a prospect of temporal as well as spiritual benefit.
>
> (Gutteridge, 1987, p. 236)

Baptized Jews founded their own support organization in 1933, renamed the *Paulusbund*, 'League of St Paul: Association of Non-Aryan Christians' in 1936 (Barkai, 1998b, p. 255; Honigmann, 1988, p. 30), distancing themselves from Jews and Jewish organizations from which they felt alienated – and which also were not likely to include people in their support networks whom they regarded as Christians. 'The name was not coincidental: it symbolized the total and complete separation from Judaism, just as Paul had separated himself in the early period of the Church' (Barkai, 1998b, p. 255).

Despite the lack of official protest against the persecution of Jews, there were individuals in the Confessing Church who were engaged in activities on behalf of Jews, mainly helping with emigration, or, when that was no longer possible, finding hiding places and providing support. The office of Dean Heinrich Grüber provided such support from 1939 until his arrest in December 1940, and after that his colleagues carried on while going underground (Gutteridge, 1987, pp. 243f.). Other individuals, such as Bishop Wurm and Pastor Karl Immer, spoke out repeatedly against the persecution of Jews, directing protest towards the state offices responsible and alerting their congregants from the pulpit. Thus, apart from a few individuals who mobilized support for Jews, many in the Protestant churches perceived Nazi antisemitic legislation and other forms of persecution as an extension of their own religious struggle as

German Christians against Jews, and many other Protestants who opposed this struggle appeared to be fighting primarily for their own survival as a church, rather than fighting the Nazis on behalf of (and alongside) Jewish Germans.

Numerous rescue efforts were conducted by individual Christians. Some of the most courageous individuals had spouses who were Jewish or had Jewish ancestry. Simply by remaining married, many were able to save the lives of their partners – whether these were Christians themselves or had remained Jewish in an inter-religious marriage. With most of German society and even the churches being inclined against them, and facing the suggestion

> to avoid marrying Jews or to separate from their Jewish partners even after many years of married life ... the available sources indicate that the great majority of Christians wedded to Jews in interfaith marriages stuck by their spouses even before they knew that they might save them by that loyalty.

> (Barkai, 1998b, p. 253)

A well-known incident in this context was the protest which wives of Jewish men staged in Berlin in 1942, in front of the building in Rosenstrasse where their husbands were interned to be deported. They demanded publicly that their husbands be released – which they eventually were, with no repercussions for them or their wives (Stoltzfus, 1996).

Efforts at Christian–Jewish dialogue about religious and theological understanding of each other in a climate of social and political antisemitism, characteristic of the Weimar years, could hardly be continued under the Nazis. The political and religious conflict regarding the 'Jewish question' had become life-threatening.

Poland 1939–45

With the beginning of the war in 1939, Poland ceased to exist as an independent state, occupied in the west by Nazi Germany and in the east by Russia. The Polish government fled to London and from there began directing resistance activities on occupied Polish territory and representing Polish interests in the international community, notably to the Allies. As such, the government-in-exile was also responsible for representing Jewish interests in occupied Poland. All Poles, with the exception of the German minority (*Volksdeutsche*), were persecuted by the Nazis, and, while Jews were singled out for immediate murder or ghettoization, slave labour and then deportation to murder sites, the Catholic intelligentsia in particular suffered deportation, imprisonment and murder in concentration camps as well. Many of the murdered

Map 10   'The Jewish death-toll 1939–1945', from The Holocaust, Maps and Photographs, *a visual narrative by Martin Gilbert, Holocaust Educational Trust, 1998. Used with permission of Martin Gilbert*

Catholics were priests. How, then, did Polish Catholics respond to the persecution and murder of Polish Jews?

The attitudes of non-Jewish Poles to the persecution of Jews were complex and diverse. For some, Jews were beyond their 'universe of obligation', partly because the prewar antisemitic propaganda had taken root, partly because they were dealing with their own concerns first. However, many Catholics, as individuals and as part of communities such as convents and monasteries, extended a helping hand to Jews, providing food and shelter, hiding children, individuals and whole families. In occupied Poland, in contrast to any other Nazi-occupied country (whether Holland, France, Denmark or Norway, to give some key examples), any aid to Jews was punishable by death – death for the whole family and for anyone else implicated. Andrzej Bryk assesses the situation Jewish and Christian Poles found themselves in as follows:

> There was a real mental confusion, an initial moral [in]ability quickly and unequivocally to recognize the intentions and consequences of the Nazi policy. The separation between the two groups was reinforced by neither having any tangible, institutional means to co-operate which predated the terror. Each could turn culturally and morally to nationalistic or ethnic traditions which underlined their differences.

(Bryk, 1990, p. 165)

In autumn 1942, '*Zegota*', the Council for Aid to Jews, was founded by Christian Poles working for the Polish underground, the *Armia Krajowa* (the Home Army), and for other resistance organizations. Linking with the Jewish underground and the Polish government-in-exile in London, the Warsaw-based *Zegota* developed a wide-ranging network, dealing with 'Legalization, Housing, Financial, Child Welfare, Medical, Clothing, Propaganda, and anti-*szmalcownik* activities [Poles co-operating with the Nazis by denouncing Jews in hiding]' (Tomaszewski and Werbowski, 1994, p. 42). The members of Zegota were not necessarily driven by philosemitic concerns. Indeed, they included nationalist Catholics who, even before the war, had advocated that Jews should leave Poland. The Nazi invasion did not change their antisemitic beliefs. Rescuing Jews was part of their humanitarian concern, integral to their Catholicism. One of the founders of *Zegota*, Zofia Kossak-Szczucka, a famous writer, wrote in 1942:

> Our feelings towards the Jews have not changed. We still consider them to be political, economic, and ideological enemies of Poland. What is more, we are aware that they consider us to be responsible for their misfortune. Why, on what grounds – that is a mystery of the Jewish soul, but it is a fact that is being confirmed again and again. The awareness of these feelings, however, does not relieve us of our duty to condemn the crime.

(Bryk, 1990, pp. 166f.)

Although *Zegota* took decisive and courageous action on behalf of Jews, this happened only after the majority of Polish Jews had already been murdered. It is possible to account for this pattern of Christian–Jewish interaction on the basis of the separation of Jews and Christians in Poland which had been enforced by each of the communities over the centuries. While there had been attempts in the prewar and interwar periods to forge closer relations between Christian and Jewish Poles, the movements counteracting this had left a greater mark on Polish society. In a situation of occupation and under constant threat of death for the smallest transgression of German orders, learnt behaviour separating Jews and Christians in Poland was increasingly difficult to shed.

> It was extremely difficult for the Poles to shake off the mental legacy of cultural anti-semitism. There was a total confusion or silence in the underground press. To admit that the Jews, if only morally and symbolically, were part of the Polish universe of obligation required the revision of anti-semitic convictions, and it required an admission that the struggle was for a culture in which Jews were equal.

(Bryk, 1990, p. 171)

Liberation and after (1945–)

At the end of the war, the Jews stranded in Displaced Persons' Camps (DP Camps) all over Europe either tried to make the journey to their prewar homes or sought to emigrate, mainly to the United States and Palestine. Thus the majority of the Jewish immigrants to Palestine before the establishment of the State of Israel in 1948 were Ashkenazim (cf. also Chapter 9). The option the DPs preferred depended largely on their relationship to their prewar national identity. While many French and Italian Jews, for example, chose to return to their prewar homes and to rebuild their lives there, reintegrating into Italian and French society because they understood themselves as French and Italian, their citizenship never having been revoked, many Jews from eastern European countries and Germany preferred emigration, feeling that their relationship with their former homeland had been irreparably damaged and all trust in the non-Jewish population had been lost.

In the newly independent State of Israel, preparations for a national commemoration of the Holocaust almost immediately developed on the basis of pre-state plans on the subject. The national memorial *Yad Vashem* ('Monument and Memorial') contains a museum surrounded by a park, with memorials to different groups of Jews affected by the Holocaust (e.g. partisans, ghetto fighters, children, the Jewish communities of the different countries) and to their rescuers, who are honoured individually as 'righteous gentiles' with plaques dotting the sides of the main paths through the site. *Yad Vashem* tells the story of the Holocaust with an emphasis on Zionism – warning against living among gentiles and underlining the need for a Jewish homeland in Palestine – and on Jewish military resistance, thereby eclipsing other perspectives on the events, notably religious interpretations of the Holocaust. However, the Jewish–Christian dimension is not totally obliterated: it finds its place in the Avenue of the Righteous Gentiles, many of the rescuers being Christians, thus creating a space in which positive consequences of prewar Jewish–Christian coexistence can be commemorated in the midst of violent conflict between Jews and Christians as part of different cultural and national groups during the Second World War.

Other national efforts to commemorate the Holocaust as an event that pertains to the contemporary societies in which Holocaust exhibitions are located are the purpose-built United States Holocaust Memorial Museum (USHMM) and the fourth floor of the Imperial War Museum in London (IWM), which integrates as well as separates the Holocaust from British perspectives on the Second World War. The mere existence of both these exhibitions emphasizes the social and cultural significance of the American and British Jewish community which includes refugees and immigrants from Nazi-occupied Europe. By devoting public money and private donations to these exhibitions, both countries not only celebrate that their Jewish communities are living in freedom from persecution and murder, but also seek to emphasize their nation's contribution to the liberation of Europe from Nazi occupation. None of the three national museums dwells on Jewish cultural and religious diversity, thereby favouring a perspective which emphasizes the similarity of 'us' and 'them', intending to break down barriers between different groups of the population and highlighting the dangers of stereotyping, suggesting that the Holocaust could happen to any of 'us' and that 'we' therefore need to uphold the ideals of liberal democracy. However, assimilation and acculturation are promoted as well, if only implicit in the moral message of the museums aimed at peaceful coexistence of different cultures as long as they all subscribe to the ideals of liberal society. Thus the possibilities and implications of difference, conflict and coexistence between cultural and religious groups in a given society are not explored.

It is difficult to speak about coexistence between Jews and Christians in post-Second World War Europe. The former European Jewish communities have been destroyed by the Holocaust, diminishing the Jewish community in Europe to the extent that the centres of Jewish life are now the United States and Israel. True, Vatican II – the last major revision of Catholic doctrine – and a number of Protestant initiatives since the 1960s have brought Christians and Jews together to dialogue. These conversations are mainly Christian initiatives – a reversal of the prewar Christian–Jewish dialogues in Germany. But, with large parts of Europe devoid of its former Jewish populations, the centre of reflections on the religious implications of the Holocaust has moved to the western world, notably to the United Kingdom and the United States. For many years, the Jewish community in postwar Germany largely comprised of DPs (displaced persons) who were not of German-Jewish origin. A connection with prewar traditions of Christian–Jewish conversations was not possible with this traumatized and, in their self-understanding, 'foreign' community. This is changing now with the immigration of Jews from the former Soviet Union. The Jewish community in Germany is the fastest growing community in Europe, numbering c. 100,000 at present. With the recent increase in numbers and a greater public profile comes a greater assertiveness on the part of the Jewish community and thus also greater attention to the conflicts surrounding Jewish life in contemporary Germany. While some thousand survivors returned to Poland, the majority decided to emigrate to the United States or Israel. Those who returned did not stay for long, but emigrated in the wake of antisemitic purges by the Communist Party in the 1950s and 1960s. As a result, the Jewish community in contemporary Poland is very small, numbering only a few thousand. However, recent years have seen an increasingly public awareness of Jewishness and the 'return' of young people to an identification with their cultural roots as well as an increased exploration of Jewish religious life. While these social and cultural movements are very much in their early stages, there is also a growing trend among the non-Jewish population in Europe to explore Jewish culture and religion (Gruber, 2002). However, to assess what has become known as Jewish–Christian relations since the Holocaust, we have to turn to religious and philosophical developments from the 1960s onwards. These are predominantly associated with Christian–Jewish conversations originating in Britain and the Unites States.

The development of Christian–Jewish relations in the international arena in the last fifty years can roughly be divided into two phases. In the wake of the Second World War and with an emerging awareness of the Holocaust, many churches felt called to issue statements that expressed their interpretation of the atrocities and of Christian antisemitism. This was the first stage of a gradual Christian re-evaluation of the churches' relationship with Jews. Statements from these years include the founding document of the Council of Christians and Jews (CCJ) in Britain (1942), the *Ten Points of Seelisberg* of the International Council of Christians and Jews (ICCJ) (1947), and the statement of the first assembly of the World Council of Churches (WCC) in Amsterdam (1948). A gap of about twenty years followed in the production of statements on Christian–Jewish relations until the mid-1960s when Vatican II issued *Nostra Aetate 4* as one of its last declarations (1965). This was followed by two documents explaining the significance of *Nostra Aetate* for Catholic teaching (1974 and 1985) and a document focusing on the Catholic Church and the Holocaust: *We Remember: A Reflection on the Shoah* (1998) (Fisher, 1999). On the Protestant side, regional churches in Europe also issued statements on Christian–Jewish relations, in particular in the Netherlands and Germany, and the WCC issued *Ecumenical Considerations on Jewish–Christian Dialogue* (1982) (Brockway, 1988; for a discussion of theological developments after the Holocaust, Chidester, 2001, pp. 546–52).

Postwar Christian–Jewish relations were characterized by intellectual rapprochement, aided by a prolonged peace in Europe, stable democracies and successful European integration. While peaceful coexistence of Christians and Jews is now the norm in Europe, because of the strength of liberal political traditions and the smallness of the Jewish minority, conflicts are never far off. These mostly relate to the memory of the Holocaust which divides Jews and Christians seemingly neatly into victims and perpetrators. Perceiving Christians as victims, as is, for example, part of the non-Jewish Polish experience of the Second World War and the Holocaust, causes repeated conflicts. The establishment of a Carmelite convent on the territory of the former Auschwitz I concentration camp, where a large number of Polish Catholics was executed, sparked a controversy in 1984 which lasted almost a decade, until the nuns finally moved to a building in the vicinity in 1993 (Rittner and Roth, 1991). Whether sites of Jewish and non-Jewish suffering in particular in Poland – such as different parts of the Auschwitz concentration camps – can or should be shared by Christians and Jews in commemoration, remains controversial. Further conflicts concern the interpretation of the Holocaust, such as the question whether the Vatican statement *We Remember* constituted an apology by the Catholic Church for failing to act on behalf of Jews during the Holocaust, or whether it circumvented the issue by admitting the guilt of individual members of the Catholic Church while exonerating the institution and its representatives (Dulles, 2001). Related to this is the controversy surrounding the beatification of Pope Pius XII. Pius XII's focus on behind-the-scenes diplomacy rather than public political intervention in 1930s and 1940s European politics, and his silence on the persecution and murder of Jews in Europe, has caused conflict between Catholics and Jews over the interpretation of his actions. Pius's defenders maintained that his diplomatic endeavours and avoidance of confrontation with the Nazi government ensured that Catholics in Germany and elsewhere were able to work with and on behalf of Jews more effectively, while not drawing attention to their efforts at protection and rescue. Others maintain that the Pope's silence signalled, at best, Catholic preoccupation with their own concerns about protection and relations with the Nazi state and, at worst, Catholic condonation of Jewish persecution and even murder (for an exploration of this controversy, see Sánchez, 2002).

This ongoing conflict between Christians and Jews is different from the other conflicts addressed in this book – it is, for instance, not a conflict between two theological positions – and different from Christian–Jewish encounters at the beginning of the twentieth century. Before the Holocaust, Christians and Jews were in conflict over coexisting with each other and forging a national and religious identity. Today, conflicts between Jews and Christians are largely independent of national politics. Now they chiefly focus on perceptions of the past. Historical behaviour of Christians is under scrutiny when the Holocaust is discussed as part of Christian–Jewish relations. The ways in which Christians made decisions about their interaction with Jews, or refused interaction, was a moral question at the time these decisions were made and it is a moral issue now, when these actions and omissions are discussed. Any interpretation of these actions is part of the interpretation of morality implicit in any decisions made. As such, the historian of the Holocaust, as well as any participant in Christian–Jewish relations after the Holocaust, is asked to make moral decisions regarding the material worked on, the tools of interpretation, and any conclusions drawn.

References

Barkai, A. (1998a) 'Population decline and economic stagnation' in M. A. Meyer and M. Brenner (eds) *German-Jewish History in Modern Times, Volume 4: Renewal and Destruction 1918–1945*, New York, Columbia University Press, pp. 30–101.

Barkai, A. (1998b) 'Jewish life under persecution' in M. A. Meyer and M. Brenner (eds) *German-Jewish History in Modern Times, Volume 4: Renewal and Destruction 1918–1945*, New York, Columbia University Press, pp. 231–57.

*Baumann, Z. (1989) *Modernity and the Holocaust*, Cambridge, Polity Press.

Benz, W. (ed.) (1991) *Dimensionen des Völkermords: Die Zahl der jüdischen Opfer des Nationalsozialismus*, Quellen und Darstellungen zur Zeitgeschichte 33, München, R. Oldenbourg Verlag.

Bloxham, D. and Kushner, T. (2004) *The Holocaust: Critical and Historical Approaches*, Manchester, Manchester University Press.

Brockway, A. (1988) *The Theology of the Churches and the Jewish People: Statements of the World Council of Churches and its Member Churches*, Geneva, WCC.

Bryk, A. (1990) 'The hidden complex of the Polish mind: Polish–Jewish relations during the Holocaust' in A. Polonsky (ed.) *'My Brother's Keeper?' Recent Polish Debates on the Holocaust*, London/New York, Routledge, pp. 161–83.

Büttner, U. (2000) '"The Jewish problem becomes a Christian problem": German Protestants and the persecution of the Jews in the Third Reich' in D. Bankier (ed.) *Probing the Depths of German Antisemitism: German Society and the Persecution of the Jews, 1933–1941*, New York and Oxford/Jerusalem, Berghahn Books/Yad Vashem/Leo Baeck Institute, pp. 431–59.

Chidester, D. (2001) *Christianity: A Global History*, London, Penguin.

Cohn, N. (1967) *Warrant for Genocide: The Myth of the Jewish World-Conspiracy and the Protocols of the Elders of Zion*, New York, Harper & Row.

Dietrich, D. J. (1988) *Catholic Citizens in the Third Reich: Psycho-Social Principles and Moral Reasoning*, Oxford, Transaction Books.

Dulles, A. R. (ed.) (2001) *The Holocaust Never to be Forgotten: Reflections on the Holy See's Document 'We Remember'*, Studies in Judaism and Christianity, New York, Paulist Press.

*Engel, D. (2000) *The Holocaust: A History of the Third Reich and the Jews*, Harlow, Longman.

Fisher, E. J. (1999) *Catholic–Jewish Relations: Documents from the Holy See*, London, Catholic Truth Society.

Gordon, S. (1984) *Hitler, Germans and the 'Jewish Question'*, Princeton, Princeton University Press.

Greive, H. (1987) 'Between Christian anti-Judaism and National Socialist antisemitism: the case of German Catholicism' in O. D. Kulka and P. R. Mendes-Flohr (eds) *Judaism and Christianity Under the Impact of National Socialism*, Jerusalem, The Historical Society of Israel/The Zalman Shazar Center for Jewish History, pp. 169–79.

Gruber, R. E. (2002) *Virtually Jewish: Reinventing Jewish Culture in Europe*, Berkeley, CA, University of California Press.

Gutteridge, R. (1976) *'Open Thy Mouth for the Dumb!' The German Evangelical Church and the Jews 1879–1950*, Oxford, Basil Blackwell.

Gutteridge, R. (1987) 'German Protestantism and the Jews in the Third Reich' in O. D. Kulka and P. R. Mendes-Flohr (eds) *Judaism and Christianity Under the Impact of National Socialism*, Jerusalem, The Historical Society of Israel/The Zalman Shazar Center for Jewish History, pp. 227–49.

Haynes, S. R. (1995) *Jews and the Christian Imagination: Reluctant Witnesses*, Studies in Literature and Religion, Basingstoke, Macmillan.

Honigmann, Peter (1988) *Die Austritte aus der jüdischen Gemeinde Berlin 1873–1941: Statistische Auswertung und historische Interpretation*, Frankfurt am Main, Verlag Peter Lang.

Hundert, G. (1986) 'The implications of Jewish economic activities for Christian–Jewish relations in the Polish Commonwealth' in C. Abramsky and M. Jachimczyk (eds) *The Jews in Poland*, Oxford, Basil Blackwell, pp. 53–63.

*Kulka, O. D. and Mendes-Flohr, P. R. (eds) (1987) *Judaism and Christianity Under the Impact of National Socialism*, Jerusalem, The Historical Society of Israel/The Zalman Shazar Center for Jewish History.

Kulka, O. D. (2000) 'The German population and the Jews: state of research and new perspectives' in D. Bankier (ed.) *Probing the Depths of German Antisemitism: German Society and the Persecution of the Jews, 1933–1941*, New York/Oxford/Jerusalem, Berghahn Books/Yad Vashem/ Leo Baeck Institute, pp. 271–81.

Kushner, T. (1994) *The Holocaust and the Liberal Imagination: A Social and Cultural History*, Oxford, Blackwell.

*Mendelsohn, E. (1983) *The Jews of East Central Europe Between the World Wars*, Bloomington, Indiana University Press.

Mendes-Flohr, P. R. (1987) 'Ambivalent dialogue: Jewish–Christian theological encounters in the Weimar Republic' in O. D. Kulka and P. R. Mendes-Flohr (eds), *Judaism and Christianity Under the Impact of National Socialism*, Jerusalem, The Historical Society of Israel/The Zalman Shazar Center for Jewish History, pp. 99–132.

Mendes-Flohr, P. R. (1998) 'Between Germanism and Judaism, Christians and Jews' in M. A. Meyer and M. Brenner (eds) *German-Jewish History in Modern Times, Volume 4: Renewal and Destruction 1918–1945*, New York, Columbia University Press, pp. 157–69.

Modras, R. (1994) *The Catholic Church and Antisemitism: Poland, 1933–1939*, Studies in Antisemitism 1, Amsterdam, Harwood Academic Publishers.

Mosse, G. L. (1970) *Germans and Jews: The Right, the Left, and the Search for a 'Third Force' in Pre-Nazi Germany*, New York, Howard Fertig.

Nipperdey, Thomas (1988) *Religion im Umbruch: Deutschland 1870–1918*, Beck'sche Reihe 363, München, Verlag C. H. Beck.

Nowak, Kurt (1995) *Geschichte des Christentums in Deutschland: Religion, Politik und Gesellschaft vom Ende der Aufklärung bis zur Mitte des 20. Jahrhunderts*, München, Verlag C. H. Beck.

Repgen, K. (1987) 'German Catholicism and the Jews: 1933–1945' in O. D. Kulka and P. R. Mendes-Flohr (eds) *Judaism and Christianity Under the Impact of National Socialism*, Jerusalem, The Historical Society of Israel/The Zalman Shazar Center for Jewish History, pp. 197–226.

Rittner, C. and Roth, J. K. (eds) (1991) *Memory Offended: The Auschwitz Convent Controversy*, New York, Praeger.

*Sánchez, J. M. (2002) *Pius XII and the Holocaust*, Washington, DC, The Catholic University of America Press.

Steinlauf, M. C. (1997) *Bondage to the Dead: Poland and the Memory of the Holocaust*, New York, Syracuse University Press.

Stoltzfus, N. (1996) *Resistance of the Heart: Intermarriage and the Rosenstrasse Protest in Nazi Germany*, New York/London, W.W. Norton & Company.

Tal, U. (1989) 'On the study of the Holocaust and genocide' in M. R. Marrus (ed.) *The Nazi Holocaust: Historical Articles on the Destruction of European Jews, Volume 1: Perspectives on the Holocaust*, Westport/London, Meckler, pp. 179–224.

Tomaszewski, I. and Werbowski, T. (1994) *Zegota: The Rescue of Jews in Wartime Poland*, Montreal, Price-Patterson.

*Young, J. E. (1988) *Writing and Rewriting the Holocaust: Narrative and the Consequences of Interpretation*, Bloomington/Indianapolis, Indiana University Press.

Asterisked items are particularly recommended for further reading.

9 Religion, conflict and coexistence in Palestine/Israel

David Herbert

The land of Israel was the birthplace of the Jewish people. There their spiritual, religious and national identity was formed. There they achieved independence and created a culture of national and universal significance. There they wrote and gave the Bible to the world. Exiled from the land of Israel the Jewish people remained faithful to it in all the countries of their dispersion, never ceasing to pray and hope for their return and restoration of their national freedom ... In recent decades they returned in their masses. They reclaimed the wilderness, revived their language, built cities and villages, and established a vigorous and ever-growing community ... They brought the blessings of progress to all inhabitants of the country and looked forward to sovereign independence.

(Israeli Declaration of Independence, 1948)

Palestine, the land of the three monotheistic faiths, is where the Palestinian Arab people was born, on which it grew, developed and excelled. The Palestinian people was never separated from or diminished its integral bonds with Palestine ... invasion, [and] the design of others ... combined to deprive the Palestinian people of its political independence.

(Palestinian National Council Declaration of Independence, 1988)

[I]f one goes reconstituting history two thousand years back there is no reason why one should not go further back, say four or five thousand years, and presently have the world ruled by militant archaeology.

(al-Kabir, a Jewish lawyer from Baghdad, *Iraqi Times* (1936), commenting on the Balfour declaration's (1917) proposal for a 'Jewish homeland' in Palestine; in Alcalay, 1993, p. 48)

We shall seek to do in western Asia what the English did in India – I mean the cultural work, not rulership and domination. We seek to extend the moral boundaries of Europe all the way to the Euphrates.

(Max Nordau, Herzl's 'chief lieutenant' (1907), in Shafir and Peled, 2002, p. 75)

A religious justification for the conquest control and settlement of the West Bank puts Judaism on a collision course with democracy.

(Ottolenghi, 2000, p. 47)

Each of these quotations provides a different perspective on the conditions in which Jews and Arabs coexist and conflict in the disputed territory of Israel/Palestine. The first two are from the declarations of independence of the state of Israel and the Palestinian National Council, precursor of the current Palestinian Authority (PA). Both refer to religion, and appeal to history to justify their claims to nationhood. While our focus here will be on religion's role in recent history (especially from 1967–2002), rather than on history as such, it is worth beginning with some reflection on contested histories and their uses, because the role of religion in Israel/Palestine is so caught up with conflicting historical claims.

Both declarations of independence demonstrate the difficulties of using history to justify contemporary political claims. First, each declaration lays claim to past national independence. Yet it is questionable whether the ancient kingdom of Israel was a 'nation' in the modern sense of the term, while under the Ottomans (1516–1921) Palestine divided into several administrative districts rather than constituting a single national community (see Map 11). This is the problem of anachronism: of imposing a contemporary political interpretative framework on past events. Secondly, the problem of historical diversity. Different peoples occupied the territory at different times, producing the need to select some periods at the expense of others to justify particular claims. This raises the spectre of countless competing and mutually exclusive nationalist claims to territory, each based on a different period, as the third quotation points out. Thirdly, the problem of producing an agreed historical account. This does not appear to diminish, in spite of the presence of much fuller records for recent events. Thus disputes between Jews and Arabs, and amongst Israeli (predominantly Jewish) historians, stem from conflicting interpretations of history which range from British promises in the First World War, through the wars of 1947–9, 1967, and 1973 and the *intifadas* ('uprisings') of 1987–93 and 2000–, to accounts of events at the Jenin refugee camp in 2002 (Silberstein, 1999; Karsh, 2000; Reinhart, 2002).

The fourth quotation hints at a fourth problem: moral evaluation of historical action varies with time and context. Thus the Israeli declaration's claim to benefit 'all the inhabitants of the land' now seems so difficult because the moral legitimacy of European colonialism has been widely undermined, in contrast to the context in which the movement for a Jewish homeland was created. Conversely, while the Palestinian declaration strikingly reflects religious diversity in contrast to the Israeli declaration's focus on Judaism, both can be seen as appeals to their different contemporary international audiences, designed to gain the widest possible international support in the circumstances of their time. In other words, both are political documents and need to be read against their different political backgrounds.

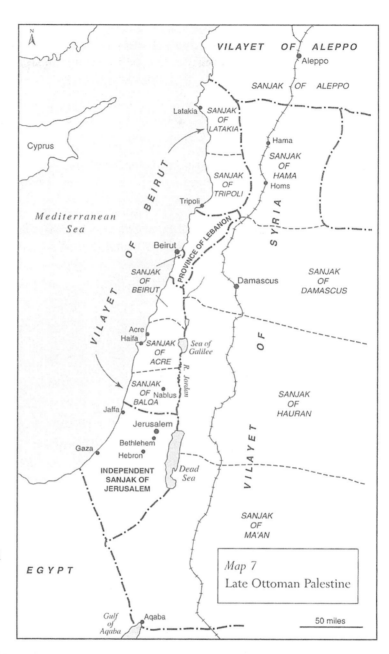

Map 11   'Late Ottoman Palestine', from Bernard Wasserstein (2003) Israel/Palestine: Why They Fight and Can They Stop?, *London, Profile Books, map 7. Cartographer: Mike Shand. Used with permission of Profile Books*

Since religious action, in so far as it can be humanly evaluated, takes place in history, the use of religion to justify political claims is subject to all these complexities. But other considerations also come into play. One is that of the tensions between religious particularism and liberal notions of citizenship. For liberal democracy, citizenship entails equal rights and freedoms for all, regardless of religious or ethnic identity, a claim which sits uneasily with the Israeli declaration's linkage of national identity to ethnicity and religion, as the fifth quotation suggests. There is also a demographic sense in which Israel's self-definition as a democratic Jewish state is under threat: trends indicate that Jews will soon be a minority of the total population of Israel and the Occupied Territories combined (Wasserstein, 2003).

Moving beyond historically and religiously based justification for action to the analysis of action itself, religion has played changing and contested roles in shaping the terms of coexistence and conflict between Jews (religious and secular) and Arabs (Muslim, Christian and secular) in Israel/Palestine throughout the twentieth century.[1] During the *Yishuv* (Jewish settlement in Israel before 1948), orthodox and traditional Jewish institutions and practices were pressed into the service of nation-building, a process consolidated with the foundation of the Israeli state. However, until the 1970s the role of religion in politics, beyond the use of religious symbols, festivals and stories as part of Israeli national identity, remained relatively limited.

Since the 1970s, however, religiously-based educational and welfare institutions, sometimes state funded, have brought support to marginal groups, amongst both Jewish and Muslim populations, and these have provided a setting for the development of radical religio-political movements that have sometimes used violent means. These include *Gush Emunim* ('Bloc of the Faithful'), an outgrowth of the Orthodox Jewish National Religious party (NRP), and Hamas (an abbreviation of *Harakat al-Muqawama,* 'Islamic Resistance Movement'), an outgrowth of the Muslim Brotherhood and notorious for their advocacy of the tactic of 'suicide bombing', or, in their terms, 'self-chosen martyrdom'. Less radical and well known, but also influential in Israeli politics is *Shas*, the religious party of the *Mizrachim* (Oriental Jews, i.e. mainly from the Arab world). We shall examine religion's role in the development and thinking of these groups, and how their influence has altered the terms of coexistence between Jews and Arabs, and sometimes led to conflict. In contrast, some religious groups have also been at the forefront of

---

[1] There is another significant religious minority in Israel/Palestine: the Druze. These people live mostly in villages to the North of Israel near the Lebanese border. They comprise about 1.2 per cent of the Israeli population (c. 70,000). The Druze broke off from the Ismaili branch of Shi'ite Islam in the eleventh century, believing the Fatimid caliph al-Hakim to have been an incarnation of God, who will return at some future point in history. In this belief, and subsequently, their theology has diverged markedly from Islamic orthodoxy: they believe in reincarnation, and do not practice some of the five pillars of Islam, including fasting during Ramadan, Hajj (pilgrimage to Mecca) or salat (5 times daily prayers). For most of their history, and partly from necessity in a Muslim-majority context, much of their belief and practice has been secret. Under Israeli administration they practice their religion more openly, and serve in the Israeli military. Because of their traditional quietism and conformity to the Israeli state the Druze have not played a significant role in the interaction between religion and politics in Israel/Palestine, and therefore are not considered further in this chapter.

attempts to promote understanding and reconciliation, including the Israel Interfaith Association and Interfaith Encounter Association.

But first, for centuries Palestine – and Jerusalem in particular – has been sacred to Jewish, Christian and Muslim faiths. Historically, competing religious claims have led to some conflict, most famously between Christians and Muslims in the crusades in the twelfth century (see Chapter 2). What is the relevance of these disputes to contemporary life? The next section will examine why historically the land has been considered holy by these three 'Abrahamic' faiths. The key events of the twentieth century will then be examined as a necessary background to understanding contemporary coexistence and conflict. Then some examples of the political mobilization of religious identity as a factor in contemporary conflict and coexistence will be examined, before briefly considering religiously inspired attempts at reconciliation. It should be noted at the outset that the aim is a modest one: to provide some insights into the role of religious factors in shaping the contemporary situation, not a comprehensive historical or political analysis.

The sacred significance of Israel/Palestine and Jerusalem

> On 28 September 2000 ... the Israeli opposition leader, Ariel Sharon, walked into the [Haram al-Sharif], surrounded by a phalanx of Israeli policemen to deliver what he called 'a message of peace'. His visit sparked off riots ... that spread to the Arab areas of east Jerusalem, the West Bank, Gaza and, for the first time, to Nazareth, Haifa, Jaffa and other Arab-inhabited areas of Israel. Within ten days the death toll in what Palestinians call the 'al-Aqsa *intifada*' approached 100.
>
> (Wasserstein, 2001, p.317)

In the last few years Israel's holy sites, and especially the Haram al-Sharif/Temple Mount in Jerusalem, have become caught up in the conflict between Arab Palestinians and Jewish Israelis. But does this recent conflict represent just the latest in a long history of clashes, or rather something different of more recent origin? This section will begin to address this question by examining the history of coexistence of the three traditions at key sacred sites, and the different senses in which they regard these sites as holy.

Judaism

> When the Lord your God brings you into the land you are entering to take possession of it, and clears away many nations

before you – the Hittites, Girgashites, Amorites, Canaanites, Perizzites, Hivites and Jebusites, seven nations greater and mightier than yourselves – and when the Lord your God gives them over to you, and you defeat them; then you must utterly destroy them.

(Deuteronomy 7:1ff, Revised Standard Version)

The land of Israel has had a continuous special status for the Jewish religion, based on narratives of redemption embedded in the Hebrew Bible, re-enacted in liturgy and founded historically on periods of occupation. These ended with the destruction of the temple in Jerusalem and the dispersion of the Jewish people after the unsuccessful revolt against the Romans in 66–70. From this period until the mid-nineteenth century, hopes for restoration looked to an eschatological, not political realization.

But from the nineteenth century, against a background of continued persecution in eastern Europe and of the development of European nationalism and colonialism, some, predominantly secular, Jews became active in promoting the idea of a Jewish homeland. These Zionists – Zion being an alternative name for Jerusalem – justified the location of this homeland in Palestine in terms of historical association rather than religious promise. Until the early twentieth century, the movement remained open to the possibility of other locations – for example, the British politician Joseph Chamberlain's suggestion of an East African site was seriously debated by the early Zionist congresses. But following the death of its most influential early leader Theodore Herzl in 1904, the Zionist Congress focused its efforts on Palestine. Furthermore, a minority of religious thinkers (e.g. Rabbi Abraham Isaac (AI) Kook, the first Chief Rabbi in British Mandate Palestine (1922–48)) also began to advocate political activism in the form of resettlement of Palestine and reinterpreted the religious tradition accordingly.

Jerusalem is sacred for Jews, Muslims and Christians and hence 'to every other human being' on earth (Hiro, 1996, p. 1). According to tradition, it is the place where Abraham offered to sacrifice his son Isaac (ibid., p. 4). In each of these traditions it is the 'navel of the earth', and the place where the last judgement and the resurrection of the dead are believed to begin. However, in Jewish tradition its prominence springs from King David's founding of a capital there, and his son Solomon's construction of the first temple (tenth–ninth centuries BCE). The temple is of spiritual importance because it is associated with God's presence on earth (Hebrew *shekinah*). This is because it became the resting place for the 'tabernacle' (mobile shrine), which had accompanied the Israelites in their wanderings around the desert under Moses, after their escape from Egypt. Thus Jerusalem became a powerful theological symbol in the Hebrew Bible (I Kings 11:13; Psalm 2:6; Jeremiah 3:16 ff.), and has remained of central symbolic importance to Jewish religious life, in spite of nearly two millennia of exile:

Figure 1 The Western Wall of Haram al-Sharif 'Temple Mount' with the Dome of the Rock in the background. Photo: © World Religions Photo Library/Osborne

> Jews faced Jerusalem when they prayed ... Biblical literature, *halakha* (Jewish law), *aggadah* (non-legal rabbinic teaching), *tefilla* (liturgy), *kabbala* (mystical writings), *haskala* (the Hebrew literature of the eighteenth and nineteenth centuries) and Jewish folklore all celebrated Jerusalem's ancient glory and mourned its devastation.
>
> (Wasserstein, 2001, p. 3)

Yet, as with the land of Israel, rabbinic Judaism distinguished between the earthly Jerusalem (*Yerushalayim shel matah*) and the heavenly place (*shel ma'lah*). Hence its central place in religious life 'was not regarded as involving any duty to gain political sovereignty over it' (ibid., p. 4). Nor was any kind of religious sovereignty claimed over the most holy site, the Temple Mount, which from the eighth century became the site of the Muslim Haram.[2]

However, from the eighteenth century the western or 'Wailing' Wall of the Temple became increasingly important as a place of prayer and pilgrimage. Traditionally believed to be the western wall of the Herodian temple, more recent archaeological evidence suggests it was a more peripheral supporting structure. Nonetheless, it was the only structure to survive the Roman attack in 70 CE, and it became a site for the lamentation of the loss of Jerusalem and for the dispersal of the Jewish people. From the early twentieth century, Jews attempted to improve

[2] 'Sacred area', containing the Dome on the Rock and al-Aqsa mosque.

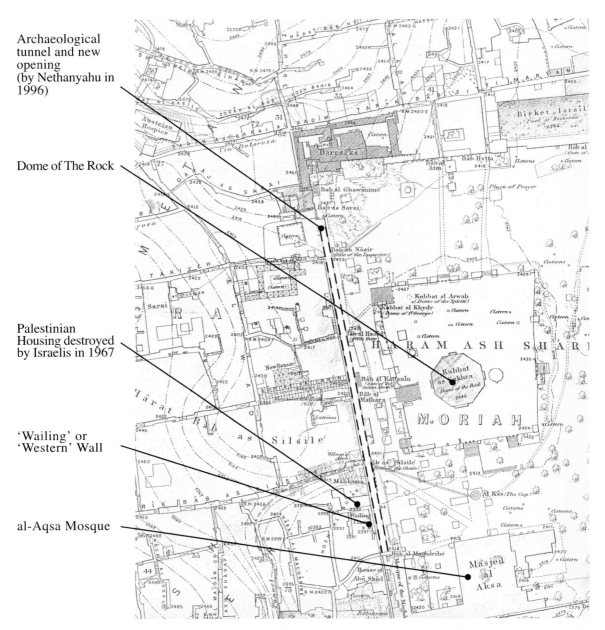

Figure 2   Plan of Temple site including added archaeological tunnel, Ordnance Survey of Jerusalem, scale 1:2500, 1864–65. Photo used with the permission of The British Library, shelfmark: Y.1115

access to the wall, and to acquire it from the Muslim trust that owned it. Indeed, agitation between the two communities boiled over into riots in 1929. Yet the status of the Haram as a Muslim holy site was not challenged until 1967, when the Israelis gained control of east Jerusalem in the Six Day War. Even then, as the site of the Temple it was regarded by many Orthodox Jews as too sacred to enter, and the Chief Rabbi forbade Jews from worshipping there (ibid., p. 319).

In 1967, the Israeli government demolished Arab housing that faced the western Wall, evicting its residents to create an open space within which Jewish worshippers could gather. The government returned the Haram itself to the trusteeship of the Muslim Council, and the Chief Rabbi's ban on entry remained in force. But from this date, small but growing numbers of militant Jewish groups have made incursions into the area and declared an intention to rebuild the temple, in some cases with support from fundamentalist Christians in the United States (Wasserstein, 2001, p. 334). Furthermore, such groups have attracted the support of prominent right-wing Israeli politicians, such as Binyamin Netanyahu and Ariel Sharon, both later to become prime ministers (ibid., p. 335).

Thus, by the late 1990s, Jewish agitation around the Haram entered the political mainstream, with a tunnel under the area ceremonially opened with Nethanyahu's approval (1996). The site was a point of contention between the Ehud Barak administration (1999–2001) and the Palestinian Authority (PA) at the Camp David negotiations in 2000. Within weeks of the breakdown of these negotiations, then opposition leader Sharon made the incursion on the Haram with which we began this section, triggering the second Palestinian *intifada*. However, this Jewish political agitation around the Haram has dismayed many secular Israelis (Reinhart, 2002, pp. 92–3).

Thus Israel's holy sites have been a cause of minor agitation for centuries, but their recent escalation into the centre stage of political conflict in Israel marks a new departure. This needs to be understood in the broader context of the development of the Israeli–Palestinian struggle in the twentieth century, and of the dynamics of contemporary Israeli society. But first we need to consider why Muslims and Christians also consider Palestine/Israel and Jerusalem to be holy.

Islam

Muslim claims to sovereignty in Palestine rest on the idea of *waqf* or 'trusteeship'. According to this religio-legal concept, lands conquered by Muslims have been permanently given by God to Muslim trusteeship. Before the nineteenth century Muslims have not often – and especially rarely in the Middle East – been either a minority or politically subordinate (Lewis, 1994). Nor has Islam often retreated from commanding the allegiance of the majority once it has become established – this has really only been the case in Spain, re-taken by

Christian rulers in 1492 (Elias, 1999, p. 14). Thus while Muslim empires have been relatively tolerant of minorities who have been accorded a protected but subordinate status (institutionalized in the *millet* system in the Ottoman Empire),[3] power sharing has not been part of this history. Palestine was under Muslim rule from the eighth to the twentieth century, with the exception of the crusader period (twelfth century), with the Ottomans as the ruling power from the sixteenth century until after the First World War. Under the *millet* system the division of society along religious lines arguably creates cultural memories which can resurface when societies come under stress under modern conditions – as in the former Yugoslavia, for example, most of which was also under Ottoman control until the late nineteenth century. More broadly, the Muslim experience of modernity, in which the idea of power sharing in the form of democracy has often arrived alongside foreign domination or influence as part of colonialism, has often been a difficult and challenging one.

Ottoman reaction to early Zionist activity is illustrated in the response of Sultan Abd al-Hamid to Herzl's offer in 1896, to buy Palestine for twenty million lire:

> Please advise him never to mention this ever. I cannot sell one inch of this country – it does not belong to me. It belongs to my people. My people acquired this Ottoman Empire by their blood, and later they fed it with their blood, and we will give our blood before we allow anyone to take it from us. ... Let the Jewish people keep their billions. If the Turkish Empire is divided, maybe the Jews will take Palestine for free, but I will not divide it except over my dead body, and I will never accept to carve it up for any reason.

> (in Cohn-Sherbok and El-Alami, 2001, pp. 96–7)

However, until the 1980s, the character of the Palestinian nationalist movement in the twentieth century was predominantly secular. This is partly because this was the dominant trend in Arab nationalism until the 1970s, and partly because of the important role of Christians in the movement, so that a nationalism based on Islam was seen as divisive. The outbreak of the first *intifada* in 1987 was to change this, because it led to the rapid formation of Islamist groups such as Hamas and Islamic Jihād. This was both a reaction to the spread of Islamic political activism across the wider Muslim world, and to the increasing role of religious mobilization in Jewish nationalism.

Jerusalem, al-Quds (literally, 'the holy', a title dating from the tenth century) in Arabic, is Islam's third holiest place, after Mecca and Medina

---

[3] The *millet* system is a form of social organization in which religious minorities live in semi-autonomous communities with their own institutions, but within a larger Muslim society.

in Saudi Arabia. In the very earliest phase of Muslim history, it was the direction towards which Muhammad's earliest followers prayed (622–24). Indeed, some have argued that there was a battle for precedence between the holy places that was not settled until the second Islamic century (the eighth century; Rippin, 1990, pp. 54–6). In Muslim tradition, the primary reason for Jerusalem's prominence is that the *Haram al-Sharif* is regarded as the place from which the Prophet Muhammad miraculously ascended into heaven during his 'Night Journey' (Qur'ān, Surah 17:1).

The two main structures on the *Haram* are the Dome of the Rock, sometimes called Omar's mosque, and the *al-Aqsa* mosque. The former is the earliest extant example of Islamic architecture, built by the caliph 'Abd al-Malik (reigned 685–705), and the rock embedded in its centre is held to be the spot from which Muhammad ascended. However, some contemporary scholars argue that the construction of the Dome of the Rock predates this association, as it is not mentioned in the earliest inscriptions (Rippin, 1990, p. 55). Arguably these inscriptions provide evidence of early inter-faith rivalry: 'do not speak of three [Gods]' one passage warns, a possible polemic against Christian Trinitarianism (ibid., p. 55). Although the Dome is sometimes called a mosque its space for prayer is limited, and the al-Aqsa mosque was constructed in the ninth century to accommodate Muslim pilgrims (Ahmed, 1993, p. 64).

Whatever the initial reason for Malik's construction of the Dome of the Rock, Jerusalem became an important pilgrimage site for Muslims. Its significance is testified to in the *hadith*[4] literature in sayings attributed to Muhammad such as:

> He who performs the pilgrimage to Mecca and visits my grave [in Medina] and goes forth to fight [in a holy war] and prays for me in Jerusalem – God will not ask him what he [failed to perform of the prescriptions] imposed on him.

(quoted in Wasserstein, 2001, p. 9)

It is the place that, another tradition testifies, was prayed at by all the prophets up to Muhammad, and is daily surrounded by a bodyguard of 70,000 angels (ibid., p. 318). However, in the eleventh century, initial Muslim resistance to the crusaders was not legitimated in terms of the sacredness of Jerusalem, but rather as a conventional defensive *jihād* (struggle) against an invading aggressor. Jerusalem's importance in Muslim literature and popular piety stems principally from the period after its recapture by Salah al-din (Saladin) in 1187.

---

[4] *Hadith* – traditions, consisting of sayings and deeds attributed to the Prophet and his companions.

Christianity

With the conversion of Constantine in the early fourth century, Christianity became the politically dominant religious tradition in Palestine, which was then part of the Roman and later Byzantine empires. It was from this period that the holy sites of Jerusalem first became important to Christians, when Constantine's mother Helena identified sites associated with key events in Jesus' life and greatly boosted the tradition of Christian pilgrimage to Palestine. She erected a shrine, later rebuilt as the Church of the Holy Sepulchre, on a site identified as the place of the crucifixion and entombment of Jesus. It was also the site of a pagan temple to Aphrodite, and thus symbolized the triumph of Christianity over paganism, reflecting wider changes in the empire. Other principal sites in Palestine also stem from the fourth and fifth centuries. These include the Basilica of the Annunciation in Nazareth (the site where an angel is believed to have appeared to Mary announcing Jesus' birth), under which the remains of a fifth-century church have been found, and the Church of the Nativity in Bethlehem, marking the place of Jesus' birth.

This emphasis on literal holy place arguably contrasts with some earlier Christian attitudes. The New Testament contains a powerful strand of allegorical interpretation that reapplied the promises to Israel in the Hebrew Bible to the church, such that literal references under what came to be seen as the 'old' covenant (or 'testament') were understood spiritually under the new covenant. For example, the heavenly Jerusalem becomes more important than the earthly Jerusalem, the spiritual 'circumcision' more important than literal circumcision, the spiritual 'temple' (Jesus' body) more important than the literal temple (Galatians 4: 21–30; Romans 2: 25–9; Matthew 26:61). We have already seen this tendency to 'spiritualize' a literal meaning in Rabbinic responses to the destruction of the temple in 66 CE, and both traditions reflect the need of minorities to adapt to a diaspora context without political power. The new emphasis on literal sacred place seems to reflect a new confidence in the material world in the Christian mainstream[5] after centuries of intermittent persecution; a similar trend can be seen in Christian art (Chapter 1).

The Byzantines lost Palestine to the Muslims in the eighth century. As we have seen, there is evidence of rivalry over holy sites in the inscriptions in the Dome of the Rock. Later, there is evidence of rivalry escalating into violence, when in 937 a Christian procession was attacked and the Church of the Holy Sepulchre burnt to the ground. We have also seen (in Chapter 2) that calls for help from eastern Christians in Palestine were one of the factors leading to the First Crusade (1096–99). However, the pattern of interaction under Muslim rule can largely be described as one

---

[5] In contrast, the origins of monasticism in this period reflect a rejection of the new worldliness of post-Constantine Christianity.

of coexistence under Muslim domination. Jews were allowed back into Jerusalem, having been banned under Rome and Byzantium, and both Jews and Christians were allowed to perform their religious duties and go about their daily lives in exchange for payment of a poll tax to the Muslim rulers. In contrast, this pattern was changed to conflict when the crusader forces of Godfrey de Bouillon captured Jerusalem in 1099, expelling all Jews and Muslims from Jerusalem, and destroying mosques and synagogues (Wasserstein, 2001, pp. 7–8).

While the crusades have had long-term consequences for the mutual perceptions of Muslims and Christians (Chapter 2), the crusaders' hold on Palestine lasted barely a century. The western Christian presence was reduced to outposts of a few Catholic orders, and eastern Christians were divided into many rival groupings. Thus in 1947 the 100,000 Christians living in the territory designated as Palestine under the British Mandate belonged to 24 different denominations, 'the result of many different historical and theological schisms' (Wasserstein, 2001, p. 20). Today they remain concentrated in the main Christian holy places of Jerusalem, Bethlehem and Nazareth. The largest group is Greek Orthodox (ethnically Arab), followed by Greek Catholic. There are also Maronites (especially near their centre in Lebanon), Armenians and Copts, while Latin Catholic (largely through holy orders e.g. Franciscans) and Russian Orthodox maintain several holy sites. Since the nineteenth-century, Protestants (Anglican and Lutheran) have had a small presence: for example, in the 1840s the Prussians and the British established a joint bishopric of Jerusalem.

Christianity has no agreed position regarding the political status of Palestine. Indeed, on this as on many political and ethical issues Christian views can be found across a broad spectrum. Western Christians, at least at a leadership level, have been deeply affected by the Jewish experience of the Holocaust on European soil, especially in the context of European traditions of antisemitism. From the Second World War until the 1980s this led to a predominantly pro-Zionist position among Protestants, and to rather later and more cautious support from the Vatican. Some Evangelical and fundamentalist Protestants are strongly pro-Zionist, because they see the return of Jews to Palestine as a sign of the second-coming of Christ. Since the first *intifada* more sympathy has been shown to Palestinians by mainstream western Christians. Eastern Christianity has been less affected by the Holocaust, and amongst eastern Christians in Palestine there is little sympathy for Zionism (Dalrymple, 1997).

Politics and population in the transformation of Palestine/Israel in the twentieth century

We have now considered some of the history of Israel/Palestine as a contested sacred site, which forms part of the background to contemporary coexistence and conflict. We now turn to the turbulent history of the twentieth century, a period of massive changes which have reshaped the map of religious diversity in Israel/Palestine. These changes are mostly attributable in one way or another to the activities and consequences of the Zionist movement, whose origins were briefly introduced above. Herzl's main legacy was to establish high level diplomacy as an essential tool to achieve Zionist goals, alongside settlement and ideological mobilization. This diplomatic activity was to prove crucial through the First World War and the British mandate that followed, and Jewish influence in this sphere contrasts with the Palestinians' lack of high-level contacts.

The First World War and the British Mandate

During the First World War, the Ottoman Empire allied with Germany against Britain, France and Russia. Under the Ottomans Palestine was divided into several administrative areas (*sanjaks*) (Map 11). During the course of the war the British sought alliances with Arab leaders in the area, and with the Zionist movement, which was particularly influential in the British foreign office (Shlaim, 2000). In the course of these negotiations the British made statements to both Arabs and Zionists (the McMahon statement (1915) and the Balfour Declaration (1917)), which each group interpreted as offering hope of some form of future political autonomy in Palestine (Peretz, 1996). In particular, the Balfour Declaration declared British approval of the establishment of a Jewish homeland in Palestine, provided this was not to the detriment of the existing population. The contradictory aspirations of these groups established tensions that were to dominate the period of the British Mandate in Palestine (Map 12).

In 1885, the population of Palestine was approximately half a million, of whom about 45,000 were Arab Christians and 25,000 Jewish, the rest being Arab Muslims and some Ottoman (Turkish) Muslim soldiers and administrators (Israeli, 2002, p. 11; Guyatt, 2001, p. 2). Most of these Jews were *sephardim*, or *mizrachim* – 'oriental' – that is from the Arab world, although some *sephardim* had come to Amsterdam and London in the sixteenth and seventeenth centuries. But the majority of European Jews who emigrated to Israel came from central Europe and were *ashkenazim* ('western' or European Jews whose ancestors had lived under Christian rulers). In successive emigrations – the Hebrew word *aliyah* has

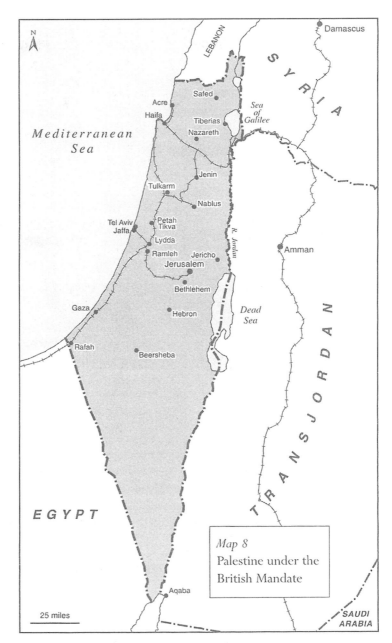

Map 12 'Palestine under the British Mandate', from Bernard Wasserstein (2003) Israel/Palestine: Why They Fight and Can They Stop?, *London, Profile Books, map 8. Cartographer: Mike Shand. Used with permission of Profile Books*

connotations of religious pilgrimage – from 1882 (in response to pogroms in Russia) through to the fifth *aliyah* in 1933–5 (in response to Nazi persecution) waves of *ashkenazi* Jews left Europe for Palestine. By 1947, with further large-scale emigration of surviving European Jews in the aftermath of the Holocaust, the Jewish population in Palestine had risen to about 600,000 (Guyatt, 2001, p. 2). During this period the Palestinian population (Muslim and Christian) had grown to approximately 800,000 (Map 13).

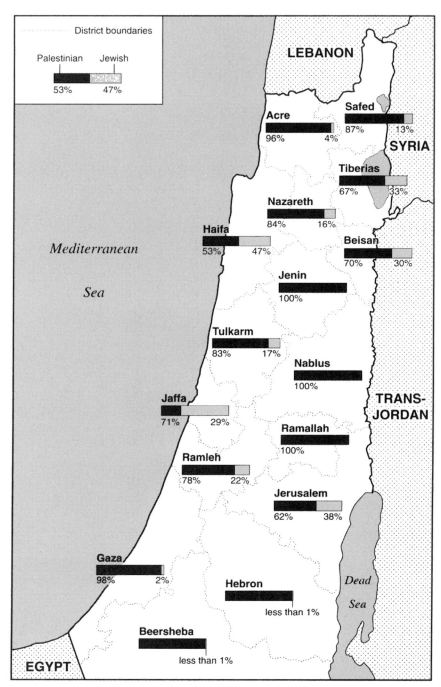

Map 13   'Palestine, 1946: population by district', adapted from Walid Khalidi, Before Their Diaspora, *published by The Institute for Palestine Studies 1984, 1991. Used with the permission of The Institute for Palestine Studies*

The War of Independence/the Disaster

Between 1947 and 1949, during a period known to Israelis as the War of Independence but to Palestinians as *al-Nakba* ('the Disaster'), approximately 700,000 Palestinians were displaced from their homes, mostly into refugee camps in neighbouring Arab states. The reasons for this displacement are still strongly contested. What is undisputed is that the Palestinian leadership rejected the partition of Palestine proposed by the United Nations and passed on 29 November 1947 (Map 14). But while Zionists have tended to put this down to Arab intransigence, others have argued that it was rejected because it was unfair: it gave the majority of the land (56 per cent) to the Jews, who at that stage legally owned only 7 per cent of it, and remained a minority of the population (Guyatt, 2001, p. 5). In the following months, Israeli settlers came under increasing attack from Palestinian militia. In response, the Jewish authorities began a policy ('Plan D') of capturing and clearing Palestinian settlements within the territory allocated to the Jewish state by the UN in order to ensure the security of Jewish settlements. While it seems that the primary intention of this policy was military, it had the effect of displacing large numbers of Palestinian civilians, as well as militia. Arguments rage over the extent to which this policy was the primary cause of the Palestinian exodus, rather than other factors such as the early departure of Palestinian leaders, or later promises of swift restoration by Arab armies. There is also argument over whether the intention was primarily military, or deliberately to depopulate Arab towns and villages. Yet another dispute concerns whether the bulk of Palestinian departures occurred before or after the outbreak of official hostilities with Israel's Arab neighbours on 15 May 1948 (Shlaim, 2000, p. 31).

Arab nations had been hostile to the creation of the State of Israel from the start, and so seeing the collapse of Palestinian resistance, neighbouring Arab states moved to direct military intervention. The proclamation of the State of Israel on 14 May was immediately followed on 15 May by declarations of war from Egypt, Transjordan, Syria, Lebanon and Iraq. The balance of forces in this war remains a contentious issue, but the outcome was the defeat of the Arab armies and the continued exodus of Palestinians. Thus when Israel signed separate ceasefires with each Arab state in 1949, the Palestinians were worse off than under the UN plan. Instead of the 44 per cent of mandate Palestine allocated in the UN plan, they ended up with only 23 per cent, and that to be administered by Egypt (Gaza) and Jordan (the West Bank) (Map 15). 700,000 Arabs had fled the territory now allocated to Israel. Estimates for the numbers of Palestinians remaining vary from 92,000 to 150,000, compared to 716,000 Jews; so between 12 and 20 per cent of the population (Shlaim, 2000, p. 54; Shafir and Peled, 2002, p. 110). Some 60,000 of these Palestinians were granted immediate Israeli citizenship; the rest had to apply under a system which made it difficult for them to qualify, but which was amended to include most in 1980 (ibid., p. 111).

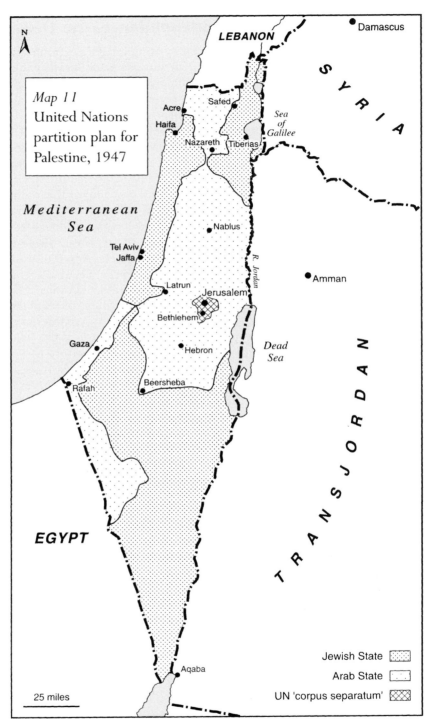

Map 14   'UN partition plan for Palestine, 1947' from Bernard Wasserstein (2003) Israel/Palestine: Why They Fight and Can They Stop?, *London, Profile Books, map 11. Cartographer: Mike Shand. Used with permission of Profile Books*

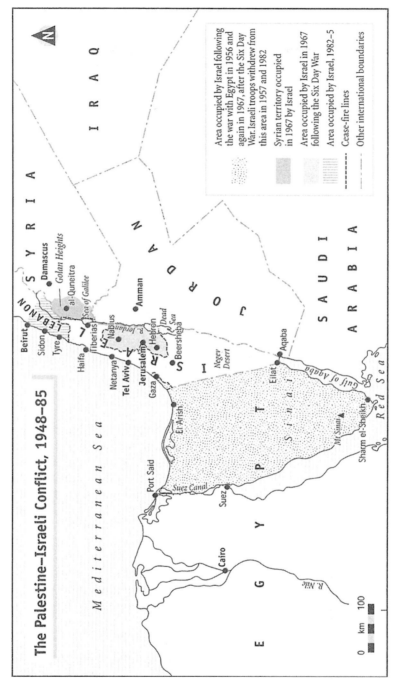

Map 15 'The Palestine–Israeli Conflict, 1948–85' from Dan Cobn-Sherbok and Dawoud El-Alami (2001)
The Palestine–Israeli Conflict (a beginner's guide), Oxford, One World Publications. Used with permission of
OneWorld

The Six Day War (1967)

The ceasefire agreements of 1949 never developed into full-scale peace treaties; instead, tensions between Israel and her Arab neighbours smouldered on for the next eighteen years, briefly igniting when Israel supported Britain and France against Egypt in the Suez crisis of 1956. In 1958 the Palestinian resistance movement Fatah was founded by Yasser Arafat. Branches were soon established across the Arab world, and formed the basis of the Palestine Liberation Organisation (PLO) (Cohn-Sherbok and al-Alami, 2001, pp. 140–2). The 'Six Day War', fought between 5 and 10 June 1967 was as intense and decisive as it was brief. In response to intelligence warning of imminent Arab attacks, on 5 June 1967 Israel launched surprise air strikes on enemy airfields. As Shlaim explains:

> The Egyptian airforce was wiped out on the ground within a few hours on the morning of 5 June, but false information was given to Egypt's allies to encourage them to join in the fighting. At noon the airforces of Syria, Jordan and Iraq started to attack targets inside Israel. Within two hours the Syrian and Jordanian forces were also wiped out, as well as the Iraqi airbase at H-3, near the Jordanian border. In all, four hundred enemy planes were destroyed on the first day of fighting, and that in essence sealed the fate of the Arab armies.
>
> (2000, p. 241)

Israel's air advantage led to the collapse of the Arab armies, so that by 10 June Israel had occupied the entire Sinai peninsula, the West Bank, and the Golan Heights. In taking control of East Jerusalem, the West Bank and Gaza, Israel took direct charge for the first time of a population of more than a million Palestinians, which has grown rapidly since (Map 15). The size of this population meant that it could not readily be absorbed into a state whose founding principles presupposed a Jewish majority. These Palestinians have been excluded from citizenship rights, but absorbed into the Israeli economy as workers, consumers and taxpayers. Israel continues with this occupation to date, in spite of UN resolution 242 (1967), which called for an immediate withdrawal. Just as the Palestinians rejected the UN plan for partition in 1948, so Israel has rejected later UN resolutions. Disputes around the interpretation of this conflict centre on whether Israel's pre-emptive strikes on Arab forces were defensively justified, or part of a prior ambition to enlarge its territories.

The October/Yom Kippur War (1973) and Camp David Peace Accord (1978)

The next major conflict was the 'October/Yom Kippur War', named after the major Jewish national and religious holiday 'the Day of Atonement'. On this Jewish holy day in 1973, Egyptian President Nasser and his Arab allies launched a surprise attack, seeking to regain what they had lost in 1967. Initial Arab gains were largely reversed, with the war resulting in

Israel's retreat from the Sinai, but not from the Palestinian Occupied Territories. The war was significant for two main reasons. In the initial Egyptian advance, Israeli lines were broken for the first time, so that in spite of the quick reversal of fortunes it is arguable that Israelis' sense of invulnerability after the comprehensive victory of 1967 was punctured. Possibly this led to more willingness to negotiate with Arab enemies, and eventually to the first full peace settlement with an Arab neighbour when the Camp David peace accords were signed with Egypt in 1978. Secondly, for the first time Arab states used their control over the world's oil supply to bring pressure to bear on the west, a factor that has arguably had long-term effects on Arab self-confidence (Milton-Edwards and Hinchcliffe, 2001, pp. 15–16).

But these Arab gains did not benefit the Palestinians; indeed, arguably they were worse off after the peace. Israel had neutralized the one Arab state (Egypt) that had posed a significant military threat, and gained credibility in the eyes of the world by making peace with an Arab neighbour, without conceding anything regarding the Palestinians. Indeed, even as Israel withdrew from the settlements it had briefly established in the Sinai, it accelerated its expansion of development in the rest of the Occupied Territories, ever more firmly entrenching Jewish settlement in these areas in spite of another UN resolution, 338 (Guyatt, 2001, p. 12).

The invasion of Lebanon, siege of West Beirut and occupation of Southern Lebanon (1982–2000)

In June 1982, in response to the Palestinian Liberation Organisation's[6] shelling of Israeli settlements in northern Israel from their positions in southern Lebanon, 'Operation Peace for Galilee' saw Israeli forces invade the Lebanon. The aim was to secure a 40km zone in southern Lebanon. But, surprised by the rapid collapse of PLO resistance and seeking to mop up PLO forces that had fled to Beirut, the Israeli Defence Force (IDF) went on to besiege the mainly Muslim Lebanese and Palestinian West Beirut, thus becoming involved in the civil war between the Muslims and Christians (mainly Maronites) on the Christian side. Trapped with the 6,000 PLO fighters in West Beirut were half a million civilians, who were killed at a rate of 200–300 per day in the bombardment, which continued until 30 August when the PLO surrendered and fled to Tunis (Guyatt, 2001, p. 18). Under the command of Ariel Sharon, Israeli troops continued into West Beirut, turning a blind eye to the Christian Phalangist massacre of at least 2,000 Palestinian elderly, women and children in the refugee camps of Sabina and Sabra on 16–17 September 1982 (Shlaim, 2000, pp. 416–18). Israeli troops withdrew from Beirut in

[6] PLO – the military and political leadership of the Palestinians in exile, founded in 1964.

1983; but in alliance with the Christian-led South Lebanese army the IDF were to remain in the 'security zone' in Lebanon until 2000, finally forced to withdraw under pressure from the Israeli left, international public opinion and continued resistance from the Shi'ite Islamic radical group Hizbullah.

The first intifada ('uprising') 1987–1993 and Oslo I (1993)

Contributory factors leading to the eruption of the first Palestinian *intifada* in December 1987 include: Palestinian despair at the expulsion of the PLO from Lebanon; frustration at continued expansion of the Jewish settlement programme in the Occupied Territories and the increasing restrictions on Palestinian life that this entailed; and a continued lack of civil and political rights and economic opportunities. The *intifada* was a spontaneous uprising of Palestinian youth against Israeli occupying forces, and has come to be symbolized in the international media by images of confrontations between well-armed Israeli soldiers and stone-throwing Palestinian youths. Through the *intifada* a number of radical Islamic groups emerged out of long-established Muslim Brotherhood activity, including Islamic Jihād and Hamas (the Islamic Resistance Movement; Mishal and Sela, 2000).

The persistence of the *intifada* and adverse international publicity led to American pressure on Israel, while the first Gulf War of 1991 exposed Israel's vulnerability to Iraqi missile attack. Military options seemed exhausted for the exiled PLO, and so a new preparedness to negotiate was found on both sides. Thus secret talks began, brokered by the Norwegian government and supported by the EU and the US, which eventually produced the Oslo peace accords of 1993. The PLO agreed to renounce violent struggle and both agreed to a staged process leading to limited Palestinian autonomy within parts of the West Bank and Gaza. The PLO returned from exile, an elected Palestinian Authority (PA) was established, and the first tentative steps of Israeli withdrawal from a small number of urban areas in Gaza and the West Bank were taken. However, discussion of central issues such as the future status of Jerusalem and the return of refugees was postponed until 'final status' negotiations, then projected for 1998.

A major obstacle to progress was the extent of Israeli settlement in the Occupied Territories. By 1993, Israel had placed 300,000 illegal settlers in these areas, and created an infrastructure to support them (Map 16). Since even minor withdrawals from recent settlements – as from the Sinai in 1982 – have provoked resistance from settlers and widespread public disapproval, any further withdrawals in accordance with Palestinian demands and UN resolutions would be extremely difficult for any Israeli government. Prime Minister Rabin agreed to a freeze on Israeli expansion, but unilaterally exempted East Jerusalem, and while

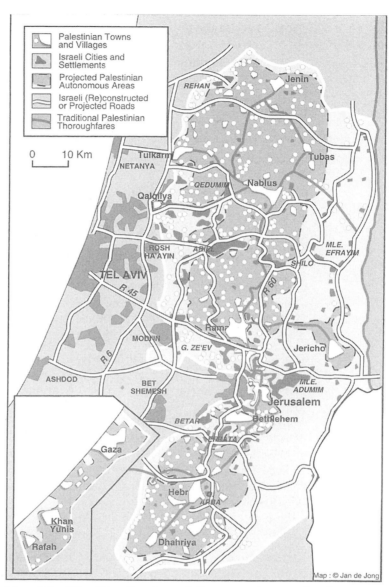

Map 16 'The West Bank and Gaza: projection for the year 2010' from Nicholas Guyatt (2001) The Absence of Peace: Understanding the Israeli–Palestinian Conflict, *London, Zed Books. Map by Jan de Jong, used with permission*

development of new sites was curtailed, expansion of existing developments continued, involving the confiscation of more Palestinian land (Guyatt, 2001, p. 31). On the Palestinian side, Hamas and Islamic Jihad opposed any compromise with Israel, and a campaign of suicide bombings which further hardened Israeli public opinion began, just as the shape of the second Oslo agreement began to emerge.

Oslo II (1995) and the Al-Aqsa intifada (2000–)

In 1995 the 'Oslo II' agreement fleshed out the phased withdrawal of Israel from substantial chunks of the Occupied Territories. 65 per cent of Gaza, where there were only 5,000 Jewish settlers, was to be handed over to the PA – but not control over crucial water supplies. Furthermore, only 25 per cent of the area of the West Bank was to be returned, and the Palestinian towns were to be (further) isolated from one another by the continued expansion of a system of Israeli-only highways (Guyatt, 2001, p. 34; Map 16). From an Israeli military point of view, this fragmented Palestinian autonomy was desirable, given the difficulties faced in maintaining order in densely populated Palestinian urban areas, while enabling consolidation of the Israeli control of access and movement. However, from the perspective of those dedicated to the expansion of Israel to its full 'biblical' boundaries it was a betrayal. Tensions were further heightened by a campaign of suicide bombings by groups such as Hamas opposed to the Oslo process, which increased the sense of insecurity within Israeli society. In this context in November 1995, Rabin was murdered at a peace rally by a student from a Jewish religious college (*yeshiva*) (ibid., p. 35).

The increase in suicide bomb attacks in the wake of Rabin's death dented Israeli confidence in the peace process, leading to the election as prime minister of the right-wing Likud candidate Netanyahu. Under American pressure, Netanyahu continued peace talks but accelerated the settlement programme, and it was expansion leading to the encirclement of Arab East Jerusalem that led to Palestinian withdrawal from the talks in March 1997 (ibid., p. 40). Talks were briefly revived in 1998, leading to the short-lived Wye River agreement in October. However, in December, the Israelis suspended the next phase of withdrawal from the West Bank, placing new conditions on the Palestinians which the latter deemed unacceptable, resulting in the breakdown of the agreement (Shlaim, 2000, p. 605).

Netanyahu was defeated in the next Israeli elections by the Labour candidate Ehud Barak in May 1999. Further negotiations with the Palestinians followed, notably in the Camp David summit in July 2000. The reasons for their collapse are disputed, with Barak claiming to have offered the Palestinians substantial concessions, but the Palestinians rejecting the proposal to relinquish all claims based on existing UN resolutions (Reinhart, 2002, pp. 55–6). The resulting frustration exacerbated by Sharon's visit to the Haram-al Sharif provoked the 'al-Aqsa' *intifada*, and the subsequent crisis saw the collapse of the Barak government, and its replacement by Sharon's Likud-led administration. To pressurize the PA to stop Islamist suicide attacks, Sharon's administration attacked Palestinian infrastructure and institutions and sought to undermine Palestinian leader Yasser Arafat. One particular incident has proved especially controversial, concerning IDF operations in Jenin refugee camp in April 2002. The facts in the case are difficult to establish, but a contemporary Amnesty International observer told the BBC there was evidence pointing to a massacre (ibid., pp. 151–70).

In spite of rapid population growth on both sides, caused principally by the immigration of Jews and a high birthrate amongst Arabs (especially Muslims), the proportions in 2000 remained similar within the 1949 boundaries, now standing at approximately 6 million Jews and a million Arabs (Shafir and Peled, 2002, p. 110). Amongst Jews the balance between *ashkenazim* and *mizrachim* has shifted so their numbers are now roughly equal, leading to challenges to the traditional dominance of the *ashkenazim*. The latter had predominated amongst the founders and leaders of the Zionist movement, and have tended to be better educated (see further below pp. 280–1). The population of the Occupied Territories has risen to approximately 3.5 million (Wasserstein, 2003).

Within the 1949 boundaries, the Christian population has grown rapidly from 34,000 to 150,000 (Dalrymple, 1997, p. 363), though more slowly than Jews and Muslims, a result of higher emigration and later marriages. Emigration has been enabled by better education (relative to Muslims) and well-established diaspora communities. The Christian exodus from the Occupied Territories has been even higher, reflecting wider trends across the Middle East (Dalrymple, 1997). The demographic shift within Israel has had political consequences leading to the loss of a Christian influence in traditional strongholds (e.g. Nazareth see Israeli, 2002); it seems likely that the political mobilization of religious identities will further hasten Christian emigration.

Religion and identity in the Palestine/Israel conflict

The sociologist Manuel Castells has distinguished two kinds of identity which are particularly relevant to understanding the role of religion in the Palestine–Israel conflict. Castells describes *legitimizing identities* as supporting the production and maintenance of organizations and institutions that support the dominant interests in a society (1997, p. 8). In contrast, *resistance identities* construct 'forms of collective identity against ... oppression' (p. 9). We shall now consider examples of the role of religion in the mobilization of both kinds of political identity in the Palestinian–Israeli conflict, and also how these two forms of identity can sometimes be intertwined.

Legitimizing identity and non-participation: Orthodox Judaism, civil religion, the Haredim and the 'secular' State of Israel

Unlike most other nationalist movements, which have sought to mobilize populations based within a fairly defined area, Zionism sought to galvanize groups of Jews who had been living in dispersion in quite different cultural settings for nearly two millennia. Not surprisingly, these groups had very little in common except for their religious heritage, and even this had substantially differentiated. The predominantly secular Zionist pioneers were therefore faced with the curious necessity of mobilizing religious symbols (e.g. Star of David, seven-branched candleholder or *menora*) and discourse (e.g. *aliya* 'pilgrimage' for emigration to Palestine; the whole exile and redemption theme) in support of their vision of a secular Israel.

But to legitimize this usage, they needed the sanction of religious institutions. An Orthodox rabbinate was established in mandate Palestine under Rabbi AI Kook (1865–1935), but Kook's pro-Zionism remained a minority position among Orthodox and ultra-Orthodox (*haredim*). Shortly before independence, Ben Gurion (soon to be prime minister) made a series of proposals to *Agudat Yisrael* (AY – or National Religious Party, founded 1912), the main Orthodox religious party, which tempted them into offering qualified practical support. This agreement was based on continuation of religious influence in four areas of public life that had developed in the *Yishuv*. These were: Sabbath observance (Saturday as a national day of rest); Jewish dietary laws (*kashrut*) to be enforced in government kitchens; religious courts to control marriage and divorce; and existing religious education systems would remain autonomous and state supported (Shafir and Peled, 2002, pp. 139–40). It should be noted that these traditions are supported to varying degrees by religious Jews from many traditions including conservatives and liberals, not just the Orthodox. Thus in a survey conducted in 1991, while only 36 per cent described themselves as 'observant' or 'largely observant', 89 per cent thought *kashrut* should be observed in civilian public kitchens. Furthermore, although not a direct poll on Orthodox privileges, 84 per cent said that they would object to their children marrying non-Jews, and 67 per cent favoured maintaining or increasing the influence of religion in public life (Levy, 1997).

Orthodox institutions can be seen as providing a core of continuity to a religious past for a civil religious framework that serves to legitimize the Israeli state's broader use of religious symbols and discourse as an integrating factor in Israeli society (ibid., p. 151; Liebman and Don-Yehiya, 1983). Such traditions and symbols range from ancient religious festivals such as Passover and the Day of Atonement (*Yom Kippur*) to places with important historical associations such as Masada and the

Western Wall, to the various forms of memorialization developed since 1948, including Holocaust and Independence days, and Jerusalem day.

Educational privilege has been particularly important in enabling the cultural reproduction of Orthodoxy – and, indeed, its mutation into extreme nationalist form, as with *Gush Emunim* (see below). There have also been attempts to extend religious influence through the other privileges – e.g. withholding *kashrut* certificates from premises on moral rather than dietary grounds (Ottolenghi, 2000, p. 46). But the main factor in increasing religious influence has been state support for religiously-based education, which extends into higher education. Indeed, this support even works against the obvious material interests of the state in the case of the exemption of *yeshiva* students[7] and Orthodox women from military service. Growing numbers (up from 2.5 per cent of those eligible for military service in 1968 to 9.2 per cent in 1999) of the former have continued their education for as long as twenty years, thus avoiding military service altogether, drawing a state subsidy, and making no contribution to the economy.

These facts raise the question of why the Israeli state continues to support *haredi yeshiva* students (ultra-orthodox Jews), many of whom refuse to recognize it. The conventional explanation is that the financial cost is relatively small compared to the benefit of the political support of the Orthodox political parties. These often hold the balance of power in Israel's proportional representation system, and in other policy areas have been relatively acquiescent (Cohen, 1997). However, the votes attracted, cost of subsidy and range of demands (especially by the *mizrachi* party *Shas*) have all increased substantially since 1988, making the 'low cost' explanation less plausible (Shahak and Mezvinsky, 1999, p. 23). Rather, some commentators argue that it is the continuing dependence of the Israeli state on religious symbols as markers of ethnic and national identity that best explains its continued material support for the *haredim*; the state is paying 'the wages of legitimation' (Shafir and Peled, 2002, p. 147). However, the state's continued reliance on 'religious capital' for Zionist mobilization has had complex and unforeseen consequences, as we shall examine in the case of *Gush Emunim*.

Thus the role of the Orthodox rabbinate and of traditional Judaism mobilized in a civil religious symbolic language, has broadly been one of legitimization of the Israeli state, in spite of the fact that the most Orthodox elements or *haredim* continue to refuse to recognize the secular state. The case of *Gush Emunim* contrasts with this, in that strong support has been given for the state's military role in expanding Israeli occupation of the West Bank, while (predominantly non-violent) resistance has been made where the state has tried to pull back from expansion. Furthermore, the *Gush* justifies its expansionist aims on

[7] Those attending a training college for Jewish religious students.

religious grounds, thus challenging the secular foundations of Israel's legitimacy.

Militant Judaism: Gush Emunim ('Block of the Faithful') as legitimizing and resistance identity

Gush Emunim was founded as a movement within the National Religious Party (NRP) in 1974. It has been the most vociferous group to argue for the extension of the boundaries of the modern Israeli state to the maximum depicted in the Hebrew Bible, and hence for Jewish colonization or 'resettlement' of the Occupied Territories. They trace their distinctive views to AI Kook, who first popularized the view that the secular founders of the *Yishuv* were God's unwitting agents in the restoration of Israel, thus harmonizing Orthodoxy with Zionism's secular roots. But AI Kook's views have been considerably developed by his son, Tzvi Yeheuda (1891–1982), who authorized the founding of *Gush*.

The religious roots of the group are in the mystical Judaism of the *kabbalah*, a medieval offshoot of Rabbinic Judaism. Rabbi AI Kook was particularly influenced by the Lurianic Kabbalah, founded in the late sixteenth century, which was also influential on other contemporary *hassidic* (mystical-devotional) groups, such as the Lubovitch sect. In the west – and especially in English language sources – *kabbalah* has predominantly been seen as a tolerant, even universalistic form of Judaism. However, commentators with access to Hebrew texts have argued that these contain xenophobic tendencies – perhaps an understandable reaction to ghettoization of medieval *ashkenazi* Judaism – which strongly influence the worldview of *Gush* followers. For example, Shahak and Mezvinsky (1999) quote from a text written by Rabbi Schneerson of the Lubovitch sect, published in Israel in Hebrew in 1965:

> [T]he body of a Jewish person is of a totally different quality from the body of [members] of all nations of the world ... the bodies [of Jews and non-Jews] only seem to be similar in material substance ... The difference of inner quality, however, is so great that the bodies should be considered as of completely different species.

> (pp. 59–60)

In *Gush* understanding, this difference should extend into the legal sphere. Thus Rabbi Ariel, the *Gush* leader in the 1980s, stated that 'A Jew who killed a non-Jew is exempt from human judgement and has not violated the [religious] prohibition of murder' (ibid., p. 71). In contrast, *Gush* Emunim Rabbi Aviner has argued that the *halacha* (Jewish law), requires the death penalty for Arabs who throw stones at Jews, because of the possible threat to Jewish life (ibid. p. 77). *Gush* settlers have shown themselves prepared to act on these views in their behaviour towards Palestinians in the West Bank.

Although these opinions can claim *halachic* legitimacy, their literal interpretation and application is accepted by only a small minority of Israeli Jews. However, while mainstream politicians have criticized such views, the Israeli state financially supports *Gush* activities, and has been influenced by and made use of *Gush* in its policy and practice in the Occupied Territories. The state supports *Gush* by funding the NRP's educational and military institutions, which range from kindergartens to a national high-school network, and include the national religious university, Bar Ilan, and exclusive military units in the Israeli army (Shafir and Peled, 2002, pp. 165–6). Furthermore, the state subsidizes *Gush* settlements in the Occupied Territories, both in land and construction costs, and through the expense of military support. In return, while *Gush* claim the mantle of the early pioneers, some have argued that they do not share the pioneers' agricultural enterprise or manual labour ethic (ibid., p.169). It is argued that they are more likely to study than work the land, but to be fair, agriculture is the only practical means of support in the more remote settlements where *Gush* predominates. As with the state's support for the *haredim*, these facts lead one to question why the state supports *Gush* settlements.

The answer seems to be that the state has used *Gush* to settle land that other less ideological settlers would be reluctant to occupy because of its remoteness from Jewish settlements, proximity to centres of Palestinian population, or lack of amenities or agricultural potential, but whose occupation has some strategic advantage. However, there has been an interactive process in defining what land is of strategic importance, because the state has in part been persuaded to settle this land by *Gush* pressure. After the military successes of 1967, the Labour government was unsure what to do with the Occupied Territories. While there was some enthusiasm for settlement as many of the leaders came from the pioneering generation, the large Palestinian population made this a problematic prospect, and in practice few Israelis except for religious nationalists were interested in settling in politically hostile and often physically inhospitable areas. Up to 1977, minister Yigal Allon's plan was largely followed. This plan saw settlement primarily in terms of defence, and involved Jewish colonization of the relatively sparsely populated Jordan rift to strengthen Israel's claim to retain this area. But it avoided Jewish settlement of the more densely populated mountainous areas of the West Bank, negotiating with Jordan to exchange some of this for peace (Shafir and Peled, 2002, p. 161).

However, even during this period of Labour government, pressure from religious nationalists led to the founding of four new settlements outside the Jordan rift, with *Gush* activists playing an important role in the three founded in 1974–7. Under Likud from 1977–1981 a further twenty-one were founded in the West Bank, more than half *Gush* affiliated. The pattern established was one that has largely continued: illegal *Gush* occupation followed by capitulation by the government, in the form of providing troops and infrastructure to support the new settlements (ibid., p. 171). This government action has been politically expedient in two senses. First, Israeli public opinion has tended to be strongly supportive of retaining all settlements once established, even though *Gush's* hard line against Palestinians and Messianic fervour are not widely shared (Shahak and Mezvinsky, 1999, p. 78). Secondly, the creation of a network of settler only roads to support the settlements has enabled the Israeli state to exert control over the movement and activities of the Palestinians, without getting bogged down in policing urban areas.

Negatively, however, the subjection of Palestinians to constant restrictions and the literal fragmentation of Palestinian society are two of the major obstacles to peace negotiations. Furthermore, while most settlement is focused on Jerusalem – of 350,000 settlers in 1999, 250,000 lived in a commuter belt around the city – it is the relatively small settlements, remote from Jewish centres of population and dominated by religious nationalists, that are the main reason for the infra-structural stranglehold on the Palestinians (Shahak and Mezvinsky, 1999, p. 79).

Thus *Gush's* influence on settlement policy illustrates how a group sustained by an ideology supported by only a small minority can exert considerable wider influence. This is possible because although few in Israeli society would be willing personally to settle the sites deep into the West Bank that *Gush* have occupied, the government and public opinion have been reluctant to act against settlers. Furthermore, *Gush* is able to appeal to more broadly shared discourses – for example, concerning the pioneering ethos, religious identification, support for the military, and security. The case of *Gush* suggests that religious identification as a basis for political mobilization can contain both legitimizing and resistance elements. For *Gush* is critical of the 'corrupt, secular' aspects of Israeli citizenship discourse, and in relation to this stands as a resistance identity. Yet it also portrays itself as the true inheritor of the pioneering ethos element of that discourse, and in this sense serves to legitimize it.

Militant Islamic resistance identity: Hamas

Hamas, an abbreviation of Harakat al-Muqawama ('Islamic Resistance Movement') grew out of the Palestinian branch of the Muslim Brotherhood (MB) in response to the outbreak of the *intifada* in 1987, and continues to identify with this movement (Mishal and Sela, 2000, pp. 16–26). The MB originated in Egypt in the 1930s, and is probably the most widespread political and social Islamic association in the Middle East (Mishal and Sela, 2000, p. 16). Although its politics have varied with time and place, it has predominantly been identified with attempts to make Muslim societies more 'Islamic' from the grassroots up, and hence MB chapters have been involved in a variety of social and education activities. Hamas retains this tradition, as two contemporary Israeli scholars observe:

> Hamas runs a network of educational institutions such as kindergartens, schools, libraries, youth and sports clubs, and adult education centers. In addition, like other Muslim Brotherhood associations in neighbouring Arab countries, Hamas provides medical services and runs hospitals as well as charities for the needy. Indeed the Intifada forced Hamas to direct larger portions of its financial resources for the welfare and support of those families whose members had been killed, wounded, or arrested by Israel.
>
> (ibid., p. viii)

Hamas has reacted against the PLO's willingness to engage in negotiations with Israel, refusing territorial compromise. Thus as well as drawing on an Islamic ethos, the movement also sees itself as the heir to the PLO's original commitment to 'liberating' the whole territory of British mandatory Palestine from the Jordan to the Mediterranean, and for the full return of refugees. Hamas justifies its uncompromising position on territory by arguing that the land of Palestine is an endowment (*Waqf*) in perpetuity to the Muslim people (Article 11 of the Hamas Charter; HC 11).[8] As we saw, Palestine was conquered and occupied by Muslims for eleven of the last twelve centuries (excepting the Crusader period), and Hamas argue that this claim should not be relinquished – Salah al-din (Saladin) and other resisters of external invaders are held up as examples for emulation (HC 34–5).

Hamas seeks an Islamic state on the whole territory of Palestine, within which Jews would be a tolerated minority. Members thus sometimes stress that their argument is not with Jews as such, but with the state of Israel, and its supporters. In this respect it differs from *Gush*, which draws on sources in the Hebrew Bible concerning the original conquest of the land by the people of Israel to argue that the people of the land (*ha'am ha-eretz*) – in this case applied to the Arab population – should be driven from the land altogether (e.g. Deuteronomy 19:1). However, in its opposition to Jewish occupation of Palestine, Hamas mobilizes anti-Jewish and not just anti-Zionist rhetoric. For example, a leaflet published in 1988 described Jews as 'brothers of the apes, assassins of the prophets, bloodsuckers, warmongers ... only Islam can break the Jews and destroy their dream' (in Mishal and Sela, 2000, p. 52). Furthermore, since Hamas extends its opposition to the Israeli state to include Israeli citizens, including civilians – hence the legitimization of suicide (or 'self-chosen martyrdom') attacks – this theoretical toleration of Jews and Judaism seem to have little practical impact.

---

[8] From Mishal and Sela, 2000, pp. 175–99.

While other MB organizations have embraced democracy where this has been seen as compatible with advancing the Islamic influence on society, elections in the Occupied Territories have posed problems for Hamas, as participation might be seen as lending credibility to a process based on an acceptance of territorial compromise. However, in 1996 Hamas decided to participate in elections by forming its own separate but related political party (Mishal and Sela, 2000, p. 140).

Hamas' Islamic ethos includes the concepts of *jihād* ('sacred struggle') and *shahid* ('martyr'), which are used to justify 'suicide' bomb attacks against Israeli targets, for which the movement is best known in the west. We shall examine in more detail Hamas' understanding of suicide bombing in Chapter 10. But in the present context of examining the role of religion in mobilizing legitimizing and resistance identities, it is the parallels with *Gush* that are most salient. Both movements have their roots in grassroots education and other community activities, with welfare playing a more prominent role for Hamas, partly because the welfare needs of Palestinians are more pressing than those of the Ashkenazi Jews who form the majority of *Gush* supporters. Both have an ambivalent stance in relation to their respective secular authorities (the Israeli state for *Gush* and the PA for Hamas). Thus both support these authorities in so far as they further their respective aims of obtaining a religious Jewish/Islamic state, but undermine their authority by legitimizing their uncompromising visions in religious terms.

Shas

Amongst Jewish religio-political groups, *Shas* represents a more typical case of resistance identity than *Gush*, in the sense that it draws its support from an underprivileged group in Israeli society – *mizrachi* Jews. In contrast, *Gush* draws almost exclusively – and exclusively at the rabbinic level – from the dominant *ashkenazi* group. There is considerable evidence that, although privileged relative to Israeli Arabs and Palestinians, *mizrachi* groups occupy a subordinate position in Israeli society. This is so both economically – from 1977 to 1996 the gap between the (mostly *ashkenazi*) rich and (mostly *mizrachi*) poor grew wider – and discursively. Thus in spite of their similar numbers *mizrachi* groups are referred to in Israeli public discourse as '*edot*', (roughly, 'ethnic groups'), a term never used to refer to *ashkenazim* (Shafir and Peled, 2002, p. 90). *mizrachim* are also concentrated in poorer new towns, and have markedly lower educational achievement – 36.6 per cent of *ashkenazim* graduated from college in 1995, compared to 10.2 per cent of *mizrachim*.

In 1984, *Shas* was formed as a political party and social movement amongst Orthodox *mizrachim*, partly in response to these conditions, and especially the lack of state welfare provision in the new towns. Thus, as well as functioning as a political party, winning four seats in the

Knesset (parliament) in the 1984 elections, *Shas* has also established welfare institutions, building on the involvement of *mizrachi haredim* in the state-supported education sector. In this pattern of political support from grassroots mobilization through education extending into welfare sectors in the face of declining state services, *Shas* resembles Hamas, although it has not used or supported non-state forms of violence. It is, perhaps, similar to what Hamas might have been had it not been for the desperate political situation of the Palestinian people. Indeed, in local politics in Israel, *Shas* and Hamas have sometimes joined forces against a common opponent. For example, in Nazareth *Shas* co-operated with Islamist parties to break the dominance of Christian politicians in local government (Israeli, 2002). This kind of co-operation with non-Jews would have been unthinkable for *Gush*, given its ideological position.

Conclusion

The Ottoman definition of minorities by religious affiliation arguably prepared the ground for political mobilization of religious identity in the twentieth century, first in the Zionist movement, which used religious symbols to cement Israeli national identity. However, this political mobilization was limited until the last quarter of the twentieth century by the secular character of dominant aspects of both Jewish (secular left-wing Zionist) and Arab (nationalist and communist) political movements. Thus, while religious institutions remained important in defining aspects of public identity and in some segments of social life, religion's role in political society remained limited; for example, only a small proportion of votes went to political parties defined along religious lines. Thus, from 1948 until the mid-1980s, relations between religions in Israel can be described as coexistence within a framework in which dominant Israeli and Palestinian political forces shared secular though competing nationalist ideologies.

In the 1970s this began to change with the rise of *Gush Emunim* in Israel, and of Islamic political revival across the Middle East. In Israel these changes were first reflected at the ballot box in 1984 and 1988, while in the Occupied Territories the outbreak of the *intifada* in 1987 marked the birth of Hamas, whose success in turn stimulated that of Islamist parties in local elections within Israel. Thus, since the late 1980s conflict between Palestinians and Israelis has escalated, and one of the major factors in this has been the rise of radical groups inspired by religious ideologies, who now represent the most intransigent elements on each side. The phenomenon of suicide bombing, a tactic used only by groups claiming Islamic inspiration in the Palestinian context – has proved particularly divisive, and will be discussed further in the next chapter in the broader context of the growth of Islamic militancy. In the process of polarization, the Christian Arab minority that once played a central role in Palestinian nationalist politics has become increasingly marginalized.

How can we make sense of the recent mobilization of religion in Israel/Palestine in terms of broader theories of religion's relation to social and political change? The development seems to stand contrary to secularization theory, which posits a broad shift towards the diminishing influence of religion in modern social and political systems (Wilson, 1992). However, some proponents of this theory do allow that where religion becomes identified with communal identity this process can be temporarily reversed, and Israel/Palestine fits this pattern (Bruce, 1996). Arguably though, seeing political mobilization of religious identity as a temporary blip in a broader shift towards secularization does not take sufficient account of the cultural character of modern social systems, and of religion's capacity to become embedded within them. For Israeli/Palestinian examples suggest that by becoming institutionalized in modern social systems (e.g. Orthodoxy in state institutions regulating marriage and nationality; Islamism in Hamas' welfare networks), religions may change the character of these systems, as well as being transformed themselves, and this dialectical process shows no evidence of grinding towards a secular end. Indeed, for Israel/Palestine we can share the conclusion of a recent study of religious adaptation and persistence in Egypt:

> [W]e cannot dismiss religious concerns as benighted survivals of earlier social stages, or merely 'inflammations' symptomatic of social pathology and political strife. Instead, we must see them as perennial questions which persist in an active manner, adapting and reproducing themselves within and between generations through increasingly complex interactions with institutions and communications media whose own advent was supposed to reduce rather than increase the influence of religious ideas in society.
>
> (Starrett, 1998, p. 91)

However, in arriving at a balanced conclusion about the importance of religious factors in shaping the conditions of conflict and coexistence, we should also consider some important non-religious factors. These include demography, economy, the environment, and culture. Demographically, the higher birthrate of Muslim Palestinians and the limited prospect of further mass Jewish immigration into Israel point towards an early resolution of the conflict being in Israeli interests. Economically, the longer Israeli occupation of the Occupied Territories continues, the more integrated the Palestinian and Israeli economies have become, especially in terms of Israeli reliance on Palestinian labour. For the Palestinians, dependence on Israel for movement and employment makes development without Israeli co-operation extremely difficult. Environmental problems are not easily resolved within political boundaries. Water supply is a good example: as a joint committee of hydrologists concluded in 1999: 'Where water is concerned, Israelis and Palestinians can be viewed as Siamese twins – two entities sharing a vital resource' (in Wasserstein, 2003, p. 97). All these factors point towards more co-operative and less conflictual forms of coexistence in the long run.

Such influences lead to the question of whether religion has or could play any co-operative role in Palestine/Israel. First, at the broad level of culture, which includes religion, while nationalist interests have tended to highlight cultural differences between Arab and Jewish populations, some have argued that both Jews and Arabs draw on a common Levantine heritage (Alcalay, 1993), and the European Union has sponsored initiatives designed to encourage co-operation by constructing a vision of a broad, shared Mediterranean culture (Wilkes, 2000).

Secondly, religion has already played a positive, if so far limited, role in promoting reconciliation. Thus, while most peace movements and collaborative ventures between Jews and Arabs have been of a secular character, there is also a tradition of inter-faith dialogue that runs back to the British Mandate period (Caplan, 1983). While this was initially restricted to academic circles, contemporary organizations such as the Israel Interfaith Association and Interfaith Encounter Association (IEA) have had a much wider reach; for example, the IEA have brought together settlers from the NRP with Hamas supporters (Wilkes, 2000, p. 130). It should be noted, however, that not all such dialogue converges towards the values of liberal democracy; Israeli (2002) has shown how a combination of Islamist and *Shas* members of Nazareth town council combined to thwart Christian plans for celebration of the millennium.

What, then, should we conclude about the role of religion in coexistence and conflict and Israel/Palestine? Our enquiries have shown that while the sacredness of the land (and especially of Jerusalem) to the three Abrahamic faiths has historically been a source of some antagonism – especially during the crusader century – coexistence under imperial systems that have sought to contain religious difference had been the norm until the early twentieth century, when the British protectorate sought to continue the imperial role in increasing tension with emerging Jewish and Arab nationalisms. Religious memory played an important but circumscribed role within Zionist discourse, while Palestinian nationalism sought to minimize religious differences in order to mobilize both Muslim and Christian populations. However, the decades since 1967 have seen increasing mobilization of both Islamic and Jewish political identities, such that the most intransigent elements of each side now claim religious inspiration. Against this politicization of religious identity, efforts have been made to promote inter-faith and inter-cultural activity and solidarity, but at the time of writing such efforts seem to be swimming against the tide of increasing political polarization, in spite of demographic, economic and ecological factors that would seem to favour more co-operative forms of coexistence.

References

Ahmed, A. (1993) *Living Islam: from Samarkand to Stornoway*, London, BBC.

*Alcalay, A. (1993) *After Jews and Arabs*, Minneapolis, Minnesota University Press.

Bruce, S. (1996) *Religion in the Modern World*, Oxford, Oxford University Press.

Caplan, N. (1983) *Futile Diplomacy*, London, Frank Cass.

Castells, M. (1997) *The Information Age: Economy, Society, Culture. Vol. 2: The Power of Identity*, Oxford, Blackwell.

Cohen, S. (1997) *The Sword or the Scroll? Dilemmas of Military Service in Israel*, Amsterdam, Harwood Academic Publishers.

*Cohn-Sherbok, D. and El-Alami D (2001) *The Palestinian–Israeli Conflict*, Oxford, One World.

*Dalrymple, W. (1997) *From the Holy Mountain*, London, HarperCollins.

Elias, J. (1999) *Islam*, New York, Routledge.

Guyatt, N. (2001) *The Absence of Peace*, London, Zed.

*Hiro, D. (1996) *Sharing the Promised Land*, London, Coronet.

Karsh, E. (2000) *Fabricating Israeli History*, London, Frank Cass.

Israeli, R. (2002) *Green Crescent Over Nazareth: The Displacement of Christians by Muslims in the Holy Land*, London, Frank Cass.

Levy, Y. (1997) 'Beliefs, observances and social interaction amongst Israeli Jews' in C. Liebman and E. Katz (eds) *The Jewishness of Israelis*, Albany, SUNY Press, pp. 1–37.

Lewis, P. (1994) *Islamic Britain*, London, I. B. Tauris.

Liebman, C. and Don-Yehiya, E. (1983) *Civil Religion in Israel: Traditional Judaism and Political Culture in the Jewish State*, Berkeley, California, University of California Press.

Milton-Edwards, B. and Hinchcliffe, P. (2001) *Conflicts in the Middle East since 1945*, London, Routledge.

Mishal, S. and Sela, A. (2000) *The Palestinian Hamas*, New York, Columbia University Press.

Ottolenghi, E. (2000) 'Religion and Democracy in Israel' in Marquand, D. and Nettler, R. (eds) *Religion and Democracy*, Oxford, Blackwell, pp. 39–49.

Peretz, R. (1996) *The Arab–Israel Dispute*, New York, Facts on File.

Reinhart, T. (2002) *Israel/Palestine: How to End the War of 1948*, New York, Seven Stories.

Rippin, A. (1990) *Muslims: Their Religious Beliefs and Practices. Volume 1: The Formative Period*, London, Routledge.

*Shafir, G. and Peled, Y. (2002) *Being Israeli*, Cambridge, Cambridge University Press.

Shahak, I. and Mezvinsky N. (1999) *Jewish Fundamentalism in Israel*, London, Pluto.

Shlaim, A. (2000) *The Iron Wall: Israel and the Arab World*, London, Penguin.

Silberstein, S. (1999) *The Postzionism Debate*, London, Routledge.

Starrett, G. (1998) *Putting Islam to Work: Education, Politics and Religious Transformation in Egypt*, Berkeley, Los Angeles and London, University of California Press.

Wasserstein, B. (2001) *Divided Jerusalem*, London, Profile.

*Wasserstein, B. (2003) *Israel/Palestine: Why They Fight and Can They Stop?*, London, Profile.

Wilkes, G. (2000) *Land of Promise and Conflict*, Module 809 of the Centre for Jewish–Christian Relations MA programme, Cambridge, CJCR. Quoted with permission.

Wilson, B. (1992) 'Reflections on a many sided controversy', in S. Bruce and R. Wallis (eds) *Religion and Modernization*, Oxford, Clarendon Press, pp. 195–210.

Asterisked items are particularly recommended for further reading.

10 Religion and contemporary conflict in historical perspective

David Herbert and John Wolffe

Why did Muslim suicide hijackers kill more than 3,000 people in the attacks on the Pentagon and the World Trade Center on 11 September 2001?[1] This compelling question of our own age echoes some of those from past eras explored in earlier chapters in this book. Throughout history violence has been committed by those acting from religious motivations and by those who have singled out particular religious groups as objects of their hatred. Single acts as appalling as September 11 are rare. Behind them, however, lie continuous undercurrents of lower intensity conflict and estrangement that establish the preconditions for such eruptions and divide cultures and nations from each other. Although the association between Islam and violence is particularly strong to contemporary western minds, other religious traditions have also historically been implicated in outrages. For example, some third century Roman emperors systematically persecuted Christians; medieval crusaders were prepared to inflict great suffering on themselves and others in the endeavour to control the Christian holy sites in Palestine; and, in carnage on a comparable scale to that in New York in 2001, 2,000 Protestants were massacred in Paris in August 1572. In slaughter of an even more horrendous order of magnitude, six million Jews perished in the Nazi death camps of eastern Europe during the Second World War. Historical examples of acts of violence in which religion was used either to justify the perpetrator or identify the victim can easily be multiplied: in this respect there was nothing new about 11 September 2001.

However, it must be emphasized that the presence of religion as a factor in situations of conflict should not be translated into a simplistic charge that religion 'causes' violence. The September 11 attacks were also driven by political concerns, above all resentment at the overwhelming geopolitical influence of the United States. A further factor was the alienated and rootless social situation of the hijackers themselves, resorting to terrorism because there seemed no other means of advancing their ideological and political aims. Parallel points can be made about other historic eruptions of violence: for example, the attack on Protestants that escalated into the St Bartholomew's Day Massacre of

---

[1] Initial estimates were approximately 5–6,000, but this steadily dropped so that by 9 January 2002, The *New York Times* reported that 2,893 were killed in the attack on the World Trade Center, including 147 on the two airplanes, and 343 City of New York firefighters. A further 184 were killed in the attack on the Pentagon, and 40 on the flight that crashed in Pennsylvania, making a total of 3,117 (Gehman, 2002, pp. 9–10).

1572 was instigated by a Roman Catholic faction associated with the Guise family, which had political as well as religious motives. The Jewish Holocaust was arguably more a product of the pathological dynamics of the Nazi regime, and of its extreme racist ideology, than of specifically religious hatred. The history of antisemitism in Catholic and Lutheran traditions was part of the background that helped to make Nazi antisemitism seem acceptable and lowered resistance to it.

Earlier chapters in this book have assisted understanding of a range of situations in which religion has been connected with violence and conflict in various historical circumstances. In this final chapter a broader perspective is developed, linking the recent to the much more remote past. In doing so a helpful starting point is the idea that every event can be looked at on three levels, first as a matter of specific decision, action or chance occurrence; secondly, in connection with the operation of general laws or wider historical trends; thirdly, as an outworking of the providence of God (Butterfield, 1979, pp. 10–11). Thus September 11 can be seen, first, as a consequence of a particular sequence of actions by a specific group of disaffected Muslim radicals; second, as a climactic manifestation of deep-seated political and religious tensions between the Islamic world and the United States; and third, either in Osama bin Laden's words, as 'America struck by God Almighty' (quoted in Halliday, 2002, p. 233) or in George W. Bush's as part of a 'monumental struggle of good and evil' in which he prayed that God would 'watch over the United States of America' (*The Times*, 13 September, 2001, p. 12; 21 September, 2001, p. 5).[2] Although historians, as such, are not competent to make judgements on the third level and would usually exercise extreme caution in making judgements at the second level, the protagonists in events themselves sometimes readily make judgements even at the third level, thus greatly raising the ideological and moral stakes.

The perceived prominence of Islam in many contemporary conflicts makes it the obvious point of departure. In the first main section of this chapter it is therefore explored as a case study, with a view both to advancing specific understanding of recent history and to suggesting insights into the wider historical problem of the perceived role of religion in violence. In approaching the topic in this way we are making no prior assumption that Islam has been in any straightforward way responsible for September 11 or other violence, but rather we are seeking to explore and test the popular perceptions that have fuelled

[2] Bush, however, was careful to avoid presenting this 'struggle' in terms of a straightforward clash with Islam: in his speech to Congress on 20 September 2001, he described the terrorists as 'traitors to their own faith' (*The Times*, 21 September, 2001, p. 5).

anti-Muslimism[3] in the west. A central theme here is the tension between a view of Islam as speaking with just one voice (univocal), and the view that the tradition speaks with a multiplicity of voices in different historical circumstances. If one takes a univocal view of Islam, then September 11 looks like an inevitable consequence of its alleged entrenched enmity towards the United States; if one regards it as multi-vocal then it looks much more like the contingent and specific actions of one particular group claiming Islamic legitimacy for their actions. Hence it is important briefly to consider the historical context and teachings of some influential Islamic reform and revival movements of the nineteenth and twentieth centuries, and to assess their contemporary legacy. The remainder of the chapter then explores the wider context, in so doing building on some themes that have emerged in the rest of the book. In particular it is instructive to consider the common characteristics of 'hate' movements such as anti-Catholicism, antisemitism, and anti-Muslimism, and to reflect on other later twentieth-century religious trends, such as the decline of Christendom in the west, and the resurgence of religion elsewhere. Has religious conflict become more widespread, or is the reality, despite September 11, a trend towards more positive coexistence? Does peaceful coexistence require religious traditions to sacrifice aspects of their historic authenticity, or is it violent conflict that is the aberration?

The case of Islam: radicals and reformers in the modern era

From Indonesia to Iraq, from Nigeria to Afghanistan, events in the last few decades have led to an association between Islam and contemporary conflict in the eyes of many observers. Above all, the tactic of suicide attack against civilian targets strikes many across the world as particularly horrific and alien. This tactic was first used in recent times by Hizbullah in the Lebanon in 1982/3, then by Islamic Jihad and the al-Aqsa brigade in Israel/Palestine and, most devastatingly, by al Qaeda against the Pentagon and World Trade Center on 11 September 2001.

It should be noted at the outset that Islamic groups do not have a monopoly on the modern use of suicide bombing or other terror tactics. For example, Tamil separatists used suicide attacks during the civil war in Sri Lanka from the mid-1980s, and atheist Russian anarchists in the late nineteenth century have been widely credited with the invention of modern terrorism (Hoffman, 1998; Townshend, 2002). But the

---

[3] An alternative term, widely used in the literature (for example, Conway et al., 1996) is Islamophobia. However 'anti-Muslimism' is preferred here, both for consistency with terms such as 'anti-Catholicism' and 'antisemitism', and because it leaves more open the key question of whether hostility is directed towards Muslims as people or Islam as a religion (see Halliday, 2002, pp. 128–30).

appearance of Islamic groups willing to use violence against civilian targets does represent part of a disturbing growth since 1980 both in the number of active international terrorist networks, and in the proportion of such groups which can be categorized as religiously motivated. As Bruce Hoffman, head of the Rand corporation's terrorism research unit, writes:

> [N]one of the eleven identifiable international terrorist groups active in 1968 could be classified as religious: that is, having aims or motivations reflecting a predominantly religious character or influence ... only two of the sixty-four groups active in 1980 could be categorised as predominantly religious ... [but] in 1995 nearly half of the fifty-six known ... could be classified as religious in character and motivation.

> (1998, pp. 90–1)

According to Hoffman, this development 'has involved elements of all the world's major faiths, and in some instances, small sects and cults as well' (ibid., p. 86). In this context, our focus on Islam in this section is not intended to single out Islam as especially prone to violence. Rather, it is to place the emergence of contemporary Islamic movements which espouse forms of violent struggle in the historical context of broader Islamic traditions, responses to modernization and western influences. In terms of Butterfield's scheme of levels of explanation, it will be argued that hypotheses offered at level two are only as good as the evidence offered to support them at level one. Thus, broad generalizations about 'Muslim civilization' or statements such as 'religion causes conflict' need to be rejected and replaced with more specific hypotheses that can be tested in particular cases.

The concept of *jihād* ('struggle'),[4] central to Islamic legitimization of the use of force, has been subject to a range of interpretations, from an insistence that *jihād* is properly only a defensive war launched with the aim of establishing justice, equity and protecting basic human rights' (Zawati, 2002, p. 111) to the view that it is properly understood as 'armed struggle for the defence *or advancement* of Muslim power ... until all the world either adopts the Muslim faith or submits to Muslim rule' (Lewis, 2003, pp. 24–5, emphasis added). Given such divergence of interpretation, one sceptical commentator argues that:

> [N]o ... essential Islam exists: as one Iranian thinker put it, Islam is a sea in which it is possible to catch any fish one wants ... [T]he answer as to why this or that interpretation [is] put on Islam

---

[4] Discussion here is restricted to the external meanings of *jihād* that sanction the use of physical force. *Jihād* also means internal struggle to overcome temptation and develop spiritual life, and external struggles for social justice that do not involve physical conflict. See also pp. 54–5 above.

resides ... not in the religion and its texts but in the contemporary needs of those articulating an Islamic politics.

(Halliday, 2000, p. 134)

Halliday's scepticism is expressed in an international context in which powerful voices both in the west and the Muslim majority world advocate 'essentialist' concepts of Islam, meaning the idea that the tradition has one single correct meaning or position on any matter, and that all other interpretations are deviant. Essentializing tendencies in the west include media presentations of Islam as a homogeneous entity, the 'Other' to the west, especially in the post-Cold War period (Said, 1997 [1981]). The increasing dominance of television as a global communication medium, and its tendency to favour clear, simple presentation of information over complex argument, leads to a propensity to reinforce existing stereotypes. There have been attempts to counter this tendency by presenting a diverse picture of Islam, for example in parts of the British media since *The Satanic Verses* controversy (1988–90). But the fact that conflict is often more 'newsworthy' than co-operation means that images of conflict tend to outnumber and outweigh more harmonious images and stories (Liebes, 1997). Beyond the mass media, international relations and popular philosophy literatures also tend to over-simplify the diversity of Islamic groups (e.g. Huntington, 1996; Berman, 2002).

In Muslim majority societies, essentialist voices include authoritarian governments keen to assert official versions of Islam, and Islamists – a broad term denoting those who argue that a return to Islam is central to Muslim revival in all areas of life – keen to challenge their authority. States have tended to use their control of the mass media to reinforce their message, with Islamist groups countering through 'micro media', such as videos and audio-tapes. Recently, rapidly expanding satellite networks such as al-Jazeera, founded in 1996, have increased access to television for Islamist voices – witness the broadcast of Osama bin Laden's videos during the conflict in Afghanistan in 2001/2 – and hence Arab audiences' access to Arabic and other language media sources from across the region and internationally (Steger, 2003, p. 7). However, in spite of this diversification, Islamist and state sources predominate, and both tend to convey stereotypical images of the west.

However, accepting that there are strong forces favouring an over-unified presentation of Islam is not the same as embracing Halliday's apparent position that Islam is purely at the mercy of its interpreters, and exerts no shaping force at all on the modern politics pursued in its name. Rather, acknowledging that there are many Muslim voices and histories, and that the presentation of Islam in the west is prone to bias and distortion, we shall seek to discover how and why it is that Islam has been mobilized in so many contemporary conflicts. This will involve brief consideration of the sacred sources on which Muslims draw, as well as historical perspectives on the troubled experiences of modernization, colonialism and de-colonization in Muslim societies.

Associations of Islam with conflict are linked to broader perceptions of Islam as an authoritarian religion characterized by harsh punishments and the oppression of women. Space does not permit detailed treatment of these issues. However, the reality informing these perceptions is strongly influenced by political and civic cultures in Muslim majority societies, and these also impact strongly on conflict within or stemming from these societies. Broadly speaking, democratization may be seen as a process in which tensions within societies come to be contained within institutions and practices that allow for the expression of different views and interests, and which facilitate the working out of disagreements through non-violent means. It is therefore important to situate our account of Islam and conflict within a broader narrative that also represents and makes sense of the co-development of Islamically inspired movements that are increasingly embracing democracy, both in theory and in practice.

Conflict and political authority in Islam's sacred sources

> When you meet the unbelievers, smite at their necks; at length when you have thoroughly subdued them, bind a bond firmly [on them], thereafter is a time either for generosity or for ransom until the war lays down its burden.
>
> (Qur'ān, Surah 47:4; translation in Sherif, 1995, p. 167)

It is ironic that in the contemporary world Islam is so often associated with conflict, because one of the main thrusts of the Qur'ān is a hatred of the *fitna* (civil war or strife) endemic amongst the nomadic tribes of the Arabian peninsula into which Muhammad was born. Against this anarchy, Islam asserts strict limits on what is permissible in warfare. Overall, the solution to *fitna* which the Qur'ān proposes is the unification of warring factions in submission to Allah. So effective in that time and place, this solution is perhaps also one of the reasons for Muslim involvement in conflict in the modern period. For, from the time of the *hijra* (622), when Muhammad's persecuted followers fled Mecca and negotiated themselves into a position of political power in Medina, the sacred sources of Islam presuppose a situation in which Islam is politically dominant, or in which it will eventually become so. The Islamic empire's expansion until 750, as far as the Indus valley to the east, and to the western tip of northern Africa and the Iberian peninsula, gave little reason to revise this perspective.

Thus by the time the Islamic expansion was halted, the connection between divine and political unity (*tawhid*), and the assumption of Muslim political authority, was well embedded in Islamic tradition. Hence in the medieval Islamic view the world was perceived as divided into *dar al-Islam* ('house of Islam') and *dar al-harb* ('house of war'), between which conflict is ameliorated only by temporary truce (*dar al-sulh*). Scholars seeking to challenge this classic division of the world need to argue that it 'was dictated by particular events, and did not necessitate a permanent state of hostility between these territories' (Zawati, 2002, p. 5). Within the politically controlled territories, peoples of recognized religious groups were allowed limited autonomy over their affairs in exchange for payment of a poll tax. Jews and Christians were initially included in this category, which was later extended by the Sannasids to Zoroastrians in Persia, and by the Mughals to Hindus in India. This autonomous status generally compares favourably with that of minorities in Christendom, but nonetheless was a subordinate role.

So until the modern era Islamic political history did not involve power sharing between groups of different religious convictions on an equal footing. This in itself is nothing unusual in the history of world religions, since pre-modern political formations tended to resolve religious differences through social stratification, whether the subordination of Jews in medieval Christian feudalism or of lower castes in the Indian caste system. It was only through the division of western Christendom brought about by the Reformation (sixteenth century) and the subsequent strife of the wars of religion that Europe developed a different way to contain religious difference – through the gradual process of religious belief and practice coming to be seen as a private rather than a public matter. This process has not occurred widely in the Muslim world. For example, a survey conducted in 1996–7 in the most populous Muslim countries found that large majorities agreed with the proposition that a 'person who says there is no Allah is likely to hold dangerous political views' (89 per cent in Egypt, 84 per cent in Indonesia, 74 per cent in Pakistan; Hassan, 2002, p. 63). Such views raise questions about the role of minorities and the development of democracy in the Muslim majority world.

Thus it is fair to say that Islam's sacred sources contain an assumption of Islamic political authority, legitimize defensive war, and for the most part have been understood as legitimizing expansive war to extend Islamic political authority.

But what of the question of so-called 'suicide bombers'? *Hadith* (sayings ascribed to the Prophet) strictly forbid suicide: for example, 'whoever kills himself in any way will be tormented in that way in Hell'.[5] However, such attackers are unlikely to construe their acts as suicide, but rather see themselves as *shahids*, 'martyrs', dying in the cause of Islam, for whom rewards are indeed offered in the afterlife (e.g. Qur'ān, Surah 3:194). The key issue here then is the motivation for an act that is likely to lead to self-destruction. If the motivation is self-destruction itself, Islam clearly

[5] Cited in Lewis, 2003, p. 119.

forbids it. But if the end is understood to be a righteous cause, Islam not only permits but praises such actions. Two questions then arise: is the cause just, and is the method of warfare an Islamically legitimate one? Early Islamic sources lay down strict rules for the conduct of warfare, and this includes the prohibition of attacks on non-combatants: for example, 'God has forbidden the killing of women and children'.[6] Clearly, such groups are amongst the targets of suicide attacks, leading critics to conclude: 'Can these [suicide attacks] in any sense be justified in terms of Islam? The answer must be a clear no' (Lewis, 2003, p. 119). Nonetheless, it was clear that Hamas in Palestine and Osama bin Laden and his al Qaeda colleagues disagreed.

For example, Dr Abdul Aziz Rantisi, a founding member of Hamas, argued that the proper term for the action of Hamas followers who deliberately blow themselves up in order to destroy Israeli civilian targets is *istishhadi* ('self-chosen martyr'), not suicide bomber. The former term denotes a choice made carefully and deliberately and understood as part of a religious obligation, in contrast to the latter's connotations of the impulsive act of a deranged individual. Rantisi's view that such attacks are justified as defensive actions against not just the Israeli government but the whole of Israeli society dedicated, as he sees it, to the destruction of Islamic nationalism. They occur not randomly, but in response to specific acts by the Israeli government, such as the assassination of leading Hamas members, killings of Palestinian civilians, and attacks by Jewish civilians on Islamic religious targets, such as the Hebron massacre in 1994 (Juergensmeyer, 2002, pp. 72–5). In the latter incident, Dr Baruch Goldstein opened fire on worshippers gathered in a Muslim holy site, the Cave of the Patriarchs in Hebron, killing 29 and injuring a further 150, before being overwhelmed and beaten to death (Hoffman, 1998, pp. 100–2).

Rantisi extends the traditional Islamic justification of violence in self-defence from the immediate threat of violence to 'defense of one's dignity and pride as well as one's physical well being' (Juergensmeyer, 2002, p. 80). In doing so he puts himself in a tradition of radical modern Islamic thought stretching back half a century to the early post-colonial period. Thus the desperate measures of the self-chosen martyrs/suicide bombers and the radical hermeneutics of Hamas spokesmen really need to be understood against a broader canvas. It is to this broader canvas of Muslim revival movements and responses to modernity and colonialism that we now turn.

Eighteenth-century revival: Wahhabism

Wahhabism is usually considered an example of a pre-modern Islamic revival movement, because its eighteenth-century origins predate

---

[6] *Hadith* cited in Lewis, 2003, p. 26.

significant European influence in the Arabian peninsula. It should be noted that this connection of modernity with Europe is posited as a matter of contingent historical origins rather than essential connection. The features of modernization, namely scientific development, industrialization and trade, stimulated by the development of capitalism, urbanization and the rapid development of communications and transport networks, may be combined with a range of cultures, and hence there are many possible modernities. This is important because one of the keys to understanding contemporary Islamic revival movements, some of which are associated with the conflicts that are the subject of this chapter, is to recognize that they are not medieval throwbacks, or even anti-modern in any straightforward sense. Most of them embrace much of modern science and technology, and they emerge from societies deeply affected by processes of modernization. They are also influenced by the same ideas with which the west responded to the experience of modernity, although the extent and nature of this influence varies and is contested. Even Wahhabism, in its contemporary Saudi form, has come to a kind of accommodation with modernity, albeit a rather peculiar one, given the ability oil money has given the ruling House of Saud to resist pressures for representation that usually follow from the growing state's requirement to impose taxation.

The origins of Wahhabism lie in ibn Abd al-Wahhab's (1703–1792) perception of the political weakness and moral corruption of the Ottoman Empire, which nominally ruled much of the Middle East in this period. This corruption he connected with religious laxity in the form of the growth of Sufi practices such as the veneration of saints and pilgrimage to their tombs. The solution he proposed was a return to the strict monotheism he saw in the Qur'ān. A key feature of his teaching was his designation of Muslims who did not conform to this ideal as unbelievers (*kuffar*), against whom *jihād* was therefore justified (al-Azmeh, 1993, p. 105). This teaching conflicted with the Sunni consensus, which since the Kharijite[7] controversy (seventh century) has been to accept that anyone who makes the confession of faith (*shahada*) is a Muslim. Although the rigour with which al-Wahhab's teaching has been carried through has varied, the designation of other Muslims as non-believers is an innovation adopted by later Islamists to justify their rejection of and rebellion against Muslim governments. To impose his vision he joined forces with a local tribal chief, Muhammad ibn Saud (d. 1765), in the Najd area of the Arabian peninsula (Esposito, 1994, p. 117). Together they attacked Sufi shrines and tombs, including the most sacred Shi'ite site, the tomb of Husayn at Karbala. By the turn of the nineteenth century the movement they created had become so powerful that in 1804–6 they occupied the holy cities of Mecca and Medina. This finally

---

[7] The Kharijites were a seventh-century group that insisted on doctrinal purity as a criterion for leadership of the Muslim community, a position which led to civil strife, and was rejected by the Sunni majority (Esposito, 1994, pp. 43–5).

roused the wrath of the Ottomans, who by 1818 had reasserted control over Arabia and executed the Saudi emir (Lewis, 2003, p. 94).

Wahhabism survived, however, and was again linked with the House of Saud when Sheikh 'Abd al-'Aziz (1880–1953) skilfully manoeuvred between the Ottomans and the British in the dying days of the Ottoman Empire (1915–21), finally consolidating his hold on the territory now known as Saudi Arabia in 1927. An agreement with Standard Oil of California in 1933 was to ensure an economic basis for this political consolidation (ibid., p. 97). Especially since the early 1970s when Saudi production of oil greatly increased and the formation of OPEC tilted the trade balance in favour of producers, the Saudis have been able to finance the building and running of mosques and the teaching of their version of Islam across the Muslim world, and amongst diaspora communities in the west. The credibility of their teaching has been enhanced by their role as custodians of the holy places. As such, Wahhabism arguably exercises a disproportionate influence in the Sunni world. Thus Lewis comments:

> Even in Western countries in Europe and America where the public educational systems are good, Wahhabi indoctrination may be the only form of Islamic education available to new converts and to Muslim parents who wish to give their children some grounding in their own inherited religious and cultural tradition ... In some Muslim countries ... the Wahhabi-sponsored schools and colleges represent for many young people the only education available ... The custodianship of the holy places and the revenues of oil have given worldwide impact to what would otherwise have been an extremist fringe in a marginal country.

(2003, pp. 99–100)

Nineteenth-century reform: Islamic modernism

The term 'modernism' here denotes the positive though selective embrace of aspects of modernity by reforming Muslims in the late nineteenth and early twentieth centuries. Whereas Wahhabism in its historical origins was a reaction to developments essentially within Muslim societies, in the nineteenth century a number of thinkers emerged who had direct experience of encounter with Europeans, and who sought to find a constructive synthesis between Islam and modernity. Particular centres of activity were the fast modernizing major cities of India and Egypt, both under increasing European, mostly British, influence. In the Indian context leading figures include Sayyid Ahmed Khan (1817–98) and Muhammad Iqbal (1875–1938), in the Egyptian context Muhammad Abduh and Rashid Rida (1865–1935). Influential in both contexts was the tireless political activist, journalist, and orator Jamal al-din al-Afghani (1838–1897), who preached his reformist message widely across Europe, the Middle East, Persia and India. We shall present a brief account of Afghani's teachings and then summarize some other main developments of Islamic modernism.

Afghani reacted to increasing European incursion on the Muslim world by arguing that Islam needed to embrace the science and technology that had enabled European advances, and as earlier Islamic empires had done. While contemporary Muslim societies had become closed to new developments Islam is, he argued, in origin and essence 'the closest of religions to science and knowledge, and there is no incompatibility between science and knowledge and the foundation of the Islamic faith' (in Esposito, 1994, p. 128). As contemporary Muslim society had stagnated in its approach to science, so its approach to law had ossified. Hence he called for a re-opening of the 'gates of *ijtihad*' (new interpretation), which had been wrongly closed by medieval *ulama* (religious scholars). At the same time, however, he appealed to contemporary *ulama* by arguing against secularists that, once revived, the influence of Islam on everyday life ought to increase rather than become privatized, and indeed embrace a total way of life (ibid., p. 127) He also saw European success as partly related to the constraints on autocratic leaders imposed by constitutions and parliamentary government. Thus he introduced several ideas that were to be taken in different directions by Islamic modernism, nationalist anti-colonial movements, and the Islamism of the late twentieth century. These include the idea of Islam as a total way of life, the need for *ijtihad*, the compatibility of Islam and science, and the drive for forms of representative government to replace authoritarian regimes.

Some of Afghani's modernist successors pushed his reforming drive further in the direction of re-thinking *sharia*. Rashid Rida developed the classical distinction between religious obligations (*ibadat* – the five pillars plus *jihād*) and rules governing social relations (*muamalat*) by arguing that while the former are immutable, the latter are subject to change. From the early years of the twentieth century, Rida became more conservative, siding with the *ulama*, stressing the total sufficiency of Islam and the dangers of westernization. After an Islamic education and study at Cambridge and Munich, Muhammad Iqbal made a similar distinction to Rida between core and peripheral aspects of Islam, but also argued that the conservatism of the *ulama* made them unsuitable to carry out *ijtihad*. Hence he proposed changing the traditional interpretation of the *ijma* (consensus) needed to make law from that of the *ulama* to that of a modern legislative assembly (Esposito, 1994, p. 138). Not surprisingly, such ideas led to conflict with the *ulama*, although they have been taken up by some Islamists. The latter, however, have tended to be critical of the modernists' close ties to colonial powers.

Twentieth-century revival and reform: Islamic fundamentalism and the roots of contemporary Islamism

Islamic modernism never developed as a mass movement, and was eclipsed at the elite level by primarily secular nationalist movements which used religion in a more superficial symbolic way, as the struggle against colonialism intensified in the middle years of the twentieth century. In the post-colonial period, however, disillusionment with these secular nationalist ideologies of both left and right grew, as through the 1960s and 1970s many parts of the Muslim world stagnated economically and military regimes allowed little democratic development. This is especially true in the Arab world (with the exception of the suddenly oil-rich Gulf states), but also of Pakistan and Iran. In the Middle East, defeat by Israel in the 1967 war was a severe psychological blow to the credibility of these governments. It was in this context that 'Islamism' emerged, with key ideas that include the concept of an Islamic state and the 'application' of *sharia*, though what is meant by these terms varies (Herbert, 2001, pp. 195–200).

The meaning of the term fundamentalism, which will be discussed further below (pp. 311–12), is contested and especially controversial when applied to Islam (ibid., pp. 173–4, 208–9). However, it may be used to distinguish between Islamists inclined to adopt a 'fixed template' approach to the application of *sharia* and Islamic governance in modern societies (fundamentalists), and those who hold that such application requires flexibility in re-interpreting Islam's sacred sources (non-fundamentalist Islamists). The term fundamentalist cannot really be used, as in a Christian context, to distinguish between those who believe in the untainted divine provenance of the Qur'ān, and the authority and authenticity of the Sunnah (traditions about Muhammad), since these beliefs are virtually universally held amongst practising Muslims. Thus, in a survey conducted in 1996–7, 97 per cent, 92 per cent and 93 per cent in Indonesia, Pakistan and Egypt respectively agreed with the statement 'The Qur'ān and Sunnah contain all the essential religious and moral truths required by the whole human race from now until the end of time' (Hassan, 2002, p. 124). The figures for the statement 'The Qur'ān and Sunnah are completely self-sufficient to meet the needs of present and future societies' were 96 per cent, 91 per cent and 85 per cent respectively (ibid.). However, the statement 'in the ideal Muslim society there will be no need to foster change' produced quite different results: 15 per cent, 70 per cent and 59 per cent respectively agreed. The issue, then, is one of the interpretation rather than authority of these sacred sources, and especially of their political implications.

The development of contemporary Islamism has been strongly influenced by two Islamic organizations formed in the late colonial period. These are the Muslim Brotherhood, founded by Hasan al-Banna (1906–49) in

Egypt in 1928, and the Jamaat-i-Islami ('Society of Islam') founded by Mawlana Mawdudi (1903–79) in Lahore in 1941 (then in India; in Pakistan from 1948). Both movements modelled themselves on the first Islamic community of the Prophet and his followers in the pre-*hijra* phase, in the sense of seeing themselves as a religious vanguard in an irreligious society dedicated to its transformation from within. Organized into a network of branches and cells, they saw religious instruction and publications, outreach work in schools and hospitals and among youth and social welfare projects as the initial means of transformation (Esposito, 1994, p. 149). Both believed this would eventually result in the creation of an Islamic state, although Mawdudi placed more emphasis on top down change, al-Banna on bottom-up transformation:

> Our duty as Muslim Brothers is to work for the reform of ourselves, of our hearts and souls, by connecting them to God the all-high; then to organize our society so that it becomes a virtuous community which calls for the good and forbids evil doing, *then from the community will arise the good state.*

(Quoted in Shadid, 2002, p. 54)

Both movements saw the doctrine of God's unity (*tawhid*) as implying a unity of religion and society, expressed in *sharia*: 'the sharia is a complete scheme of life and an all embracing social order' (Mawdudi quoted in Esposito, 1994, p. 150). This meant that while both accepted the modernist reinterpretation of consultation (*shura*) and consensus (*ijma*), extending both from the community of scholars to the whole people, and hence embraced a sort of democracy, the decision-making powers of any representative body would be circumscribed by *sharia*. This has become a hugely influential position in the Muslim world. For example, the Cairo Declaration of Human Rights, presented by the member states of the Organisation of the Islamic Conference to the United Nations in 1993, made all rights asserted within it subject to being 'in accordance with *sharia*' (in Herbert, ed., 2001, p. 67).[8]

While the Muslim Brothers grew rapidly to become a mass movement with perhaps a million members by the late 1940s and branches across the Middle East, the Jamaat remained primarily an elite phenomenon in Pakistan, though later to spread to the west through the South Asian Muslim diaspora. Although neither is a political party, both have been drawn into politics. In Pakistan, the Jamaat often opposed governments for failing to 'Islamize' sufficiently, and frustration drew them into electoral politics, where they had limited success. Although occasionally arrested, they were mostly able to work within the system, but lost some credibility after they supported Zia al-Haq's authoritarian regime (1977–88). The Muslim Brothers have found it more difficult to work within the Egyptian system.

---

[8] For discussion of the CDHR, see Herbert, ed., 2001, pp. 80–6.

In the turmoil that succeeded the Second World War, frustration at the Egyptian government's failure to establish an Islamic state led to violence: in December 1948 a Brother assassinated the Prime Minister Mahmoud Fahmi al-Nuqrashi Pasha, and in a subsequent apparent revenge attack al-Banna was assassinated by police (Shadid, 2002, p. 55). In 1952 Gamal Abdel Nasser drew on Brotherhood support in his initial seizure of power, but soon clamped down on them. The Brotherhood's next leader, Sayyid Qutb (1906–66), formerly an employee in the Ministry of Education, was imprisoned for most of the 1950s and 1960s, and finally was hanged for plotting to assassinate Nasser. Qutb's time in jail served the Islamist cause well in the long run, however, for while there he wrote some of the movement's most influential works, including a monumental thirty-volume Qur'ānic commentary and, perhaps most influentially of all, *Milestones* or *Signposts*. Qutb rejected al-Banna's idea that Islamization can occur purely from below. Rather, action at the level of the state is required, and this means revolution. To support this, Qutb made the same powerful ideological move as the Wahhabists, which was to break with Sunni tradition's acceptance that all who declare the *shahada* are indeed Muslims, and argued that unless they live by *sharia* they must be judged unbelievers, against whom *jihād* is obligatory. Like the Wahhabists, he also saw contemporary Muslim societies as *jahiliyya*, in need of cleansing.

For reasons of space, the account here focuses on developments in Sunni Islam, since Sunnis comprise approximately 90 per cent of the world's

Figure 1   Portrait of Sayyid Qutb (1906–66). Photo © AP/Wideworld

Muslim population. However, Shi'ite Islam has also had a significant effect on shaping the politics of the contemporary Muslim majority world, largely because of the influence of the Iranian revolution in 1979. This has been described by historian Eric Hobsbawm as 'the first major twentieth century social upheaval rejecting both the traditions of 1789 [secular republican] and 1917 [communist]' (1994, caption to plate 30). As a social revolution in the name of Islam, leading to the overthrow of the Shah who had long been supported by western countries including the United States, the event was a major confidence boost for growing Islamist movements across the world.

Differences of belief have to some extent limited the direct dissemination of ideas from the Iranian revolution across the Sunni world. For example, the messianic belief in the future coming of the Mahdi (rightly guided leader), and Khomeini's notion of the rule of the *faqih* (expert in Islamic law) are specific to a Shi'ite context (Esposito, 1994, p. 178; Utas, 1999, p. 172). Nonetheless, the themes of opposition to anti-western 'imperialism', the need for an Islamic alternative to both capitalism and communism, and for a radical reinterpretation of Islamic tradition to meet contemporary needs articulated by the revolution's main intellectual exponent, the Sorbonne educated Ali Shariati (1933–77) transcends Sunni–Shi'ite differences. Alongside Qutb and Mawdudi, Shariati has become one of the main influences on contemporary Islamism.

The two paths of contemporary Islamism: violence and democracy

Qutb's legacy to the Brotherhood, and indeed to Islamism generally, has been a sharply divergent one. One path has been the violent political Islam most familiar in the west, but another has been to accept Qutb's message that action at the level of the state is needed to complement grassroots action, but to articulate this in terms of support for democracy rather than revolution, and to reject Qutb's labelling of most Muslims as unbelievers and of Muslim society as *jahiliyya*. The violent and reformed faces of contemporary Islam not only share their origin in alternate readings of Qutb, but also in the breakdown of traditional structures of authority in Islamic teaching. As we have seen, the monopoly claimed by the *ulama* (religious scholars) to interpret Islam's sacred sources was challenged by the modernists. But while modernist opinions remained confined to an elite, al-Banna's adoption of the modernist reapplication of *shura* (consultation) and *ijma* (consensus) from the *ulama* to the *umma* (Islamic community), spread that challenge to the masses. It is possible to exaggerate the extent of the decline of the authority of the *ulama*. One poll conducted in 1996–7 found that 53 per cent, 55 per cent and 40 per cent in Egypt, Indonesia and Pakistan respectively said they had a lot of trust in the *ulama*, and only 19 per cent, 18 per cent and 21 per cent no trust, which compares favourably with state institutions (Hassan, 2002, p. 158). However the *ulama*'s monopoly on interpretation is being broken down in a process greatly accelerated by the spread of information technologies across the Muslim world, enabling the easy circulation of a range of alternative perspectives. 'The upshot of all these changes is that at the beginning of the twenty-first century, Islamic authority has badly fragmented and competing *fatawa* [legal opinions] are flying thick and fast' (Murphy, 2002, pp. 97–8). This process has been likened to the European Reformation, itself enabled by the printing press (McLuhan, 1962; Sardar, 1993; Starrett, 1998; Eickelman, 1998). Just as the mechanical reproduction of texts greatly increased the scriptural literacy of sixteenth-century northern Europeans and led to a plethora of pamphlets on religious and political matters, so the electronic reproduction of voice, image and text greatly increased circulation of religious and political ideas in the late twentieth-century Muslim world. The effect has been to stimulate the most creative and destructive, brilliant and ignorant, interpretations of Islamic tradition. It has been both a democratization and 'anarchization' of the interpretation of Islam.

One notorious example of this interpretative freedom was when in the late 1970s Mohammed Abd al-Salam al-Farag, a self-styled handy-man preacher in a family-built mosque in Cairo's slums, produced a pamphlet. This simplified Qutb's argument and developed its own, based on a novel reading of a thirteenth-century Islamic scholar ibn Taimiyya. Farag drew the conclusion that 'We have to establish the rule of God's religion in our country first ... There is no doubt that the first battlefield for *jihād* is the extermination of these infidel leaders' (in Shadid, 2002, p. 76). Inspired by the pamphlet a young army officer, Islambuli, approached Farag with a plot to assassinate Anwar Sadat, Egypt's president since 1970. On 26 September 1981, while taking part in a parade past the president, Islambuli and three accomplices halted their armoured car and hurled grenades – supplied by Farag – at Sadat, killing him and several of his entourage (ibid., p. 78).

No significant uprising followed, and Islambuli and his accomplices were executed the following year. But the incident demonstrated to other militants the 'lesson' that every terrorist organization across the world had learned before: that with little prior preparation a small group could grab the attention of the world and, maybe, change the course of history. Such violence was to plague Egypt until the late 1990s, and was to spread to other countries across the Middle East and eventually beyond. A great catalyst was the Afghan war against the occupying Soviets. This conflict was widely seen among Muslims as a legitimate *jihād*, and, throughout the 1980s, thousands of young men from across the Muslim, and especially Arab, world went to Afghanistan via training camps in Pakistan in search of glory in victory or death, inspired by Qur'ānic verses such as: 'God has promised reward to all who believe, but he distinguishes those who fight, above those who stay at home, with a mighty reward' (Qur'ān, Surah 4: 95). A decade of war created a body of

Figure 2   This homepage of a website based in Qatar illustrates how by the early twenty-first century Muslims were effectively using new media. Islam Online sees itself as both a source of information for Muslims themselves and as a means of promoting better understanding of Islam among non-Muslims

battle-hardened men for whom violence had arguably become a way of life, and a minority of whom contributed to the creation of a floating, stateless set of Islamist networks responsible for attacks such as the bombing of the World Trade Center in 1993 and the Egyptian Embassy in Pakistan in 1995 (Berman, 2002, p. 85).

Among the volunteers was Osama bin Laden, a civil engineering graduate and son of a Yemeni businessman, who had made his fortune in the Saudi building boom of the 1970s, and of a Syrian mother. Bin Laden had gone to Afghanistan in 1979, taking some of his family's bulldozers with him to help make roads, tunnels and storage depots for the *mujahideen* cause. Later, he apparently distinguished himself as a military commander of considerable bravery. On his return to Saudi Arabia he was much in demand as a speaker, with as many as 250,000 of his (now banned) tapes distributed (Shadid, 2002, p. 87). On these tapes, anti-American sentiment is evident, for example: 'When we buy American goods, we are accomplices in the murder of Palestinians' (ibid.). But such views were (and are) not unusual in the Arab world. However, bin Laden's vocal objections to American troops being stationed on Saudi soil after Iraq's invasion of Kuwait in 1990 led to censure by the Saudi authorities and his flight to Sudan in 1991. As his denunciations continued, his Saudi-based assets were seized and in 1994 his citizenship was revoked. Such actions reflect not only American pressure but Saudi self-interest, as in the early 1990s the Saudi authorities were being challenged by, and then suppressed, internal Islamist dissent. Throughout the 1990s, initially from his Sudanese base and later from Afghanistan, where he supported the Taliban, bin Laden assisted Islamic militant causes across the Muslim world from Algeria to Chechnya, Bosnia to Kashmir, as well as the bombings of US embassies in Kenya and Tanzania in 1998. According to Turabi, the Islamist leader of Sudan who harboured him for much of the 1990s, bin Laden is a fighter rather than a visionary, lacking any coherent aim or programme beyond a hatred of Israel, America and Saudi corruption (ibid., p. 89).

In an effort to make sense of the bin Laden phenomenon, some western commentators have argued that Islamic radicalism is best understood not as a distinctively Islamic, but rather as an essentially western-inspired movement (Berman, 2002; Gray, 2003). These groups have been compared to fascist and communist totalitarianism, because of their willingness to impose a utopian vision on society, regardless of the human cost. They have also been compared to late nineteenth-century Russian revolutionary anarchists, both because of their use of spectacular violent tactics, and their belief that the world can be re-made through such actions. These authors draw on evidence that al Qaeda operatives lived, worked or travelled or were trained in the west, as have Islamist-inspiring authors from al-Afghani to Qutb. Indeed, the latter spent a year in the US, and was appalled at its materialism and sexual licence. Thus it has been argued that Qutb's activist interpretation of the Qur'ān was inspired by existentialism, and that he shared in the totalitarian 'cult of death' (Ruthven, 1997, p. 6; Berman, 2002, p. 120). In this sense, extrapolating a little, and like Nazism in particular, radical Islam may be seen as a modern movement that lays claim to tradition but is in fact 'de-traditionalized'. It is a product of cultural dislocation brought about by rapid modernization and the humiliation of colonization (in the case of early Islamists like Qutb), economic crisis and military defeat.

In at least one respect this largely speculative argument fits well with evidence on the ground, in the sense that while al Qaeda's actions have struck a chord with widespread anti-western sentiment, al Qaeda operatives have mostly been young men dislocated from the 'Arab street', or local Muslim communities, by periods of work, study or fighting abroad, and out of touch with more recent developments there. Thus, close observers of the Middle East see an irony in al Qaeda's prominence at a time when Islamic militancy in much of the Middle East is evolving towards a more democratic politics, except in Palestine and Saudi Arabia where opportunities for democratic development are particularly restricted (Starrett, 1998; Roy, 1994; Murphy, 2002; Shadid, 2002). Much as bin Laden claims to speak for Islam, both he and al Qaeda's recruits are disembedded from the 'Muslim street', or local contexts. However Berman and Gray make no distinction between forms of radical Islam, and their analysis applies less well to more embedded militant movements, and completely fails to acknowledge the much larger phenomenon of democratizing Islamism, resulting in a very biased presentation.

The only territorially located Islamist movements that continue to inspire suicide attacks, Palestinian Hamas and Islamic Jihād and Chechen Islamist movements are certainly not out of touch with the Muslim street. In Palestine, as we saw earlier, suicide bombing is read as self-chosen martyrdom, one fruit of Islamic interpretative anarchy and continued Israeli oppression. Terrorism itself can be defined as 'A strategy of violence designed to promote desired outcomes by instilling fear in the public at large' (Reich in Whittaker, 2003, p. 1). This implies a lack of political power to achieve 'desired outcomes' by other means – certainly lack of capacity to impose their will by conventional military methods. Thus Islam may be associated with particularly feared forms of violence – random attacks against civilian targets, for example – partly because of the powerlessness of many Muslim groups. This has certainly been the case in Palestine, where several decades of struggle against Israeli occupation of the West Bank and Gaza seem only to have tightened the Israeli stranglehold.

But, finally, let us briefly consider democratizing Islamism, a phenomenon claimed to be far more widespread than militancy, and increasingly successful in local and sometimes national politics both across the Middle East and in the wider Muslim world, from Turkey to Indonesia. In each case the entry into democratic politics has built on a history of social activism (Herbert, 2001; Shadid, 2002). As Shadid argues:

Since 1979, despite staggering failures in Sudan and Iran and setbacks in Egypt and Turkey, Islamism has become part of mainstream life, a vibrant, diverse socioreligious movement that claims its own modernly educated intellectuals, cadres and institutions far removed from the militancy for which it is best known in the West.

With that evolution has come maturity, namely in the politics of Islamism. In Jordan, Yemen, Egypt and Kuwait, Islamic parties that trace their roots to the once-violent Muslim Brotherhood, arguably Islam's most influential movement, have all undergone striking transformation, competing in elections and making notable gains through the ballot box.

(2002, p. 4)

Democracy certainly remains a contested concept across much of the Muslim world. Its association with the west, and unease about perceived dependence on the whims of majorities, are barriers to its acceptance. But several reasons, both pragmatic and principled, led to its increasing endorsement by Islamists during the 1990s. One is the experience of so many Islamist activists, who see democracy supporting human rights as their best chance to avoid the perils of authoritarian regimes. Another is that, aware of Islam's popular base, democracy is seen as the best route to power. But would Islamists then use democracy as a means to gain power only then to reject it, as was alleged by the military who seized power in Algeria in 1993 after polls predicted an Islamist victory?

In fact, there is evidence of an increasing readiness in Islamist circles to engage in a principled defence of democracy. There is also evidence of a growing recognition that Islam's sacred sources do not dictate any particular form of governance (Ayubi 1991, Tibi, 1998). In Egypt, for example, Sheikh Yusuf al-Qaradawi has issued a *fatwa* against those who see democracy as a form of unbelief. After differentiating the idea of democracy from its western manifestations, al-Qaradawi argues that 'even though Islam does not specifically designate democracy as a form of rule, it offers a legitimate and effective way to institutionalize the abstract concept of *shura*' (quoted in Shadid, 2002, p. 69). Such careful distinctions, acknowledging absences in the Qur'ānic text and recognizing the importance of historical context and development, move beyond both earlier crude Islamist assertion, such as the claim that Islam already possesses the perfect form of democracy in the concept of *shura*, and blanket condemnations of democracy as western or a product of unbelief. Furthermore, the ideas of Qaradawi and others are being widely debated on the Muslim street (ibid.).

Thus Islam's relationship to contemporary conflict needs to be understood against a background of the differing responses to modernity of which the Muslim majority world is now thoroughly a part. While traditional readings of Islam's sacred texts legitimize defensive and arguably offensive war to spread Islamic dominion, there is no apparent theological justification for the terrorist attacks of 11 September 2001. However, the loosening of traditional Islamic interpretative authorities has given rise both to extremist militant readings and innovative democratic interpretations of these texts. The former are arguably influenced by counter-Enlightenment currents in western thought (existentialism, fascism, anarchism). Through such readings, Islamism has played a role in the production of Islamic terrorism. But, far more influentially across the Muslim majority world, this same interpretative anarchy has also produced Islamisms that arguably present the best prospect for democratization in the Muslim majority world, and hence for the containment of conflict in democratic institutions and the enabling of peaceful coexistence.

Finally, for our consideration of modern Islamically-inspired movements, a methodological point that springs out of reflection on the sources used to put together this section. In this process, a range of sources has been used, including overviews of Muslim history, broad historical surveys of ideas, international relations literature, and detailed ethnographic studies. Viewing contemporary political Islam in the context of reform and revival movements from the eighteenth to twentieth centuries has enabled us to see current developments as driven by forces both internal and external to the Islamic tradition. Clearly, modern Islamism is a product of global interaction, yet if we look at it only as a product of global currents we miss its distinctiveness and lose sensitivity to diversity and new trends that local, detailed studies reveal. Yet without the broader canvas we may miss real connections between, for example, Islamism and western political thought. So, the general lesson would seem to be that looking at any one kind of literature – for example, general works by non-specialist authors seeking to explain the rise of militant Islamism – results in a distorted picture: methodological eclecticism is important in arriving at a balanced view of a phenomenon.

Perceptions and realities

The rise of Islamism in the Muslim world has been paralleled by growing alarm in the west. In 1993 the defence correspondent of the *Herald Tribune* wrote:

> Muslim fundamentalism is fast becoming the chief threat to global peace and security as well as a cause of national and local disturbance through terrorism. It is akin to the menace posed by Nazism and fascism in the 1930s and then by communism in the 1950s.

(Quoted in Halliday, 2002, p. 111)

The use of such language by a respected journalist in a heavyweight newspaper was evidence of the increasing pervasiveness of anti-Muslimism. The events of subsequent years, culminating in the September 11 attacks have reinforced this trend. In 1996, a report identified four leading features of Islamophobic perceptions:

1   Muslim cultures seen as monolithic and unchanging;

2   claims that Muslim cultures are wholly different from other cultures;

3   Islam perceived as implacably threatening;

4   claims that Islam's adherents use their faith mainly for political or military advantage.

(Conway et al., 1996, p. 8)

It should immediately be apparent from the analysis in the preceding section that none of these perceptions commands much objective validity. Muslim cultures are diverse and unstable, as a result of sharing many of the pressures for rapid change also experienced in western cultures. While al Qaeda and other extremist groups are indeed implacably threatening towards the west, these are not representative of the Muslim world as a whole. Some Muslims (like some Christians) indeed used their faith for political or military advantage, but their actions should not be seen as characteristic of the majority of the adherents of Islam.

Some of the earlier chapters of this book suggest a longer historical framework in which contemporary anti-Muslimism can be viewed. Anti-Catholicism, as explored in Chapter 4, shares many of the same features. A perception that Catholicism is 'monolithic and unchanging' is apparent in an inability to distinguish between general characteristics of all Roman Catholics, and specific actions and attitudes of individual Roman Catholics at a particular moment in history. Thus, for example, the burnings of Protestants in Mary I's reign are divorced from their historical context, and seen as indicative of what would happen if Roman Catholicism ever again gained political power in England. There is also a sense that Catholic cultures are 'wholly different', evident for example in the belief of many Ulster Protestants that their own culture would be incompatible with life in a united Ireland in which Catholics were a majority. The sense of 'implacable threat' is apparent too, in the way that in the eighteenth and nineteenth centuries in Britain and North America, in the absence of major explicit challenges from Catholics, the belief that they were engaged in nefarious conspiracy very much kept anti-Catholic fear and hostility alive. Finally, the charge that faith was subordinated to political or military ends was a stock-in-trade of Protestant polemic, notably in anxiety about the Pope's dual role until the later nineteenth century as a temporal ruler as well as a spiritual leader, and in a suspicion of predominantly Roman Catholic states such as Spain and Austria.

A similar parallel can be drawn with the antisemitism that, as shown in Chapter 8, established the preconditions for the Holocaust (for an overview see Cohn-Sherbok, 2002). Hatred and fear of the Jews can be traced back to biblical times, with the specifically religious complaint that they rejected and murdered Christ merging into a range of racial stereotypes, including a sense of Jewish culture as wholly alien, and fear that their perceived financial power and political scheming were part of a conspiracy for world domination. The historical persistence and strength of antisemitism had a particularly tenuous relationship to the reality that Jews were a dispersed ethnic and religious group, a vulnerable minority in most societies, lacking military or conventional political power. In the early twentieth century, the widespread circulation of the fabricated 'Protocols of the Elders of Zion', originating in St Petersburg in 1903, gave popular credibility to the idea of a Jewish world conspiracy (Cohn, 1996). Even in the aftermath of the Holocaust, antisemitism has still been evident in Europe, although it has declined in the US (Cohn-Sherbok, 2002, pp. 318–24), but the creation of the State of Israel and the occupation of the Golan Heights and the Palestinian territories have fuelled its resurgence as a potent force in the Arab world. Here again the perception of a monolithic and implacably threatening force recurs (ibid., pp. 325–42). Diversity of Jewish opinion is ignored, while the attitudes of religious extremists and the heavy-handed actions of the Israeli army in the occupied territories are seen as evidence of generalized irrevocable hostility to Muslims.[9]

Instances of hatred and paranoia in which religion is implicated could be multiplied, including also, for example, the former Yugoslavia and the Indian subcontinent. All have distinctive and contingent elements, and need to be studied in detail if they are to be fully understood. Nevertheless, a broad comparative perspective is also useful in identifying some common causes and characteristics. A recurrent characteristic of societies where such attitudes are prominent has been contested or insecure religious, cultural and national identities. Only in a minority of instances is there a clear objective contest over territory or sovereignty, but such situations, when bound up with religion, give rise to particularly intense and entrenched conflict, as in Bosnia, Northern Ireland, Kashmir and Israel–Palestine. Much more widespread are situations where, although territory is not in dispute, a religious minority is perceived as a challenge to essential communal identity. Thus, between the first and third centuries, Christianity was persecuted because it was seen as *superstitio* that threatened the traditional public worship

---

[9] While some Israeli actions have tended thus to fuel Arab antisemitism, there is nevertheless nothing inherently antisemitic about measured criticism – which may well be expressed by Jews as well as non-Jews – of specific policies of the Israeli government or of Zionist political agendas.

(*religio*) of the pagan Roman Empire. Medieval Christendom's need for religious uniformity during its crusades against Muslims led to violence against its own Jewish minorities, above all at the time of the launch of the First Crusade in 1096. This process has been described as an 'internalization of holy war' (Riley-Smith, 2002). Eighteenth-century Britons, conscious of their own cultural diversity and religious divisions, found common cause in hostility to Roman Catholicism. 'Protestantism was the foundation that made the invention of Great Britain possible' (Colley, 1992, p. 54). Similarly, in the US in the nineteenth century, large-scale immigration from Europe presented a challenge to coherent national identity, leading to the nativist assertion of Protestantism as a distinctive American characteristic (Billington, 1938). In Germany in the interwar period, a divided and insecure society, with a legacy of confrontation between Catholic and Protestant, was fertile soil for Nazi assertion of a common Aryan identity founded in irrevocable hostility to the Jews. 'The Third Reich's solution to the Jewish question, although neither spontaneous nor "popular", nonetheless employed violence of a kind that was not foreign to the German past' (Levy, 2002, p. 187).

The recurrence of such attitudes throughout history does not explain the similar sense of confrontation between Islam and the west around the turn of the third millennium, but it does highlight the need to distinguish popular illusions, compelling though they may be, from realities, and to look at the environment that contributes both to anti-Muslimism and to anti-western feeling in Islamic countries. The previous section demonstrated the diversity and volatility of Muslim responses to modernity since the late eighteenth century, but it remains to consider some parallel tensions and changes in other religious cultures. There is no space here to consider important geopolitical questions, such as the implications of the collapse of the Soviet Union, or economic ones, relating above all to the west's need for Arab oil, but in pursuing this book's primary emphasis on religion, three significant trends merit exploration.

First, there is what can best be encapsulated by the phrase 'the decline of Christendom', analysed with reference to Britain in Chapter 6, and evident as a general process throughout western Europe (McLeod and Ustorf, 2003). Some years ago scholars would have written of a lengthy process of 'secularization' but, for the reasons given in Chapter 6 by Parsons, this concept now seems increasingly problematic. In explaining the collapsing influence of the churches, the emphasis has shifted from sociological processes to more abrupt cultural changes. Moreover the decline of Christen*dom*, by which is meant a sense of society and culture being founded in Christian tradition and values, does not necessarily imply disaster for Christian*ity* as a committed and explicit belief system. However, it does imply a retreat into a counter-cultural or sub-cultural environment, although that can be seen as completing a kind of full circle, to the situation of Christianity in the first three centuries of its existence before Constantine. At the same time, Christendom in Europe is being succeeded not by a wholly secular culture, but by one in which a plurality of beliefs and practice exists, including other major world religions, and the diversity of spiritualities and beliefs apparent in the 'Mind, Body, Spirit' sections of any large bookshop. In a context of such religio-cultural complexity and turmoil, the apparent certainty and universal relevance claimed by Islam was deeply alien and disconcerting. When in 1989 Muslims condemned Salman Rushdie's novel *The Satanic Verses* because of its allegedly insulting treatment of the Prophet Muhammad, their most uncomprehending opponents were not Christians but secular liberals, tolerant of diversity of belief, but not of absolute dogmatic claims. Conversely, from a Muslim perspective, a dechristianized west is liable to seem more alien and threatening than a Christian one had been and no longer entitled to the respect that Islam historically accorded to the other 'peoples of the Book'.

Secondly, and paradoxically, there has been widespread religious resurgence, especially in the non-western world. It is a huge irony that after the great European missionary endeavours of the colonial era had brought only a limited harvest of conversions, the decline of both empire and traditional missions in the second half of the twentieth century was accompanied by a dramatic expansion of Christianity in regions such as sub-Saharan Africa and East Asia. By the turn of the millennium Christianity's numerical centre of gravity shifted decisively to the developing world. At the centre of this Christian revival and reorientation was the Pentecostal movement, which in 2002 'on a conservative estimate includes about a quarter of a billion people' (Martin, 2002, p. xvii). According to one version of history, Pentecostalism originated in Los Angeles, California, in 1906, but its distinctive emphasis on empowering personal encounter with the Holy Spirit had many antecedents in the Christian tradition, and its spread during the twentieth century should be seen as quite as much a multi-centred phenomenon of simultaneous (re)discovery as of diffusion from a single source (Wolffe, 2002). Not only has Pentecostalism led to Christian advance in territory historically associated with other traditions – such as African indigenous religions, Buddhism and Confucianism – but it has meant a marked shift of character within Christianity, notably in historically Roman Catholic Latin America. In the meantime, this expansion of Protestant Christianity has had its parallels in numerous other religious traditions, not only, as explored above, in Islamic revivalism in the Arab world and elsewhere, but in, for example, the recovery of Orthodox Christianity in Russia, in India in an increasingly exclusivist politicization of Hindu religious identity, and a growth in vociferous ultra-orthodox Judaism. A French scholar, Gilles Kepel, coined the phrase '*la revanche de Dieu*' ('the revenge of God') to characterize this very widespread phenomenon, which seems to fly in the face of western-centred assumptions about the inexorable secularization of the world (Kepel, 1994). Moreover, as Kepel shows, religious resurgence has been a strong counter-current even in the developed world, especially in the US, where from the 1950s

Figure 3   The banner advertising a Pentecostal rally was photographed in Muanar in southern India in February 2001, one illustration of Christian expansion in the non-western world. Photo: John Wolffe

onwards, a range of Christian Evangelical and Pentecostalist movements became increasingly influential, commanding the loyalty of around a quarter of the population in the mid-1990s (Brouwer, Gifford and Rose, 1996, p. 3).[10] Conversion has, at least in the broad sense the word is used in this book, indeed become a global trend in the last quarter of the twentieth century.

In discussing this plethora of seemingly parallel movements, both academics and journalists have made extensive use of the controversial concept of 'fundamentalism'. In its narrowest Christian theological sense, the word refers to a specific movement in early twentieth-century American Protestantism, which advocated a return to perceived 'fundamentals', above all a belief in the inerrant authoritative status of the Bible (Wolffe, 2002, p. 19). In its broadest journalistic sense, 'fundamentalism' is a term used to refer to virtually all the resurgent

[10] The estimation of the numbers of American Evangelicals is a vexed and complex question, and figures vary according to the measure used, which may be self-identification, membership of particular denominations and/or organizations, or the profession of particular beliefs. Applying these various measures, calculations range from 11.9 per cent to 39 per cent of total population (Wolffe, 2002, pp. 49–50).

religious movements of the late twentieth century. In between these two extremes of usage has been an endeavour exemplified in the massive Fundamentalism Project, conducted at the University of Chicago in the early 1990s, to use the concept as a meaningful cross-religious and cross-cultural category of analysis, requiring a definition that is broad enough to work for a variety of religious traditions, but not so expansive as to become meaningless and merely polemical.[11] Details of such a definition are inevitably debated, but consistent features are a characterization of fundamentalists as responding to a sense of crisis in their religious identity, fighting to preserve what they see as the essential features of their tradition against a hostile outside world, and defining their values and community tightly so as to ensure the maintenance of their spiritual and moral purity. The points that fundamentalists seize on as essential may well distort the historic emphasis of their parent tradition and hence place them at odds with genuine traditionalists. They also tend in practice readily to adopt many structural features of modernity, such as the sophisticated use of mass media and other technologies, while their ideological preference for a simplified and, on their own terms, orderly religious mindset has also been characterized as distinctively modern. Fundamentalism thus is but one strand, albeit an important and conspicuous one, within the wider pattern of religious resurgence (Marty and Appleby, 1991, pp. viii–x, 817–33; Parekh, 1992).

For the majority of fundamentalists the sense of being embattled remained metaphorical, but their states of mind provided fertile soil for the growth of the kind of religious hate movements discussed above. Moreover, their activities were apt to fuel external stereotyping of their own tradition. Sometimes, however, because of the perceived need to fight rather than admit any compromise, religion of this kind was an important factor in leading to actual violence, as in the case of global Islamic terrorism, already explored above. There were also notable instances in India, particularly when Sikh extremists, with a conservative religious agenda, took refuge in the Golden Temple at Amritsar in 1984. Against a background of violent clashes with the police and other Sikh and Hindu groups, this action brought to a head the alarm of the Indian government about the aspirations of Sikh separatists for an independent state in the Punjab. The army was accordingly ordered into the Temple and the consequent destruction and loss of life within the precincts of Sikhism's holiest shrine gave rise to widespread outrage. After the subsequent assassination of the Prime Minister, Indira Gandhi, by her Sikh bodyguards, there were massacres of Sikhs in Delhi, a serious breach in the hitherto peaceful coexistence of Hindus and Sikhs in India. In 1992, Hindu activists were responsible for the demolition of the Babri mosque at Ayodhya, to the outrage of Muslims (Madan, 1997). In the US intense Christian fundamentalist opposition to abortion has given rise to

---

[11] For an alternative discussion of the Fundamentalism Project see Herbert, 2001, pp. 173 and 208–10.

direct action, sometimes taking the extreme form of shootings of doctors and others involved in the work of abortion clinics. Here, too, fundamentalist readings of the Bible led, especially in the aftermath of the Six Day War of 1967, to considerable apocalyptic expectation, associated with an uncritical support for Israel because of its perceived divinely appointed role in the events expected to lead up to the end of the world (Ariel, 2002). This stance reinforces a sense of wider conflict with Islam. It has even been suggested that rival Christian, Islamic and Jewish fundamentalist claims to the Temple Mount/*Haram al-Sharif* are likely to lead to globalized military conflict, the biblical Armageddon (New, 2002). It is crucial to recognize, however, that such potentially explosive fundamentalism, while the most disturbing aspect of the late twentieth-century religious resurgence, has remained an extreme rather than representative tendency. It is equally important to appreciate that the historical record shows it to be a religious pathology potentially at least inherent in all traditions, rather than something to which Islam is uniquely or particularly prone.

Thirdly, issues relating to women and gender have assumed increasing importance in religion. At one level this is a change in perceptions rather than realities, given that half of humanity has always been female and in most traditions and historical contexts women have been rather more than half of the active adherents of organized religion. On the other hand, in nearly all traditions at most times in history, leadership has been exclusively or predominantly male and the formal power exercised by women has been relatively circumscribed. What was new in the twentieth century was the extent to which, in the west at least, this situation began to be perceived as a major issue rather than simply the way things are. Thus, as we saw in Chapter 6, arguably a decisive factor in the 'death of Christian Britain' in the secular context of sexual 'liberation' and equal rights was the reluctance of many women to continue to accept either the subordinate religious roles that they had traditionally undertaken or the religiously constructed moral, cultural and sexual identities they had traditionally been assigned. They accordingly either opted out of organized Christianity altogether or, as described in Chapter 7, sought to exercise an equal role with men in the leadership and control of the churches, thereby bringing to life the latent conflict in religious patriarchalism.

In other cultures and traditions, meanwhile, the continuing ascendancy of religious teachings that emphasized the pivotal importance of family life and motherhood, and the destructive nature of unregulated female sexuality, defined and limited the roles of women not only within religious organizations, but also in the wider society. The reaffirmation of such outlooks in the face of modernity has been particularly associated with fundamentalist movements, which are even seen by some feminist scholars as primarily driven by a neo-patriarchal backlash against the expanding rights of women (Brasher, 1998, p. 19). Nevertheless, women committed to such forms of religion continued to acquiesce in the more circumscribed functions allowed to them. A 1996 study of Egyptian and Iranian women showed that the majority had internalized a sense of motherhood as the core of their personhood, while even in the US where such lifestyles were much more a matter of conscious choice, fundamentalist women were shown to be generally accepting of their imposed limitations (Gerami, 1996, pp. 154–5). Indeed, religious organizations could offer considerable benefits to women: in late twentieth-century Latin American Pentecostalism, as in nineteenth-century British Evangelicalism, they provided a sphere of safety in which their human and spiritual dignity was recognized even if it was seen as different from that of men. In such contexts, the responsible patriarchalism of organized religion could act as a check on the irresponsible patriarchalism of the wider society. There was also potential to gain a sense of empowerment through religious activities led by women for other women (Brasher, 1998, p. 181). Just as there has been recognition by historians of the important role of the churches in the origins of feminism in the UK and the US (Rendall, 1985), it has been observed that in the Middle East the Islamic revival of the late twentieth century helped to politicize women, gave them a better understanding of sacred texts, and helped to lay the groundwork for indigenous women's movements (Gerami, 1996, p. 156).

The contrast between 'liberated' western Christian women and 'oppressed' women in other religions is therefore a great deal less clear-cut than it might appear at first sight. Nevertheless, perceptions that link fundamentalism in general and Islam in particular to the mistreatment of women are widespread, making an interesting parallel with past charges against Roman Catholics. They gained some credibility from a stereotyped view of the situation of women in Iran after the revolution of 1979 and, in the late 1990s, from the extreme case of the Taliban in Afghanistan. Hence the gender conflict, while having its own dynamic, served to reinforce other forms of religious conflict.

This section has highlighted the pervasiveness and power of entrenched preconceptions in the recent history of religion. Thus we have considered the liberal assumption of the inevitable secularization of the world; the stereotype that sees implacable hostility in a particular religious group – Catholics, Jews or Muslims; the powerful conviction of fundamentalists that they are the only legitimate interpreters of a tradition; the feminist apprehension that organized religious structures are wholly opposed to women's interests. When such preconceptions become entrenched they serve as a filter to block out alternative perspectives or contradictory evidence. When applied to people, they tend to result in stereotyping that ignores individual characteristics or differences. When they collide, the potential for conflict is considerable. Nor can they easily be removed: in many cases they are so deeply held that they appear to be realities, and confronting them is likely only to lead to their deeper embedding, as opposition is read as confirmation of the truth of one's position. Certainly there is evidence that in some cases deeply and widely-held preconceptions have weakened over time, for example, Protestant anti-Catholicism, and the belief in early modern Europe that religious uniformity is essential for political stability. However, the widespread reinforcement of stereotypes has also occurred in the recent past, as with the growth of Muslim antisemitism, deriving more from modern European sources than from Islamic tradition, in the wake of the creation and development of the state of Israel.

The 'clash of civilizations' and the coexistence of religions

In 1993, an American expert in international relations, Samuel P. Huntington, published an article entitled 'The clash of civilizations' (Huntington, 1993), which, later expanded into a book (Huntington, 1996), has been an influential interpretation of the global situation at the close of the twentieth century. Huntington's central thesis was that in the future 'The great divisions among humankind and the dominating source of conflict will be cultural' and 'The fault lines between civilizations will be the battle lines of the future' (Huntington, 1993, p. 22). Religion, according to Huntington, is 'a central defining characteristic of civilizations' (Huntington, 1996, p. 47). Accordingly he gave considerable attention to '*la revanche de Dieu*', seeing it as pervading every continent and recasting human life, in reaction 'against secularism, moral relativism and self-indulgence' and reaffirming 'the values of order, discipline, work, mutual help, and human solidarity' (Huntington, 1996, p. 98). While he perceived numerous potential clashes of civilizations, his dominant preoccupation was with that he saw between Islam and the west, seeing it as a 'deeply conflictual' and historically entrenched hostility between opposed cultural traditions, which was far more than a matter of 'violent Islamic extremists' and 'fundamentalism' being opposed by 'the CIA or the U.S. Department of Defense' (Huntington, 1996, pp. 209, 217).

The view of relations between Islam and the west taken in this chapter is a different one. Whereas, to revert to the three levels of explanation enunciated at the beginning, the emphasis here has been on specific movements and trends that led to a sense of confrontation at the end of the twentieth century, Huntington sees a general historical law of antagonism between Islam and the west. There is a danger that such a use of the second level of explanation by western opinion-formers could be self-fulfilling in shaping the attitudes of both western intelligentsia and popular opinion, in a parallel way to that in which Osama bin Laden's use of the third level of explanation, explicit reference to the intervention and purposes of God, has helped him to mobilize wider Muslim support for his terrorist acts. Huntington's argument, however, is problematic, not only because it is founded on a stereotyped view of

Islam, but also because of his equation between Christianity and 'the west' (Huntington, 1996, p. 209; Chee Pang Choong, 1998). In reality, as we have seen, Christianity has become much more geographically and culturally widespread, while western culture has become less founded in Christianity, increasingly diverse, and accommodating to significant religious minorities, including Muslim ones. Such trends have deep historical roots: as shown in Chapter 3, in seventeenth-century Britain there had been some notably positive attitudes towards Jews and Muslims, just as in the same period the Muslim Ottoman Empire allowed freedom of worship to Christians. If there is such a thing as a clash of civilizations, it is not the same thing as a clash of religions.

Indeed, the case studies explored in this volume include numerous further examples of coexistence, widespread both in time and space, between pagans and Christians in late fourth-century Antioch, between crusader settlers and Muslims in twelfth-century Palestine, between Hindus and Christians in nineteenth-century Calcutta. This last example, as explored in Chapter 5, is particularly suggestive in that it shows how creative interactions between two traditions established new religious directions that enriched and diversified both. Within Hinduism, the universalizing outlook promoted by Rammohun Roy and Vivekenanda (despite the chauvinistic undertones of his glorification of India) was a significant counterweight to the more exclusive and nationalist constructions of the tradition associated with the Arya Samaj (founded 1875) (Madan, 1997). Similarly, a rounded view of Muslim–Christian relations in the later twentieth century needs to move beyond seemingly polarized 'fundamentalisms' to recognize the enormous diversity of opinion in both traditions and acknowledge the genuine advances in dialogue made in the 1970s, 1980s and 1990s, even as in other quarters anti-Muslim and anti-western sentiments gathered momentum (Goddard, 2000, pp. 142–76). Diversity within Judaism is apparent between the exclusive ethos of the *haredim* and *Gush Emunim*, and the advocacy by Jonathan Sacks, Chief Rabbi of Orthodox Jews in the British Commonwealth, of mutual recognition of the 'dignity of difference' as a means of avoiding the 'clash of civilizations'. Sacks's view that religious diversity should be positively welcomed and fostered is especially significant coming from a man who represents a relatively conservative strand in his own tradition, and who explicitly repudiates relativism (Sacks, 2002, pp. 51–5). Thus at the dawn of the twenty-first century, as in the various earlier eras and contexts studied in this book, there remains considerable scope for peaceful and mutually enriching coexistence. At the same time the actuality and potential for conflict remains considerable. History provides no blueprints for the future, but it does present some horrifying examples of how abrupt and extreme conflict can be, as in the degeneration of the largely peaceful, albeit tense, coexistence of Christians and Jews in interwar Europe into the cataclysm of the Holocaust. There is no room for complacency, but neither is there need for despair.

References

Al-Azmeh, A. (1993) *Islams and Modernities*, London, Verso.

Ariel, Y. (2002) *Philosemites or Antisemites? Evangelical Christian Attitudes Towards Jews, Judaism and the State of Israel*, Jerusalem, Vidal Sassoon International Center for the Study of Antisemitism.

*Ayubi, N. (1991) *Political Islam*, London, Routledge.

Berman, P. (2002) *Terror and Liberalism*, London, Norton.

Billington, R. A. (1938) *The Protestant Crusade 1800–1860: A Study of the Origins of American Nativism*, New York, Macmillan.

Brasher, B. E. (1998) *Godly Women: Fundamentalism and Female Power*, New Brunswick, NJ, Rutgers UP.

Brouwer, S., Gifford, P. and Rose, S. D. (1996) *Exporting the American Gospel: Global Christian Fundamentalism*, London, Routledge.

Butterfield, H. (1979) *Writings on Christianity and History* (ed.) C. T. McIntire, New York, Oxford University Press.

Chee Pang Choong (1998) 'Samuel Huntington's Clash of Civilizations and its implications for Christian identity in Asia', in M. Hutchinson and O. Kalu (eds) *A Global Faith: Essays on Evangelicalism and Globalization*, Sydney, Centre for the Study of Australian Christianity.

Cohn, N. (1996) *Warrant for Genocide: The Myth of the Jewish World Conspiracy and the Protocols of the Elders of Zion*, London, Serif.

Cohn-Sherbok, D. (2002) *Anti-Semitism: A History*, Stroud, Sutton.

Colley, L. (1992) *Britons Forging the Nation 1707–1837*, New Haven, Yale University Press.

Conway, G. et al. (1996) *Islamophobia: Its Features and Dangers*, London, The Runnymede Trust.

Eickelman, D. (1998) 'Inside the Islamic Reformation', *The Wilson Quarterly*, vol. 22, no. 1, pp. 80–9.

Esposito, J. (1994) *Islam: The Straight Path*, 2nd edition, Oxford, Oxford University Press.

*Gehman, H. (2002) 'September 11: the terrorist attack on America', in I. Markham and I. Abu-Rabi (eds) *September 11: Religious Perspectives on the Causes and Consequences*, Oxford, One World, pp. 1–19.

Gerami, S. (1996) *Women and Fundamentalism: Islam and Christianity*, New York, Garland.

*Goddard, H. (2000) *A History of Christian–Muslim Relations*, Edinburgh, Edinburgh University Press.

Gray, J. (2003) *Al-Quaeda and What it Means to be Modern*, London, Faber.

Halliday, F. (2000) *Nation and Religion in the Middle East*, London, Saqi.

*Halliday, F. (2002) *Two Hours that Shook the World: September 11, 2001: Causes and Consequences*, London, Saqi.

*Hassan, R. (2002) *Faithlines: Muslim Conceptions of Islam and Society*, Oxford, Oxford University Press.

*Herbert, D. (2001) 'Representing Islam: The Islamisation of Egypt 1970–2000', in G. Beckerlegge (ed.) *From Sacred Text to Internet*, Aldershot, Ashgate, pp. 161–217.

*Herbert, D. (ed.) (2001) *Religion and Social Transformations*, Aldershot, Ashgate.

Hobsbawm, E. (1994) *Age of Extremes: The Short Twentieth Century (1914–1991)*, London, Michael Joseph.

Hoffman, B. (1998) *Inside Terrorism*, London, Indigo.

Huntington, S. P. (1993) 'The clash of civilizations', *Foreign Affairs*, vol. 72, no. 3, pp. 22–49.

Huntington, S. P. (1996) *The Clash of Civilizations and the Remaking of World Order*, New York, Simon and Schuster.

Juergensmeyer, M. (2002) *Terror in the Mind of God: The Global Rise of Religious Violence*, Berkeley, London, California University Press.

Kepel, G. (1994) *The Revenge of God: The Resurgence of Islam, Christianity and Judaism in the Modern World*, Cambridge, Polity.

Lewis, B. (2003) *The Crisis of Islam*, London, Weidenfeld and Nicolson.

Levy, R. S. (2002) 'Continuites and discontinuities of anti-Jewish violence in modern Germany, 1819–1938', in C. Hoffman, W. Bergman and H. W. Smith (eds) *Exclusionary Violence: Antisemitic Riots in Modern German History*, Ann Arbor, University of Michigan Press.

Liebes, T. (1997) *Reporting the Arab-Israeli Conflict: How Hegemony Works*, London, Routledge.

McLeod, H. and Ustorf, W. (2003) *The Decline of Christendom in Western Europe 1750–2000*, Cambridge, Cambridge University Press.

Madan, T. N. (1997) 'Religion, ethnicity and nationalism in India', in M. E. Marty and R. S. Appleby (eds) *Religion, Ethnicity and Self-Identity: Nations in Turmoil*, Hanover, NH, University Press of New England.

Martin, D. (2002) *Pentecostalism: The World their Parish*, Oxford, Blackwell.

Marty, E. and Appleby, R. S. (1991) *Fundamentalisms Observed*, Chicago, University of Chicago Press.

McLuhan, M. (1962) *The Gutenburg Galaxy: The Making of Typographic Man*, Toronto, University of Toronto Press.

*Murphy, C. (2002) *Passion for Islam: Shaping the Modern Middle East: The Egyptian Experience*, London, Scribner.

New, D. S. (2002) *Holy War: The Rise of Militant Christian, Jewish and Islamic Fundamentalism*, Jefferson, NC, McFarland.

Parekh, B. (1992) *The Concept of Fundamentalism*, Leeds, Peepal Tree.

Rendall, J. (1985) *The Origins of Modern Feminism: Women in Britain, France and the United States, 1780–1860*, Basingstoke, Macmillan.

Roy, O. (1994) *The Failure of Political Islam*, Cambridge, MA, Harvard University Press.

Riley-Smith, J. (2002) 'Christian violence and the crusades', in A. S. Abulafia (ed.) *Religious Violence Between Christians and Jews: Medieval Roots, Modern Perspectives*, Basingstoke, Palgrave.

Ruthven, M. (1997) *Islam: a Very Short Introduction*, Oxford, Oxford University Press.

Sacks, J. (2002) *The Dignity of Difference: How to Avoid the Clash of Civilizations*, London, Continuum.

Said, E. (1997) *Covering Islam: How the Media and Experts Determine How We See the Rest of the World*, London, Vintage.

Sardar, Z. (1993) 'Paper, printing and compact discs: the making and unmaking of Islamic culture', *Media, Culture and Society* 15, pp. 43–60.

*Shadid, A. (2002) *The Legacy of the Prophet: Despots, Democrats and the New Politics of Islam*, Oxford, Westview.

Sherif, F (1995) *A Guide to the Contents of the Qur'an*, Reading, Ithaca.

Starrett, G. (1998) *Putting Islam to Work: Education, Politics and Religious Transformation in Egypt*, Berkeley, Los Angeles and London: University of California Press.

Steger, M. (2003) *Globalization: A Very Short Introduction*, Oxford, Oxford University Press.

Tibi, B. (1998) *The Challenge of Fundamentalism: Political Islam and the New World Disorder*, Berkeley, University of California Press.

Townshend, C. (2002) *Terrorism: A Very Short Introduction*, Oxford, Oxford University Press.

Utas, B. (1999) 'Iran, Afghanistan and Tajikistan', in D. Westerlund and I. Svanberg (eds) *Islam Outside the Arab World*, London, Curzon, pp. 166–89.

Whittaker, D. (2003) *The Terrorism Reader*, London, Routledge.

*Wolffe, J. (2002) 'Evangelicals and Pentecostals: indigenizing a global gospel', in J. Wolffe (ed.) *Global Religious Movements in Regional Context*, Aldershot, Ashgate.

Zawati, H. (2002) *Is Jihad a Just War?*, Lampeter, Edwin Mellen.

Asterisked items are particularly recommended for further reading.

List of maps

Index